# Business
## in
# Context

# Business in Context Series

Editors

**David Needle**
Head of Undergraduate Studies
East London Business School
University of East London

**Professor Eugene McKenna**
Chartered Psychologist and Emeritus
Professor
University of East London

**Accounting in a Business Context
(2nd Edition)**
Aidan Berry and Robin Jarvis
ISBN 0 412 58740 8, 400 pages

**Economics in a Business Context
(2nd Edition)**
Alan Neale and Colin Haslam
ISBN 0 412 58760 2, 336 pages

**Behaviour in a Business Context**
Richard Turton
ISBN 0 412 37530 3, 400 pages

**Law in a Business Context**
Bill Cole, Peter Shears and Jillinda Tiley
ISBN 0 412 37520 6, 256 pages

**Business in Context
(2nd Edition)**
David Needle
ISBN 0 412 4840 2, 400 pages

**Quantitative Techniques in a Business
Context**
Roger Slater and Peter Ascroft
ISBN 0 412 37570 2, 416 pages

**Human Resource Management in a
Business Context**
A. Price
ISBN 0 412 37230 3, 384 pages

Books in the series are available on free inspection for lecturers considering the texts for course adoption.
Details of these, and any other International Thomson Business Press titles, are available by writing to the
publishers (Berkshire House, 168-173 High Holborn, London WC1V 7AA).

# Business
## – in –
## Context

## AN INTRODUCTION TO BUSINESS
## AND ITS ENVIRONMENT

### SECOND EDITION

## David Needle

### INTERNATIONAL THOMSON BUSINESS PRESS
### I ⓣ P An International Thomson Publishing Company

London • Bonn • Boston • Johannesburg • Madrid • Melbourne • Mexico City • New York • Paris
Singapore • Tokyo • Toronto • Albany, NY • Belmont, CA • Cincinnati, OH • Detroit, MI

**Business in Context**

Copyright © 1989 , 1994 David Needle

This edition first published 1994 by Chapman & Hall

I ⓣ P   A division of International Thomson Publishing Inc.
The ITP logo is a trademark under licence

*British Library Cataloguing-in-Publication Data*
A catalogue record for this book is available from the British Library

*Library of congress Catalog Card Number:* 94-71064

**First edition 1989**
Reprinted 1991 (twice), 1992
Second edition 1994, 1995
Reprinted by International Thomson Business Press 1996

Typeset in 10/12pt Palatino by Best-set Typesetters Ltd., Hong Kong
Printed and bound in Hong Kong

**ISBN 0-412-48410-2**

International Thomson Business Press
Berkshire House
168–173 High Holborn
London WC1V 7AA
UK

International Thomson Business Press
20 Park Plaza
14th Floor
Boston MA 02116
USA

To Jacquie

# Contents

# List of case studies

# Series foreword

This book is part of the Business in Context series. The books in this series are written by lecturers all with several years' experience of teaching on undergraduate business studies programmes. When the series first appeared in 1989, the original rationale was to place the various disciplines found in the business studies curriculum firmly in a business context. This is still our aim. Business studies attracted a growing band of students throughout the 1980s, a popularity that has been maintained in the 1990s. If anything, that appeal has broadened, and business studies, as well as a specialism in its own right, is now taken with a range of other subjects, particularly as universities move towards modular degree structures. We feel that the books in this series provide an important focus for the student seeking some meaning in the range of subjects currently offered under the umbrella of business studies.

With the exception of the text, *Business in Context*, which takes the series title as its theme, all the original texts in our series took the approach of a particular discipline traditionally associated with business studies and taught widely on business studies and related programmes. These first books in our series examined business from the perspectives of economics, behavioural science, law, mathematics and accounting. The popularity of the series across a range of courses has meant that the second editions of many of the original texts are about to be published and there are plans to extend the series by examining information technology, operations management, human resource management and marketing.

Whereas in traditional texts it is the subject itself that is the focus, our texts make business the focus. All the texts are based upon the same specific model of business illustrated in Figure 1.1. We have called our model Business in Context and the text of the same name is an expansion and explanation of that model.

The model comprises four distinct levels. At the core are found the activities which make up what we know as business and include innovation, operations and production, purchasing, marketing, human resource management and finance and accounting. We see these acti-

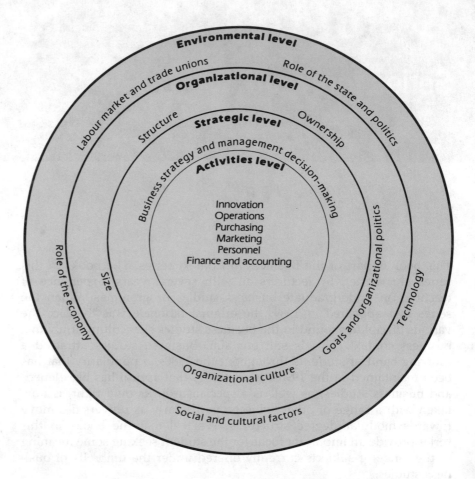

vities operating irrespective of the type of business involved and are found in both the manufacturing and service industry as well as in the public and private sectors. The second level of our model is concerned with strategy and management decision-making. It is here that decisions are made which influence the direction of the business activities at our core. The third level of our model is concerned with organizational factors within which business activities and management decisions take place. The organizational issues we examine are structure, size, goals and organizational politics, patterns of ownership and organizational culture. Clear links can be forged between this and other levels of our model, especially between structure and strategy, goals and management decision-making, and how all aspects both contribute to and are influenced by the organizational culture. The fourth level concerns itself with the environment in which businesses operate. The issues here involve social and cultural factors, the role of the state and politics, the role of the economy, and issues relating to both technology and labour. An important feature of this fourth level of our model is that such elements not only operate as opportunities and constraints for business, but also that they are shaped by the three other levels of our model.

This brief description of the Business in Context model illustrates the key features of our series. We see business as dynamic. It is constantly being shaped by and in turn shaping those managerial, organizational and environmental contexts within which it operates. Influences go backwards and forwards across the various levels. Moreover, the aspects identified within each level are in constant interaction with one another. Thus the role of the economy cannot be understood without reference to the role of the state; size and structure are inextricably linked; innovation is inseparable from issues of operations, marketing and finance. The understanding of how this model works is what business studies is all about and forms the basis for our series.

In proposing this model we are proposing a framework for analysis and we hope that it will encourage readers to add to and refine the model and so broaden our understanding of business. Each writer in this series has been encouraged to present a personal interpretation of the model. In this way we hope to build up a more complete picture of business.

Our series therefore aims for a more integrated and realistic approach to business than has hitherto been the case. The issues are complex but the authors' treatments are not. Each book in this series is built around the Business in Context model, and each displays a number of common features that mark out this series. First, we aim to present our ideas in a way that students will find easy to understand and we relate those ideas wherever possible to real business situations. Second, we hope to stimulate further study both by referencing our material and pointing students towards further reading at the end of each chapter. Third, we use the notion of 'key concepts' to highlight the most significant aspects of the subject presented in each chapter. Fourth, we use case studies to illustrate our material and stimulate further discussion. Fifth, we present at the end of each chapter a series of questions, exercises and discussion topics. To sum up, we feel it most important that each book will stimulate thought and further study and assist the student in developing powers of analysis, a critical awareness and ultimately a point of view about business issues.

We have already indicated that the series has been devised with the undergraduate business studies student uppermost in our minds. We also maintain that these books are of value wherever there is a need to understand business issues and may therefore be used across a range of different courses including some BTEC Higher programmes and some postgraduate and professional courses.

David Needle and Eugene McKenna
January 1994

# Preface to the first edition

The origins for this book lie in a course I taught for a number of years to undergraduate business studies students. That course was called 'Business and its Environment' and it attempted to introduce students with little prior notion of business to the major business activities. An important theme of the course was the interrelated nature, both of the activities themselves, and of their dealings with the strategic, organizational and environmental contexts in which they operated. A second important theme was the identification of what was considered at the time to be key issues in business, such as the interest in small firms and in Japanese management. These two themes are the basis of *Business in Context*.

The course was always a challenge to teach, but almost impossible to support with reading material sympathetic to its aims. Students were faced with daunting reading lists, and I was faced with a growing criticism from students over the lack of a textbook. This book is an attempt to stifle those criticisms and happily coincided with the plans of Van Nostrand Reinhold (later Chapman & Hall) to broaden their activities in the business and management field.

Like many authorship ventures the book has been slow to arrive and confirmed my deepest suspicions as to why the writers of textbooks often hunt in pairs.

In teaching the aforementioned course I developed a model to show the complex workings of business. With a few refinements the model forms the basis of the Business in Context series and is the main linking factor in that series of related texts. This book, the first in the series, presents a detailed examination of the workings of that model, stressing the interrelationship between business activities and the various contexts in which they operate.

While the origins of this book relate to a specific course, the growth of business studies as a discipline, or group of integrated disciplines (a debate I shall not prolong), means that ever more students are in need of a book which at least attempts to introduce them to the complexities of their chosen subject. I strongly maintain that this book is suitable for any course where an understanding of the integrated nature of business activities is required, and particularly where students need to develop perspectives on key business issues. Most undergraduate business studies programmes contain such courses, and this is the main market at which this book is aimed. It is also suitable for some BTEC, post-graduate and professional programmes.

As we state in the series editor's foreword, business is treated throughout the series in its widest possible context, and this book is no exception, including as it does illustrations drawn from a variety of contexts. One of the interesting features of the 1980s is the convergence of all types of organization towards similar methods of operation either by choice or through the pressure of external influences. Certainly, whatever our perspective, many educational establishments are currently displaying the kinds of strategies we normally associate with more traditional businesses.

As with any book which takes the broad sweep that this one does there is bound to be a great deal of selectivity. This is true of the material in general but particularly true of the various illustrations I have used. The main criteria for their inclusion is that they interested me. Many are attributed to their rightful source, but many are the product of years discussing business issues with students, friends and colleagues. It is an author's privilege to claim for him- or herself the ideas of others. I acknowledge all those sources here. The only reason for their inclusion is that they should stimulate the reader's own thoughts to develop new perspectives on business issues.

David Needle
January 1989

# Preface to the second edition

In the five years that have elapsed since the first edition, the world has undergone a number of significant political changes. The Communist bloc has collapsed, and with it, the Berlin Wall and the former divisions between West and East. Germany has been reunified and, in many parts of former Eastern Europe, cultural factionalism and developing capitalism have brought new tensions. Alongside this the European Community, through the Maastricht Treaty, has strengthened its resolve for increasing unity. Influential political leaders such as Thatcher and Gorbachev have been ousted from power, and Reagan's successor in the US Presidency failed to gain re-election after a term in office.

While the impact of many of these changes will need time to assess, an attempt is made to introduce the more obvious changes in this edition, particularly in a much expanded Chapter 2. The previous edition was written at a time when the full impact of political changes in the UK under Margaret Thatcher were being assessed. This edition examines that era in terms of its policy implications for business, more especially in Chapters 2 and 3. Expanded treatment is given to economic issues, the EC, culture at national and organizational levels, innovation, quality and several other areas. The former chapter on personnel has been revised to accommodate the increasing focus upon human resource management. New cases have been added on the sterling collapse, London Zoo, British Airways, Hoover, Glaxo and management in South East Asia. The last case has been informed by my experience of teaching on the University's MBA programme in Singapore. As always, the main aim of this book is to stimulate thought and to enable readers to develop new perspectives on business issues.

David Needle
January 1994

# Acknowledgements

There are many who deserve my thanks for helping me write this book. The students and staff at the University of East London assisted me in developing many of the ideas which resulted in the first edition. For this edition, I thank, particularly, Sukhdev Johal for his assistance in compiling the economic data in Chapter 2.

As with the first edition, I owe the biggest debt to my wife, Jacquie, both for her support and her own knowledge of business issues.

# The concept of Business in Context

**1**

The major theme of this book, and of the series of which it forms a part, is that businesses are complex. They cannot be understood by reference to their activities alone. These activities, which include innovation, production and operations, marketing, human resource management, finance and accounting and so on, take place in a series of contexts. It is our contention that they can only be understood fully when those contexts within which they operate are also understood. In this first chapter we will explain what we mean by business and identify the relevant contexts. It is also our contention that the relationship between business activities and these contexts is dynamic.

In the foreword we introduced a model of business around which this and other books in the series are based. We present the model once again in Figure 1.1 and use it to illustrate the elements of this dynamic relationship. The workings of the model are explained by two case studies. The first concerns changes that have occurred in the shipping industry over the last 25 years, while the second focuses more specifically on a single organization, News International, and the events surrounding a major dispute with its workforce in 1985. We introduce briefly two theoretical approaches to the analysis of business organizations; the systems and contingency approaches. These are often used as the starting point for our analysis throughout this book and reference will be made to them in other chapters. We will conclude this first chapter by outlining the layout of this book.

## Businesses and their contexts

The popular image of a typical business firm is invariably that of a manufacturing industry, and probably large-scale mass production at that. In this text we hope to present a broader view of business. Businesses operate in all kinds of areas, including manufacturing industry, but also embracing such activities as retailing, banking and other financial services, transport and so on. The publishers of this book are engaged in a business activity, involving the production, marketing and selling of books to generate income to make both profit and finance future operations. Businesses also vary considerably in terms of size. Indeed, in recent years the focus has shifted away from large-scale operations and small businesses have become popular with governments and academics alike and, accordingly, will be acknowledged in this text.

| | |
|---|---|
| **KEY CONCEPT 1.1**<br>*Business* | A business is the organized effort of individuals to produce and provide goods and services to meet the needs of society. We view business as a broad concept, incorporating profit-making concerns such as manufacturing firms and banks, and non-profit-making concerns such as schools and hospitals. |

The image that businesses are exclusively profit-oriented will also be challenged. Business systems and methods operate in all kinds of organization. Many institutions of higher education operate with budgets in excess of £40 million, and represent fairly complex organizations in which all the activities normally associated with business may be identified. For example, there are few colleges who do not market their courses, or from time to time experience the kind of industrial relations problems normally associated with manufacturing industry. Hospitals too are large, complex organizations experiencing the type of management problems found in businesses anywhere. In recent years this has been acknowledged by the creation of new hospital top management posts, many of which have been filled by candidates from the private business world. In any case, the distinction between profit and non-profit organizations has become increasingly blurred. All universities and colleges are actively engaged in income generation through selling their services to business firms. The growth of medical provision outside the National Health Service has seen the growth of profit-oriented private hospitals which compete in the market place for customers and advertise their wares.

As we can see from Figure 1.1 we have identified a number of business activities. In this book we deal with them under five main groups; innovation, production, marketing, human resource management and accounting. Each of these groups is sufficiently broad to cover a number of related functions. For instance it is acknowledged that purchasing is an important business activity, but it is dealt with under the heading of production for the purposes of this text. The production function itself is regarded in the widest operational context and as such is present in all forms of business organization. There are two points to consider when examining business activities. First, they interact with one another, so that operational decisions influencing the quantity and quality of the goods produced and the services provided will have significant implications for the other functional areas. Second, as we have already indicated, these activities do not exist in a vacuum, but are shaped by and in turn shape the contexts within which they operate.

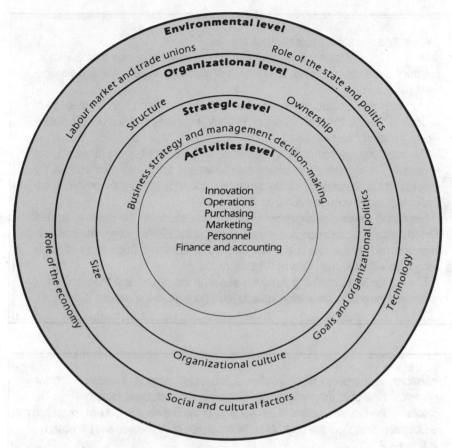

Labour market and trade unions
Role of the state and politics
Structure
Ownership
Business strategy and management decision-making

**Activities level**

Innovation
Operations
Purchasing
Marketing
Personnel
Finance and accounting

Role of the economy
Size
Goals and organizational politics
Technology
Organizational culture
Social and cultural factors

Environmental level
Organizational level
Strategic level

*Figure 1.1*   The Business in Context model.

In our Business in Context model we have identified three types of context; strategic, organizational and environmental. We will deal briefly with each of these in turn.

At the strategic level we are concerned with those management decisions, and the influences on those decisions which determine the direction of business activities. Strategic decisions will influence such factors as the product range, the amount spent on advertising, the recognition of trade unions and so on. Strategies are often a question of reconciling opportunities and constraints which exist within both the organization and the environment in which it operates. The managing director of a small firm with a potentially profitable innovation often faces a strategic dilemma. Its organizational size means that expanding production capacity is impossible and its credit standing is such that it may be unable to raise sufficient development capital. The availability of finance is, in any case, a function of the economic and political climate. Alternatives might be to sell the idea for development by a larger firm or simply accept a merger with the larger organization; both of which may be personally unacceptable to the owner of the small business. In this way, strategic issues are inseparable from the

**KEY CONCEPT 1.2**
*Business activities*

We identify a number of major business activities.

*The innovation function* is concerned with the development of new business ideas, in terms of products, processes, and methods of marketing, organization and management (Chapter 5).

*The production function* comprises those activities concerned with the creation of goods and services through the bringing together and mixing of a number of resource inputs, including materials, labour, finance, and plans (Chapter 6).

*The marketing function* deals with all those activities which relate directly to the consumer. These involve researching the market and using that information in the development of the product, pricing, promoting, and ensuring that the product eventually reaches the consumer (Chapter 7).

*The human resource management function* is concerned with the planning, acquisition, development, utilization and reward of an organization's human resources. An important part of the role is the management of conflict through those activities associated with industrial relations (Chapter 8).

*The finance and accounting function* deals with the raising and management of funds, and the production of information to facilitate these two processes (Chapter 9).

**KEY CONCEPT 1.3**
*Interaction*

Interaction is a process which involves a two–way influence. It occurs when two elements are able to exert influences which bring about changes in each other. The process of interaction is central to the workings of the Business in Context model and is illustrated throughout this book, as in the interaction of businesses and the economy in Chapter 2.

**KEY CONCEPT 1.4**
*Strategy*

A strategy comprises a set of objectives and methods of achieving those objectives. A strategy is usually formulated by top management and is based on a mixture of careful analysis of the environment and the organization (Key concepts 1.5 and 1.7), the personal preferences of the managers involved, and a process of negotiation with other interested parties such as shareholders and trade unions (Chapter 4).

organization and environment in which they operate, and can in fact alter those two other contexts. It is widely accepted that the structure of a firm is often a product of its strategy (Chandler, 1962). The overseas investment strategies of large multinational corporations have been seen to have considerable influence on the economic and political affairs of other nations, especially those in the Third World.

At the organizational level we are concerned with such issues as size, ownership, goals and structure. Many such issues are inter-related. The public ownership of business firms may well mean the pursuit of social as well as business goals, and publicly owned firms invariably

> An organization refers to the way in which people are grouped and the way in which they operate to carry out the activities of the business. We define the key elements of the organization as the goals of the business and the way they are formulated, ownership and control, size, structure and organizational culture (Chapter 3).
>
> **KEY CONCEPT 1.5**
> *Organization*

have bureaucratic structures. This is partly a function of organizational culture, and partly a function of the large scale of most public-sector operations. All firms as they increase in size tend to adopt more formalized structures. Such organizational factors can place limitations on the nature of business activities; formalized structures can inhibit certain types of product and process development; the existing size can be a restriction on expansion as we saw in our illustration of strategic issues. In more general terms these organizational factors combine with management strategy to create distinctive organizational cultures.

> The environment includes all those elements which exist outside the organization and which interact with it. These interactions occur on three levels: at the local level, as with competition among firms offering the same product in the same market; at the national level, as with the influence of government policy; and at the international level, as through the operation of multinational companies or the interchange of business ideas from different countries. We define the key elements of the environment as the economy, the state, technology, labour and cultural factors relating to specific societies or nations.
>
> **KEY CONCEPT 1.6**
> *Environment*

We have identified five factors which operate at the environmental level; the economy, the state, labour, technology and culture. Some of these factors are deliberately broad. The state includes discussion of government, legal and political issues; labour takes into account both the workings of the labour market and the activity of trade unions; culture includes both social factors related to business as well as those issues which differentiate businesses in different countries. As with the other factors in our model there is considerable interaction between these various environmental factors. The membership and power of trade unions is a function of the level of economic activity and the restrictions imposed by the law, which in turn reflects the policy of governments. The composition of the labour market reflects changes in technology, and the mobility of labour within different countries varies with the social and cultural traditions of those countries. Technological innovations are often motivated both by declining economic fortunes and by direct state intervention. Similarly we can cite illustrations of the interaction between the environment and our other contexts. The technological complexity of the product market in which the firm operates will largely determine the extent of its research and development activity, and hence its strategies and structure. In traditional manufacturing industry, a strong trade-union presence will determine the size, shape, policies and activities of the human resource management department. Goals, size, structure and activities all tend to change as the economic environment changes.

The interplay which typifies the relationship between business activities and the contexts in which they operate will be a constant theme in this book. We will attempt to show that many of the relationships are two-way. The economic environment referred to above not only shapes businesses, but is in turn a product of business activity. Changes in technology are products of innovation activity at the level of the firm. We are thus able to build up a model of business as a constant interplay of interactions and influences.

We are able to illustrate the workings of the model by reference to two cases, the first concerning the worldwide shipping industry and the second focusing on a single, albeit large firm in the newspaper industry. In both cases we will explain the events and central issues, following this with an analysis of each case using our Business in Context model as a framework.

## The shipping industry

The shipping industry referred to in this case is that industry concerned largely with the transport of goods by sea, and not to be confused with shipbuilding. The information for the case is taken largely from a study of the shipping industry, titled *Innovating to Compete* (Walton, 1987). Walton examines eight countries; Denmark, Holland, Japan, Norway, Sweden, United Kingdom, USA and the former West Germany. The choice of the eight nations is significant in that they represent the world's traditional merchant fleets and accounted for 74% of the entire world tonnage in shipping prior to the Second World War. Since the war the powerful position of these shipping nations has been challenged by a variety of factors. By 1973 their collective tonnage had fallen to 43% and by 1983 to 26%. The case study identifies those factors and examines the strategic responses of the shipping companies concerned. It should be remembered that while merchant fleets are invariably linked to nation states, shipping is operated as a business and shipping companies are privately owned.

In Walton's study, two phases were to be identified, the first 1963–73, and the second 1973–83.

### Period 1: 1963–73

For the eight nations listed above, this period was one of economic prosperity. The demand for shipping exceeded supply and that demand was increasing throughout this period at a rate of 7% a year. It was also a period in which unemployment was extremely low and the shipping industry faced intense competition for its labour from land-based industries. The lure of seafaring had declined with the prospect of long periods away from home and the increasing development of functional ports in unglamorous locations away from the main centres of urban life. Furthermore, time spent in port had been sacrificed to the fast turn-around of vessels to save cost and maximize operational time. Combined with these factors was a growing resistance to the quasi-military regime of the merchant navy, especially in the face of attractive job opportunities elsewhere. Labour shortages became the norm in the shipping industry of all these nations. Under such conditions the bargaining power of trade unions is substantially strengthened, as was the case in the majority companies covered by the study. Wage rates were increased to attract and keep labour, with a corresponding increase in costs. Nevertheless demand for shipping was still high and the industry remained relatively healthy with increased costs being borne by the customer through increased freight charges.

## Period 2: 1973–83

1973 was a watershed for the shipping industry in the eight nations. The problems caused by the high costs of labour were superseded by very high interest rates and a dramatic increase in the cost of fuel. Unfortunately as far as these developed countries were concerned, price competition within the industry had increased through the activity of two types of new entrant.

First, there had been the fast growth of shipping operating under 'flags of convenience'. Such shipping is associated with such countries as Liberia and Panama, where the cost of registering and insuring ships is much lower than in traditional shipping nations. The advantage to the shipowner is not just in terms of registration and insurance. The regulations which cover shipping operations and shipboard practices tend to be far less restrictive, and labour tends to be cheaper too. A country like Liberia has actively marketed this service and sees it as an important source of foreign investment. Under such a mechanism, overheads and labour costs are kept to a minimum, and shipping operating under a 'flag of convenience' is able to enter the marketplace offering an attractive price to the customer. It is hardly suprising that the eight nations saw a defection of shipowners from their fleets to such 'flags of convenience'. The bulk transport of the world's oil supply quickly became the prerogative of the Liberian tanker fleet, heavily underwritten and supported by the major multinational oil corporations.

Second, certain governments, particularly those of the former Soviet bloc nations and those of developing countries, see their own shipping industry as a means of achieving highly prized international recognition. The industry becomes both metaphorically and literally a flag-carrier for its sponsoring nation. Government-backed shipping from such countries has, like the 'flags of convenience', reduced the price and widened the choice for the customer.

The problems facing the eight nations were therefore intensified and by 1983 the entire industry was suffering from problems of over-capacity. This became particularly acute as the decade from 1973, unlike its predecessor, marked a decline in the demand for shipping.

## The strategic options of shipping companies in the established nations

We can see that a combination of rising labour costs, rising fuel costs, high interest rates, cheap competition and overcapacity had seriously weakened the competitive position of the eight developed nations in Walton's study. Those firms still operating were faced with a number of options in order to maintain their competitive position. The strategic options and the problems associated with them may be identified as follows.

- Some firms found that the move towards much larger vessels enabled them to achieve economies of scale and compete on price. Such an option was not available to all due to the very high investment costs needed for this type of strategy.
- Some governments decided to assist their own shipping industry by setting up subsidies and by granting generous tax allowances. Protectionist strategies and trade agreements have been used to safeguard the position of national fleets. Such agreements might include the provision that all coastal traffic should use national carriers, or that the exchange of imports and exports must be accompanied by a corresponding exchange of shipping services. While some governments were committed to such policies, others showed a complete disinterest and, in some cases, ideological opposition to state intervention.
- A popular strategy involved product specialization. Some companies decided that they could not compete with developing nations and 'flags of convenience' in the transport of bulk cargoes or in the oil tanker trade. Instead, they opted for those cargoes requiring specialist facilities and handling, such as liquid gases and other dangerous chemicals; or they chose to operate with highly mixed loads in relatively small batches. However, overspecialization can be threatened by the lack of demand and the cost of transporting loads in small batches raises its own logistics problems.
- A classic response to the problems of labour shortages and increased labour costs was process innovation. Containerization has been a popular option in many cases; cargoes come ready packed in large containers, reducing the need for dock and shipboard handling. Inevitably, containerization was supported by the development of the 'roll on–roll off' process, where the containers are driven directly on ship and unloaded by container lorry, obviating the need for cargo handling at all. Such developments have been matched by the automation of shipboard engineering, control and monitoring processes and changes in telecommunications rendering traditional methods of ship-to-shore communication redundant. In all cases such innovations reduced the need for labour or enabled

formerly specialized tasks to be substituted by those with a lower skill requirement. However, such changes carry high investment costs and often meet employee resistance to change, more especially union opposition to both reduced manning levels and more flexible work practices.

- In shipping, as with all industries, technical innovations invariably offer the possibility of organizational changes to underline the advantages of the former. In particular, automation and changes in telecommunications introduced the possibility of flexible manning, and hence even greater labour savings. Some companies went even further and attempted to introduce permanent crews operating as a team and ensuring continuity of labour, a radical innovation in an industry built on a history of casual hiring. The move towards teamwork was a deliberate attempt to improve the quality of working life and was accompanied, in some cases, by the creation of less hierarchical organizational structures. These new structures offered more opportunity for delegated authority and participation. Some companies saw such moves as inevitable to match conditions in shore-based industries and to change the merchant navy's image of authoritarian man-management systems to attract labour. Bringing about such changes is not without its difficulties. The very structures that are identified for change are likely to provide the biggest obstacle. The shipping industry is typified by highly bureaucratic structures and shipboard relations steeped in naval tradition where ship captains are highly resistant to participative forms of management.

The options are not mutually exclusive and some shipping companies had pursued all five options in an attempt to maintain their competitive position. Far from being mutually exclusive, some of the options were dependent upon the support of others for maximum effectiveness. The major point of Walton's study is that competitiveness can only be achieved when technical innovations are accompanied by organizational innovations. Our point in using this case is that it serves as a useful illustration of our model of business. It is to this aspect we now turn.

## The shipping industry in a business context

### Environmental aspects

**Economic** factors have had a significant impact on the shipping industry during the period of the study and illustrates, among other things, the interplay of selling price, wage costs and competition. With a buoyant demand the industry could combat labour-market shortages by higher wages offset against increased freight charges. With increased competition together with falling demand other strategies became imperative for business survival.

The state through the activity of national governments has had a major impact on the fortunes of individual shipping companies. This occurs in a number of different ways. One key variable would seem to be a nation's economic structure; support for the shipping industry assumes a greater importance when shipbuilding and oil interests are at stake. The governments of developing countries and those of the former Soviet bloc have seen shipping as a matter of national prestige and have supported it accordingly. The response to increased competition by the eight industrial nations has tended to vary with differing levels of state intervention. Denmark, Holland, Japan and the USA have received most government backing and protection, and it is these four nations that have been most successful in preserving their tonnage. Nation states have also laid down regulations governing the activity of shipping in the interests of those employed and the environment. Sometimes such regulations have stood in the way of organizational changes, especially those involving reductions in manning levels. Conversely it is the very lack of such restrictions that has made 'flags of convenience' attractive to some shipowners.

The technological aspects of this case centre around process innovations aimed at reducing manning levels and costs. Some of these innovations such as containerization and 'roll on–roll off' are direct responses to shipping industry problems. Others, such as automated control systems and communication systems, are the adaptations of state-of-the-art technology for use by the shipping industry.

Labour issues represent a key element in this case. The difficulty in attracting labour to the shipping industry in the period 1963–73 was a major incentive for technical and organizational innovation. The case also illustrates the links between economic conditions, labour-market forces and trade-union power.

In terms of culture, the study compares the different responses of eight nation states to the same problem. These differences do not always follow the expected pattern. For instance, the USA, not known for its state intervention, has taken several steps to protect its merchant fleet, with a subsequent increase in its share of world shipping. A major cultural difference that does occur is that which marks out those nations in the developing world and the former Soviet bloc from the eight industrially developed nations of the study. An interesting feature of the case from a cultural point of view occurs not at the national but at the industrial and organizational levels and will be dealt with in the next section.

## Organizational aspects

The organizational aspects of this case are dominated by issues relating to structure. Environmental influences, especially those concerned with competition, new technology and the labour market, together with the individual company's strategic response, have resulted in changes in the organization structure of many shipping firms. The major changes have been the breakdown of a traditional hierarchical naval structure with its emphasis on formalization, specialization and authoritarian management style. In its place have emerged much more flexible structures with an elimination of class barriers between officers and ratings, much greater job flexibility and delegation of authority. The case therefore shows the inter-related and interactive nature of environmental and organizational aspects.

Overall the changes identified above represent a major attempt to change the **organizational culture** of individual shipping companies as part of a strategic response to a weakened competitive position.

The case also shows how **goals** differ between shipping companies in different nations. The eight nations appear to be linked by the super-ordinate goal of survival, while the state sponsorship of shipping in the former Soviet Bloc identifies political as well as business goals. While the survival and competition goals of the shipping companies may find broad agreement, the means through which such goals may be achieved does not. Unions may oppose manning reductions and flexible work practices; some management may resent a shift away from authoritarian naval traditions; national governments, trade unions, and many seamen may object to the migration of shipowners to 'flags of convenience'. The last illustration of goal conflict also raises the issue of **ownership** versus control. Owners faced with problems of profitability may seek solutions that are unpopular to other interested parties.

**Size** is an important variable in the shipping industry. The sheer scope of operations and the investment costs of fitting out a large ocean-going vessel tend to favour the large company. This relationship has been further underlined by the costs of containerization, automatic control systems and the like. Additionally a fair proportion of shipping trade is associated with large multinational corporations like the oil companies. There are, however, niches in the industry for the smaller operator, such as tramp-steamer operations where goods are transported on an irregular basis up and down the same stretch of coastline.

## Strategic aspects

In our presentation of this case we have isolated from Walton's study a number of strategic responses employed by shipping companies to maintain their market position during a period of change from 1963 to 1983. The case is a good illustration of the role of strategy in our model of business.

First, we can see how strategic options were formulated in response to environmental conditions. In this way shipping companies are adapting to the environment in which they find themselves and conforming to a classic contingency response. However, an important theme of this book is that the relationship between the business environment and business strategy is not just a case of the environment determining strategy. Here we can see that some firms responded to rising costs by transferring the registration of their ships to 'flags of convenience'. The strategy of some shipping companies thus became an additional competitive factor to which other firms had to respond; a case of strategy changing the business environment. In the same way, decisions to change to container cargoes would affect the interplay between shipping, port and other transport industries.

Second the case illustrates the inter-relationship between strategic and organizational aspects, especially structure. We have already noted Walton's main conclusion concerning the interplay between technical and organizational innovations. This is not simply a case of structure following strategy, but structure being an integral part of that strategy.

### Functional aspects

The case illustrates the interplay between the functional areas of our model and the environmental, organizational and strategic aspects identified above.

The **production** function in many of the companies had undergone quite radical changes in both the nature of the product (e.g. containers, specialist chemicals) and the nature of the operating process (e.g. roll on–roll off, automated engineering control systems). Moreover, changes in the organization structure had significant impact on the way work was organized (e.g. flexible manning). Many of these changes are the direct result of product and process **innovation**.

In terms of **marketing**, increased price competition from 'flags of convenience' and other nations has forced many shipping firms in the eight countries to seek new, more specialized markets to replace those, like the oil tanker trade, which are no longer profitable for them. There is a clear interplay between marketing and production through product innovation. The development of containerization, for example, has particular implications for distribution.

Changing **human resource** policies are a key feature of the case. These include flexible work allocation, a more participative management style and an attempt to eliminate casual hiring practices. A focus on personnel issues reveals how not all elements of the business model fit neatly together. Changes which reduce the need for labour are likely to meet with trade-union opposition; calls for workforce participation may be strongly resisted by some management, especially in an industry like shipping, influenced by traditional practices.

**Accounting** decisions lay behind most if not all of the strategic options pursued by the shipping companies in this case. The industry in these eight nations was in slump and profit margins had dwindled. The case reveals that not all the options would be cost-effective for all companies, and a divestment of assets may be the only viable solution.

## News International and Wapping

For almost a year every Saturday evening the residents of a fashionable warehouse conversion on the edges of London's docklands were denied free access to their property. The residents' access was blocked by mass picketing resulting from an industrial dispute between News International and its former Fleet Street employees over the printing of newspapers at the company's newly commissioned Wapping plant. In this section we will examine the background to the dispute and the events from December 1985 to February 1987. Although what has become known as the Wapping dispute focuses on the events of that period, the seeds of that dispute were laid much earlier. As with the shipping industry we will see how this case illustrates our model of business.

News International is a company controlled by Rupert Murdoch, Australian by birth but with recently acquired American citizenship, and with considerable newspaper holdings in Australia and the USA. The British company controls three daily newspapers, *The Times*, *Today* and the *Sun*; and two Sunday newspapers, the *Sunday Times*, and the *News of the World*. The *Sun*, the *Sunday Times* and the *News of the World* are the best selling newspapers of their type in Britain and *The Times* is arguably the nation's most famous daily paper.

In 1978 land was purchased in Wapping with a view to building a large printing works using the latest technology in newspaper production and construction began within two years. At that time News International owned just the *Sun* and the *News of the World* and the plant was part of plan to increase both the output and the size of both newspapers. In 1981, the company purchased both *The Times* and the *Sunday Times*, in the face of accusations that News International would be operating a monopoly against the public interest. Once again there was a desire to increase both the production runs and the size of both newly acquired newspapers. In all cases the size of the newspapers and the quantity of production were restricted by the size of the existing plants around the Fleet Street area of central London and what management saw as uneconomic manning levels imposed by the trade unions. The issues of new technology and trade union control over work practices lay at the heart of most major national newspaper disputes. No national paper was immune and in 1985 alone 95.6 million copies were lost to industrial disputes of one type or another.

## A little background

The major technological innovations were direct input and photocomposition. This means that the printing operation could in effect be carried out by journalists or typists, eliminating the need for traditional print working through a method referred to as 'cold-type' printing. Computer keyboards and VDUs are used to input material to be stored on a central computer which also contains programs for page composition. The computer prints off its stories and advertisements on photographic paper, which are then pasted up to form the eventual pages of the newspaper. These are photographed and a negative is produced. The negative is converted into a flexible polymer plate to be clipped to the existing presses for the printing to commence.

Under this method around 3000 lines a minute could be typeset compared with seven lines per minute using the conventional technique, with the added advantage that stories and whole pages could be changed and mistakes corrected quickly and cheaply. Such methods had been used by American newspapers since the early 1960s. In Britain however, the introduction of new technology had been slow. There was a strong adherence to the traditional process of using lino-type, a method involving the creation of the type from molten lead, sometimes known as the 'hot metal' process. This method is labour-intensive and is often performed by compositors using equipment some fifty years old. The new generation of printing presses are much cheaper and can therefore be scrapped when further technical im-provements are made. Even where photocomposition had been in-troduced, the process was not used to its full potential as, under management–union agreements, keyboard operations were still being performed by print workers and not journalists or typists.

The printing industry is one of the most traditional of the craft in-dustries and has a long history. The print unions have been vigilant in maintaining control over the apprenticeship system, entry to the pro-fession, and over the way the job is done. These are traditional craft controls aided by the rigid enforcement of a union closed shop. Such controls were greatest in Fleet Street where job entry was reserved only for existing members of a recognized trade union (a pre-entry closed shop). The two major unions were the National Graphical Association (NGA), covering the printers themselves and the Society of Graphical and Allied Trades (SOGAT 82), covering dispatch, distribution and clerical workers.

In this way the union controlled work allocation and above all, man-ning levels for each job. Frequent management complaints concerned overmanning and the inability to implement changes that would in-variably be accompanied by uneconomic manning requirements. There was considerable resistance to the introduction of new technology, as this would effectively reduce the craft control of the job and make it accessible to those not trained as printers.

Despite management's frequent complaints, the situation was largely of their own making. Concessions to trade-union control of manning levels had been made due to the highly competitive nature of the national newspaper industry, the highly perishable nature of the product, and the need for maximum flexibility, especially when dealing with late changes in news items. Competition was not just for readers, but for advertisers. Lost production could never be regained and lost distribution could not be sold at a later date. These factors also gave the trade unions considerable strength in wage negotiation and Fleet Street workers were able to achieve higher rates than those earned by other print workers.

It was partly competition which led to Fleet Street management adopting a new approach to the introduction of new technology. The relative cheapness of cold type over hot metal reduced one of the major barriers to entry to newspaper production. The initial challenges came in the provinces with the growth of the 'free newspaper' industry. These are essentially cheaply produced local papers where advertising takes precedence over news items. The income from advertising is such that the newspapers can be distributed free to all householders in a given area. This sharpened competition in the local paper market. The response among some existing local papers was to force through the introduction of new technology. The *Nottingham Evening Post* in the face of union opposition from the NGA simply replaced the print workers.

The real focus was in 1983 with the case of the Messenger group of free local newspapers in south Lancashire and its proprieter Eddie Shah. In expanding his distribution and introducing direct input printing he overcame bitter opposition from the NGA. He was backed in his quest by new laws redefining industrial disputes and imposing greater restrictions on picketing, drawn up by a government intent on curbing the power of the unions. The NGA were fined by the courts and Shah achieved all his objectives. He built upon his success with the local newspaper industry and launched a new national daily paper *Today*, using new technology and non-traditional workers in a labour force one-tenth the normal size for such a newspaper. At the same time plans were announced for the launch of other new daily and Sunday national papers. Although Shah's ownership of *Today* was brief and unprofitable (he sold the paper to Lonrho, who in turn sold it to News International), the relationship between Fleet Street management and the print unions had changed irrevocably. At the same time Express newspapers announced plans to reduce its workforce by 30%.

Competition came not just from within the industry but through the coverage and the expansion of the television news services. The advent of breakfast television posed an even greater threat to an already declining total newspaper readership. The newspaper industry needed new technology to provide a better quality product with clearer newsprint and sharper pictures and an ability to respond quickly to changing news stories.

## Events at Wapping

Before Murdoch's acquisition *The Times* had attempted to force the new technology issue, but an 11-month shutdown in 1978 altered very little and the NGA retained exclusive control over typesetting operations. The completion of the plant at Wapping and the expense involved in interest payments alone gave new urgency to some form of agreement with the print unions. However, negotiations to move the production of the *Sun* and *News of the World* broke down in early 1984. The unions had refused to give way on the issue of manning levels and demarcation. Murdoch was clearly frustrated by the failure to reach agreement and, undoubtedly spurred by Shah's action against the NGA, ensured that Wapping was protected against the action of pickets. During the dispute the building was popularly known as 'Fortress Wapping'. Plans were laid to treat Wapping as a greenfield site for the production of a new London evening paper staffed with non-Fleet Street people. At the time the unions saw this as a diversion to mask the true intention of transferring production of all four newspapers to Wapping.

Whatever the intention, Murdoch was determined to introduce total management control over manning levels and achieve total labour flexibility. News International terminated all its existing collective agreements with the unions with the aim of replacing them with a legally binding contract and a no-strike clause, the elimination of the closed shop, and binding arbitration in the case of a dispute. The penalty for breaking the agreement would be instant dismissal for individuals and the right to sue the union for unlimited amounts. Such a strategy was calculated to confront the unions on the issue of job control and not surprisingly was rejected by NGA and SOGAT 82. The two unions insisted that any move to Wapping should be accompanied by no redundancies and the maintenance of existing work practices. As a result, Murdoch declared that negotiations were over and gave his print workers six months' notice and no option of jobs at Wapping.

One union, the Electrical, Electronic, Telecommunication and Plumbing Union (EETPU), was prepared to negotiate on the basis of the new proposals, much against the advice of the trade-union movement's central body, the TUC. For some time the electricians' union had been keen to expand its membership in new areas and viewed its members as key workers in all workplaces increasingly operating under the demands of new technology. One of those areas was printing, and the union had even gone so far as to provide training for its members in newspaper production.

Electricians were recruited by News International initially to commission the new presses. However, by the end of January 1986 the Wapping plant was producing the four newspaper titles amid much secrecy, using electricians recruited from outside London and transported daily by an organized bus network. This led to considerable recriminations within the trade-union movement and calls to expel the EETPU from the TUC. They were eventually expelled at the 1988 TUC Conference. The move had also affected the journalists on all papers. Many moved to Wapping for increased salaries but several refused to work under the new arrangements. For their part the print unions held a secret ballot which showed that most were in favour of strike action. Picket lines were set up outside Wapping and SOGAT attempted to prevent the distribution of the newspapers with the help of the transport workers union (TGWU). Both unions were countered by the law. In the case of the TGWU the threat was sufficient, but SOGAT was fined £25 000 and had its assets sequestrated by the High Court for persistent attempts to prevent newspaper distribution.

By the following month News International agreed to the involvement of ACAS. The main issue that emerged was that of redundancy payments for those on strike. The company had always maintained that those choosing this course of action forfeited their right to severance pay and had effectively dismissed themselves. The company did offer the unions the old *Sunday Times* printing plant so that they could set up their own newspaper staffed by the displaced workforce. The offer was rejected by the unions, who insisted on the maximum number of workers being taken on at Wapping and generous redundancy payments for the rest. Increasingly, however, the union position was being undermined by events elsewhere. New technology agreements were being reached with unions at the Express and Mirror newspapers and several national newspapers announced their own plans to move to Docklands. In all cases the owners saw the move as an opportunity both to expand and negotiate fresh deals with the trade unions.

By May 1986 the company made what they claimed was a final offer in a bid to end the picketing at Wapping. This comprised a redundancy payment deal totalling £50 million, an opportunity for all workers to apply for vacancies at Wapping as and when they arose, a withdrawal of all legal actions against the unions, and a promise to review the issue of union recognition after a year. The offer was rejected. Picketing was intensified, accompanied by a significant involvement of the police and further legal proceedings to prevent the picketing taking place. As a result of these proceedings SOGAT estimated its losses at £1.5 million. The estimated costs of policing the dispute up to June 1986 were £1 million.

In September News International made a revised offer of redundancy payments to the dismissed workers, again rejected by the NGA and SOGAT 82. The mounting costs of the dispute sought SOGAT to appeal for funds among its membership nationwide. The appeal was rejected.

The first anniversary of the strike in January 1987 was accompanied by the largest mass picket to date and extremely violent clashes between the police and the pickets. Part of the violence was undoubtedly attributed to a growing frustration among the workers and a realization that the unions could no longer afford to continue. The cost of legal proceedings, the general cost of running the dispute, and an impending contempt of court action was too much for the NGA and SOGAT to bear and would have resulted in the elimination of all their assets. By February 1987 both unions, along with the journalists' union accepted a redundancy package for the dismissed employees and the dispute ended.

## The News International case in a business context

The case illustrates all aspects of our Business in Context model.

### Environmental aspects

**Economic** factors are represented by the highly competitive nature of the newspaper industry. The high potential profit from a national title led to fierce competition for circulation and advertising. Traditionally this resulted in a fierce rivalry and lack of cooperation between the owners. The availability of new technology combined with external competition from television and radio meant that technological changes were sought to reduce costs and maintain profit levels. Furthermore, the relative cheapness of that new technology lowered a significant barrier to entry, thereby increasing competition. This has broken the oligopoly of Fleet Street and led to new national titles as well as major changes in regional newspapers resulting from the growth of the free newspaper industry. In a much broader sense, a high level of unemployment may have increased the resolve of the electricians' union to expand its field of activity and influenced the lack of wider support for the printworkers in their dispute. (A good summary of such changes and their impact on management strategy in particular can be found in Oram (1987).)

The state had a considerable influence on events at Wapping both directly and indirectly. There was a direct involvement through the policing of the dispute with extensive costs over a period of a year. The Employment Acts of 1980 and 1982 and the Trade Union Act of 1984 brought about changes in the legal definition of a dispute, and placed restrictions on both picketing and the formation of a closed shop. The unions were challenged on the legality of their dispute and were found wanting. The subsequent clashes between the unions and the courts led to substantial fines being imposed, which eventually brought an end to the dispute. Prior to the events at Wapping, the government of the day had, in 1981, become embroiled in a monopolies issue when News International negotiated to buy *The Times* and *Sunday Times* when it already owned the biggest selling national and Sunday papers. The deal was allowed to go through on the undertaking of editorial freedom for the newly acquired titles. More sceptical observers, like Harold Evans (successively the editor of the *Sunday Times* and *The Times*), saw the acquisition as a reward for News International's editorial support for the government in the previous general election (Evans, 1983). Whatever the situation, this aspect of the case raises the important issue of the relationship between politics and the press.

Technology, or more specifically the introduction of new technology, was a central issue in this case. Changes in the technology of newspaper production brought about the possibility of changes in work allocation. The elimination of traditional printing work through the substitution of direct input and photocomposition challenged the job control of the print workers and ultimately the bargaining position of their trade union. Printing operations could now be performed by journalists and typists, considerably reducing operating costs and presenting much greater scope for editorial changes, allowing newspapers to be much more responsive to changes in the news and hence the needs of the market place. Traditional craft unions like the NGA do not yield their historical controls willingly, hence the intensity and at times the bitterness of the dispute. New technology also gave management a new strategic weapon in dealing with the trade unions and was doubtless seen by some as a means of gaining greater control over costs and workplace practices, especially manning levels. (A much more detailed account of changing technology in the newspaper industry and its impact on labour can be found in Martin (1981).)

Labour issues, as we can see, are inseparable from those relating to technology. New methods not only mean changes in work allocation, but also an ultimate reduction in the number of jobs. The bargaining position of the trade unions was being challenged on the issue of job control at a time when their response was further weakened by high levels of unemployment. The case is not simply a matter of management versus the unions, but illustrates the complexity of the dispute on the union side. The Fleet Street workers had, for a very long time, considered themselves to be the 'aristocrats of labour', positioned at the very top of the printing hierarchy (Bassett, 1986). This had often rankled with printworkers outside London, and may have explained their reluctance in giving full support to their Fleet Street colleagues.

The *Independent* newspaper, launched in 1986, was printed at regional sites away from London, and its management had little difficulty in gaining the agreement of NGA and SOGAT 82 on the use of the new technology. Quite apart from the differences among the printworkers themselves, their position was further challenged by the willingness of the electricians to be trained in newspaper operations. This forms part of a much broader debate within the trade-union movement, as individual unions, mindful of a declining membership, seek to insure their own future by offering the kind of stoppage-free deals sought by management. In the case of Wapping the EETPU were more than happy to replace the printworkers and on a broader front to see themselves ideally placed to become the key trade union of the future in workplaces increasingly controlled by computers. Changes in the trade-union movement are thus reflecting wider occupational changes. For the future, a weakened NGA and SOGAT 82 may be forced to merge and widen their appeal to attract new members. This would further dilute the traditional power base of the craft union in printing.

The aspect of culture is relevant to this case in at least two ways. First, we have the issue of the distinctive culture of Fleet Street, brought about by the competitive nature of the industry and the job control of the craft unions. Work practices, manning levels and wage rates have marked off Fleet Street from the rest of the British newspaper industry. The distinctive Fleet Street culture has been especially resistant to change and thus a major factor in the dispute. Second, comparative studies of the newspaper industry reveal marked differences between Britain and other countries, notably the USA (e.g. Griffin, 1984). The newspaper industry in the USA has embraced new technology with little union opposition. Moreover, in Britain there is much greater evidence of cooperation and solidarity between print workers, ancillary staff and journalists than exists in most other societies.

## Organizational aspects

While the case clearly shows the interaction and influence of the environmental aspects of our model, there are significant organizational influences at work too.

In terms of **size**, though News International's British operation were considerable, part of the motivation behind the move to Wapping lay in the desire to expand. At its previous locations around Fleet Street the opportunities for expansion were denied both by available space, limiting production capacity and distribution, and by manning agreements limiting the size of each edition.

The change to Wapping and the adoption of new printing technology had clear implications for organizational **structure**. A much more flexible structure has emerged for the newspaper industry. The role of the journalist has potentially broadened to assume responsibility for typesetting as well as content. The electricians have emerged as a fast-growing occupational group within the industry. Such changes in work allocation also have implications for management control.

Changes in the newspaper industry have been related to major changes in the ownership of national titles. The acquisition strategies of News International led to the grouping of five major titles under a single ownership. More significantly, the ownership style was one that had developed in Australia and the USA, where new technology in the newspaper industry was well established. Ownership changes away from Fleet Street were also having an impact. We have already made reference to the catalytic effect of Eddie Shah, but ownership changes in some local newspapers like the *Notts Evening Post* led to a much more aggressive style by management, especially towards trade unions and the introduction of new technology.

Changes in ownership often went hand in hand with changes in goals. Historically newspapers have often been regarded as a special kind of product under the control of individual press barons, such as Lord Beaverbrook at the *Daily Express*. As such, profit goals have co-existed with the less common business goals of political, social or moral reform. Increasingly major titles have come under the control of business groups in which newspapers represent just one of a highly diversified stable of products. An extreme case here would be the holding company Lonrho's acquisition of the *Observer* Sunday newspaper. It is unlikely that such changes have taken place without a corresponding elevation of purely business goals. The case illustrates goal conflict in various ways. At its most obvious this is represented by the unions' need to retain job control in the face of mangements' desire to reap the cost savings of new technology. The NGA and SOGAT's goal of union solidarity is sharply contrasted with the EETPU's goal of expansion. From an industrial-relations perspective the case is interesting in revealing how goals shift as disputes develop; in this case from issues of job control to the negotiation of an acceptable redundancy package.

## Strategic aspects

We have seen that changes at News International and in Fleet Street generally have been part of a pattern of interrelated environmental and organizational factors. These changes have resulted in changed culture within national newspaper organizations. A significant contribution to that changing culture has been the changes that have taken place in management strategy. In general terms Fleet Street management appears to have shifted from a reactive, crisis-induced strategy to one typified by long-term, planned technological and organizational change. A combination of a technological imperative and market and economic conditions has led management to adopt a more confident and, as some would term, aggressive approach in dealing with the trade unions. A widely voiced speculation concerning the strategic implications of News International's move to Wapping was that it represented a deliberate confrontation with the trade unions as a prelude to changing work practices once and for all. The unions certainly believed that Wapping was never intended for a new evening paper and that all along it was designed as the operating centre for the company's major titles. Certainly the initial management proposals, effectively removing the union's traditional control of work practices, were ones to which the union were never likely to agree.

Aside from management, the case is an interesting illustration of strategy from a trade-union perspective. Trade unions are faced with the problem of declining membership in an unfavourable economic and political climate. Like businesses in a declining market they have to be very careful about their choice of strategic option. In such a situation the case of new technology presents an interesting dilemma; its acceptance by unions would inevitably entail job losses, yet a refusal to negotiate may have far more serious consequences for the future bargaining position of the union. Just as some businesses find declining markets favourable for growth, then some trade unions can take advantage of a seemingly disadvantageous conditions by proposing deals acceptable to management. In this way the EETPU has embarked upon a fairly vigorous growth strategy, not only securing recognition rights, but in doing so creating work for electricians.

## Functional aspects

At the heart of management strategy in this case are the implications for the functional operations of business. All our functional areas are implicated by News International's move to Wapping.

**Innovation**  Changes in News International's operations have obviously been made possible through process innovations in the newspaper industry. Other types of innovation are illustrated by this case, more especially the entrepreneurial activity of industry newcomers like Shah, attempting to break the traditional Fleet Street monopoly on national newspaper titles.

**Production**  The new site operating under the latest technology offers management a speedier and more flexible operation with a capability of increased capacity. The new location offers all the benefits of a green-field site, with particular improvements in the supply of raw materials and the distribution of the finished product.

**Marketing**  In marketing terms, the case illustrates how the need for change has arisen through increased competition and reduced barriers to entry for would-be competitors. The new printing processes offer the reader and the advertiser the potential for a much improved product.

**Accounting**  Major motivations behind changes in the newspaper industry have been declining readership and reduced profits. The cost of setting up a new operating plant and its commissioning with state-of-the-art technology represents a considerable short-term investment with a potential for long-term cost saving. It is however important from a management perspective that operations commence at the new plant as soon as possible.

**Human resources**  The case focuses around the industrial relations aspects of the transfer to Wapping and the introduction of new technology. The marketing and accounting factors identified above put pressure on the need for a speedy agreement with the unions. On the other hand the setting up of a greenfield site has presented management with an ideal opportunity to introduce a completely new set of personnel and industrial relations policies.

| | |
|---|---|
| **KEY CONCEPT 1.7**<br>*The systems approach* | The systems approach is a view of business involving two related concepts. First, businesses are made up of a series of interactions (Key concept 1.3), involving the various business activities (Key concept 1.2), the various aspects of the organization (Key concept 1.5), and aspects of the environment (Key concept 1.6). What we identify as a business is the sum total of all these influences and interactions. Second, the systems approach views business as a series of inputs from the environment, internal processes and eventual outputs. |

| | |
|---|---|
| **KEY CONCEPT 1.8**<br>*The contingency approach* | The contingency approach focuses on the relationship between the organization and its environment. It embraces the notion that business activities and the way they are organized are products of the environment in which they operate. The most successful businesses are therefore those which are organized to take advantage of the prevailing environmental influences. |

## The systems and contingency approaches

We have stressed both in the series editor's foreword and elsewhere in this introductory chapter that the various elements of our model interact with one another and influences go backwards and forwards across the various levels (see Figure 1.1). We are presenting an interaction–influence model. The idea of such a model for businesses is not new but forms the basis of the systems and contingency approaches, which have been developed as part of organization theory. It is not our intention to present either a comprehensive review or a critique of these two approaches. Instead we present a brief summary of their main ideas. Their importance as far as we are concerned is that they offer the student of business an important framework for analysis.

The systems approach assumes that all organizations are made up of interdependent parts which can only be understood by reference to the whole. As such, organizations may be analysed in terms of inputs, processes, and outputs as we illustrate in Figure 1.2. We can see from this that there are many similarities with our own model.

The development of systems thinking from an organizational perspective starts with the analogy of the firm as a living organism. To be effective, the firm, like the organism, must adapt to its environment in order to survive. The inputs, processes and outputs must be balanced so that the firm can obtain equilibrium, especially with its environment. The application of the systems approach in organizational analysis first gained prominence through the utilization of a socio-technical systems perspective. This is based on the assumption that the social system of the firm and its technical system interact in a complex way. The approach was popularized in the work of the Tavistock Institute and its associated researchers throughout the world (see for example Trist and Bamforth, 1951; Rice, 1958; Emery and Thorsrud, 1976). Unless the social system and the technical system work in harmony, a firm will be inefficient.

The contingency approach can be traced through the work of Woodward (1965), and Burns and Stalker (1966), although the term itself was popularized in the work of Lawrence and Lorsch who wrote,

> Organizational variables are in a complex interrelationship with one another and with conditions in the environment. If an organization's internal states and processes are consistent with external demands . . . it will be effective in dealing with the environment.
>
> (Lawrence and Lorsch, 1967, p. 157)

The contingency approach starts with an analysis of the key environmental variables which shape the organization. It then proceeds with the assumption that the successful firms are those which adapt to the key influences and achieve some kind of best fit with their environment. This approach has been very influential in the area of corporate strategy. The strategist attempts to match the environmental

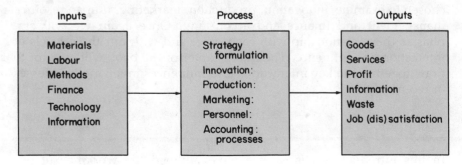

*Figure 1.2  A systems view of business*

opportunities and threats with the organization's own strengths and weaknesses to develop an optimum strategy for the firm in question.

Both the systems and contingency approaches are based on the concept of an organization interacting with several key elements in its environment and adapting to them. Some writers (e.g. Burrell and Morgan, 1979, pp. 164–81) regard the contingency approach as an extension of the systems analysis of organizations. Both approaches have been criticized for focusing on a limited range of environmental variables, for being deterministic and for ignoring both the influence of the organization on its environment and the values and behaviour of management and the workforce. It is our view that such criticisms place unnecessary limits on the use and value of both approaches. In developing our model of business we wish to use systems and contingency thinking to present a broad analytical framework, enabling us to gain a greater insight into the way businesses operate. We are concerned to show, however, that businesses, while influenced by their environments, are not wholly determined by them. Business strategies can and do influence environmental contingencies.

## The layout of this book

The chapters which follow will analyse each of the various elements of our Business in Context model. After examining these elements students are recommended to return to the Shipping and News International cases presented in this opening chapter.

Chapters 2 to 4 will look at the environmental, organizational and strategic contexts respectively. The variables identified in Figure 1.1 will be examined in turn. In our discussion of these variables certain issues emerge which call for more detailed consideration. For example, in our treatment of culture as an environmental variable we deal at some length with the phenomenon known as 'Japanese Management', and in viewing size as an organizational variable raise the topic of small businesses. Such issues are chosen for their topicality, but, more significantly, that they further illustrate the workings of our Business in Context model by drawing together the various activities and their contexts.

Chapters 5 to 9 will focus on the functional areas of business we have chosen to examine; innovation, production, marketing, human resource management and finance and accounting. Once again we will emphasize their relationship with each other and with our three levels of interaction and influence. The final chapter of the book will attempt to draw together the key interactions and influences involving businesses in recent years.

## Summary

In this introductory chapter we have outlined the workings of our Business in Context model and in so doing mapped out the rest of this book. In the model we identify a number of key variables which interact with business. We have arranged these variables in a series of levels, which we have termed environmental, organizational and strategic. We believe that our understanding of the way businesses and their key activities operate is enhanced by placing them in this contextual framework.

The workings of the model can be seen by reference to two cases. The first deals with the shipping industry and in particular the impact of the recession and increased competition on the shipping fleets of eight industrially developed nations. The second case looks at a single company, News International, and focuses on the events surrounding relocation, technical change and a major labour dispute in 1985. The theoretical underpinnings of the model are discussed with reference to the systems and contingency approaches to organizational analysis.

## Further reading

Although they concentrate more upon organizations, their processes and theories, two other texts can be recommended for attempting to integrate their subject matter giving fresh insights into the complexities of business. These are John Child, *Organization: A Guide to Problems and Practice*, 2nd edition (Harper & Row, 1984), and Sandra Dawson, *Analyzing Organizations*, 2nd edition (Macmillan, 1992). Those students seeking more background to the systems and contingency approaches should look at G. Burrell and G. Morgan, *Sociological Paradigms and Organization Analysis* (Heinemann, 1979), and two seminal studies in the area; T. Burns and G. Stalker, *The Management of Innovation* (Tavistock, 1966) and J. Lawrence and P. Lorsch, *Organization and Environment* (Harvard University Press, 1967). More information on the shipping industry case can be found in R. E. Walton, *Innovating to Compete* (Jossey-Bass, 1987), while aspects of the News International case can be found in R. Martin, *New Technology and Industrial Relations in Fleet Street* (Clarendon Press, 1981).

## Discussion

1  We have identified five environmental and five organizational variables in our model. By necessity these represent broad categories. What are the possible elements which might be considered under the various headings in our model of business?
2  Using the way we have analysed the two cases as your guide, take in turn an industry, a firm and a specific issue, and analyse each using the Business in Context model.
3  What is the value of the systems and contingency approaches to an understanding of business?

# 2 The environment and business

In Chapter 1 we introduced the model which forms the basis of our analysis of business. In this chapter we focus on a major element of that model, namely the environment. We define the environment as comprising all factors which exist outside the business enterprise, but which interact with it. As we pointed out in the last chapter, all firms are to a greater or lesser extent constrained by the environment within which they operate, but the activities of businesses themselves also change that same environment. This two-way process is an important theme throughout the book.

In devoting just one chapter to the business environment, the material is necessarily highly selective. Five key areas have been identified, namely the economy, the role of the state, technology, labour and culture. We devote a section to each of these topics and identify issues which illustrate the interaction between the firm and its environment. Each of the areas selected also interact with the others as the matrix presented in Figure 2.1 shows.

For the business manager, the environment therefore comprises a number of key variables which interact with the business either singly or jointly. The complexity does not end there. These interactions may occur on a number of different levels, as shown in Figure 2.2. First, a firm interacts with a local environment, in which expansion plans may need approval from the local council, and where its marketing and personnel strategies will be significantly influenced by firms operating in the same local market. Second, interaction occurs in a national environment, influenced by such matters as government laws, bank interest rates, the rate of inflation, and national trade-union policy. Third, we have the international environment in which the firm may be affected by international money exchange rates, the competition from cheap labour economies, and the regulations of supranational bodies such as the European Union. As a general rule, the ability of managers to influence their environment diminishes as they move further away from the local environment. As with all such rules there are exceptions, since the ability to influence the environment tends to increase with the size of the firm. We shall see in our discussion

| | LABOUR | TECHNOLOGY | STATE | ECONOMY | |
|---|---|---|---|---|---|
| **STATE** | | | | The extent and direction of state intervention in the economy. The power of the multinationals in influencing policy. | S T A T E |
| **TECHNOLOGY** | | | State support of innovation and technical change and the specific impact on certain industries e.g., defence. | The impact of innovation on economic growth. | T E C H N O L O G Y |
| **LABOUR** | | The impact of technical change on skills and trade union policy towards such changes. | Government policies to direct the supply of labour. Legislation to regulate trade union activities. | The impact of the economy on the type and levels of employment. | L A B O U R |
| | Cultural influences on personnel and industrial relations strategies. | The impact of changes in technology on society. Cultural attitudes towards technology. | Cultural explanations for the differences between nations regarding state intervention. | The nature of the economy shaping family life e.g., agricultural vs industrial societies. The influence of cultural values on the directions of economic development and specialization. | C U L T U R E |

*Figure 2.1* The interaction of environmental factors: some illustrations.

of multinationals in the next section that the management of larger conglomerates can exert influences which extend beyond national boundaries to change international economics and politics.

We will deal with each of our five variables in turn. As we stressed in Chapter 1, each of them represents broad categories; for example, the role of the state will deal with issues pertaining to the general political environment. The chapter closes with a treatment of 'Japanese management', not only because this is an important topic within any discussion of cultural influence an the diffusion of business ideas, but also in that it represents a fascinating case study of a business community being shaped by and shaping its environment.

## The economy and business

With many aspects of our environment we are faced with the immediate problem of deciding where the environment ends and business begins

*Figure 2.2* Levels of the environment.

and vice versa. In looking at the relationship between business and the economy this becomes particularly acute since much of what we label as the economy is the product of business activity. By the same token, business enterprises are influenced significantly by economic developments. Figure 2.3 is an attempt to illustrate this relationship in the form of a simple model. In this section we will examine the model by focusing largely on the experience of Britain in the post-war period, although, inevitably, comparisons will be drawn from other countries. Britain along with most capitalist countries is an example of a mixed economy, where free enterprise is mixed with state involvement through public ownership, legal regulation, and various forms of planning and direction. In the 1980s attempts were made through government policy to change the balance of that relationship to favour the workings of the free market. For this reason there is considerable overlap between the economy and the role of the state, dealt with in the next section. Obviously a much fuller account of the relationship between business and the economy can be found in the economics text in this series (see Neale and Haslam, 1994).

The economy interacts with businesses at all three levels depicted in Figure 2.2. At the local level, immediate competitive issues related to firms operating in the same product market are the most significant. If the Virgin record store in London's Oxford Street reduces the price of all its compact discs by £1.00, then the management of the large HMV store just down the road must determine their most appropriate strategic response. This may involve adopting the same price strategy or it may involve a more selective strategy offering larger discounts on big selling items. In the 1960s labour shortages meant that firms actively competed for labour and often increased pay and bonus rates to attract labour from their competitors. Such competition can reach particularly fierce proportions and many firms prefer to cooperate rather than compete on issues like price or wage rates. In this way businesses form themselves into cartels which may be an effective way of controlling the immediate competitive environment, and perhaps the wider environment too, as in influencing government policy. There are several examples of groups of local grocers being formed to buy in bulk from

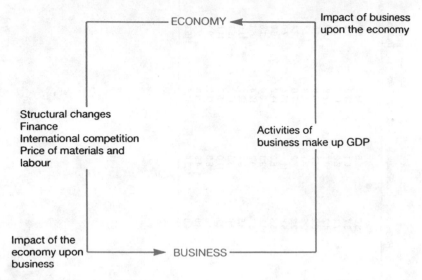

*Figure 2.3*  Business and the economy.

suppliers in an attempt to keep prices down and combat the threat posed by large supermarkets. We deal with the competitive environment in more detail in Chapter 4 and students are referred to Porter's model illustrated in Figure 4.3. For the rest of this section we will illustrate the relationship between the firm and the economy by focusing on issues mainly, but not exclusively, at the national and international levels.

## The impact of business on the economy

All businesses produce goods and services and provide employment. In doing so they contribute to a nation's income, its capital assets, and its economic growth. Economies are often compared on the basis of their gross domestic product (GDP), the sum total of the net outputs of each sector of the economy. In Tables 2.1 to 2.3 we show levels of GDP growth and the GDP per head of population (GDP per capita) for a number of selected countries over a 15-year period. The countries represent a number of advanced industrial economies including the USA, Japan and a selection from Europe. These are presented alongside a number of countries from the Far East, selected as an economically buoyant region. The three sets of figures show how similar data may be presented in different ways.

In Table 2.1 we present the growth of Real GDP from one year to the next. 'Real' GDP is the term used to describe the level of GDP where the calculation has taken account of inflation factors which may distort the true picture. The interest in Table 2.1 lies in the quite considerable growth in the Far Eastern economies compared to that of the more advanced nations, supporting the contention of economic buoyancy,

**Table 2.1**  Percentage growth in real GDP year on year, 1975–91

| | France | Germany | Italy | Japan | Spain | UK | US | China | Indonesia | Malaysia | Philippines | Singapore | South Korea | Thailand |
|---|---|---|---|---|---|---|---|---|---|---|---|---|---|---|
| 1975 | 5.7 | 4.6 | 8.0 | 2.7 | 4.5 | 2.5 | 5.5 | 6.0 | 2.0 | 22.6 | 8.0 | 9.6 | 18.7 | 9.7 |
| 1976 | 3.1 | 2.9 | 3.6 | 3.0 | 1.9 | -0.7 | 4.9 | 7.7 | 10.7 | 9.9 | 3.7 | 6.1 | 17.0 | 8.2 |
| 1977 | 4.3 | 4.6 | 5.5 | 5.8 | 2.1 | 6.6 | 5.1 | 6.7 | 10.7 | 11.7 | 7.4 | 6.2 | 17.7 | 12.1 |
| 1978 | 2.6 | 3.9 | 6.5 | 4.4 | 1.1 | 3.1 | 0.1 | 9.1 | 21.1 | 18.2 | 4.2 | 10.7 | 8.8 | 4.2 |
| 1979 | -0.1 | -5.1 | 3.3 | 0.6 | 0.2 | -0.7 | -4.1 | 4.3 | 20.3 | 7.6 | -5.2 | 12.7 | -5.6 | -1.6 |
| 1980 | -0.6 | 4.0 | 0.2 | 2.4 | -2.4 | -1.5 | 1.5 | 4.2 | 14.0 | -1.5 | 2.2 | 8.1 | 2.9 | 2.4 |
| 1981 | 2.5 | -1.7 | 0.8 | 2.1 | 0.8 | 0.4 | -2.1 | 6.7 | -1.8 | 2.7 | 2.2 | 7.2 | 7.0 | 2.4 |
| 1982 | 0.8 | 1.7 | 1.3 | 2.2 | 1.1 | 4.4 | 4.8 | 9.7 | 11.1 | 7.8 | 5.8 | 11.1 | 13.4 | 7.0 |
| 1983 | 1.4 | 2.5 | 3.4 | 4.4 | 1.5 | 1.2 | 6.4 | 16.7 | 4.8 | 9.5 | -5.5 | 6.3 | 11.2 | 6.0 |
| 1984 | 1.8 | 1.8 | 2.3 | 4.5 | 3.2 | 3.3 | 3.2 | 9.9 | 3.1 | -2.8 | -11.5 | -3.3 | 8.6 | 1.8 |
| 1985 | 5.2 | 5.7 | 4.9 | 3.8 | 5.3 | 4.1 | 3.7 | 5.9 | 0.0 | -8.3 | 5.7 | -0.7 | 12.4 | 6.1 |
| 1986 | 1.9 | 3.2 | 4.4 | 4.0 | 6.2 | 5.5 | 2.6 | 7.1 | 11.3 | 10.9 | 8.5 | 9.7 | 12.7 | 11.6 |
| 1987 | 4.4 | 3.9 | 5.6 | 5.9 | 6.0 | 5.8 | 3.8 | 2.8 | 5.4 | 11.2 | 7.6 | 15.5 | 10.2 | 15.7 |
| 1988 | 4.0 | 3.1 | 2.8 | 4.3 | 5.0 | 1.6 | 2.1 | -2.4 | 10.8 | 8.6 | 2.7 | 11.0 | 5.7 | 11.8 |
| 1989 | 1.9 | 5.4 | 3.3 | 4.2 | 4.2 | -1.9 | -0.2 | 9.7 | 9.8 | 10.5 | 1.8 | 8.3 | 11.2 | 9.1 |
| 1990 | 1.2 | 4.5 | 2.3 | 3.0 | 3.3 | -1.1 | -1.3 | 9.7 | 8.1 | 8.2 | -3.0 | 4.9 | 9.5 | 9.3 |
| Total | 40.1 | 44.9 | 58.2 | 57.2 | 44.1 | 32.7 | 35.8 | 113.7 | 141.3 | 126.6 | 34.6 | 123.4 | 161.5 | 115.9 |

*Source:* Calculated from *IMF Statistics Yearbook*, 1992.

and the relative low rate of growth of the UK compared with its European and Japanese competitors.

In Table 2.2 GDP is expressed in the same currency (US dollars) and as per head of population. The same data are expressed as percentages in Table 2.3, using the USA as a base against which all others are compared. The data reveal a number of interesting points. First, we have the growth of the Japanese economy compared with its major rivals. Second, the levels of GDP per capita reflect closely the growth rates depicted in Table 2.1 for the advanced economies but reveal a very different picture for the rest. With the one exception of Singapore, Tables 2.2 and 2.3 depict the relatively low levels of GDP per capita for the Far Eastern countries. While growth has been significant since 1975 it has started from an extremely low base. Even for one of the so-called 'economic tigers', South Korea, levels of GDP per capita fall far short of the more mature economies. This comparison is brought into sharper relief when GDP per capita is expressed as a percentage of the USA. We return to these economic issues in the Far East and the particular case of Singapore in Case 2.4.

Key issues for business managers are also key economic issues. These may be identified as products, productivity, markets, profits and the supply of labour. These themes re-emerge when we discuss the role of the economy in the chapters on the various activities of business. For example, in Chapter 5 we examine the view that economic growth is dependent upon product and process innovation.

## The impact of the economy on business

There are a variety of ways in which economic changes have affected businesses in this country. We will illustrate these changes through the changing nature of world economies, including structural changes, the supply and price of raw materials, increasing international competition and the emergence of the multinational as a powerful influence. The case of the multinational illustrates the difficulty of isolating business and environmental influences. Many businesses in this country have undoubtedly been influenced by a world economy increasingly dominated by multinational corporations. These same multinationals are themselves businesses with the ability to influence national and international economies.

Changes in the world economy have, for a country like Britain, led to major structural changes involving the decline of the manufacturing sector (de-industrialization) and the growth of the service sector, especially the financial sector. In turn these changes have had a significant impact on levels of employment, causing high levels of unemployment in those areas formerly dominated by traditional manufacturing industry, while creating many new jobs in the emerging financial services industry. We deal with these issues in more detail at the end of this section on the economy.

The availability of key resources cannot only have a significant influence on the fortunes of individual firms, but can also lead to

**Table 2.2** GDP per capita in US dollars (average rate)

| | France | Germany | Italy | Japan | Spain | UK | US | China | Indonesia | Malaysia | Philippines | Singapore | South Korea | Thailand |
|---|---|---|---|---|---|---|---|---|---|---|---|---|---|---|
| 1975 | 6482 | 6749 | 3832 | 4479 | 2945 | 4249 | 7338 | 165 | 225 | 785 | 376 | 2497 | 599 | 355 |
| 1976 | 6724 | 7229 | 3773 | 4980 | 3006 | 4138 | 8104 | 166 | 279 | 899 | 419 | 2590 | 807 | 395 |
| 1977 | 7349 | 8391 | 4344 | 6072 | 3322 | 4610 | 8963 | 189 | 335 | 1045 | 467 | 2821 | 1024 | 449 |
| 1978 | 9066 | 10416 | 5321 | 8455 | 3993 | 5832 | 10031 | 222 | 368 | 1265 | 524 | 3342 | 1360 | 532 |
| 1979 | 10890 | 12348 | 6624 | 8727 | 5290 | 7529 | 11058 | 262 | 359 | 1576 | 625 | 3974 | 1724 | 593 |
| 1980 | 12322 | 12396 | 8022 | 9070 | 5651 | 9619 | 11890 | 299 | 491 | 1785 | 672 | 4865 | 1643 | 688 |
| 1981 | 10757 | 11015 | 7223 | 9943 | 4876 | 9236 | 13180 | 278 | 608 | 1768 | 720 | 5699 | 1801 | 730 |
| 1982 | 10130 | 10609 | 7116 | 9169 | 4696 | 8689 | 13566 | 269 | 611 | 1843 | 735 | 6181 | 1893 | 732 |
| 1983 | 9607 | 10660 | 7337 | 9944 | 4063 | 8238 | 14533 | 284 | 540 | 2025 | 639 | 6964 | 2062 | 796 |
| 1984 | 9082 | 10050 | 7247 | 10538 | 4074 | 7705 | 15980 | 287 | 542 | 2226 | 589 | 7432 | 2230 | 813 |
| 1985 | 9487 | 10266 | 7430 | 11118 | 4310 | 8172 | 16934 | 275 | 531 | 1994 | 562 | 6911 | 2277 | 724 |
| 1986 | 13206 | 14542 | 10544 | 16345 | 5977 | 9923 | 17736 | 262 | 476 | 1723 | 534 | 6848 | 2574 | 793 |
| 1987 | 15962 | 18102 | 13238 | 19736 | 7558 | 12124 | 18695 | 279 | 441 | 1912 | 581 | 7742 | 3171 | 912 |
| 1988 | 17181 | 19390 | 14603 | 23630 | 8883 | 14573 | 19997 | 341 | 480 | 2047 | 648 | 9387 | 4168 | 1097 |
| 1989 | 17190 | 19057 | 15122 | 23319 | 9782 | 14655 | 21202 | 376 | 528 | 2158 | 708 | 10877 | 5025 | 1252 |
| 1990 | 20098 | 23460 | 18986 | 23799 | 12613 | 17038 | 22062 | 325 | 598 | 2381 | 719 | 12933 | 5692 | 1429 |
| 1991 | 21196 | 24421 | 19936 | 27137 | 13511 | 17711 | 22449 | 321 | 667 | 2590 | 716 | 14467 | 6539 | 1631 |

*Source:* Calculated from *IMF Statistics Yearbook*, 1992.

**Table 2.3**  GDP per capita in US dollars as a percentage of United States, 1975–91

| | France | Germany | Italy | Japan | Spain | UK | US | China | Indonesia | Malaysia | Philippines | Singapore | South Korea | Thailand |
|---|---|---|---|---|---|---|---|---|---|---|---|---|---|---|
| 1975 | 88.3 | 92.0 | 52.2 | 61.0 | 40.1 | 57.9 | 100.0 | 2.3 | 3.1 | 10.7 | 5.1 | 34.0 | 8.2 | 4.8 |
| 1976 | 83.0 | 89.2 | 46.6 | 61.4 | 37.1 | 51.1 | 100.0 | 2.0 | 3.4 | 11.1 | 5.2 | 32.0 | 10.0 | 4.9 |
| 1977 | 82.0 | 93.6 | 48.5 | 67.7 | 37.1 | 51.4 | 100.0 | 2.1 | 3.7 | 11.7 | 5.2 | 31.5 | 11.4 | 5.0 |
| 1978 | 90.4 | 103.8 | 53.1 | 84.3 | 39.8 | 58.1 | 100.0 | 2.2 | 3.7 | 12.6 | 5.2 | 33.3 | 13.6 | 5.3 |
| 1979 | 98.5 | 111.7 | 59.9 | 78.9 | 47.8 | 68.1 | 100.0 | 2.4 | 3.2 | 14.3 | 5.7 | 35.9 | 15.6 | 5.4 |
| 1980 | 103.6 | 104.3 | 67.5 | 76.3 | 47.5 | 80.9 | 100.0 | 2.5 | 4.1 | 15.0 | 5.7 | 40.9 | 13.8 | 5.8 |
| 1981 | 81.6 | 83.6 | 54.8 | 75.4 | 37.0 | 70.1 | 100.0 | 2.1 | 4.6 | 13.4 | 5.5 | 43.2 | 13.7 | 5.5 |
| 1982 | 74.7 | 78.2 | 52.5 | 67.6 | 34.6 | 64.0 | 100.0 | 2.0 | 4.5 | 13.6 | 5.4 | 45.6 | 14.0 | 5.4 |
| 1983 | 66.1 | 73.4 | 50.5 | 68.4 | 28.0 | 56.7 | 100.0 | 2.0 | 3.7 | 13.9 | 4.4 | 47.9 | 14.2 | 5.5 |
| 1984 | 56.8 | 62.9 | 45.4 | 65.9 | 25.5 | 48.2 | 100.0 | 1.8 | 3.4 | 13.9 | 3.7 | 46.5 | 14.0 | 5.1 |
| 1985 | 56.0 | 60.6 | 43.9 | 65.7 | 25.4 | 48.3 | 100.0 | 1.6 | 3.1 | 11.8 | 3.3 | 40.8 | 13.4 | 4.3 |
| 1986 | 74.5 | 82.0 | 59.5 | 92.2 | 33.7 | 55.9 | 100.0 | 1.5 | 2.7 | 9.7 | 3.0 | 38.6 | 14.5 | 4.5 |
| 1987 | 85.4 | 96.8 | 70.8 | 105.6 | 40.4 | 64.9 | 100.0 | 1.5 | 2.4 | 10.2 | 3.1 | 41.4 | 17.0 | 4.9 |
| 1988 | 85.9 | 97.0 | 73.0 | 118.2 | 44.4 | 72.9 | 100.0 | 1.7 | 2.4 | 10.2 | 3.2 | 46.9 | 20.8 | 5.5 |
| 1989 | 81.1 | 89.9 | 71.3 | 110.0 | 46.1 | 69.1 | 100.0 | 1.8 | 2.5 | 10.2 | 3.3 | 51.3 | 23.7 | 5.9 |
| 1990 | 95.2 | 106.3 | 86.1 | 107.9 | 57.2 | 77.2 | 100.0 | 1.5 | 2.7 | 10.8 | 3.3 | 58.6 | 25.8 | 6.5 |
| 1991 | 94.4 | 108.8 | 88.8 | 120.9 | 60.2 | 78.9 | 100.0 | 1.4 | 3.0 | 11.5 | 3.2 | 64.4 | 29.1 | 7.3 |

*Source*: Calculated from *IMF Statistics Yearbook*, 1992.

structural changes. In 1973 OPEC representing the oil-producing countries decided to restrict the supply of oil, with a subsequent dramatic increase in price. The impact on businesses in this country were several. Increased costs were passed on in the form of increased prices, or resulted in reduced profits, with some firms unable to compete. Some industries sought substitute products with corresponding increases in demand for products of the coal and gas industries. Rising petrol prices meant increased costs of transport and led to major product changes in the car industry. These changes were even more significant in the USA with a dramatic reduction in car size and the imposition of a national speed limits on all roads, which stands to this day. When Britain became a major oil producer, changes in the price of oil had an effect upon the exchange value of sterling. An exchange rate strengthened by an oil economy meant that British exports became more expensive and particularly damaging for those businesses who depend for a large proportion of their revenue on exported goods. The whole issue of the exchange value of sterling is presented in more detail in Case 2.1, which charts the fall of the pound against other major currencies in 1992 and the impact this had for certain types of business.

Changes in the car industry and the problems brought about by shifting exchange rates identified above are linked to a marked increase in the international dimension of most types of business. This has taken the form of a dramatic growth in international competition, initially from Japan, but more recently from other South East Asian economies such as Taiwan and Singapore. (Case 2.4 examines issues of business and management in South East Asia.) The decline in competitiveness of many of Britain's industries, such as shipbuilding, motorcycles, domestic electrical products and cars, has been attributed to the rise of cheap labour economies, especially those in the Far East, or the product superiority of manufacturers such as Japan and West Germany. However, our perspective of international competition must be revised constantly, so dynamic are the forces at work. Whilst de-industrialization in many 'advanced economies' was linked to a switch of manufacturing to those aforementioned cheap labour economies, such economies are becoming less cheap and far from lagging behind, they are taking the lead in certain areas of manufacturing technology and product development.

| **KEY CONCEPT 2.1** *The multinational corporation* | A multinational firm is one that operates from bases in a number of different countries. While small businesses can and do operate multinationally, most multinationals are large corporations with diverse interests coordinated by a centrally planned global strategy. Multinationals tend to compete in oligopolistic markets. In recent years there has been a shift in emphasis away from American multinationals to focus on the multinational growth of SE Asian companies, especially the Japanese. |
|---|---|

## The multinational corporation

An important aspect of international competition has been the market dominance of the multinational corporation. Trade and finance have always been international, but it was not until the post-war period that the large American conglomerate with its divisionalized structure was attracted to expanding European markets. While Europe initially provided an open door to American investment, later protectionist policies set up by the then European Economic Community accelerated the growth of American subsidiaries in Europe. Similar developments took place involving Japan. The coordination of multinational activities was enhanced by developments in communications and especially in information technology.

The multinational has had a significant impact on national economies in a variety of ways. Multinational companies tend to be very large; for example it is often quoted that Exxon and General Motors have annual turnovers in excess of the GNP of all but 14 nation states. While they tend to be highly diversified, multinationals tend to concentrate in oligopolistic industries, those dominated by a few large companies, where the general pattern of competition is through expensive product development and expensive promotional strategies. The multinational corporation is able to draw upon a worldwide pool of skilled labour and exploit the advantages of centralized control and a centralized research and development function. Business empires are thus based around a centrally planned global strategy. Such a process has been formalized through the planning process of companies like 3M (Case 4.2). As a result of the economic and political dominance of multinationals they have been viewed as a key device in the diffusion of management ideas and methods.

Certain changes have taken place in the development of multinationals. The USA is still dominant but has been joined by the expansion of the Japanese and European multinational. The focus for the location has also shifted, from Europe, then to Canada and Latin America, and most recently to South East Asia. Along with this shift in location has gone a marked change in rationale. Initially multinationals grew to exploit local markets and raw materials. The emphasis is now upon manufacture and in particular on specialization, either through product specialization in the case of the car industry or the more general location of labour-intensive industries in low-wage areas, as with the manufacture of video-cassette recorders. Some writers (Adam, 1975; Harrison, 1985) see this shift in production as following a set pattern occurring in traditional declining labour-intensive industries with a reasonably long product life-cycle or in the labour-intensive aspects of the more technologically based industries as with electronics or car manufacture. Both the shift in location and the emphasis on reduced costs has had a considerable impact upon the ability of non-multinationals to compete in manufacturing industry and upon levels of employment in the West, and especially Britain. Such specialization is often cited as a strategy of the multinational corporation itself, but this is not always the case. As part of its economic plan the Singapore Government deliberately set out to attract multinational firms to establish manufacturing bases. The policy was highly selective and only those firms operating in high-tech product markets were encouraged (Case 2.4 has further details).

Much has been written about the impact of the multinational corporation on the economy of Third World countries (for example, Harrison, 1985). While involvement in the Third World is done with the cooperation of host governments, leads to an inflow of capital, provides local employment and improves the balance of payments, there are considerable problems involved. These include the exploitation of natural resources, allegations of bribery and corruption, the expatriation of profits, price speculation, the tendency of multinationals to move both capital and financial assets to gain the most favourable tax and exchange rate advantages and so on. In general Third World economies become dominated by companies whose primary aim is the maximization of profit when those countries might benefit more from a planned, local approach to development.

The two cases of resource allocation and the internationalization of capital through multinational expansion show how economic developments can have an impact upon businesses in a single nation state. To these can be added the influence of world financial markets on business investment and, for most countries, increasing attempts to control the economy through state intervention. This aspect will be dealt with in the next section.

Multinationals continue to play a significant part in the UK economy. With the single exception of the USA, Britain invests more overseas than any other country. As for inward investment, Britain's attraction to foreign investors is bettered only by the USA and Canada. Apart from the obvious contribution foreign multinationals have made to UK employment, Britain's active role in multinational activity appears to have done little to enhance its economic position. The investment activities of UK firms overseas appears to be confined to portfolio investment only and where manufacturing is concerned the focus has been on low-tech goods for local markets. In both cases the contribution to GDP and balance of payments has been negligible. While the attraction of foreign manufacturers to the UK is encouraging, the marked trend is towards highly specialized aspects of a particular industry. This could result in a highly fragmented manufacturing base, an inappropriate base for sustained manufacturing growth. It is to this aspect that we now turn.

## The impact of a changing economy on British business

> If you want to buy a small business, buy a large one and wait.
> (New English proverb)

Green (1989b) argues that the major changes in the UK economy since 1970 have been the decline of manufacturing and the growth of the service sector; the growth in numbers of long-term unemployed; the weakening of trade unions; and the shift from public to private owner-ship. We will deal with the last two aspects elsewhere in this chapter and here focus on the shift away from manufacturing to the service sector, and on rising unemployment. In the next section we argue that such changes are political and ideological as well as economic.

The decline of manufacturing industry in the UK has been well documented. Since the 1950s UK industry has lost market share to overseas competitors. In shipbuilding the UK was the world's leading exporter in 1950, yet in six years its market share fell from 38% to 14%. In 1955 the UK produced 70% of the world's motorcycles, but was unable to meet the challenge first from the Italians and then from the Japanese. UK manufacturers retreated up market only to be pursued and overtaken by the Japanese in every market segment. Case 2.2, Norton-Villiers-Triumph, explores the political dimension of the decline in motorcycle manufacture but an interesting dimension is the link between R&D and market share, an aspect explored in more detail in Chapter 5. In the late 1970s Norton-Villiers-Triumph employed 100 staff in R&D, while its Japanese competitors, Honda and Suzuki, employed 1000 each (Bowen, 1992).

While market share has declined, the domestic consumption of manu-factured goods has increased. From 1973 to 1988 domestic expenditure on manufactured goods increased by 30% while domestic output re-mained about the same (Wells, 1989). The impact of this has been a rise in imported goods and a worsening of the balance of payments deficit.

Apart from market share, the numbers employed in manufacturing is a good indication of the relative health of the manufacturing sector. Table 2.4 shows the decline of numbers employed in manufacturing since 1971 relative to those employed in the USA, Germany and Japan. While other countries have maintained their employment base in manufacturing, the UK has lost 40% of its manufacturing workforce. As we can see, the decline in manufacturing employment was most severe during the recession of 1980–82. Optimistic commentators point to the impact such changes have had in clearing out ineffective and inefficient firms and how some firms and even entire industries are now more efficient and competitive. While this may be true there is a real danger that manufacturing capacity has been lost to such an extent that it will be difficult to recover. As Wells (1989) states,

> UK manufacturing production which remains at the end of the Thatcher decade may well be leaner, fitter, have a higher level of labour producti-vity and be more profitable than before – but it is totally inadequate in terms of the volume of its internationally competitive capacity.
>
> (Wells, 1989, p. 58)

The decline of manufacturing has been contrasted with the rise in the service sector of the economy. For example, while all employment fell by 6.2% between 1979 and 1986, employment in the service sector rose by 6.6%. In some sectors such as financial services the increase in employment has been quite dramatic accompanying the deregulation by the government of financial markets. The growth of the service

**Table 2.4** Employment in manufacturing

| | UK | USA | Germany | Japan |
|---|---|---|---|---|
| 1971 | 100 | 100 | 100 | 100 |
| 1972 | 97 | 103 | 98 | 99 |
| 1973 | 98 | 108 | 98 | 100 |
| 1974 | 98 | 108 | 96 | 99 |
| 1975 | 93 | 98 | 89 | 94 |
| 1976 | 90 | 102 | 87 | 91 |
| 1977 | 91 | 106 | 86 | 90 |
| 1978 | 91 | 110 | 86 | 89 |
| 1979 | 90 | 113 | 86 | 88 |
| 1980 | 85 | 109 | 87 | 89 |
| 1981 | 78 | 108 | 85 | 90 |
| 1982 | 73 | 101 | 82 | 91 |
| 1983 | 69 | 99 | 78 | 91 |
| 1984 | 67 | 104 | 78 | 92 |
| 1985 | 67 | 103 | 79 | 94 |
| 1986 | 65 | 102 | 80 | 94 |
| 1987 | 64 | 102 | 80 | 93 |
| 1988 | 65 | 104 | 80 | 94 |
| 1989 | 65 | 104 | 82 | 96 |
| 1990 | 64 | 103 | 84 | 97 |
| 1991 | 60 | 99 | 85 | 100 |

*Source: Datastream international.*

sector of the economy undoubtedly has its roots in the historical de-velopment of the British economy. The City has always been a focus of attention due to early British dominance in world trade and the inter-national role played by sterling. Later in the chapter we also explore the view that core cultural values of the British have favoured the development of the service economy at the expense of manufacturing.

High levels of unemployment are however a fairly recent phen-omenon. Between 1948 and 1966 the average rate in Britain was 1.7% with only 1.1% in 1966. Along with other industrial countries, levels of unemployment have risen sharply since then with an official figure of 3.25 million people being out of work in 1982, representing 13% of the working population. (Other figures vary considerably, unemployment statistics being very much a part of a wider ideological debate.) While the extent of unemployment has fluctuated since 1982 there has been a steady increase in the numbers of long-term unemployed. Various policies have been initiated to deal with the problem, including government training schemes, regional aid, increasing public investment and direct state intervention to support ailing firms. Some of these aspects are dealt with in the next section.

Over the last ten years the impact of the above economic changes on a major UK employer, such as Ford Motor Company, have been considerable. No one single factor has been dominant as most of the influences have operated interactively. Along with the rest of UK manufacturing, capacity at Ford Motor Company has been reduced. This in turn has led to a reduction in the range of models produced and in the labour force. The decline of manufacturing throughout the UK has meant that the company has gone further afield for the sourcing of its components and hastened the trend towards the internationalization of manufacturing. The decline of the UK manufacturing base has also meant a decline in the numbers being trained in up-to-date manufacturing skills. Despite the large pool of unemployed labour there is a reduced pool of labour in certain manufacturing skills. The growth in financial services has not gone unnoticed by manufacturing concerns themselves and Ford have joined the growing trend by expanding its activities in this area. Along with other employers Ford have experienced fewer industrial relations problems. Weaker trade unions, unemployment and growing international competition have contributed towards a more cooperative industrial relations climate and management have been able to introduce changes in areas such as flexible labour practices, that would hitherto have been impossible. Wage settlements too have been lower.

In some cases the above has contributed to a more cost-effective manufacturing industry, but for a company such as Ford there is also a considerable loss of potential through the under-utilization of existing plant and capacity.

## Does manufacturing matter?

To some the growth in the services sector of the UK economy is seen as compensation for the decline in the manufacturing base and simply part of the process of evolutionary economic change. However, several arguments are put forward for the importance of manufacturing in a healthy economy. Only manufacturing can add value to raw materials, and in doing so can provide jobs in numbers that can never be matched by the service sector. While most if not all of manufacturing output can be traded as exports, this is not the case for services. Some estimates put the extent of tradeable services as low as 20% of the total. As Bowen (1992) writes, 'you cannot pay for Japanese cars with British hairdressing'. In many other countries, the health of the service sector depends ultimately on the health of manufacturing industry. In Germany some 50% of the demand for services comes from the manufacturing sector itself (Hahn, 1993).

For reasons such as these successive British governments have been urged to lend greater support to manufacturing industry. It is to this

| KEY CONCEPT 2.2<br>*The State and<br>business* | The State comprises parliament, the judiciary, the civil service, police and armed forces and so on. Traditionally there have been tensions between the State's need to direct the economy and regulate business and the wishes of the business community to pursue their interests with a minimum of State intervention. Nevertheless, State intervention is a feature of business life and is inevitable in a country such as the United Kingdom where the State is a major employer. Intervention occurs through the legal regulation of market transactions, inventions and employment contracts and through the State's attempt to influence demand both as a consumer and via government economic policy. The business community in turn attempts to influence the State by adopting the various tactics associated with pressure groups. Increasingly, business comes under the influence of the policies of supranational bodies, such as the EC. |
|---|---|

and other aspects of the state's involvement with business that we now turn.

## The state and business

Taking his lead from Max Weber, John Scott (1979) defines the state as that body which has a monopoly over taxation, the money supply, and the legitimate use of violence. The state is normally thought of as comprising the executive, parliament, the civil service, the judiciary, the armed forces and the police. It would be wrong to perceive the state as a united body. Tensions can and do occur, as between parliament and the civil service or between parliament and the judiciary. Variations in policy often result from differences in political ideology. These differences are apparent not only between parties, but also within the same party, as revealed in Case 2.2; or as shown by the policies of the Conservative government since 1979, which has pursued policies radically different from those of its post-war predecessors irrespective of party loyalties.

We have already noted that the state interacts with business through its management of the economy. The state's influence can also operate at a highly localized and immediate way as the following example shows. In the 1960s the Ministry of Transport had a policy of employing independent firms to act as consultants in the testing of government construction projects such as roads and bridges. The policy coincided with a massive expansion in motorway construction. This resulted in a business boom period for a number of civil engineering firms. Testing contracts were usually given to a small proportion of the larger firms in the industry and, for some firms, this government work accounted for 75% of the annual turnover. In 1986 the Government, as part of its policy to encourage greater competition, decided to invite bids for such consultancy work from any civil engineering contractor. The firms which had previously relied on such work as a major part of their income were faced with the prospect of either losing out to new competitors or accepting reduced profit margins through having to lower their consultancy fees. In either case, management were forced to rethink their strategies significantly.

In this section we will deal with aspects of the state's activity at both national and local levels in terms of the state's attempt to intervene in business and the attempts made by business managers to influence the workings of the state. Throughout this book we illustrate the interaction of the state and business by examining the relationship through its impact on the various business activities in chapters 5 to 9. We extend the concept of state intervention at the end of this section by examining briefly the role of two supranational bodies, GATT (the General Agreement on Tariffs and Trade) and the European Union.

Before we examine more closely the relationship between the state and business it is important to consider the broad ideological underpinnings that have informed state involvement in business in the UK this century. The dominant ideology has been that of liberal pluralism.

For liberals, the state is concerned with the maintenance of order and with providing conditions so that business can prosper. The state is seen as a neutral umpire in a pluralist society dominated by voluntary cooperation and exchange, where differences are never fundamental. Under a liberal view of the state, intervention is necessary; to protect the workings of the free market against forces which might otherwise disrupt it, such as excessive monopoly power of either business or trade unions; to provide and/or control goods and services to individuals such as defence and education, where provision by other means would be impossible or inappropriate; and to take a longer term view of economic, social, and environmental change than individual businesses are capable of doing. The liberal perspective allows wide variation, from a highly directive economy to one in which the free market is encouraged to operate unfettered by government controls.

Those criticizing this perspective argue that the state tends to operate to preserve the *status quo*, that groups in society rarely have equal power to support voluntary cooperation and exchange, and that ultimately the state is not neutral. Marxists take this view a stage further and argue that the state is the instrument of the ruling class in an essentially exploitative society, where massive inequalities exist. Under a Marxist view of the state, intervention is necessary to maintain the *status quo* in favour of the dominant class. The state will therefore intervene to protect investments or prevent strikes.

Whichever perspective is adopted, it is clear that this century has seen an increase of state intervention in Britain, much of it aimed specifically at business.

## State intervention and business

An examination of UK state intervention in business this century reveals a progression through four stages. Winkler (1977) describes the first three of these as facilitative, supportive and directive. The fourth stage exhibits a radical departure from its predecessor both ideologically and economically and was ushered in with the election of Margaret Thatcher in 1979. We deal with each stage in turn.

The facilitative phase involved minimum intervention, largely through law and order, taxation and currency protection. The primary concern was for the smooth operation of the market. Two factors emerged to challenge this policy; an increase in industrial concentration resulting in large firms being able to override market competition, increasing economic crises of the 1920s and 30s with sharp rises in the level of unemployment, and, ultimately, the Second World War.

Economic crises in particular led to the state adopting a much more supportive role towards business. State policies followed the Keynesian belief that the free market was unable to solve the problems of unemployment and that increasing state intervention was required to redistribute wealth and create employment. The policy was ultimately challenged by a progressively weaker industrial base and the rise of international competition. The state therefore took upon itself to pursue a more directive line.

Increased direction in the 1960s gained broad support, even from groups not normally associated with such a policy, like the Federation of British Industry (a predecessor of the CBI), and the Conservative government in its setting up of the National Economic Development Council in 1962. Directive policies included attempts to restructure business, the promotion of mergers to encourage both economies of scale and innovation, and incomes policies.

Such state direction in business has been labelled as corporatism. This is essentially an attempt by the government to achieve stability by integration, involving representatives of business and trade unions in the economic decision-making process. Corporatist states tend to favour central planning and the use of extra-parliamentary bodies such as 'quangos' to make decisions. Crouch (1978) has suggested that most countries in Western Europe have set up corporatist machinery at some time in the post-war period, with perhaps Holland and West Germany experiencing most success. In Britain, integration has traditionally been resisted by both business and trade unions and attempts at corporatism have failed either through the refusal of one or other of the groups to participate or a lack of consensus. One of the more recent attempts at integration occurred when the Labour government of 1974–9 launched its 'social contract', a device to control the economy with the cooperation of the trade unions through wage restraint. The plan ultimately failed (and the government along with it) with rising inflation being met by ever-increasing wage demands. Some writers are pessimistic about the role of the state in corporatist societies, feeling that a failure of consensus may result in an increasingly directive state and the hastening decline of parliamentary democracy.

The lack of consensus highlights one of the major difficulties of state intervention in business. Jessop writes of the British government attempts to influence the direction of business to solve the economic crises of the 1960s and '70s, far from industrial policy being a consensual panacea for solving the British crisis, it is a major focus of economic, political and ideological struggle.

(Jessop, 1980, pp. 47–8)

## Thatcherism and the New Right

Whatever consensus existed in post-war Britain, it was threatened by a series of economic problems that emerged in the 1960s and continued through the 1970s. The problems included rising levels of inflation, wage claims and unemployment; low productivity and a worsening balance of payments deficit. The Labour government of the 1970s was embarrassed first by the intervention of the International Monetary Fund in the conduct of its economic affairs and second by a series of strikes, especially in the public sector, during the winter of 1978–9. The latter, in particular, saw a weakening of the traditional alliance between the Labour Party and the trade unions, challenged the 'social contract', referred to above, and did much to bring about a change of government.

The first government of Margaret Thatcher introduced an economic doctrine that owed much to the free-market ideas of Hayek and Friedman. State involvement with business was seen as being incompatible with efficiency and freedom and measures were taken to 'get the state off our backs' and to control those elements which were likely to interfere with the freedom of both markets and individuals. A number of policy measures were introduced to achieve the government's goals and included the following.

- Monetarist policies were used to tackle inflation, comprising the gradual reduction of money supply and the cutting of public expenditure to reduce the excess of expenditure over taxation, and hence the public sector borrowing requirement (PSBR).
- A number of supply-side measures were taken with the primary objective of stimulating economic growth. Taxation was cut between 1979 and 1988 with the base rate falling from 33% to 25% and the top rate moving from 83% to 40%. The tax cuts were intended as an incentive for those out of work to return to the job market and on the assumption that the extra funds available would be invested in business growth. The work incentive was further strengthened by a series of welfare benefit cuts. In addition to these measures, steps were taken to reduce the power of the trade unions, to deregulate and privatize a number of industries and to encourage entrepreneurialism through the growth of the small business sector. The changes in trade-union power are dealt with later in this chapter and in Chapter 8. Privatization and small businesses are covered in Chapter 3.

The economic doctrine pursued has been labelled 'the New Right', championing as it does market and individual freedoms and the abstention of the state. The UK was not alone in taking this line

Similar policies were being pursued by the Reagan administration in the USA and by the Kohl government in Germany.

In a number of areas the policies achieved their stated objectives. The PSBR was reduced from 5.89% of GDP in 1980 to 1.98% in 1988. Inflation fell from 18% in 1980 to around 2% in the first quarter of 1993. Policies on trade-union reform, privatization and deregulation were carried out as planned. However, any assessment of government policy is difficult. To ask whether policies have been successful begs a number of questions. We must ask: successful for whom, by what criteria, and at what price? The policies have attracted their critics, who feel that they have done little to enhance UK competitiveness; that they have led to the demise of UK manufacturing industry and to a rise in unemployment; and that while some have gained, the lower income groups have experienced a worsening of their standard of living.

## Difficulties with state intervention

The problems involved in assessing the impact of Thatcherism on UK business and the debate generated illustrates some of the difficulties associated with the state's interaction with business. The impact of government policy upon business activity is often difficult to measure and direct relationships can be difficult to prove due to the large number of other variables which can and do affect the situation. There are other difficulties. While the government since 1979 has been re-latively consistent in its policies, this has not always been the case. Differences both between and within political parties have resulted in different approaches to intervention as can be seen in Norton-Villiers, Case 2.2 and with INMOS, Case 5.2. The business community may oppose attempts by governments to control it. The majority of owners and managers of business have an ideological attachment to *laissez-faire*. In addition, as we saw in the previous section, multinationals tend to have a greater allegiance to their own corporate goals than those of any single nation state.

In the preceding section we have attempted to chart the attempts by the UK government to influence business activities in a number of different ways. We shall now attempt to classify the main types of state intervention.

## Types of state intervention

**Collective provision** The most obvious form of state intervention is through the provision of those goods and services which would other-wise be too expensive, or too dangerous, or just ineffective if left to private control. Such aspects would include defence, the police, health, welfare and housing. The extent and nature of such collective provision is a matter of political and ideological debate. The British government since 1979 has pursued a policy of reducing its collective provision as we will see when we discuss privatization in Chapter 3.

**The state as employer**   The proportion of the working population employed by the state has rose from 2.4% in 1851 to 24.3% in 1975. Policies of privatization since 1983 have led to reductions in those directly employed by the state, but it remains a major employer with a profound affect on the labour market. The government since 1979, while formally rejecting incomes policy as a mechanism of control, has attempted to hold down wages in the public sector as part of its policy of reducing public expenditure. This has resulted in major confrontations with such groups as the miners, nurses and the teachers.

**The state as consumer**   The case of the civil engineering contracts cited in the introduction to this section is a clear illustration of the state's operating as a consumer of business services. As a major employer, the state is also a major purchaser of office equipment and many businesses rely on government contracts as a major source of revenue. The state through its involvement in defence, health and education has a significant influence on the direction of innovation (Chapter 5 has a more comprehensive review of this aspect).

**Legal regulation**   The legal regulation of business is extensive and complex. The law of contract is used to regulate the marketplace. Company law deals with such issues as the protection of consumers through the regulation of monopoly power, rules governing the provision of company information and so on. Labour law deals with both the protection of the individual worker and the regulation of collective bargaining. Patent law exists to encourage innovation by granting monopoly rights to patent-holders. Illustrations of such legal provisions may be found in the chapters dealing with specific business activities. Some laws operate as constraints while others exist specifically to aid industrial development. The Norton-Villiers-Triumph case is a good illustration of how the Industry Act 1972 was used by the government to assist a single firm in the West Midlands. The government wished to help BSA/Triumph motorcycle manufacturers, but was prevented from giving a grant under regional aid policy as the West Midlands was not designated a special area. Instead, the government was forced by its own laws to aid the entire industry; hence its wish to see all three motorcycle manufacturers merged as one company (Sandberg, 1984). With privatization new forms of regulation have been added to protect the consumer and regulatory bodies have been set up for all those public utilities now under private control.

**Demand management**   All governments attempt to influence and control economic growth, the balance of payments, wage and price stability and the level of unemployment. A variety of measures are used, including fiscal measures such as taxation, monetary measures such as the control of credit, and direct measures such as import controls and assistance to specific firms. We have seen already how the government of the UK has, since 1979, attempted to stimulate economic growth through its monetarist and supply-side policies.

Through taxation and monetary policies the government is able to raise revenue to finance its activities and also to achieve specific objectives, as through the lower rates of taxation levied on food as opposed to tobacco. Successive governments have given aid either for specific purposes, such as innovation (Chapter 5 contains a full discussion of this), or to assist a particular firm or an entire industry. In the 1960s, the Labour government targeted the nuclear, motor vehicles and electrical industries for special assistance, while the 1970 Conservative government targeted the machine-tool industry and woollen textiles. During that period specific firms were given substantial state aid under what was popularly known as the 'lame duck policy'. These firms included Rolls-Royce, British Leyland, British Steel, Upper Clyde Shipbuilders, and Chrysler. Such support for individual firms is ideologically incompatible with the kind of 'New Right' economic policies outlined above. In addition, aid to individual firms may be constrained by the regional policies established by the EC. While the 'New Right' rejects the kind of direct intervention seen in the 1960s and early '70s, the UK government has targeted the smaller firm for special attention, as part of its commitment to the growth of entrepreneurialism. The small firms policy will be discussed more fully in Chapter 3.

**Training**   Government concern about skills shortages and the lack of adequate training in the UK has been a recurrent theme since 1852 and a number of more recent studies have pointed to the greater attention devoted to training by our competitors (for example, Handy, 1987 and Steedman and Wagner, 1987). Successive governments have attempted to redress this balance by such measures as the Education Act 1944, the Industrial Training Act 1964, the creation of the Youth Training Scheme, and, more recently, the introduction of the National Curriculum in schools and the move towards a national system for the accreditation of vocational skills (NVQs).

**Protection**   Governments have to varying degrees attempted to protect their industries against what is viewed as unfair competition from overseas firms and indeed other governments. One direct measure is the use of import tariffs and controls such as quota restrictions. Government representatives will also attempt to influence the policies of supranational institutions such as the EC or GATT to ensure a level playing field for the conduct of international trade.

**Marketing**   Most governments actively support their own businesses in exporting goods and services. Diplomatic services will inevitably involve a trade function and embassies will act as host to trade delegations as well as influencing foreign governments and businesses through a range of diplomatic connections.

**Advisory services**   In addition to its policies of regulation and assistance, the state offers various types of advice to business people. Such advice ranges from overseas trade, as identified above, to dealing with industrial relations problems.

## The business community as a pressure group

So far this section has concentrated on the way the state attempts to influence business. We now turn our attention to the ways in which the state can be influenced by the business community acting as a pressure group, or more correctly, as a series of pressure groups.

We have already noted that businesses in this country are traditionally resistant to state control and are generally committed to a *laissez-faire* economy; and that as a pressure group, businesses tend to be fragmented with no powerful central body to coordinate policy. Indeed some evidence suggests that British industry is a singularly unsuccessful pressure group because of this fragmentation, and tends to extert pressure only in response to crises (Grant and Marsh, 1977).

However, as with all pressure-group activity there is both a difficulty in observing it and in measuring its effect. We can only make deductions based upon open, formally reported attempts to influence. The business community tends to be secretive and many attempts to influence government policy are undoubtedly covert and informal. Nonetheless the business community represents an important source of revenue via taxation and borrowing to enable the state to fund its activities, and for this alone constitutes an important political lobby.

**CASE 2.1**
***Black Wednesday and the collapse of the pound***

In the four months leading up to September 1992 the British Government under Prime Minister John Major was optimistic that their economic policies would bring about a long awaited recovery. The Government was re-elected in the previous April when many predicted a clear defeat. Both inflation and interest rates had fallen, and Germany with the strongest economy and strongest currency in Europe was experiencing economic problems following re-unification. The Prime Minister himself had begun a six-month presidency of the European Union and to the UK media he had expressed a prediction that sterling would once again emerge as the leading European currency.

Britain was a member of the European Monetary System (EMS) within which 11 EU members operated fixed exchange rates within agreed margins of fluctuation. This was known as the Exchange Rate Mechanism (ERM). The German Deutschmark, as the strongest currency, was the benchmark against which all other currencies were measured. By Wednesday, 17 September, the pound had reached its ERM floor level of DM2.77 on the foreign-exchange market. The Chancellor of the Exchequer Norman Lamont attempted to support the falling pound by using UK foreign currency reserves to buy sterling. Estimates ranged from £10 billion to £15 billion as to the money spent. Interest rates were immediately raised from 10% to 12% with a further 3% increase promised the following day. This had no impact on the downward trend of the pound and it fell to DM2.68 almost immediately. By the end of the next day it had reached DM2.62 and closed the week at DM2.61. The pound also fell against the US dollar, from US$1.92 at its highest point in the week to US$1.74 by the close. The EU Monetary Committee met during the week and Britain requested a lowering of German interest rates to save the falling pound. This was not forthcoming and Britain, along with Italy, temporarily left the ERM, while Spain devalued by 5%.

There are several reasons for the fall in sterling and the decision to withdraw, albeit temporarily, from the ERM. One of the major factors was a problem in the German economy. The cost of unification with the former East Germany was considerable, not least of which was the Government's support of the old East German currency, assimilated into the German system on a par with the Deutschmark. The subsequent increase of cash in the German economy had led to an increase in the demand for goods which supply could not meet. This in turn led to price increases and the German economy was faced with an inflation rate of 4.8%. While not large by world standards it was for the Germans, who possess a fear of inflation linked to the problems of the 1930s. In order to combat inflation, the German Government raised interest rates to 9.75%. The strength and stability of the Deutchmark has always seen it as the favoured currency for investors. As a result of the rise in the German interest rate, other countries were forced to do likewise to prevent their currencies being sold to buy Deutchmarks. The USA was one country that did not raise its interest rates. Economic policy in the USA saw low interest rates as a means of stimulating an economy in recession. With low interest rates firms might be encouraged to borrow money to invest in new products and processes or to expand existing businesses. Interest rates in the USA had fallen to 3% and US investors seeing the rise in German interest rates bought marks. As a result the Deutchmark became even stronger.

Three other events occurred around 17 September 1992 that added fuel to the sterling crisis. The Italian lira was also in trouble in the ERM and the currency was devalued by 7%. Experts were quick to point to other currencies in trouble, with the pound as the prime candidate. There was also considerable speculation about a forthcoming French referendum on the Maastricht Treaty, an important plank in the EU's move towards greater unity. The referendum was an attempt by the French Government to strengthen its own position by gaining popular support fur its policies on EU unity and the move towards a single European currency. However, the polls were predicting a close vote. This in turn caused further speculation on the money markets with the growing weakness of lira and sterling. At the same time there was a leak of an interview that Deutchebundesbank President, Helmut Schlesinger, had allegedly given to *Handelsblatt*, the German business paper, and to the *Wall Street Journal*. While the precise details of the text were disputed, the message given by the media was that he believed that sterling should be devalued along with the lira.

The factors identified above were cited as the prime reasons for speculation and foreign exchange activity leading to the fall in the value of the pound. However some saw these events as triggers which exposed Britain's fundamental problem, its weak economy. Many dealers and economic experts considered the pound to be overvalued at DM2.77, particularly since imports were greater than exports despite a fall in UK spending. A UK interest rate of 10% was also viewed by many as an obstacle to economic recovery. The two-year membership of the ERM had, for some, masked the problem of an overvalued currency that events of the week of 14 September had simply exposed.

Contributory factors were undoubtedly the structure of the UK financial market and the increased sophistication of information technology. A previous Conservative Government under Mrs Thatcher, as part of its commitment to free markets, had deregulated the financial markets and abolished exchange controls. This had made it easier for investors to buy and sell not only shares but currencies as well and had led to a dramatic increase in both financial services firms and the number of dealings. Most of these firms had access to the latest information technology. This has made possible electronic international money transfers and provides instant information on such deals and anything else which might affect the market. The slightest change in patterns of buying and selling currency is known instantly around the world, as are the actions of governments and even rumours. In this way a slight shift in the value of the pound can easily turn into a major movement. The actions of Chancellor Lamont to stem the fall of the pound were known at once around the world, and probably interpreted as a sign of panic, resulting in further sales of sterling.

The immediate impact of the pound's fall and the UK Government's decision to leave the ERM was profit for the dealers and a loss to the UK economy of between £750 million and £1 billion on its own dealing to protect sterling. Share trading increased, as did fears among the business community of higher inflation and even higher interest rates that both would hinder economic recovery. However, not all were threatened. Firms such as Shell, BP, British Aerospace, Rolls-Royce Aero-engines and British Airways conducted their businesses to a greater or lesser extent in US dollars, and thus the sterling value of their dealings would rise. Some firms with a large US market, like Jaguar, anticipated increased sales. Overall, however, the UK imported £17.3 billion and exported £14.6 billion worth of goods to Germany and imported £13.7 billion worth of US goods as opposed to exporting £11.3 billion. Unless the balance in the volume of goods were to change, the impact of a lower pound would be a widening of the trade deficit.

In the UK much party political capital was made of the Government's failed economic policies of stable exchange rates and lowering interest rates. In Europe there was much bickering. John Major blamed the Germans for maintaining high interest rates and there was an intensification of the debate on Maastricht, the ERM and even the whole issue of European unity.

Ultimately it would appear that market forces, so beloved of John Major's predecessor, had operated against government policy. Sterling had probably entered the ERM at too high a rate. Almost certainly this affected UK competitiveness and had prevented interest rates coming down below 10%. As Ruth Lea, the Chief Economist for Mitsubishi Bank, stated, 'the ironic thing is that we may get an economic recovery because the Government's policy failed' (*Independent*, 18 September 1992).

Almost a year later, in August 1993, the pound was valued at DM2.54 and US$1.48, and the UK interest rate was 6%. High German interest rates persisted and the French franc was under pressure to devalue along with the Spanish pesata, the Portuguese escudo and the Danish krone. Speculation was rife as to the future of the ERM, with a number of countries threatening to leave.

(*Sources: Financial Times*, The *Independent*, The *Independent on Sunday*, The *Observer* 17–20 September 1992, 1–3 August 1993)

We have suggested that, for the most part, firms tend to be reactive rather than proactive as far as the state is concerned and seem more concerned to predict changes in the political environment than to initiate those changes themselves. In this way the tobacco manufacturers predicted increased government regulation of their industry and took measures both to diversify and transfer attention to growing Third World markets. The same companies reacted successfully to increased restrictions on tobacco advertising by expanding their interests in sport sponsorship to maintain a high public profile. Some companies, of course, are more successful than others in resisting state intervention. Multinationals can use their protected status as members of another sovereign state to limit the extent of intervention in those countries in which they operate, and, by transferring funds from country to country, can minimize tax liabilities. The Swiss pharmaceutical company Hoffman-la-Roche successfully defended itself against the probing of the British Monopolies Commission in 1971 on the grounds that the British government had no legal right of access to information belonging to a Swiss company. The case was considerably hampered by a lack of vital financial information. (For a fuller account of this case see Stopford *et al.*, 1980.)

Political risk assessment is a technique or series of techniques used by some firms operating in an international environment, particularly where there is considerable investment planned, as in the establishment of a new manufacturing plant. Risk assessments would be built into the strategic plan and would assess the stability of the country as well as the chances and likely impact of a change in regime. At a more detailed level risk assessment will attempt to predict policy changes and their impact upon operations. There have been a number of well documented cases where a change of government has resulted in the expropriation or nationalization of assets, as has occurred in such countries as Chile, Egypt, Iran, Iraq and Nigeria. Other risks can incorporate such diverse events as civil war, the kidnapping of key personnel and associated ransom demands, restrictions on borrowing, trade-union activities, and policy changes concerning the hiring of local staff. Such assessment is far from easy. Governments can change without any fundamental shift in economic policy and the nationalistic rhetoric of some politicians may threaten foreign investment in the run up to an election, but be entirely supportive once power has been achieved.

Once genuine risks are forecast then management will wish to take some measures to prevent them. Real pressure-group activity exists where the business deliberately attempts to control the political environment in which it operates. In the UK there are a number of groups who attempt to influence government policy. These include professional groups such as the British Medical Association and employers' associations such as the Engineering Employers Federation. The Confederation of British Industry (CBI) addresses a range of economic and business issues, although its impact as a national body is often weakened by the rather fragmented demands of its constituent industrial groups.

Such groups operate by lobbying government bodies to secure some kind of advantage or to protect themselves from what they see as unfair competition. Thus the fishing industry in both Britain and the rest of Europe is persistently lobbying for increased protection through the extension of territorial waters. As well as lobbying some firms seek political influence through their donations to political parties. In the

UK donations usually favour the Conservative Party and in the 1990s there have been well-publicized donations from such firms as United Biscuits, Glaxo, British Airways, Rolls-Royce, Hanson and Forte. The Labour Party, while not receiving funds from industry, has been keen to listen to the views of its representatives in an attempt to broaden the party's electoral appeal after 15 years in opposition.

Not all attempts to influence the state are the products of group pressure. We have already seen the influence of the multinational corporation, and the major firms in any country will make some attempt at influencing government policy and may even be consulted. Individuals too represent an important channel of influence. Many references are made to the 'old boy network' that operates in government and business circles and several firms take more direct action by enlisting the services of a member of parliament on its board of directors.

British Airways prior to privatization set up a powerful lobby to protect its own position. The Civil Aviation Authority had published a report recommending that British Airways should give up some of its routes to its competitors, particularly local routes to provincial airlines and international routes to its main competitor, British Caledonian. The report also recommened that British Airways should move some of its services from Heathrow to Gatwick Airport and allow its competitors to move into Heathrow. The lobby was successful and a government White Paper on airline competition policy favoured British Airways. Some sources indicated the active role played by the then BA Chairman, Lord King, who was a personal friend of the then Prime Minister. The government decision effectively prevented British Caledonian from expanding and did much to prepare for its eventual takeover by BA following privatization.

In recent years a number of firms have emerged, which operate as professional lobbying consultants. Clients include not just private-sector organizations, but local authorities who wish to influence government policy on such issues as the dumping of nuclear waste and are resisting proposals to create nuclear waste sites in their area.

We can see that businesses attempt to influence the state in a variety of ways; through personal influence, by gaining media coverage for their views, by taking out expensive advertisements, by hiring consultants, and by submitting letters to the press, often enlisting the support of other interested parties. The timing of such attempts to influence can be crucial. In 1987 two studies emerged with the expressed intention of influencing government policy on the training of managers. The publication of both reports coincided with a general election campaign with a substantial loss of impact.

So far in this section we have focused on the way the state exerts its influence over the business community and vice versa. GATT and the European Community operate as supranational bodies which increase the complexity of the interaction between the state and business. We deal first with GATT and then proceed to examine the EU.

## GATT

GATT is the General Agreement on Tariffs and Trade. It was founded as a supranational body shortly after the Second World War. Alongside the World Bank and the International Monetary Fund it was set up as part of the Bretton Woods system for the management of the post-war economy. GATT was seen as a temporary stage in the creation of a World Trade Organization. It was not until the conclusion of the Uruguay Round of GATT talks in 1993 that this became a reality. GATT was originally founded on the twin assumptions that trade is associated with wealth and that an increase in trade between nations meant a reduction in the risk of war. These assumptions were born out of the experience of the 1930s when many nations sought to protect their own economies during depression through the imposition of high import tariffs and through the experiences of global war in the 1940s.

GATT operates from a headquarters in Geneva and agreements are reached through a series of 'Rounds' of which there have been eight since 1945. Each round seeks to pursue the basic objectives by furthering the liberalization of trade. In general GATT operates by:

- establishing rules which govern trading behaviour between nation states;
- attempting to liberalize trade through tariff and quota reduction;
- offering a legal framework and a court for the settlement of disputes;
- monitoring trade agreements and government policies, especially those which may contravene the GATT objective of further liberalization.

Since its foundation GATT has grown to embrace 105 nation states and at least 90% of world trade. Supporters of GATT point to the dramatic reduction in tariffs and the equally dramatic increase in world trade since the war. Others are more sceptical, highlighting the emergence of trading blocs as proof of the continued existence of protectionism, the success of countries such as Japan in resisting foreign imports and the growth of informal agreements outside the jurisdiction of GATT. Such an agreement would include the 'gentleman's agreement' between Britain and Japan and between the USA and Japan to limit unofficially the import of Japanese cars. Such agreements are contrary to the spirit of GATT.

The most recent 'round' began in Uruguay in 1986 and took seven years to reach its conclusion at the end of 1993. This particular round has concerned itself with the usual tariff issues, but has also tackled foreign investment, patents and copyright, trade issues concerning service industries and agriculture. It is this last issue, among others, that has resulted in the Uruguay talks taking so long to reach a conclusion. Throughout the world agriculture is the most highly subsidized of all industries and any proposal to reduce subsidies and hence liberalize trade have met with stern opposition and ultimately deadlock, resulting in the talks exceeding their deadline date. Even though the

Uruguay round was completed at the very end of 1993 it was done so amid much last-minute compromise. Even then the agreement must be ratified by the respective governments of the parties to the talks and it will probably take a further two years for the measures to be put into place. This lengthy process and the difficulties in reaching an agreement calls into question the ability of GATT and its successor, the World Trade Organization, to regulate international business and trade and has caused one reporter to comment somewhat sarcastically,

> Amid the crumbling of the post-war order, GATT is a laudable example of continuity and stability. The Soviet Union has disappeared, the Gulf War is over, Yugoslavia has disappeared and still 105 negotiators cannot decide what to do about farmers.
>
> (Andrew Marshall, *Independent on Sunday*, 18 October 1992)

## The European Union

The current European Union embraces 12 nation states. In Table 2.5 we identify the stages in the growth of the European Union since the 1950s. The EU was formed out of post-war idealism as a means of putting an end to war between European nations and to assist in the post-war political, social and economic reconstruction of Europe. Politically the EU saw itself a third major power bloc alongside the USA and the USSR. Economically there was a desire to capitalize on the largest market in the advanced industrial world. Protectionism was sought both against a buoyant Japanese export trade and in response to increasing protectionism on the part of the USA. By the late 1980s, the EU comprised 326 million people compared with 240 million in the USA and 125 million in Japan. From a UK perspective the incentive to join lay in the potential of a growing European market to compensate for declining commonwealth market.

While the initial impetus for the creation of the EU was economic (it was originally known as the European Economic Community), the EU has formally embraced social and legal issues as well. Social issues pertaining to the workplace have been grouped together under the collective banner of the Social Charter, to which the UK has been unable to subscribe, the only EU member so to do.

The political changes that took place at the end of the 1980s and into the early 1990s are likely to change the face of European business, and with the reunification of Germany, a former communist state has been brought into the EU. Predictions have been made that it will not be long before countries such as Hungary, Poland and the new states which were formerly Czechoslovakia will petition for membership. There is, however, much uncertainty. The future of many of the former communist states, particularly those in the old USSR, is as yet unclear, new business opportunities have been hyped, and the existing members of the EU have found agreement difficult on currency and employment issues. This was the context within which discussions took place in the Dutch town of Maastricht in 1992 to produce the Treaty on European Union, intended as a strengthening of EU provisions to achieve even

**Table 2.5** Stages in the development of the European Union

| | |
|---|---|
| 1952 | The European Coal and Steel Community formed by BELGIUM. FRANCE, WEST GERMANY, ITALY, LUXEMBOURG and NETHERLANDS. |
| 1957 | The above six countries sign the Treaty of Rome and establish the European Economic Community. The UK, invited to participate, withdraws from the talks at an early stage. |
| 1958 | The European Economic Community comes into being. |
| 1973 | The EEC six are joined by DENMARK, IRELAND, and the UNITED KINGDOM. |
| 1981 | GREECE joins. |
| 1986 | SPAIN and PORTUGAL join. |
| 1987 | The Single European Act is passed to create a single market by the end of 1992. |
| 1992 | The Treaty on European Unity, also known as the Treaty of Maastricht. |

greater unity. The Treaty dealt with the workings of the EU institutions, with economic and monetary union, with social policy and with foreign and security policy.

In this section on the EU we will examine its objectives, the mechanisms through which those objectives are achieved and focus on specific key issues, most of which lay at the heart of the debates surrounding the Maastricht discussions.

## EU objectives and instruments
The key objectives of the EU include:

- the maximization of the advantages accruing from the free movement of goods, finance and people;
- the increase of competition and demand;
- the maintenance of stable prices and high levels of employment;
- the coordination of the policies of individual governments and their central banks.

Such objectives rest on a number of assumptions. First, it is assumed that the reduction in trade barriers will lead to increased competition, which will drive more efficient methods of production and result in better quality products at cheaper prices. This in turn will lead to an increase in demand. Second, it is assumed that a united Europe will offer considerable economies of scale and eliminate the waste associated with nation states operating independently. (A full account of these debates may be found in Cecchini, 1988.)

The main instruments through which these objectives are to be achieved are contained within the Treaty of Rome 1957, the Single European Act 1987, the Social Charter and the Treaty of Maastricht, the

Treaty on European Unity 1992. A primary objective is seen as the removal of obstacles to free trade, and hence there are proposals to eliminate frontier controls and work permits and to harmonize both taxation policies and technical standards. The creation of a single European technical standard for car manufacture would, for example, eliminate the need to produce different types of headlamps for the same model of car to meet the various legal requirements in different European countries. The elimination of such differentiation would reduce costs and likely lead to increased demand.

The degree to which such instruments have been introduced has varied according to the nature of the proposed change and between member nations. Not all countries have embraced the proposals as readily as others. The UK has failed to agree to the provisions of the Social Charter and opted out of the Social Chapter of the Maastricht agreement. A particular contentious issue is that of monetary union and, as we saw in Case 2.1, this seems increasingly difficult to achieve in the short term. It is to this and other issues we now turn.

## EU issues

Businesses have been influenced by a certain harmonization that has taken place in company law, employment law, accounting practice, taxation and the role of financial institutions. There has been significant cooperation over policies concerning industrial development, regional aid and environmental protection. In the same way that business interests lobby national governments, attempts are made to influence EU policy. Nonetheless there would appear to be two major problems for businesses in dealing with the EU. The first concerns the bureaucracy and somewhat protracted decision-making mechanisms of EU institutions while the second concerns the conflict of interests between the constituent nation states. At the root of this conflict is the key issue of sovereignty. The European Commission and Parliament will assume powers that formerly belonged only to democratically elected governments of individual nation states. A third kind of problem relates to the differences that exist within the EU. Between countries there are considerable differences in geographical size, population, resources, living standards and a whole range of economic variables that present difficulties in the move to a level playing field.

We will illustrate some of the difficulties by focusing upon monetary union, competition policy and workplace issues.

Members of the EU possess a common unit of currency, the Ecu. While it does not exist in monetary form it is used for transactions between member states. The European Exchange Rate mechanism (ERM) is an attempt to keep the exchange rates of currency between member countries within fixed limits. The problems associated with the ERM have been well documented in Case 2.1. While the ERM has its detractors the major objections are usually reserved for the proposals associated with European Monetary Union. (EMU) and the creation of a single European currency. Those in favour of EMU see advantages in terms of increased competition and trade, the reduction of transaction costs, increased certainty in planning, the reduction of inflation and the necessity for greater political cooperation. The detractors point to the problems of maintaining comparable interest rates as seen within the ERM in 1992 and 1993 and that there would be unequal costs and benefits. In particular the fear is that EMU would strengthen considerably an already strong German economy and its central position in the European economy. For the British government EMU is seen as a loss of sovereignty and hence political control and democratic accountability. For this reason Britain has acted as the chief opponent to full-scale monetary union.

Competition policy of the EU has the avowed aims of preventing cartels, of controlling monopolies, especially state-controlled monopolies, and of restricting state aid to certain industries thereby creating unfair competition. Despite such aims there are many cases of protectionism and unfair competition within the Union. One reason for the demise of the British coal industry lay in the availability of cheaper coal elsewhere and the subsidies offered to coal producers in Germany.

The Social Chapter of the Treaty on European Unity building on the 1989 Social Charter deals with issues relating to wages and workplace conditions. The treaty seeks to harmonize practices not only on wages and conditions but also on equal opportunities and mechanisms for consultation between management and labour. The UK alone has opted out of this element of the treaty, an act which has provoked much criticism. The problems of unequal wages and conditions were highlighted by the decision of Hoover in 1993 to move 450 jobs from its factory in Dijon in France to Cambuslang in Scotland. This was done on the basis that wages and, in particular, associated benefits are up to 30% cheaper in the UK than in parts of the EU. Around the same period, Philips moved 150 jobs from Holland to the UK at Blackburn. Such transfer of labour for cost advantages has been dubbed 'social dumping' and threatens to undermine one of the key elements of European harmony.

| **KEY CONCEPT 2.3** *Technology* | Technology is a broad concept referring to the application of available knowledge and skills to create and use materials, processes and products. Technology is often accorded a dominant role in business and is often viewed as determining products, processes, organization structure and the individual's attitude to work. While there are situations where the prevailing technology is undoubtedly influential, it is the product of human endeavour and many managers do have a choice.<br><br>*New technology* refers to the application through computers of miniaturized electronic circuitry to process information thereby giving managers greater potential flexibility in and control over work operations.<br><br>*Information technology* links new technology with telecommunications to enhance the quantity, quality and speed of transmission. |

# Technology

Technology tends to be a somewhat mystical concept, no more so than when we speak of 'new technology' and 'high technology', overused and underdefined phrases. We hope to shed some light on what technology represents and where it stands in relationship to the firm in its environment.

The concept is popularly used to imply some form of process, invariably machinery-based, so we think of lathes, assembly lines, computers, and cash dispensers. In this way technology represents the application of science and engineering for use in business. However, technology not only refers to the artefacts themselves, but also to the way they are used and the theories governing their application. Human knowledge is therefore an essential ingredient of technology. We often distinguish between manufacturing firms according to the nature of the product, especially its constituent materials and its level of sophistication. We can therefore speak of material and product technology. On a much broader scale we distinguish between societies according to their sum total of knowledge and skills and the application of these for the benefit of that society. This too is known as technology. From a business perspective we can therefore speak of technology as the application of available knowledge and skills to create and use materials, processes and products.

Technology is closely associated with production systems, representing both an input and a transformation device. It is also central to the process of innovation. These concepts are developed further in Chapters 5 and 6. In this section we look at more general issues in the way technology and business interact, and focus on issues associated with 'new technology' and 'information technology'.

---

In 1972 the Conservative government, worried about the collapse of the BSA/Triumph motorcycle manufacturers, decided to aid the entire industry by assisting the formation of a merger between BSA/Triumph and Norton Villiers. The new company known as Norton-Villiers-Triumph (NVT) was launched in 1973 backed by £4.8 million from the government and £3.4 million from the Norton Villiers parent company. The new firm employed 1750 people in three plants, two ex-BSA/Triumph (Meriden and Small Heath) and the other ex-Norton (Wolverhampton).

Faced with intense Japanese competition for the mass bike market NVT's strategy was to concentrate on larger 'super bikes', mainly for the American market. The company would stress its craftsmanship image. To assist its policy, the decision was made to close the largest production plant at Meriden. The reasons behind this decision were the high cost of overheads, representing 50% of BSA/Triumph's losses, low productivity, a high incidence of industrial unrest, and a lack of space for expansion. The aim was to be in profit within three years and to expand on two sites within six years.

The new company was formed during the July shut-down at Meriden and faced an immediate strike there over holiday pay. Announcement of the closure was delayed

**CASE 2.2**
*Norton-Villiers-*
*Triumph*

until the strike was settled, when the government pledged its help with shut-down arrangements. The union at Meriden refused to accept the proposals and initiated a work-in, blockading not only their own management but parts and drawings for other factories, in particular affecting operations at Small Heath.

Workers at Meriden wanted to set up a cooperative and in October 1973 offered £1 million in exchange for NVT guaranteeing a market for Meriden bikes. The offer was rejected and redundancy notices were served on the employees in November. The redundancy notices were accepted but the blockade continued amid considerable media attention. The government intervened resisting NVT's management's request for an eviction order. The Department of Trade and Industry (DTI) acted as facilitator in talks between NVT management and union leaders and despite much management scepticism, the cooperative were given until the following April to acquire the plant.

The agreement took eight weeks to draft, both sides blaming the other for the delay, by which time NVT and the proposed cooperative faced a number of problems. The affair had drained NVT's working capital, especially as the country was faced with a three-day working week resulting from petrol shortages and a miners' strike. Workers' redundancy money to be used to buy the company was largely spent on living expenses, the company was unable to supply working capital and the government was unwilling to underwrite the exercise. The plan was saved during the General Election campaign of February 1974 when the cooperative agreed to lift the blockade in return for first option on Meriden's assets.

The election of a new Labour government resulted in the reorganization of the DTI. A newly created Department of Industry, headed by Labour left-wingers Benn and Heffer, resulted in increased sympathy for Meriden, backed by an ideology that opposed closures on financial grounds only. Benn proposed further public funding of the cooperative. Meanwhile the blockade continued and NVT obtained a court injunction. The union refused to take action until the government funded the enterprise. However, Benn used his personal influence over the workers, the blockade was lifted and the injunction was not served.

The cooperative appeared to be launched with government financial backing and the appointment of a politically sympathetic manager. The scene now shifted to Small Heath whose workers opposed the plan demanding that Meriden's products be sold by NVT, and that jobs be secured with government funding at their plant. Such opposition was grounded in the growth of Meriden at the expense of Small Heath when both were owned by BSA, the lack of solidarity shown by Meriden workers when job losses occurred at Small Heath, and the fact that the recent blockade had seriously affected operations at Small Heath. The Small Heath workers threatened their own work-in and blockade.

The government asked NVT to prepare a three factory plan, but at the same time launched the cooperative with a grant of £5 million. The new NVT plan estimated the need for additional government financial backing to the tune of £12–15 million. The Small Heath workers refused to agree unless job guarantees were made and the investments were made in their plant.

In December 1974, the Meriden cooperative reinstated its blockade and NVT continued to lose money. The managing director of NVT blamed government intervention, and in particular the conflict between economic and ideological motives, from preventing his taking action to solve what he saw as a domestic industrial dispute.

(*Source*: Sandberg, 1984)

## Technology: determinant or choice?

A classic view of technology is that it exists as an environmental constraint which becomes the dominant feature of all businesses. Firms operate within certain technological imperatives which shape not only the products and the processes they use, but the structure of the organization, relations between people, and individual job satisfaction. Such a view can be found in the work of Joan Woodward (1965) and in Robert Blauner's classic but flawed sociological study of alienation (1964). Galbraith (1972), too, painted a picture of markets being dominated by technological considerations rather than consumer choice.

Woodward in particular has been very influential. Her classification of small batch, mass, and process production has featured in most text-books on management and organization since the 1960s and this book is no exception (Chapter 6 has a more detailed description of these three types). To Woodward, technology not only determined organization structure, but the relationship between individual departments and the focus of each business. In small batch firms, product development and technical sales were the key issues; in mass-production organizations, fragmentation led to tensions between departments, a source of potential conflict; in process organizations, once the system has been created, high volume sales become the key issue. The relationship between technology and structure was, according to Woodward, crucial to the success of a business. In her study of manufacturing firms in south-east Essex she found that the most successful firms financially were the ones which conformed to the organizational type most appropriate for their technology.

Joan Woodward viewed technology as a determinant of both organization structure and the range of possible strategy alternatives. Woodward has been labelled a contingency theorist, yet, as we saw in Chapter 1, the contingency approach puts forward a view of business whereby activities at the level of the firm result from the interrelationship of a number of variables such as technology, the behaviour of competitors, the role of the state and so on. The end result is supposedly strategic choice for the individual manager following from an analysis of relevant variables. Woodward's view of technology would appear to give the manager no choice at all. Technology is dominant and managers fail to adapt to it at their peril.

We offer two challenges to this view of technology. First, we look briefly at its relationship with organizational size and second, we view technology as an element of strategic choice.

The first challenge to the notion of an all-pervasive technology is offered by those who champion size as a more influential variable than technology (for example, Hickson *et al.*, 1969). Studies such as these conclude that technology may well be an important determinant of the structure and work patterns in smaller plants, but as firms increase in size, it is size itself which becomes the more dominant influence. We examine the variable of size more fully in the next chapter.

We suggested earlier that technology has a certain mystical quality determining the structure and processes of business as the climate and weather determine agriculture. The knowledge, skills, artefacts and processes that make up technology are, unlike the weather, products of the kind of people who operate technological systems. The assembly line is not a technological imperative, but a device created to satisfy the pressures of mass markets and a product of the foresight of entrepreneurs like Ford and the skill of designers who made the process work. Viewed in this way, technology is not a determinant of business, rather a product of the way managers respond to other environmental influences. Furthermore, the kind of technology employed by businesses may be a matter of strategic choice. The application of socio-technical systems analysis offers managers the possibility of changing the prevailing technology to suit the needs of their own particular workforce and the prevailing social situation in which they operate. Increasingly technology and, more especially information technology, is used as a strategy for competitive advantage. We see this to good effect in Case 2.3, Thomson Holidays, where an on-line computerized booking system was established linking individual travel agents to the central booking facility, thereby giving Thomson the edge in the market place over its rivals.

While we cannot afford the space for a full academic debate on the role of technology and offer a complete critique of contingency and socio-technical systems theory, we may conclude that the relationship between technology and business is highly complex, certainly involv-

---

**CASE 2.3**
*Thomson Holidays*

This case deals with the introduction of the Thomson Open-line Programme, a computerized reservation system giving travel agents instant and direct access to the company. In this way, customers are able to book their holiday through their local travel agent and obtain immediate confirmation. Such systems were not new. Computerized reservation had been used by airline companies for some 15 years before Thomson's decision to adopt the technology. Thomson were not even first tour operator, as a similar system was already operated by Olympic Holidays. However, Thomson were the first major holiday company to introduce a direct access computerized booking system that was adopted by a large number of travel agents, and which became the industry standard.

Thomson Holidays is part of the International Thomson Organization. The company, with interests in newspapers, publishing and oil, did not enter the travel business until 1965 with the acquisition of Universal Skytours and Britannia Airways. After a shaky start and several managerial changes, the company emerged as one of the United Kingdom's largest operators, largely as a result of a vigorous price-cutting campaign in the early 1970s, backed by attention to customer feedback and quality improvement. With the collapse of Clarksons, its major rival, Thomson Holidays became the top company in 1974 and now commands a market share in excess of 33%, far ahead of its closest rival the International Leisure Group. As well as being a tour operator, the company has developed in all aspects of the travel industry. In Britannia Airlines it controls the largest holiday charter company in the country. Portland Holidays is one of the largest companies selling holidays direct to the public and, in Lunn Poly, the company owns one of the largest multiples of travel agents.

Prior to the introduction of a computerized system, holiday booking was done either by telephone or entirely on the basis of a booking form. This information was handled centrally and all booking data were kept on card index. The first technological change came in 1976 with the introduction of the Thomson Reservation and Administrative Control System (TRACS). TRACS established a computer network linking head office with ten regional centres, through which bookings were made by the travel agents. The company bought existing software used by the airline KLM but had underestimated the degree of customization required and the software was almost completely rewritten.

TRACS was viewed by management as a success and was seen as a major factor in the company's keeping ahead of its rivals in the turbulent environment of rising oil prices in the 1970s and the subsequent impact on the cost of air travel. Errors in bookings and administration were reduced, credit control was improved, and the system was popular with travel agents. Central booking staff were reduced by approximately two-thirds and those remaining in post had their jobs enhanced as they now operated as a direct interface between the company and travel agents. The person heading the introduction of TRACS was promoted to Systems Director, recognition by the company of the strategic importance of IT.

When TRACS was introduced in the mid 1970s, networking technology was relatively unsophisticated. By the end of the decade, the Post Office had launched Prestel, a nationwide on-line processing system with low-cost terminals. This effectively paved the way for a considerable growth in national computer networks. Thomson extended TRACS to a large number of travel agents through the Thomson Open-line Programme (TOP). The relatively low cost of the on-line system did not limit its use to just the larger multiples in the travel agency business. The accessibility to the small independent travel agency of its computer booking system was an important strategic objective for Thomson.

The company hoped to build upon the efficiency and effectiveness of TRACS, not least the cost savings. TOP became a corporate priority receiving direct top management support and a project team was set up drawing upon staff from all parts of the organization as well as recruiting staff with specific expertise from outside. This was vital given the decision to develop the company's own network, based largely on its experience with TRACS. Travel agents were closely involved throughout the development stage and all participating agents received comprehensive training. TOP was widely publicized by Thomson and the company received a great deal of favourable press coverage. The intended image was created of a company that was not only a leader in the holiday business but also a leader where technology was concerned.

TOP was introduced in 1982 with 2200 participating travel agents. Within a year 3584 agents were involved covering 61% of all bookings. Telephone bookings were withdrawn altogether in 1986 and by 1988, 95% of all bookings were made through the on-line system. The overall cost of introducing TRACS and TOP has been estimated at a little over £20 million. Between 1978 and 1987 there was a 400% increase in business and Thomson's market share rose from 18% to 29%, with a further rise to 33% by 1990. Throughout this period staffing had remained fairly constant at around 800 and Thomson estimate savings in the region of £28 million.

(*Source*: Peltu and Land (1987), Daniels (1991).)

ing the interrelationship of other variables like size and management choice, and one which cannot be reduced to a simple notion of determinism. A good illustration of this complexity is provided in Chapter 5. Using Rothwell's illustration of the development of railways, we conclude that innovation is neither technology-led nor market-led, but a complex interrelationship of those and other variables, such as the availability of finance and cheap labour (Rothwell and Zegveld, 1981).

An analysis of the role of technology in many organizations offers us insights into a highly dynamic process. A rival tour operator to Thomson Holidays may well feel it necessary to develop its own on-line reservation system to maintain competitiveness. In this case the rival management are confronted by the twin forces of available technology and competition. Management must then evaluate the costs of introducing the new reservation system against the costs of not introducing it, the kind of system to buy and precisely how it will be used in their organization. Thus far technological and competitive determinism have interacted with management decision-making and choice. Once a decision is reached then the new technology assumes a new dynamic, that of reshaping the organization and offering possibilities of new ways of working. At this stage the new technology must interact with the prevailing organization culture and organization politics. This explains why, in some organizations, groups may resist technological change, as in the case of the Fleet Street newspaper industry.

## New technology and information technology

New technology represents yet another elusive and imprecise term, used in a variety of different ways. In this book we take it to refer to the application through computers of miniaturized electronic circuitry to process information. We therefore find 'new technology' in a variety of business and non-business settings. In banking and finance, it has enabled money markets all over the world to be linked with instant access to information and especially market changes. The speed with which changes can be registered with the subsequent speed of response has been cited by some as a major contributory factor behind steep stock-market falls in all major markets during the latter part of 1987 and the fall of sterling and associated ERM crisis in 1992 (Case 2.1 offers more details). In retailing, 'electronic point of sale systems' (EPOS) provide instant information on sales trends, cash flows and stock levels. In manufacturing, computer-controlled machines, robotics, and entire computerized flexible manufacturing systems have greatly enhanced a firm's response to changing market demands and improved product quality. In the office, the introduction of word-processing systems can greatly speed up typing operations, especially where large numbers of standard letters are involved, and E-mail systems can reduce the amount of paperwork in circulation.

The concept of new technology is often linked to that of information technology. The above illustration from banking and finance shows how miniaturized electronic circuitry has been combined with developments in telecommunications to broaden the information processing capacities of a single computer system.

Child (1984b) and Earl (1989) give us some clues to the popularity of new technology and information technology for businesses, in that they offer the following:

- the opportunity of gaining competitive advantage by offering a product or a service that no-one else is able to provide;
- the improvement in productivity and performance;
- the improved quality of both system operation and system outputs;
- increased efficiency through reduced operating costs and reduced manning levels;
- improved information and diagnostic systems leading to improvements in management control;
- the opportunity to develop new ways of managing and organizing.

The kind of advantages outlined above offer to management, cost reduction and increased profitability; to the workforce, increased job satisfaction; and to the customer, better quality goods and services at competitive prices. Such opportunities were sought and largely gained by Thomson Holidays in Case 2.3. In the early 1980s, Surrey County Council set up a centralized word processing unit to undertake much of the work done by existing typing pools in a number of different departments. The intention was to meet user needs more effectively than previous systems and to create a more satisfying work environment. The County Council saw benefits of the new system in terms of a much quicker turn-round of work, particularly on standard items; improved quality necessitating less time in checking and correcting; a closer relationship between operator and user with a clearer identification of priorities and a better understanding of user needs; more flexible working allowing peaks of work to be smoothed and priorities to be dealt with; and increased job satisfaction among the staff involved (Smith, 1982).

There are however a number of problems which may be created by the introduction of new technology. While desktop computers and word-processors can be relatively cheap labour-saving devices for the office, the introduction of entire manufacturing systems based on new technology can be prohibitively expensive. In general terms, the introduction of new technology in the office incurs much lower costs than in manufacturing. The availability of a wide variety of software has reduced considerably the cost of establishing computerized systems. However, the costs of adapting the software to meet local specifications can add greatly to the cost of implementation. Considerable costs were borne by Thomson Holidays in adapting existing software already being used by airline companies. We have made reference to the use of computer control, robotics and flexible manufacturing systems in Chapter 6. Likewise the problems of skills training and industrial relations are dealt with in Chapter 8. Students seeking information on these aspects are advised to refer to the relevant parts of these chapters. The one area where there is considerable controversy is the impact of new technology on labour, and it is to this we now turn.

## New technology and labour

There would appear to be three perspectives on the impact of new technology on labour. First we have the kind of view associated with such writers as Braverman (1974). New technology is seen as a de-skilling agent reducing the amount of discretion an individual has over his job, at the same time increasing management control over both work process and the worker. The labour force has been reduced with the greatest effects of both deskilling and job losses being felt by skilled craft workers. The second perspective offers an optimistic scenario. New technology is seen as creating new opportunities for the work-force in the form of new and different types of labour with opportunities for existing workers to learn new skills. The third perspective is also optimistic, viewing new technology as a liberating device, eliminating the need for human labour in repetitive, dangerous or unpleasant tasks. The evidence supporting these three perspectives is mixed. We will view the effect on the numbers employed, on the type of jobs involved, and on the content of those jobs.

In terms of the numbers employed, the introduction of new technology in manufacturing industry has resulted in some job losses (Daniel, 1987). Predictions of actual numbers vary but most studies stress that actual losses occur mostly in lower skilled jobs and are generally fewer than envisaged. A survey of the period 1981–3 estimated a net loss of 34 000 jobs but at the same time stressed that this represented only 5% of all job losses in manufacturing (Northcott and Rogers, 1984). This view is reinforced by Daniel (1987). He acknowledges the difficulty of isolating the impact of new technology and claims that its impact on job losses is much less than other forms of change, notably declining markets. He also found that actual dismissals were very rare and that reductions were generally met by redeployment, early retirement and (in some cases highly attractive) voluntary redundancy schemes. In the service sector, predicted job losses have not occurred. The introduction of new technology has been used to increase productivity and provide an improved service retaining existing employment levels or, in the case of banks, by providing new types of customer service requiring more, not fewer staff (Williams, 1984). The study by Daniel (1987) found that the use of computers and word-processors in offices led to a general increase in staff. In Case 2.3, the Thomson's computerized booking system resulted in staff reductions, when it was first introduced. However, over time the increase in the volume of bookings meant that staffing was restored to its former level, with the staff handling a far greater volume of work than previously.

The impact of new technology varies greatly according to the type of job. In general, the demand for unskilled labour has fallen while that for skilled labour has risen. Far from causing mass unemployment this has led to job shortages in some areas, notably computing and renewed attempts to raise skill levels through training opportunities (Chapter 8). This uneven impact has in some cases led to a transfer of skills from one group of workers to another. Wilkinson (1986) points out that the introduction of the computer control of manufacturing equipment (known as 'numerical control' and 'computerized numerical control') has shifted the skill from the craft jobs on the shop floor to the computer programming skills of the office. There are variations within manufacturing industry; Northcott and Rogers (1984) found that where microprocessors were part of the manufacturing process then job losses resulted, but in those industries which used microprocessors as part of the product, then job gains were made. The same study found that the introduction of new technology generally called for more flexible skills and work practices.

The debate about job numbers is matched by that concerning job content. The implication of the point made by Wilkinson in the last paragraph is that for some shopfloor workers deskilling has taken place. However, the PSI survey from 1980 to 1984 concluded that on balance advanced technology has enriched the jobs of those affected in both manual and office settings, with greater possibilities being afforded the latter group. In deference to Braverman the survey does make the distinction between enhanced satisfaction in terms of job content and reduced autonomy through the centralization of management control. In manufacturing, automation has greatly enhanced the work environment of jobs such as paint spraying. In the office the use of word processors has reduced the drudgery of typing numerous addresses. Nevertheless the benefits derived through the introduction of such advanced systems can be offset by the cost in manufacturing, and by the time taken to encode information in the office, before such benefits can accrue.

The main point to be taken from all the studies is that new technology should not be viewed deterministically. Its impact is based on a number of different factors including the nature of the product and service, the type of organization involved, the management strategy employed, and the attitude of trade unions and employees. Surrey County Council's adoption of a centralized word-processing system in the 1980s highlights a number of these points. In this case, the introduction of word-processing was carried out in the context of introducing new methods of working through the introduction of work teams; the union was involved in the planning process; and the employees themselves were largely self-selecting.

We end this section on new technology by raising two related and fundamental issues.

First, we may conclude that the job losses arising directly from the introduction of new technology are much less than originally envisaged and must be viewed in the context of job losses resulting from other causes, and in the light of job gains in skilled occupations and service industries. Three notes of caution have been sounded.

- While there has been a transfer of labour from the manufacturing to the service sector, it remains to be seen how long this will continue (Wilkinson, 1986).
- New technology is generally associated with growth industries. Rather than focus on job losses perhaps we should be more concerned about the lack of job gains (Daniel, 1987).
- In terms of job losses the hardest hit group has been the low-skilled workers. Since female labour is over-represented in such jobs, the introduction of new technology may have a significant impact on unemployment levels among women workers (Williams, 1984).

Second, the point has been made that whatever the effect upon labour through the introduction of new technology, the failure to embrace it will be much more wide-ranging (Williams, 1984; Wilkinson, 1986). Williams writes as follows.

> . . . if the United Kingdom introduces new technology more slowly than other industrialised nations, there will be a real danger of job losses through declining competitiveness without the wider benefits which new technology can bring.

(Williams, 1984, p. 210)

---

| **KEY CONCEPT 2.4** *A trade union* | A trade union is a group of employees who formally come together to achieve mutual goals. Such goals normally include job protection, improving pay and conditions and attempting to influence management decision-making. In the United Kingdom, trade-union membership cuts across individual firms and entire industries, although different patterns exist in other countries, notably industrial unions in Germany and company unions in Japan. There is considerable ideological debate concerning the influence of trade unions in business decisions. |
| --- | --- |

---

## Labour

Labour interacts with business through the workings of the labour market and through the activities of trade unions. Aspects to consider are the changes in both the level and nature of employment and the role played by trade unions in the operation of business. The labour factor itself interacts with other elements in our environment, so levels of employment are also affected by state intervention and the introduction of new technology. The type of employment in a particular labour market is a product of these and cultural factors. Firms themselves influence the workings of the labour market through various management strategies of recruitment training and payment. Variations in management strategy also account for the way different companies handle issues of industrial relations. In this section we will look at two aspects of labour; employment trends and the power of trade unions in influencing management decisions. A more detailed discussion of personnel and industrial relations strategies may be found in Chapter 8.

## Employment trends

We have seen elsewhere in this chapter that changes in the economy have significant effects on both the type and levels of employment. The changes affecting Britain, and indeed many other industrialized nations, may be summarized as follows.

- In the 1960s and 1970s considerable job losses were experienced in the primary sector (mining, agriculture, fishing etc.). During that period the primary sector workforce was cut by one half, although, largely through mechanization, its share of total output was increased. In the 1990s further employment losses were incurred by the primary sector through an extensive programme of pit closures in the coal-mining industry.
- The process of de-industrialization has led to considerable job losses in the manufacturing sector. Table 2.4 shows how manufacturing industry has shed 40% of its labour since 1971. The extent of job losses in manufacturing is viewed by some as unusual in an industrialized country (Edwards *et al.*, 1992). A fuller discussion of the de-industrialization process is offered in the first section of this chapter.
- Job gains have been experienced in the tertiary sector of the economy, particularly in the financial sector, catering, the professions and professional services.
- Many changes in the nature of employment are attributable to changes in technology. References to this are made throughout this book and aspects of new technology have been dealt with earlier in this section.
- There is some evidence that firms in this country and elsewhere are following the Japanese practice of establishing a dual labour market comprising a trained core of employees supported by workers on a less permanent basis. A fuller discussion on flexibility is presented in the following chapter. Over the last decade there has been a marked increase in the numbers of part-time workers and several firms already express a clear preference for part-time employees. (The Orlake records case in Chapter 6 illustrates this.)
- Related to the increase in part-time workers and the rise in long-term unemployment among males, there has been an increase in women workers from 33% of the work force in 1951 to 48% in 1990 (Edwards *et al.*, 1992).

## Trade unions

Trade unions are formally organized groups of employees with the aims, among others, of job protection, the improvement of pay and conditions, and the widening of industrial democracy. Such aims often bring unions into conflict with their employers, a conflict normally resolved by a process known as collective bargaining. We will examine first the changing nature of trade-union membership before assessing the power unions can use to influence business decisions.

**Table 2.6** Trade-union density as a percentage of the working population, 1913–92

| | |
|---|---|
| 1913 | 23 |
| 1920 | 45 |
| 1933 | 22 |
| 1945 | 38 |
| 1964 | 44 |
| 1974 | 50 |
| 1979 | 55 |
| 1983 | 50 |
| 1985 | 46 |
| 1988 | 42 |
| 1992 | 36 |

*Sources*: Price and Bain (1983), *The Employment Gazette*.

Trade union membership has grown considerably this century as we see in Table 2.6. However, such data must be viewed with a little caution as trade-union density is calculated in different ways. The table does offer a broad view of growth and decline. A number of key changes are summarized as follows.

- There are marked variations in union membership in different types of employment. In coal mining, union density has consistently stood at over 90%. A high density can also be found in local government and the engineering industry. Low levels of membership are found in retailing, and hotel and catering.
- The number of unions has declined from 1323 in 1900 to 393 in 1983 and to 275 at the end of 1991. This change is attributable to a mixture of amalgamation and structural changes in the economy. De-industrialization has accounted for the loss of a number of specialist unions in manufacturing. The amalgamation process has meant that the growth of the firm has been matched by the growth of the large trade union. At the peak of membership in the late 1970s, the biggest union, the Transport and General Workers Union, almost topped 2 million members. Table 2.7 shows the top ten trade unions in terms of membership.
- Unions in older established industries, such as coal mining and the railways, have suffered large membership losses as employment has declined, while union growth has been most marked in the white-collar sector and among public employees. More recent membership increases are to be found among part-time workers and female employees of all types. Between 1990 and 1991, at a time of general membership decline, female trade-union membership rose by 20 000. Despite these growth trends there is clear

**Table 2.7** Top ten unions by membership in 1991

| | *Thousands* |
|---|---|
| Transport and General Workers Union | 1127 |
| GMB | 863 |
| National and Local Government Officers Association | 760 |
| Amalgamated Engineering Union | 623 |
| Manufacturing Science and Finance Union | 604 |
| National Union of Public Employees | 551 |
| Electrical Electronic Telecommunication and Plumbing Union | 357 |
| Union of Shop Distributive and Allied Workers | 341 |
| Royal College of Nursing of the UK | 293 |
| Graphical Paper and Media Union | 282 |

Since 1991, the National and Local Government Officers Association has merged with the National Union of Public Employees and the Confederation of Health Service Employees to form UNISON, now the largest union in the UK.

evidence that trade unions are failing to secure members in many new areas of employment (Edwards *et al.*, 1992).

- The major change since 1980 has been the overall marked decline in membership. Between 1979 and 1991, trade unions lost 3.7 million members, some 25% of the total (Bird *et al.*, 1993). In each year during that period there has been a consecutive fall in total membership.

- Along with the decline in membership there is evidence that collective bargaining has also declined (Millward *et al.*, 1992). This is the traditional mechanism used by unions to negotiate wages and conditions with management and many firms are clearly seeking alternative ways of wage determination.

Union growth and decline have mirrored economic, political, and social changes. Increasing levels of unemployment have not only led to a reduction in trade-union membership but undoubtedly weakened their bargaining power. Two other developments may be noted. First, the influence of unions has been further weakened by the dismantling of many tripartite forums, associated with the Labour governments of the '60s and '70s, and hence the removal of unions from the political arena and the development of economic policy. Second, following the pattern set by American and Japanese multinationals, it is not unusual to find firms with no trade union representing the workforce, or where a union does exist, it operates under single union, no-strike agreements. These strategies are analysed in Chapter 8. Despite this weakening of trade-union power there is still a concern that unions often operate against the interests of private property and the public at large. This has been a key theme in the Government's policies since 1979. It is to this issue of trade-union power we now turn.

## Trade-union power

Any debate about trade-union power seems to be based upon assumptions about a balance of power and management's right to manage. At an obvious level trade unions do have influence. For example, wage rates in general are higher in unionized firms than in non-unionized firms in the same industry, and certain groups such as the Fleet Street print workers have resisted technical change in their industry. The union supporter would doubtless claim that the trade union acts as an important check and balance in management decision-making, preventing management from acting unreasonably and improving the quality of the decisions made.

Some, however, regard trade unions as being too powerful. This is a particular view of the 'New Right'. Their belief is that unions disrupt the mechanisms of the free market, particularly by pricing jobs according to bargaining strength rather than demand. This favours only a minority, pricing jobs out of the market and adding to the problems of unemployment. In addition, individual freedoms are challenged by strikes affecting the supply of goods and essential services. As a result, unions are viewed as privileged members of society whose power needs to be curbed. The Employment Acts of 1980, 1982, 1988, 1989, 1990 and the Trade Union Act of 1984 were introduced to effect such controls. (Those seeking further analysis of this position are referred to Shonfield, 1968; Hayek, 1984; and Conservative government policy 1979 onwards.)

This view in turn has been challenged on the basis that unions are only concerned with marginal issues, such as minor changes in rates of pay and conditions, or the resistance of change in highly specific areas. The challenge further argues that unions are relatively unconcerned about wider issues of management control and industrial democracy. By contrast, it is believed that management wield considerable power, which is actually strengthened by the formal procedures used in dealing with unions; most procedures attempt to protect the status quo, thereby favouring management. The introduction of formal procedures tends to push the conflict away from its source, away from the traditional basis of union strength, the membership, so that it is dealt with by top management in negotiation with full-time union officials, not involved in the original dispute. (A further analysis of this position may be found in Hyman, 1972; Fox, 1974b; and Goldthorpe, 1977.)

The debate about union power will doubtless run and run since it is all a question of ideology. Many of the arguments above have their roots in different values and party politics. This influences not only the position taken, but the way facts are selected and interpreted. As with all influences on the management decision-making process there are insuperable problems of measurement. Even then we have to be content with observing the formal procedures when so much influence is undoubtedly the product of informal communication.

Whichever view is taken it is clear that, since the early 1980s, management's hand against the unions has been strengthened by rising levels of unemployment and changes in labour law. In addition, an increasingly competitive product market has led firms to seek greater flexibility both in the labour force itself and in working practices. Unions, weakened by membership losses and fearing job losses, have agreed to many such changes. Some view this state of affairs as permanent, while others see reasons for the decline of unions as a temporary phenomenon, linked to specific factors that will change over time.

---

Culture represents all human activity that is socially, as opposed to being genetically, transmitted. Cultural influences therefore pervade all areas of business life. A particular interest in business is the extent to which we can learn from the business experiences of other cultures and transplant ideas developed by businesses in one culture and use them in a totally different setting. It is for this reason that many people have sought to understand the reasons for post-war business growth in Japan and Germany and, in particular, the interest shown in Japanese management methods.

**KEY CONCEPT 2.5**
*Culture*

---

## Cultural influences and business

Culture may be defined as that part of human action that is socially as opposed to genetically transmitted. It comprises ideas through which we perceive and interpret the world, symbols we use to communicate these ideas, and institutions which enable individuals to become socialized and satisfy their needs. Trompenaars (1993) recognizes that culture operates in three layers. At its most visible it represents those artefacts and goods that most readily distinguish one culture from another, such as architecture, food, ceremonies and language. At a deeper level it comprises our notions of 'right' and 'wrong', our norms, and our notions about what is 'good' and 'bad', our values. Many problems associated with the relationships between people of different cultures stem from variations in norms and values. At its deepest level, however, culture comprises a set of basic assumptions that operate automatically to enable groups of people to solve the problems of daily life without thinking about them. In this way, culture is that which causes one group of people to act collectively in a way that is different from another group of people.

Culture is a highly complex subject and interacts with business in three different ways.

● Our socialization, the influences which shape our behaviour in a particular social setting, will determine our individual orientations to work.

- We tend to see organizations as societies in microcosm with their own specific cultures and ways of transmitting these cultures to their members. In some companies, like Hewlett-Packard, the creation of a corporate culture is seen as a priority and a great deal of time, effort, and expenditure is given to induction and training (Case 3.5).
- We use culture as an analytical device to distinguish one society from another.

We deal with the concept of organizational culture in the next chapter and focus here on the third meaning of the term, viewing the wider cultural environment as one of the influences which shape business. Culture is of course the most pervasive of our five environmental factors in the model, having an impact on the other four. Factors such as the role of the state, the application of technology, and the orientations of the labour force to their work can all be viewed as being culturally determined. As with the other elements of the model the relationship with business is not just one-way. The way businesses conduct their affairs affects and often changes the particular culture in which they operate; the operation of the multinational corporation in the Third World being a case in point.

Interest in cross-cultural research blossomed in the 1960s following the popularity of the convergence thesis; a claim that the imperatives of industrialization would eventually cause all industrialized liberal democracies to become more like one another. The contending views of convergence versus cultural diversity are often referred to as the 'culture free' versus the 'culture specific' debate. In the following sections we examine briefly the main points in that debate and attempt to draw some conclusions.

## The 'culture-free' hypothesis

A visitor to the Ford car plant at Dagenham in the UK will find many features that Ford has in common with a General Motors car plant in the USA, a Renault factory in France, a Volkswagen operation in Germany, a Toyota plant in Japan, and the Proton Saga factory in Malaysia. Such features include a common technology, similar types of organization structure, individuals with similar skills and job titles, and work being carried out in much the same way. The culture-free hypothesis argues that businesses in the same sector in all countries are converging on similar types of technology, strategies and forms of business organization. Moreover, some believe that the speed of this convergence is increasing as a result of the growth of global travel and global communications.

For the manager, the key advantages of convergence are that ideas and techniques developed in one cultural or national setting may be transferred to another and used effectively. Furthermore, developing nations are able to learn from those more advanced countries and thus benefit from the mistakes of others. Such thinking is clearly behind the adoption by British and American firms of Japanese techniques such as quality circles and just-in-time and the focus on American theories of motivation by British management trainers. Belief in the transferability of techniques has led management to turn elsewhere for solutions to problems.

In the late 1980s management at the Ford plant in Dagenham wished to reduce the average time for resetting the presses and turned to international comparisons for assistance in tackling the problem. The time taken to change the set-up of metal presses at the beginning of the production process is a key element in the overall efficiency of that process. Such changeovers are frequently necessary given the large number and variety of metal parts in a modern motor car and delays at this stage have an impact on the entire process. It was found that Ford workers at the Genk factory in Belgium could, with similar technology, effect the changeover in approximately half the time of the Dagenham workers. As a result, a massive training exercise was undertaken and every member of the linesetting teams (those responsible for setting the presses) at Dagenham was sent to observe the Belgian operation. Lessons were learnt and the time was improved in the UK. However, the improvements did not match the time taken by the Belgian workers which suggested that there may be less tangible cultural factors accounting for the difference in the set-up times in the two countries.

The underlying theory behind all the above is that convergence on a particular type of technology and business organization is more significant than the cultural features of a particular society. The key elements in the convergence process are technology, the growth of big business and professional management and the impact of multinationals. The arguments were first developed by Kerr *et al.* (1973) and Harbison and Myers (1959). The main imperative of all nations was seen as efficient production and the key elements were developments in science and technology that were available to all. Businesses in all nations, faced with the same problems, adopted the same solutions. These included increasing size, increasing specialization and formalization, the development of similar systems of authority, occupational types and structures and adopting similar systems of education and training. To Kerr *et al.* the ultimate development was that of industrialism which would transcend differences formerly ascribed to culture and political economy.

Support for the convergence hypothesis may be found in the universality of similar forms of productive technology, in the growth of big business and the multinational with global influence and in the growth of professional management with increasing influence. The assumption is widely held that the theories and approaches to management and organization were universal, and that the same recipes (usually American) could be applied irrespective of the cultural context.

## The culture-specific hypothesis

Hofstede (1980a, 1980b) believes that there are significant national differences in the way people approach work and organizations.

Hofstede's major work was based around a survey carried out between 1967 and 1973 of 116 000 employees of IBM across 40 different countries. The survey was an attempt to measure a number of cultural variables and hence determine the extent to which business activities were culturally defined. IBM is noted for its distinctive corporate culture and the deliberate strategy of developing that culture irrespective of national boundaries. Hofstede was dealing with an organization which had the same technology in all locations, the same organization structure and jobs and pursued the same strategies. The conditions were ripe for convergence. However, Hofstede found differences which could be explained by reference to four variables.

**Power distance**   This is the extent to which members of a society accept that power is distributed unequally in organizations. In all societies there is inequality between people, be it based upon physical, economic, intellectual or social characteristics. Hofstede found societies like France, Mexico and Hong Kong where the power distance is large and formed the basis of social relations. In those societies such as Germany, Sweden and the USA, the power distance was small and such societies were noted for their attempts to reduce inequality.

**Individualism**   Individualistic societies such as the USA and the UK are depicted by a preference for looking after yourself or your immediate family group, a belief in freedom and a tendency towards a calculative involvement with work organizations. Collectivistic societies such as India, Singapore and Mexico show concern for a much wider group and emphasize belongingness which can extend to organizations.

**Uncertainty avoidance**   This is the extent to which members of a society feel uncomfortable with uncertainty. Members of societies displaying strong uncertainty avoidance, as in Argentina, Switzerland and Japan, tend to be anxious about the future and have an inability to tolerate deviant ideas. Weak uncertainty avoidance as displayed in Hong Kong, USA and Thailand is associated with a willingness to accept new ideas and take risks.

**Masculinity**   Masculine societies such as Japan, USA and Germany tend to display a preference for achievement, assertiveness and material success and display a strong belief in gender roles. Feminine societies like Sweden and Holland place more emphasis on the quality of life, care for others and equality, more especially between the sexes.

These variables shape the values and hence the behaviour of people operating in work organizations and enable us to explain differences in the way different countries conduct their business affairs. They may also explain why work systems developed in one country will not work in another. For example, Hofstede reported that American car workers from Detroit working at the Saab-Scania plant in Sweden disliked the work system which placed a great deal of emphasis on group work. The Americans, with the exception of one woman, were much happier with a system which stressed individual achievement. Hofstede noted that many management theories originated in the USA. The USA is typified by ratings that are below average for power distance and uncertainty avoidance, above average for masculinity, and has the highest rating on measures of individualism than any other country in Hofstede's survey. American motivation theory has been particularly influential and, in particular, the approaches of Herzberg, McClelland and Vroom reflect typically American features. These are the need for individual achievement and performance (high individualism and masculinity) and involve the acceptance of risk (weak uncertainty avoidance). The implication is that such theories will not work so well in societies that are more collectivistic and feminine and whose people are risk avoiders.

The 'culture-specific' hypothesis claims that cultural influences in different societies will result in different styles of organization behaviour and different patterns of organization structure, as well as variations of influence in the business environment, such as the role of the state or trade unions. As a result, the policies of multinational corporations may well need to vary in different countries and managers operating out of their home environment need specific training in cultural differences. This latter theme has been taken up by Fons Trompenaars (1993).

Trompenaars, like Hofstede before him, believes that much of management behaviour is culturally determined and that the key to successful international management lies in the understanding of these cultural differences. Trompenaars uses an anthropological approach and attempts to examine cultural differences in the way we relate to others, in our attitudes to time and in our attitudes to the environment. The few examples presented below offer a flavour of this type of approach.

In terms of how we relate to others, Trompenaars focuses upon five variables relating to how we use rules, individualism, how public and private we are, the extent to which we show emotion and the extent to which we are achievement-oriented. For example, in countries such as the USA, Switzerland and Germany, the prevailing culture is much more universalistic and rules are applied irrespective of the situation. On the other hand, cultures such as Malaysia and Indonesia tend to apply rules in a much more particularistic fashion and personal relationships can be more important in some situations than the rules governing conduct. In such universalistic cultures greater use is made in business of lawyers and contracts and in multinational operations, the head office plays a more directive role. Cultures also differ in the way they display emotion. Neutral cultures such as those in Northern Europe and Japan tend to keep feelings hidden and debate and argument are seldom personalized. On the other hand emotional cultures such as those found in Italy or Latin America show their feelings and find it difficult to distinguish between issues and personalities. In some societies such as Japan much more emphasis is placed upon age, seniority, status and professional qualifications whereas in others, like the USA, respect tends to be earned on the basis of job performance. There may also be very different approaches to policies of pay and promotion. Such differences as illustrated above can have a significant influence on doing business with people from a different culture, and on the operation of multinational corporations.

The implications of a culture specific approach are twofold. First, we must be extremely cautious in the way we borrow business and management ideas from other cultures. A management technique developed in one country may only work in that country because it is based upon a particular set of cultural values. The failure in the UK and the USA of many attempts to introduce Japanese style quality circles was due, in the main, to an incomplete understanding on the part of the adopters of the particular cultural values underpinning such an approach. The technique could be transposed but the conditions necessary for healthy growth could not. Second, in our dealings with people from other cultures we must recognize that differences do exist and be prepared to adjust behaviour and expectations accordingly. This is the theme of many recent initiatives in training for international management.

## Towards a mixed approach

While convergence as an idea represents a somewhat superficial analysis, we have seen that its practical implications are that because industrialized societies are moving in the same direction, we may therefore learn from the mistakes of others further along the route. We have seen also that the supporters of the 'culture specific' hypothesis believe that specific aspects of business are especially susceptible to cultural and national influences. As well as the work of Hofstede and Trompenaars, studies have identified the most likely as attitudes to work, management behaviour, organization structure, industrial relations, recruitment and training (see, for example, Brossard and Maurice, 1976; Child and Kieser, 1979; Sorge and Warner, 1980). If we accept the culture-specific hypothesis then we need to be cautious in our approach to managerial panaceas. Useful ideas and methods may be transplanted but care must be taken to see that they have been adapted to the new cultural setting and that there is an understanding of the supporting conditions needed for their development.

Reality of course never fits neat conceptual explanations. Both our models may be used to explain the rapid emergence of Japan as an industrial nation. Elements of its business organization, management techniques and state machinery have been imported from other cultures, while other elements are clearly products of its own cultural past. Its late start to industrialization enabled businesses to learn from the mistakes made in more advanced countries such as Britain, USA and Germany. The specific elements of the Japanese culture undoubtedly gave these ideas a fresh impetus, so much so that the West has in the 1980s become fascinated by Japanese business methods. This is the reason that books on business and management have, since the 1970s, paid homage to the phenomenon we call 'Japanese management'. This topic has assumed great importance in academic, business and political circles and we devote much of our review to it.

For this we make no excuses, for a study of Japanese business and management practices is truly a study of 'business in context', for nowhere is the inter-relationship between business activities, management strategies, organizational culture and environmental factors more clearly illustrated.

This mixed view is taken by Dore (1973) in his comparison of a British and a Japanese factory in the electronics field. He found similarities in the technology and in the complex nature of work organization. In the case of Japan, he noted the impact of late development and that ideas had been borrowed from the UK, Germany and the USA. However, significant differences were found in motivation, recruitment, training and supervision. Dore noted that late developers can overtake their mentors, when they in turn become the focus of attention for would-be copiers. This is clearly the case with Japan.

Such a mixed approach may also be found in Case 2.4, where the development of Singapore owes much to both the traditional cultural values associated with Confucianism and the impact of foreign multinationals.

In illustrating the relationship between culture and business we examine specific aspects of Britain and Germany, and offer a cautionary note on the dangers of cross-cultural comparison. We end the chapter with our analysis of Japanese business and management.

---

**CASE 2.4**
*Business and Management in Singapore*

An examination of Tables 2.1, 2.2 and 2.3 in the main text reveals the remarkable growth of South East Asian economies and in particular the economic strength of Singapore, second only to Japan in the region, and with a GDP to match many of the older industrialized nations. The growth of the Singapore economy is associated with a number of interrelated factors, including geography, politics, culture and the influence of multinational corporations from a variety of countries.

Singapore is a relatively small island of some 2.5 million people linked to the Malaysian Peninsula by road and rail. Its geographical position has made it an important staging post for world shipping. Singapore was established as a trading post by the British in 1819 and expanded rapidly in the 1860s as a result of increasing trade with China and Japan and the opening of the Suez Canal. This growth was consolidated by the exploitation of rubber and tin in the surrounding regions, with Singapore operating as a vital export channel. This economic expansion led to considerable immigration to an almost uninhabited island. The majority of immigrants were Chinese, reflected in the ethnic mix of the population today with 76% Chinese, 15% Malay and 7% Indian. In 1959, Singapore achieved self-government and in 1963 joined the Malaysian Federation. The political alliance with Malaysia was short-lived and Singapore became a fully independent nation state in 1965.

Throughout the 1950s and the early 1960s there were a number of key problems to be faced. Britain withdrew and relations with Malaysia were problematic. The country had no natural resources and there were insufficient jobs in trading to support the population. The domestic market of two million people was small by international standards and the country was facing increasing competition from growing economies in the SE Asia region. Politically the country was far from stable and its businesses were dogged by a number of labour-relations problems.

Following independence in 1965, there has been uninterrupted economic growth, almost 10% per year on average. Between 1990 and 1992 inflation was never more than 3% while wages rose by 9% a year. In 1992 unemployment was less than 2%. In 1990 Singapore attracted $1 billion worth of new investment, 80% coming from overseas. Singapore is now the second largest port in the world, the third largest refiner of oil, and produces most of the world's computer disc drives.

The continued economic growth has been attributed to a number of factors. The dominant philosophy, which underpins the core cultural values, is Confucianism. This has been the basis of much of Chinese education and social organization for two thousand years and its influence is apparent in China, Hong Kong, Taiwan, Korea and Japan, as well as Singapore. There are a number of key values associated with Confucianism. These are adaptation to the world about us, harmony and social order, family and friends, education, duty and hierarchy, rule by humanity and moral persuasion, meritocracy and the supremacy of ethical standards. In business and economic life, such values are seen in loyalty to the nation' rulers and the support of officialdom, loyalty to the firm by a hard-working and responsible workforce, the importance of family firms, thrift, adaptable entrepreneurs, and a concern for education and self-improvement.

Undoubtedly in Singapore there is a commitment to the goals of the government that is rare in other countries, although high levels of labour turnover as a result of labour shortages suggests that loyalty to the firm can be compromised. The concern for education is evident in a population eager to accumulate qualifications and by a massive state support of schools, polytechnics and universities, as well as training for industry. The people are clearly hard-working and thrifty. The Singaporeans save a higher proportion of their income than anyone else, assisted largely by the state-run Central Provident Fund (CPF), which takes around 40% of wages. The CPF then provides finance for home ownership, interest on savings and acts as a retirement pension fund. Withdrawals are also possible to buy blue-chip stock. Family firms play an important part in the economy of Singapore and there are many large and powerful Chinese businesses. Some of these businesses are linked to Chinese clans, to which people belong on the basis of their family origins, traced back to a particular village in China. Among the Chinese there is also some evidence that business specialism is linked to groupings of people who speak the same Chinese dialect. For example, Hokkien-speaking people tend to dominate in banking, finance and trade. However there is also evidence to suggest a weakening of such traditional networks and value systems. Many of the new generations have acquired university education, often overseas, and experiences have been broadened beyond traditional values. In several local firms family control is being replaced by professional management.

Two other factors are often cited for the economic growth of Singapore, These are the roles played by the state and by the multinational corporations. Since independence, Singapore has been effectively a one-party state, with control in the hands of the People's Action Party (PAP). Opposition parties do exist but their parliamentary representation is negligible. State leadership has been highly directive and proactive particularly in defence, education and training and the economy. Many Singaporeans work directly for the state and government employment tends to attract the most talented from the population. The economic policies embrace the attraction of foreign direct investment and the establishment of a number of government-linked companies.

Some of these, like Singapore Airlines, are highly successful and pursue policies that are both aggressive and progressive. As well as the government-linked companies, the state plays a part in local investment through the Development Bank of Singapore. In more recent years economic policy has involved a closer relationship with Malaysia and Indonesia, to broaden both the product and labour market. Much of Singapore industry's unskilled labour travels daily across the causeway linking Singapore to Malaysia and the government has backed offshore manufacturing in both Malaysia and the nearby islands of Indonesia. The labour-relations problems of the 1950s and early 1960s have disappeared, not least because trade unions are part of the state apparatus and a senior ranking government minister is head of the trade-union movement.

For many years Singapore has been an attractive location for multinational investment and many leading firms from the USA, Japan, Germany and the UK have manufacturing operations on the island. There are now over 3000 foreign firms operating in Singapore, attracted by a number of features. Singapore is viewed as a very safe and relatively attractive posting for expatriate employees. There are tax incentives and the state provision of factory shells and related infrastructure. The Singaporean government has been quite selective in its dealings with multinationals favouring high-tech, capital-intensive firms. Such companies have also been attracted by the political stability of the country and the absence of effective opposition either from political parties or from hostile trade unions. The available local labour force is generally well educated and well trained, although there are labour shortages and competition for highly skilled managerial and technical talent is fierce.

(*Sources*: *The Singapore Yearbook*, 1991 and 1992; Chong Li Choy, 1990; Wong Kwei Chong, 1991.)

## The British and business

A popular topic that emerged in the 1980s, and has continued ever since, is the search for an explanation of Britain's economic decline (Wiener, 1981 and Gamble, 1985). Wiener uses cultural variables to explain an economic phenomenon. He believes that the British are no good at business because their hearts are not really in it. The prevailing values in Britain are those espoused by the land-owning gentry and as a consequence, business and especially industry are rejected as being representative of something fairly unpleasant. The consequences of this prevailing attitude are that the pursuit of economic gain is half-hearted and talent is directed away from industry. Government and the professions are favoured as occupational routes, capitalists aspire to be land-owning gentry, and the education system is dominated by a public-school ethos which shuns science, technology, business and industry. While university graduation rates are comparable to those in former West Germany, only 0.7% of British students are engineering graduates compared with 19% in Germany (OECD, 1993). Moreover almost 40% of German managers have an engineering degree. Our half-hearted approach to business is consolidated by leaving management to the sometimes gifted but, most times, untrained amateur.

While it is not the job of this text to examine contending theories of Britain's economic decline, views such as those expressed by Wiener have a certain appeal. They are easy to understand and focus on easy targets, such as the public-school system and the land-owning gentry. However, the hypothesis is highly speculative, difficult to verify and probably represents an exaggerated and idealized view. There is no explanation for the success of British entrepreneurs, the energy which accompanied the industrial revolution, nor the economic growth of the banking and finance industries in the post-war period. While it is true that the best products of our education system tend to be attracted not to industry but to the civil service and the professions, that situation is also true of Japan, a country we tend to hold as our economic role model.

Despite such criticisms of hypotheses such as Wiener's, there are cultural elements which seem to have a significant impact on business. The class structure of this country provides us with greater insights into the relationship between management and workers. Certainly we assume that anyone with the 'right' background and a reasonable level of education can assume managerial responsibilities with no professional qualifications or training, a view taken up in recent reports on the state of management training in this country. On average, a manager in this country will receive one day of formal training per year. Charles Handy has referred to the British view of management as 'something that happens to decent people at a certain stage in their life'. On a more general level, the British labour market has experienced a continuous shortage of technically skilled manpower ever since the last war, despite attempts to remedy the situation through legislation (the Industrial Training Act 1964) and a considerable amount of political rhetoric. A country which appears to take its training more seriously is Germany and it is to this we now turn.

## Germany: a training ethos

Compared with their British counterparts managers in Germany are qualified to higher educational levels. Approximately 80% of German managers are graduates, while Britain boasts fewer than 50%. The degrees are vocationally oriented with engineering and other technical subjects predominating. Generally the managers better qualified educationally hold the more senior positions in the hierarchy and have risen through the ranks rather than by switching companies as is the norm in Britain and the USA (Lawrence, 1980; Child *et al.*, 1983). It is quite common to find German managers who have preceded their degree by some kind of technical apprenticeship, and if we include compulsory national service for men, it is understandable that management positions may not be assumed until the age of 30.

Germany lays great store by its system of youth training referred to as the 'dual apprenticeship system'. A very high proportion (around 85%) of all school-leavers who do not go on to higher education enter a three-year apprenticeship across a range of occupations (Casey, 1986).

The apprenticeship involves training in a mixture of job-specific and general work skills with one day a week spent in a specialist vocational college. The scheme has been successful in supplying the labour market with skilled workers that are easy to retrain because of the presence of general work skills and the emphasis on attitude training. The scheme is supported by government, employers, the education system and trade unions. Not least in this support is that of the trainees themselves whose acceptance of initially low wages helps fund the scheme. For example, a 16-year-old trainee in Germany can expect to receive only 25% of the adult wage for the job, compared with 50% in Britain (Casey, 1986). It is this social acceptance of training costs against likely future benefits that does much to underpin the system. No such ethos exists in Britain, and attempts at introducing youth training schemes have met with a consequent unenthusiastic response.

Such differences between Germany and the UK have been used by some studies to explain the differences in strategies, export performance and profitability of German and British industries. Training and skills were particularly significant in explaining such differences in the German and UK kitchen industries (Steedman and Wagner, 1987).

## The difficulties involved in using culture as a variable

Culture remains a fascinating concept but a difficult analytical tool. The following points attempt to give some indication of the difficulties involved.

- Many studies which use culture as a central concept tend to define culture in rather broad, generalized terms. In many instances it is a kind of residual variable, a catch-all to explain away differences that cannot be explained by differences in the economy, technology, role of the state, size of the firm and so on.
- Comparisons with other countries are often difficult because of the different rules governing the collection of data. Thus, strike statistics are notoriously difficult to compare because different countries use different yardsticks to define and measure a strike.
- Cultural comparisons tend to be made from the perspective of one culture only. We may make conclusions about another culture based on our own values. A study of the car industry worldwide showed that European and US manufacturers outperformed the Japanese on criteria they deemed most relevant; profitability measured by accounting ratios. The Japanese, however, laid greater store by market penetration and growth, and on these criteria easily outperformed the European and American manufacturers (Bhaskar, 1980).
- In many cases language presents a serious barrier to full understanding. Certain concepts do not translate easily. 'Technik' is a central concept to German manufacturing, yet has no direct translation in English.

- We have seen that we possess preconceived notions about other cultures, often expressed as stereotypes. These can creep into our analysis and become self-fulfilling prophecies; we see what we expect to see. Our ready acceptance of such stereotypes prevents us from digging more deeply. For instance, an analysis of German management will reveal a much greater formality in superior–subordinate relations than exists in Britain or the USA. We may conclude from this that the Germans have less interest in man-management, when all evidence points towards good working relations existing in German firms. Such stereotypes are often deliberately used in training, when preparing managers for cross-cultural management, as we saw in our discussion of the work of Trompenaars. Clearly such approaches need to be used with considerable caution.
- Cultures can and do change over time and our perceptions can become dated. For example, management students in Singapore are keen to challenge Hofstede's classification that places Singapore as a culture possessing a low-risk avoidance and thus typified by a willingness to take risks. They claim that while that may have been true in the early stages of independence in the late 1960s, the prevailing culture of the 1990s is much more risk-averse and conservative.

## Japanese business and management

> Explaining the heady success of Japanese manufacturing has, in recent years, virtually replaced baseball as our national pastime. The trouble is, however, that American managers cannot agree among themselves on the rules of this new competition, the current score, or even the precise type of game in which they are involved.
>
> (Wheelwright, 1981, p. 65)

The quotation by Steven Wheelwright is appropriate for two reasons. First it introduces the notion of Japanese industrial success and second identifies the problems that we in the West have of understanding and interpreting that success. These problems have done little to deter those willing to offer us an explanation. Management literature since the late 1970s has been preoccupied with Japan. Serious and popular newspapers alike have jumped on the bandwagon and television documentaries have followed the fortunes of British recruits to Japanese multinationals as they exchange Newcastle Brown Ale for sake. Despite such exposure, our knowledge of Japanese management, while much greater, appears to have done little for our real understanding. In many respects Endymion Wilkinson's quote is still valid.

> I examine the European image of Japan and find it composed of an arsenal of stereotypes founded on the shifting sands of indifference, ignorance, prejudice, and fear, rather than on any effort to seriously understand the Japanese.
>
> (Wilkinson, 1983, p. 17)

The stereotypes to which Wilkinson refers have changed dramatically over the years from a manufacturer of cheap, unreliable products, to a menacing military and then economic imperialist, to a currently fashionable view of Japanese management science as the panacea for the ills of Western capitalism.

Even allowing for the difficulties of comparing the economies of different nations it is clear that Japan has emerged in the post-war period as the world's second largest economy behind the USA. There is a widely held view that this is some kind of post-war miracle in which a modern Japanese economy arose from the ashes of a completely devastated country. A similar view is often proffered for the former West Germany. Indeed, respective accounts of the two countries sometimes vie for the greatest extent of devastation, and hence a claim to the greater 'miracle'. In both cases, the foundations of a strong economy were laid much earlier. Nevertheless, post-war growth has been significant and in Japan's case, particular advances were made in the period 1955–61 (Armstrong *et al.*, 1991). Tables 2.1–2.3 presented earlier in this chapter plot the growth of the Japanese economy since 1975. Although there has been a marked reduction in that growth in recent years, there remains a fascination in the way that the Japanese organize their business affairs. We offer a flavour of the complexity and paradoxes of that area known as Japanese management. We will do this by looking at various explanations that have been offered for Japanese economic success, ending with a brief look at the experience of Japanese firms in Britain and the process known as 'Japanization'.

The various explanations that we will deal with are cultural, political, economic and organizational in nature. Additionally a more radical explanation will be offered, but first we turn to attempts which focus on the social and cultural background of the Japanese themselves.

## Cultural factors

According to Ronald Dore in his excellent book *British Factory – Japanese Factory*, Japan has benefited greatly from the 'late industrialization effect', whereby the diffusion of ideas from advanced industrial societies into totally different settings gives those ideas a new impetus (Dore, 1973). In the case of Japan, Dore believes, the system has developed to permit a culturally conservative society to adjust to rapid technical change. The core values that are often quoted as shaping Japan's particular response to industrialization are 'loyalty', 'dependence', and 'duty' resulting in an importance being attached to vertical relationships. This would explain the Japanese loyalty to the group be it the country, the family, or their company. Both historically and emotionally Japan is a closed society, due largely to a sense of isolation and a lack of resources. The resulting insecurity has led the Japanese to place more emphasis on bank savings than their counterparts in other industrial nations and to adapt quickly to changed conditions. When we view these characteristics alongside the core values it may well explain the tendency of the people to give their wholehearted support be it to Imperial decree, government decisions, or company initiatives.

## The role of the state

Historically the state has always had a significant role in the development of the Japanese economy. The big five companies known collectively as the 'Zaibatsu', which dominated the Japanese economy in pre-war times, developed with the specific assistance of the government. Their legacy today is in the large holding companies at the heart of the Japanese economy.

A central feature of the state's influence is the role played by the civil service, in particular the two departments known in the West as MITI (Ministry of International Trade and Industry) and MOF (Ministry of Finance). Between them they help coordinate and direct Japan's economic strategy. Specifically, MITI targets those industries that are internationally competitive as in the case of cars and micro-electronics. Industries operating in preferred sectors are offered prime locations, are allowed to expand, receive tax relief on modernization programmes, and MITI ensures that such industries get first priority as far as foreign investment is concerned. The department has been especially active in encouraging cartels both for purposes of rationalization and for exploiting world trading conditions, both occurring in the case of the shipbuilding industry. As part of this strategy there is marked lack of assistance for those businesses operating in non-designated sectors of the economy. In Chapter 5 we examine the role of the state in R&D and the establishment of research cartels among major manufacturers in a given sector.

MOF controls the Bank of Japan, which in turn has significant influence over the 12 major commercial banks and hence the direction of investment. It is important to know that in Japan, banks are the major shareholders in industry and commerce, individual investment playing a very minor role indeed. This system is actively encouraged by the intervention of MOF. Additionally, with MITI, MOF assists in the process of channelling foreign investment to high priority companies, especially when capital is short, and targets Japanese investment abroad, in particular to those areas rich in the kind of natural resources coveted by Japan.

Japanese banking is not only influential in the investment process, it plays a major part in survival of some firms under threat of closure. In the mid-1970s Toyo Kogyo, the producer of Mazda cars faced bankruptcy with a 1975 loss of US$ 70 million, resulting largely from increased wage costs at a time of dramatic fall in sales and export orders. The Sumitomo Bank, a major shareholder, stepped in and initiated a major turnaround operation. Matsuda, the controlling influence for 45 years was forced to withdraw, and family control was handed over to the Sumitomo Bank. New management was installed by the bank and there was a marked change in both business strategy and management style. Autocratic and paternalistic control was replaced by a more open style with greater emphasis on communication and team-building. As a result of the bank's intervention, the company not only survived, but developed a new range of models which enhanced greatly their export performance and world standing (Pascale and Rohlen, 1983).

The activities of the civil service take place within a highly stable political framework, the Liberal Democratic Party having held power since 1955. The state in Japan represents a network of influence between politics, the civil service and business operating a system of targeted development and trade protection at home, with selective investment overseas. Elites within this system tend to circulate; the civil service recruits top graduates from the best universities, the most successful of which tend to move at a later stage in their careers to politics or business. Such relationships are ripe for those who favour conspiracy theory and images have been painted of a mafia-style command economy. However, the images do not bear close examination. Conflict exists, not only between business and the state, but also between companies themselves competing for the same markets. The ruling party, the LDP, is far from a cohesive body, and consists of different factions competing for power. Moreover, the 1993 elections saw a serious challenge to its overall majority for the first time since 1954 and its parliamentary majority was reduced to marginal proportions.

Nevertheless it is still the largest parliamentary party by far and any challenge will depend on the willingness of opposition parties to collaborate with each other. The view of a highly directive state is also challenged by the success of industries outside the favoured sectors, such as hi-fi, pianos, television manufacture, and above all motorcycles. Nevertheless, the state has played an influential role in the development of the Japanese economy, particularly in accelerating market forces. A legacy of this is the continued dominance by big business, which could well benefit from their influence with MITI and MOF to the detriment of the small business sector.

## Economic organization

Duality is the central theme which dominates Japanese economic life. This duality operates both in the organization of the manufacturing sector and in the labour market. Every large firm in Japan uses a large number of smaller firms as sub-contractors. For example, Nissan uses 150 different sub-contractors within a 50 km radius of its plant at Oppama, with the result that only 30% of the Nissan car is actually manufactured in its own plant; this compares with 40% at Austin-Rover (Hetherington, 1986). Other writers have noted that it is not unusual for a firm employing 1000 workers to have 160 sub-contractors (Armstrong *et al.*, 1991). In this way a hierarchy of manufacture is built up, with larger firms sub-contracting to smaller and so on. In every case, the relationship between the firm and its supplier is carefully specified, with deliveries being requested not by the week or even day, but by the hour. Furthermore it is quite usual for the purchasing company to get involved in work organization and job design in the sub-contractor's factory, often in an attempt to reduce costs and hence the price of supplied parts.

Such a system tends to favour the large corporation, and the Japanese economy is indeed dominated by big businesses operating as giant holding companies controlling a number of (often) highly diversified firms. For example, the Sumitomo Group has divisions dealing with mining, cement, chemicals, electrical goods and heavy industries; the Mitsubishi Group deals with chemicals, glass, rayon, paper, automobiles, steel and heavy industries. Additionally, both these groups along with the other large holding companies have banking, insurance and real estate divisions (Sato and Hoshino, 1984). The role of banks as major shareholders has already been mentioned, but here we have a case of banking operating as yet another division of the holding companies. This not only gives such firms access to sources of investment, but places them at the centre of a network of information. The relationship with sub-contractors is further cemented in that the bigger firms, often through their banks, are major shareholders in the smaller companies. In general the relationship is very close and 'parent' companies tend to be very loyal to their sub-contractors. In recession it is not unnatural for sub-contractors to be supported and protected by the major company, who will often reduce its own labour force to cut costs rather than sever the link with its supplier.

As for the labour market itself, a great deal of publicity has been given to the Japanese concepts of lifetime employment and seniority payment systems. However, such benefits only apply to the minority of Japan's workforce and a dual labour market operates. The system works as follows. The labour force is divided into 'permanent' and 'temporary' workers. The 'permanent' workers have tenure and receive the pay and welfare benefits normally associated with Japanese firms, while those classed as temporary workers have no such security, have few employment rights and enjoy none of the benefits of their permanent counterparts. According to such rare accounts as Satoshi Kamata's experience as a temporary worker for Toyota, the lot of the temporary worker is far from idyllic (Kamata, 1983). Precise statistics concerning the proportion of workers in each category are difficult to obtain, but various accounts estimate the 'permanent' group to represent around 35% of the total workforce, although this varies considerably according to the size and nature of the organization. A major firm like Nissan will have 'permanent' employees in the majority, perhaps around 75%, the remainder being made up of workers who are classed as temporary. Nissan's major sub-contractors will likewise have a large proportion of 'permanent' staff, but further down the sub-contracting hierarchy the proportion of 'temporary' workers rises sharply, many smaller firms having no 'permanent' workers whatsoever. No farm workers and very few women in Japan have 'permanent' status.

We will look at the negative aspects of this dual system later. From the point of view of the country's economy there would appear to be some advantages to this economic organization, not least of which is a built-in elasticity to cope with changing demand. A firm like Nissan will cope with increased demand by taking on more temporary workers and either increasing its number of sub-contractors or placing greater demands on its existing suppliers. Reduced demand will be met by lay-offs of temporary workers, although, as we have noted, a corresponding reduction in orders to suppliers may not take place. The system would appear to succeed because of the privileged position and economic strength of the larger companies and the ready supply of temporary workers, a proportion of whom aspire to 'permanent' status, and a proportion who are basically farm workers seeking seasonal work. Such a model of a flexible labour force has found favour with many Western employers and it is an issue we will discuss in the next chapter.

## Organization style and management strategies

A number of aspects of Japanese company life have been identified by various writers as playing a significant role in the economic growth of Japan (for example, Dore, 1973; Pascale, 1978; Ohmae, 1982; Sethi *et al.*, 1984). These aspects are identified below.

**Personnel policies** These are often the most publicized aspects of Japanese firms, but as we have seen, they only really apply to about a third of the workforce. They include: lifetime employment, pay based on seniority, an attention to employee welfare, and fringe benefits such as company housing and holidays. Recruitment and selection tend to be rigorous even for comparatively low-level employees. As we show in the case study of Nissan (Case Study 2.5), the selection of supervisors is a highly competitive affair, candidates being subjected to a battery of tests and strenuous interviews. The selection process for all workers is followed up by an equally rigorous training programme where employees are expected to master most aspects of a particular process. The emphasis is clearly on flexibility, reinforced, in most cases by an absence of organization charts and job descriptions.

**Industrial relations** All Japanese trade unions are company unions and employees have no choice as to which union they join. Not surprisingly, plant level industrial relations are comparatively harmonious and are more akin to joint consultation than collective bargaining. Disputes do occur at national level, but they tend to be highly predictable affairs based on annual pay negotiations (referred to as the 'Spring Offensive') or about the size of the autumn bonus. Since the early 1980s the unions have been increasingly opposed to Japanese investment overseas, but carry little political clout to affect policy.

**Decision-making** 'The process of communication within a Japanese organization is very much akin to the mating dance of penguins' (Sethi *et al.*, p. 37). As this quotation implies there is considerable ritual and a great deal of consultation. Much attention has been focused on consensus and collective decision-making (*ringi sei*), when, in practice there would seem to be considerable initiatives and decisions taken by top management alone. However, the consultation process (*nemewashi*)

**CASE 2.5**
*Nissan UK*

Nissan, the major Japanese car manufacturer, produced its first British-built car at its plant in Tyne and Wear in April 1986. The firm was coveted by several county councils seeking to stimulate business and employment in their areas and competition to attract a major company like Nissan was fierce.

The plant uses robots for welding and has a fully automated paintshop, but these are hardly unique features in modern car manufacture. For many the real difference at Nissan lies in its approach to industrial relations and its personnel policies.

Acknowledging the traditional labour-relations problems with the car industry in Britain and a strike frequency of over seven times the norm for manufacturing industry, the company on the advice of personnel director, Peter Wickens, opted for the recognition of a single union only. The policy alternatives of either a non-union shop or the recognition of several unions were felt to be recipes for antagonism and chaos respectively. The competition for union recognition among trade unions hungry for members was considerable. Nissan represented a potential of 2700 new members when most trade unions were losing members at an alarming rate. Recognition was eventually achieved by the Amalgated Union of Engineering Workers (AUEW) and a deal embracing terms and conditions of employment was signed between the union and company representatives before production started in 1985. The deal was unique both for the car industry and for the AUEW.

The agreement between the union and the company lists certain key principles upon which it is based. These include mutual trust and cooperation; a commitment to quality, productivity, and competitiveness, using modern technology; a need for change and flexibility to maintain the competitive edge; a belief in open and direct communications. Most significantly there is an adherence to the avoidance of any action which interrupts the continuity of production and the union's recognition of management's right to make the final decision in the best interests of the company.

These principles have been reinforced by several mechanisms. First, terms and conditions form part of a two-year agreement, which is binding on both sides and includes a no-strike clause for the duration of the agreement and during any negotiation or arbitration. Second, in exceptional circumstances, when agreement cannot be reached ACAS will be called upon to arbitrate, but a straight choice must be made between the two alternatives in a system of pendulum arbitration. Third, negotiations are made between the company and the Works Council, not the trade union. The Works Council is made up of elected representatives, each representing part of the plant. Although the election is supervised by the union, representation is open to all employees. In fact one estimate has put union membership at only 18%. As well as negotiating salaries and conditions, the Works Council concerns itself with issues of productivity, quality and planned change.

The personnel practices are also new to the car industry. All employees are treated as single-status, share the same canteen, wear the Nissan blue uniform, and all receive annual salaries paid in equal monthly instalments. Employees are not required to clock on and are only asked to clock off when overtime is being worked so that a record may be kept. Workers are paid a guaranteed week of 39 hours. Management has retained the right to review both the clocking-on procedure and the guaranteed week in the light of operating experience, and to lay workers off without notice should production be disrupted by industrial action either at Nissan itself or one of its suppliers.

Competition for jobs at Nissan has been high. In an area of 20% unemployment an estimated 3500 applied for the first 22 supervisory positions. An estimated 11 000 applied for the 240 production jobs. Selection processes were exacting. The potential supervisors were all put through a series of psychological tests, while the production workers were narrowed down through successive hurdles including pencil and paper aptitude tests and at least two interviews for short-listed candidates. The emphasis was on seeking employees with a strong positive commitment to the goals of the company, thereby reducing future potential conflict. Apart from the management, nearly all recruits were under 40 years old, few had previous experience in the car industry and only a minority were unemployed. By comparison, the senior management nearly all had motor industry experience and were recruited from such companies as Ford, Austin Rover and Rolls-Royce. In total the company started with three British and four Japanese directors.

Peter Wickens has claimed that Nissan's policies are not peculiarly Japanese, and feels them to be a distillation of American, German and British as well as Japanese methods. Indeed, he operated similar policies in his previous employment with a North Wales-based American company, Whatever the origins, the novelty of Nissan's approach lies in its single union, no-strike deal and in its insistence upon absolute commitment to the goals of productivity, quality and continuity. The approach has formed the basis of its advertising campaign orchestrated by Saatchi & Saatchi under the slogan, 'They don't half work'.

(*Source*: Burrows, 1986; Tighe, 1986.)

is very important and large numbers of workers do in fact participate. The consultation process is part of a corporate culture, which is typified by an absence of class divisions and which is reinforced by the trappings of egalitarian society, including company uniforms for all, compulsory exercises for all at the start of the day, and a sharing of the same canteen facilities.

**Production orientation** For many, the attention paid to the production function is the key to Japanese manufacturing prowess and export success (for example, White and Trevor, 1983; Hayes and Wheelwright, 1984). While attention has been focused on specific techniques such as 'quality circles' and 'Just-In-Time', the essence is almost certainly a meticulously planned, integrated system, in which attention to quality plays a central role. To this we must add an orientation to product innovation which pays particular attention to the needs of the customer. A pivotal figure in this production system is the first line supervisor, which perhaps explains the attention paid to his selection. The production orientation is supported by a system which places considerable emphasis on rules, regulations and discipline. Dore's comparison of Hitachi with English Electric noted, in the Japanese case, the emphasis placed on attendance and timekeeping and the willing participation by Japanese employees in the widely found practice of sacrificing holidays in favour of the company (Dore, 1973). British companies dealing with the Japanese for the first time are often astonished at both the time spent in planning and the inordinate level of detail involved in the planning process. A more detailed review of Japanese production methods can be found in Chapter 6.

**An Investment in R&D**   In Chapter 5 in Tables 5.3, 5.4 and 5.5 we show the extent of innovative activity through a series of patent indicators. There is clear evidence to suggest that the Japanese place a higher priority on new product development than any other nation.

The result of these organizational features and management strategies has been the creation of the firm as a community and a high level of identification with the company on the part of individual employees. There is however an alternative explanation for Japan's economic growth.

## Japanese management: an alternative view

The cultural, political, administrative, economic, organizational and strategic factors identified above, have all been cited as explanations for Japanese economic superiority over the West. Kamata's view of life as a temporary worker for Toyota, with accounts of production speed-ups, excessive overtime and the oppression of the bachelor dormitory paints an entirely different view (Kamata, 1983). Other analyses, some of them Marxist in their approach, conclude that Japan's economic success is based on carefully planned exploitation (especially Armstrong *et al.*, 1991).

This exploitation takes several forms. First, the 'temporary worker' is exploited in terms of his lack of security and must bear the brunt of any recession; a case could even be made for the exploitation of the 'permanent' employer through an employment system which ties him to a single employer. Second, the larger firms exploit the dependent position of the smaller firms through the system of satellite sub-contractors. Third, we have the suppression of independent trade unions which render plant level collective bargaining somewhat meaningless. The particular system of company unions has its origins in a four-month dispute in 1953 involving workers at the Nissan car factory. The dispute led to a lock-out by management that was backed by the major shareholder, the bank, and the USA authorities. The stipulation for a return to work was the acceptance by the workforce of a company union with the motto 'those who truly love their union love their company' (Hetherington, 1986). Other companies took Nissan's lead and set up their own unions. Finally it has been argued that the economic system exploits the cultural characteristics of the Japanese people themselves, namely their loyalty, discipline and commitment to national goals.

It is difficult for someone brought up and operating in a particular culture and value system to draw accurate conclusions about the exploitation that is supposed to occur in an entirely different cultural context. More accounts like Kamata's would be welcome, especially since it dates from the early 1970s.

We do however have experience of Japanese methods in the United

Kingdom through the operation of companies such as Nissan, Sony and YKK, many of which have been manufacturing from British bases for a number of years. It is to this aspect we now turn.

## Japanization and the experience of Japanese firms in Britain

In recent years the concept of 'Japanization' has emerged, referring to two related phenomena. First, it refers to the process of Japanese foreign direct investment (FDI), by which Japanese firms set up operations overseas. Second, it relates to the process whereby Japanese business and management methods are practised in other countries either as a direct consequence of FDI or through the process of cross-cultural transference as mentioned earlier in this chapter. As far as the UK is concerned (and perhaps other countries as well), the favourable reception given to Japanization in the manufacturing sector by government, employers, employees and, in some cases, trade unions, appears to rest on two assumptions. First, it is believed that Japanese manufacture overseas will increase the value added in the host country by stimulating economic growth and employment and by reducing the number of Japanese imports. Second, there is a belief that Japanese manufacturing methods set the kind of examples that the rest should follow.

A study of Toshiba Consumer Products (UK) Ltd revealed specific features about their operation including the absence of job descriptions at any level, a periodic review of the company plan with all employees, a much greater application of planning techniques than is normally associated with a British firm, with a much closer relationship between manufacturing and sales, and a corresponding attention to consumer needs, product design and quality (Taylor, 1984). While there was no company union, there was recognition of a single union only (the EETPU) and an agreement for pendulum arbitration, a system referred to in Chapter 8, and in the case study (2.5).

A series of studies of Japanese manufacturing plants and financial concerns in the United Kingdom concluded that many features associated with Japan, namely a stable, highly committed workforce, complete cooperation in change, and low levels of conflict, simply do not exist over here (White and Trevor, 1983). Nevertheless these Japanese firms do exhibit higher levels of productivity than their British counterparts. In achieving these levels of productivity, White and Trevor found that typically Japanese employment practices such as the lifetime employment and the seniority principle were not used, but that great attention was paid to selection and training. They found no real difference in levels of employee satisfaction, but the real distinction lay in certain work practices. These were a highly organized approach with an emphasis on fine detail, the elevation of quality as the top priority and a much greater sense of discipline throughout the various organizations. They noted a quite exceptional acceptance of management authority, which tended to be more favourable the greater the Japanese presence, almost as if employees were more willing to legitimize the position of Japanese managers than their British counter-parts. White and Trevor attributed this to the greater egalitarianism displayed by the Japanese and the greater willingness on the part of the Japanese manager to get involved in the operations. As the authors note:

> The predominant response of employees was one of approval and often some pride at being part of such an exceptional effort.
>
> (White and Trevor, 1983, p. 130)

Studies of the introduction of Quality Circles in British factories tend to reinforce this view (Bradley and Hill, 1983; Collard and Dale, 1985). It is not the shop-floor employee who is resistant to 'Japanese' methods, but the reasons for the failure of quality circles is often attributable to a mixture of management fear and scepticism resulting in a lack of support on the part of the managers and suspicion on the part of the employees.

The conclusion drawn from such studies is that successful transfer of certain Japanese methods is possible to British institutions. The main elements would appear to be a careful attention to detail in the pro-duction process, a greater investment in training and a much more egalitarian approach to management. White and Trevor believe that the essence of the Japanese system shifts the emphasis to micro issues at the shop-floor level. In so doing, the system fits in with the prevailing industrial relations culture in Britain. There may be elements which are too embedded in the cultural values of the Japanese and which will be difficult to transfer. These include the stability of employment, the strong company identification and work ethic and the ability of Japanese managers to employ a management style that is a mix of paternalistic, disciplinarian and egalitarian methods.

Such perspectives on the advantages of Japanization are not shared by all. Williams *et al.* (1992b) are particularly sceptical. They produce evidence to show that 70% of Japanese overseas investment is in non-manufacturing areas such as financial services and the purchase of land, activities that do not create jobs. They claim that the influence of Japanese firms has been exaggerated by the media since Japanese firms employ only 0.6% of the UK workforce and only 1.1% in the USA. Moreover, the value of Japanese exports is 40 times that of goods produced by Japanese firms in the UK. They argue that the majority of manufacture carried out in UK-based Japanese manufacturing outlets is the assembly of parts made in Japan and that attempts to limit the extent of such sourcing have been unsuccessful. Contrary to popular belief they found that Japanese manufacturing in the UK, especially among the car companies, was not particularly profitable. In a re-examination of Japanese manufacturing effectiveness in the car industry they claim that, Toyota excepted, some European manufacturers such as BMW perform better than the Japanese in such areas as stock turnover and work in progress, traditional measures of manufacturing effectiveness.

While the expansion of Japanese multinationals in Britain is part of the general process of the internationalization of the Japanese economy, two additional factors stand out. First, the interest Japanese firms have shown in Britain is seen as a mechanism to circumvent EC trade restrictions on Japanese imports. This has resulted in many joint ventures between British and Japanese firms, as between Austin Rover and Honda in the development and manufacture of the Rover 800 series, and the Triumph Acclaim before that. Second, those Japanese firms that have established themselves in Britain have tended to favour development areas where government grants and other advantages are available. There is, however, an alternative and perhaps more cynical interpretation that has more to do with the exploitation hypothesis, previously mentioned. The development areas, such as the North-East of England and Scotland, have high levels of unemployment. It is undoubtedly much easier to ensure the compliance of a workforce and the cooperation of trade unions, even to somewhat alien work practices when the alternative is long-term unemployment. There is no doubt that the situation also favours the company in its relationship with its local suppliers. When suppliers are struggling to survive in a harsh economic climate, it is much easier for the purchaser to negotiate contracts that are highly favourable to him or her in terms of price and delivery.

However, there is evidence in the North-East of England that many of the workers taken on by Japanese firms are neither unemployed nor refugees from the most depressed industries such as mining and shipbuilding (Tighe, 1986). There is also little evidence to suggest that the Japanese are treating English suppliers any differently to those in Japan, where exacting cost, quality and delivery requirements are the norm. Moreover there is significant evidence that Japanese companies are giving customers what they require, with a growing trend towards the customization of products for local markets.

Further insights into the Japanese in Britain may be found in the Nissan case (Case Study 2.5).

## Japanese management: some conclusions

The specific nature of Japanese culture, state intervention, the subcontracting system, the dual labour market, management strategies and practices, company unions, and the exploitation hypothesis have all been used individually or in combination to explain the post-war growth of the Japanese economy. All contain elements that are highly plausible, and in all probability the real explanation is a complex interaction of all factors, with some factors being more important than others at particular times.

Many in the West, including business leaders, politicians and some academics would like to reject the cultural hypothesis, since this offers us little hope of practical gain, unless we all become Japanese. We have noted already that interest in the Britain centres on two phenomena:

- the expansion of Japanese multinationals, the subsequent employment of British workers, and the introduction of Japanese management practices;

● the use of 'Japanese management' practices by management in British firms.

The conclusion drawn by such writers as White and Trevor and Hayes and Wheelwright is that there is nothing peculiarly Japanese about the way they run their businesses. The emphasis is on high growth and market penetration; a concern for long-term as opposed to short-term profits; a concern for labour productivity and costs; a concern for quality, employee selection and training; and an emphasis on incremental product improvement. Commitment on the part of employees is based largely on the egalitarianism of factory life, which leads to an acceptance of a highly disciplined regime. The implication is that British firms could follow suit with economically beneficial results.

A number of factors temper this enthusiasm. First, the elements mentioned above may well represent excellent management practice, but their successful application in Japan may be due to a supportive state, a particular form of economic organization, and draw upon specific characteristics of the Japanese people. Second, such methods have assumed greatest interest in the West at a time of high unemployment and the weakened bargaining position of employees and trade unions. Third, writers such as Williams *et al.* (1992) have questioned both the contribution of Japanese firms to the UK economy and the effectiveness of their practices.

Most significantly, the system would seem to be under threat in Japan itself. The world economic recession and competition from lower cost countries such as Korea and Taiwan have led to firms experiencing losses for the first time, rising unemployment, resulting in early retirement programmes and redundancy of some 'permanent' workers. At the other end of the scale, there are labour shortages created by the introduction of labour mobility in some high-technology sectors. All these factors lead to a weakening of the ties that bind the Japanese worker to his company. The recession in the 1990s has been particularly damaging to Japan's domestic markets in consumer electronics and cars. In 1993, Matsushita Electric, the world's largest consumer electronics group, announced a 60% fall in profits for the final quarter of 1992. Also in 1993, Nissan closed one of its manufacturing plants cutting its workforce by 5000, some 9% of the total. For smaller car companies such as Isuzu and Subaru the 1990s became a battle for survival. In 1990, Isuzu posted losses of US$ 387 million. In many parts of Japanese manufacturing there were severe reductions in overtime and bonus payments, a major component of salaries.

Despite the recession, Japanese firms continue to place a high priority on R&D activities, an issue we discuss at greater length in Chapter 5. Even though making record losses, Isuzu were continuing with plans to invest US$ 900 million in new product development. Changes have also occurred in the structure of the Japanese economy with a shift away from manufacturing towards financial services. In 1987, Nomura Securities made more money than Toyota and Nissan combined. This sector, however, has been beset with problems of a different kind. In 1991 Nomura were found guilty of dealing with criminal syndicates and of giving illegal payments to some of their biggest clients to offset investment losses. As a result, MOF suspended Nomura from trading for a period of six weeks. Further disclosures of a similar nature were made involving other securities firms such as Nikko, Daiwa and Yamaichi. This resulted in a loss of confidence worldwide, but the size and influence of the firms involved probably lessened the damage.

Undoubtedly time will tell whether the phenomenon we call Japanese management represents a new era in management strategy and employment practices, is simply exploiting favourable conditions, or is merely yet another passing management fad that is as susceptible to the forces of economic recession as any other. There is evidence that, fed on tales of Japanese economic problems and inefficiencies, enthusiasm for things Japanese has waned. Other fads such as corporate culture and total quality management have emerged to capture our interest. However, we should not lose sight of the fact that the Japanese economy is still immensely strong in comparison to its competitors, and that many of the more recent fads have much in common with the style and techniques we have come to associate with 'Japanese management'.

## Summary

In this chapter we have identified five key aspects of the environment, namely the economy, the state, technology, labour and culture. For each of these we have selected issues which highlight the interaction between business enterprises and the environment in which they operate.

The **economy** is viewed as a product of its constituent business activity as well as exerting considerable influence upon the way businesses operate. These influences work through resource availability and allocation, international competition, especially via multinational enterprises, the extent of state direction and levels of employment. Major changes have taken place since 1979 involving both the structure of the UK economy and the relationship between the economy and the state.

The **state** is examined from the perspective of increasing intervention as an employer, a collective provider, an adviser, a legal regulator, and most significantly for business as a demand manager. Business interests for their part attempt to influence government policy through pressure-group activity with mixed results. Businesses also interact with supranational bodies such as the EU.

**Technology** is viewed as the application of available knowledge and skills to create materials, processes and products. It is viewed both as a constraint and an opportunity as well as a product of innovation by business. New technology is seen as an opportunity for businesses to reduce costs, while increasing the quality of their products and the effectiveness of their service. Evidence concerning its impact on both job content and levels of employment is mixed.

The relationship between business and labour is seen through the workings of the labour market and the influence of trade unions. Changes in the economy have resulted in changes in the type and availability of jobs. Trade unions are seen both as a constraint and an aid to management decision-making, but the debate on their ultimate power and influence founders for lack of evidence and the inevitability of ideology.

Culture is viewed as a pervasive factor shaping the entire environment of business. Dominant cultural aspects of society leave their mark upon businesses operating in that society and lead to certain generalizations about the value different societies place upon business. Interest in culture has been stimulated by the prospect of learning from others and transplanting business methods from one society to another, as with the popular pastime of analysing Japanese business methods. This book joins in that pastime by giving its own account of Japanese business. This is not only illustrative of the cultural debate but also represents an extended case of the way businesses in a particular society interact with key elements of that society.

## Further reading

The relationship between the economy and business and the role of the state are well treated by P. Armstrong *et al.*, *Capitalism Since 1945* (Basil Blackwell, 1991), F. Green (ed.), *The Restructuring of the U.K. Economy* (Harvester Wheatsheaf, 1989) and D. Childs, *Britain Since 1945: A Political History* (Routledge, 1992). A good source for issues relating to the EC is R. Welford and K. Prescott, *European Business: An Issue-based Approach* (Pitman, 1992). C. Randlesome, *Business Cultures in Europe* (Butterworth/Heinemann, 1991) is an effective bridge between EC issues and the more general issues relating to culture. Although dated, J. Woodward, *Industrial Organization: Theory and Practice* (OUP, 1965), is a good account of the influence of technology on business organization, while illustrations of the impact of new technology can be found in B. Wilkinson, *The Shopfloor Politics of New Technology* (Heinemann, 1983) and M. J. Earl, *Management Strategies for Information Technology* (Prentice Hall International, 1989). Good sources for labour and trade-union issues are S. Kessler and F. Bayliss, *Contemporary British Industrial Relations* (Macmillan, 1992) and Millward *et al.*, *Workplace Industrial Relations in Transition* (Dartmouth, 1992). An interesting account of the impact of culture on business in Britain can be found in M. J. Wiener, *English Culture and the Decline of the Industrial Spirit 1850–1980* (CUP, 1981), while excellent sources for culture in general are G. Hofstede, Motivation, leadership and organization: do American theories apply abroad?, *Organizational Dynamics* (Summer, 1980) and F. Trompenaars, *Riding the Waves of Culture: Understanding Cultural Diversity in Business* (Economist Books, 1993). Good treatments of Japanese management include R. Dore, *British Factory – Japanese Factory* (University of California Press, 1973) and M. White and M. Trevor, *Under Japanese Management: The Experience of British Workers* (Heinemann, 1983).

## Discussion

1  In what ways can a business influence its immediate economic environment through its R&D, production, marketing and personnel strategies?

2  Using the illustrations of (a) a mass producer of cars, (b) a university, and (c) a small accountancy practice, examine how a firm interacts with its economic environment at the local, national and international level.

3  Examine the major structural changes that have affected the UK economy since 1979? What has been the cause of such changes and how have they affected manufacturing firms?

4  To what extent is the state a facilitator and to what extent a constraint in the operation of a business? What does the Norton-Villiers case (2.2) tell us about the state's involvement with business?

5  Using the three illustrations offered above in topic 2, identify how management could influence the state and the directions this influence might take.

6  Examine Case 2.1. What are the key issues and what are the implications of such events for businesses in the UK and for the future of the EC?

7  Identify the various types of change that are likely to occur from the introduction of new technology. What opportunities and threats exist for management and the workforce? What problems will be created and how may they be overcome?

8  Examine the major changes in the labour market and trade unions in the last 20 years. What impact have such changes had on the operation of business at the level of the individual firm? Was the British Government in the 1980s justified in introducing laws to restrict the freedom and powers of trade unions?

9  How useful is the concept of culture in explaining the way businesses operate in different countries? To what extent can business ideas and management techniques developed in one cultural and national setting be transferred to another?

10  Examine the environmental influences which lay behind Nissan's decision to open a new plant in the North-East of England (Case 2.5). What does the case tell us about Japanese management methods?

# 3 Organizational aspects of business

In the last chapter we examined aspects of the environment which interact with business. Such aspects constitute the outer level of our model. In this chapter we examine a second level of interaction and influence belonging to the organization itself. We will consider five aspects in our model; goals, structures, size, ownership and organization culture.

As with other aspects of our model there is considerable interaction and overlap between these organizational issues. As well as pointing out the areas of overlap in each individual section, the way that issues relating to goals, ownership, structure and size come together is examined in more detail through the concept of organization culture. In addition, we highlight two specific issues, the public sector and small businesses, both of which illustrate the complex nature of these organizational relationships. The public sector has been chosen since it is a good illustration of the interaction and tensions both within the organizational elements, as well as those operating between the organization and its environment. In addition, government policy of privatization, deregulation and the commercialization of the public sector has meant that the distinction between public and private concerns is becoming increasingly blurred, further justifying our focus. The treatment of small businesses raises contemporary economic and political debates as well as highlighting the very specific nature of business problems found in this sector.

## Goals

In this section we shall examine the nature of goals, the purposes they serve and how they emerge. We shall also consider the potential problem arising from a number of different goals operating in the same organization. We often speak glibly of organizations like Marks & Spencer, British Rail, or even our own college as having goals. However, we ought not to ascribe behaviour to abstract entities such as organizations. Goals should always be attributable to some person or

**KEY CONCEPT 3.1**
*Organizational goals*

The stated goals of an organization exist to give direction to the activities of its members. In many companies, goals comprise both an overall statement of intent, sometimes referred to as a mission statement, and a set of more detailed objectives to guide strategic planning. Since many organizations are made up of different interest groups the formulation of goals can be a highly political process. This can cause conflict but the goals of most businesses are generally accepted as being those of the senior management team. There has been a renewal of interest in the role of goals to shape the culture of an organization. We deal with this aspect in our discussion of organizational culture (Key concept 3.6).

**CASE 3.1**
*Illustrations of company goals*

**A statement of company objectives by J. Sainsbury PLC**

To discharge the responsibility as leaders in our trade by acting with compete integrity, by carrying out work to the highest standards, and by contributing to the public good and to the quality of life in the community.

To provide unrivalled value to our customers in the quality of the goods we sell, in the competitiveness of our prices and in the range of choice we offer.

In our stores to achieve the highest standards of cleanliness and hygiene, efficiency of operation, convenience and customer service, and thereby create as attractive and friendly a shopping environment as possible.

To offer our staff outstanding opportunities in terms of personal career development and in remuneration relative to other companies in the same market, practising always a concern for the welfare of every individual.

To generate sufficient profit to finance continual improvement and growth of the business whilst providing our shareholders with an excellent return on their investment.

(*Source*: Annual Report and Accounts, 1988)

**The stated aims of Rank Hovis McDougall**

The business of the Rank Hovis McDougall Group of companies is to process and market a wide range of food products in the United Kingdom, Europe, the United States, the Far East and Australasia.

Our aims are:

- to provide attractive and wholesome food products at prices which represent good value for money;
- to provide our employees with worthwhile jobs in safe working conditions at fair levels of pay;
- to provide our shareholders with an acceptable return on the money they have invested in the Group;
- to provide for the long-term growth and stability of the Group in the interests of customers, employees, and shareholders alike.

(*Source*: Annual Report and Accounts, 1988)

**Rhône-Poulenc: extracts from the Chairman's message, 1986**

In this changing world our ambition is to lead the Rhône-Poulenc group along exceptionally vigorous lines to place it among the world leaders in each of the fields in which it excels. Our strategy can be summed up in three points. They are concomitant and complementary.

We must first increase the high-value added activities where Rhône-Poulenc already holds considerable know-how and strong markets . . . To succeed in these fields means continuing to pursue our capital expenditure program as well as continuing our substantial commitment to Research and Development . . . to sign research agreements . . . with the international academic world . . . seizing every opportunity for external expansion through acquisitions.

Secondly we reinforce our upstream activities . . . our chemical business in major intermediates, both organic and inorganic, areas in which we hold positions of leadership and where we have been able to set extremely competitive cost prices. To do this we must unceasingly pursue the improvement of our manufacturing processes. We must maintain here high levels of investments in productivity and capacity, and exercise a particularly rigorous industrial management policy.

Lastly we want to free ourselves from activities which are too far removed from our fundamental business or facing severe economic problems.

(*Source*: Company Report and Accounts, 1986)

group. Case 3.1 illustrates the goals of three organizations, two explicitly stated (Sainsbury, the supermarket chain, and Rank Hovis McDougall, the food processors) and the third extracted from the Chairman's statement (Rhône-Poulenc, a French multinational with interests in chemicals, fertilizers, pharmaceuticals and computer tape and discs).

The renewal of interest in the role played by goals in influencing the behaviour of organization members has been highlighted through the concept of the 'excellent company' (see for example Peters and Waterman, 1982). In companies like IBM, Hewlett-Packard, and Boeing you will find clearly articulated goals which are so dominant that they appear to have a life of their own irrespective of the personnel involved. Closer examination will certainly reveal that such goals are carefully formulated by the chief executives of such companies as part of a policy of establishing a set of dominant values which guide the behaviour of every organization member. As with all organizations, the main purpose of goals is to give members a sense of direction and to reduce ambiguity and conflict.

Managers who use goals in this way make the assumption that the clear formulation of goals will influence performance. This assumption has been translated into a set of techniques aimed at influencing the behaviour of individual members, known as 'Management-by-Objectives' or MBO (Drucker, 1964). Where MBO is used, the goals for the organization as a whole are generally broken down into individual goals or targets for each manager, forming an entire network of interconnected and internally consistent goals. The most effective MBO schemes tend to be those where there is some measure of negotiation between manager and subordinate over the precise nature of the goals to be achieved by the subordinate. This raises two points; that goal formulation is part of a political process and that goal achievement is undoubtedly related to the extent to which goals are shared by members of the organization.

However, the evidence on the influence of goals on performance is mixed, and even where such a relationship can be shown, it is unclear how it works. The use of goals to determine performance is easiest to understand where jobs are straightforward so that clear targets can be set and performance measured. Many jobs are more complex and performance measurement is difficult to achieve. Furthermore, employees may be expected to achieve a number of different goals which could conflict with one another or with those of other workers. We shall see that for some organizations internal consistency is difficult to achieve in the face of considerable inter-personal and inter-departmental conflict. The extent to which goals can be used to motivate performance is also a function of management behaviour and individual expectations.

Not every company has such clearly identified goals. For many small firms (as well as some larger ones), goals remain the unstated intentions of the owners; they may be thought of only in the vaguest of terms; employees may be completely unaware of them, and may give priority to their own personal goals, sometimes bringing them into conflict with management. A review of most companies' annual reports will reveal that the explicit statement of the goals is usually marked by its absence (the cases of Sainsbury and Rank Hovis McDougall are the exception rather than the rule). Instead the various missions, objectives and strategies must be extracted or at best implied from the various statements by company chairmen and operating reports (the case of Rhône-Poulenc providing a much clearer exposition than most).

## The nature of goals

> We consider goals to be the ultimate, long-run, open-ended attributes or ends a person or organization seeks.
>
> (Hofer and Schendel, 1978, p. 20)

Allowing for the contention that organizations can engage in goal-seeking behaviour, this definition sees goals in terms of the future orientation of the company, but stated in rather loose, broad terms. The examples in our case illustrate this point. A popular notion is that business firms should possess some superordinate goal, namely the maximization of profit. This view has been challenged. Some, like Handy (1993), see profit as a by-product of other goals like survival, market expansion and enhancing reputation. Marris (1964) sees profit as less important than growth. In any case the profit notion is entirely inappropriate for those public-sector organizations where goals of service take precedence over all others.

Hofer and Schendel (1978) make the distinction between goals, objectives and strategies. Goals themselves are seen as being unbounded, generalized statements of intent, whereas objectives represent those intentions that can be measured within a certain time frame. Strategies are seen as the processes by which goals are determined through the adoption of certain courses of action and the allocation of resources. We examine strategies more thoroughly in Chapter 4.

Richards (1978) distinguishes between closed- and open-ended goals. Closed-ended goals are those which have clearly defined and measurable targets to be achieved within a stated time period. By contrast open-ended goals are the type which include some broad statement of intent such as the pursuit of excellence. This broader view of goals has sometimes been defined as a firm's 'mission', which would seem to equate with Hofer and Schendel's concept of a goal. A mission has been described as a master strategy which has a visionary content, and which overrides all other types of goal (Richards, 1978).

Despite the confusion over terminology we can therefore see a kind of hierarchy developing which comprises different types of goals, as follows:

Another classification made by Perrow (1961) distinguishes between 'official' and 'operative' goals. 'Official' goals are the statements of intent which occur in official documents and are the type illustrated by our case illustrations. 'Operative' goals on the other hand reflect the behaviour that is actually occurring, and which may in fact conflict with the official intention. To Perrow the development of a package of operative goals was the process of corporate strategy formulation. This process is developed in the following section.

## How goals are developed

Our understanding of how goals develop owes much to the work of Cyert and March and their *Behavioural Theory of the Firm* (1963). They see organizations as being formed around individuals and groups who combine to pursue mutual interests as coalitions. The interests need not be shared but the coalition is recognized by all participating interest groups as the most effective way of achieving their goals.

An interest group may be an entire department, such as marketing or research and development, or it might be a particular section within that department such as a project team. It may even be a less formal grouping of managers within a department who collectively wish to pursue a specific policy. The creation of such interest groups may be a deliberate structural device. For example, senior management at Procter & Gamble felt that its interests could best be served through the creation of teams based around a single product or groups of products. The aim was the creation of healthy competition between product teams, and a competition and justification of resource allocation which would operate in the best interests of the firm as a whole. A more detailed discussion of the relationship between goals and structure may be found in the next section.

Interest groups can emerge due to the complexity of the organization's task and/or its environment, requiring a degree of internal specialization, to deal with specific problems, such as product development, or external bodies such as banks. Interest groups may also develop informally, cutting across formal structures.

Each interest group will determine its goals by reference to the information it collects. Such information generally includes comparative data on other organizations on such issues as price, product design, and criteria for success. Many interest groups for example establish their goals in relation to competing groups in the same organization. The important point made by Cyert and March is that groups deliberately limit strategic choice by selecting information from the range available and having decided upon a course of action, often fail to consider alternative strategies. This is perfectly understandable given the range of information and the time available to make decisions. Such a process is sometimes referred to as bounded rationality.

Interest groups combine to form coalitions and in any one organization there will be a number of such coalitions. They are created by a process of influence, negotiation and bargaining between different interest groups. It is out of this process that the goals emerge which guide the behaviour of organization members. However in any one organization there is usually a group that may be identified as a dominant coalition. Once established, the dominant coalition will set up procedures to ensure that their goals are pursued by the organization as a whole. Such criteria will normally include establishing the procedures for staff selection, promotion, and reward as well as laying down the rules of operation. The dominant coalition usually comprises, therefore, the senior management of an enterprise. However, certain groups align themselves with top management to ensure their goals are well represented. Even in those organizations where decision-making proceeds along more democratic lines, as in institutions of higher education, the various coalitions will compete for membership of key committees at which decisions about such issues as resources are taken.

In short, the ability of groups to pursue their goals depends upon the power they wield in the organization, which may depend on a number of variables; such as their position in the hierarchy; the skills of group members; the resources they command; whether or not their role is seen as legitimate by the rest of the organization members.

It is inevitable that different coalitions will pursue different interests and that some will compete. The process of influence, negotiation and bargaining may be termed organizational politics. Such a concept tends to be viewed pejoratively and political activity in business firms is often seen as a problem. Yet if we subscribe to the views of Cyert and March the process is an inevitable prelude to goal-setting. Nonetheless the potential problem of goal conflict will now be explored through the examination of multiple goals.

## Multiple goals

In any organization made up of different interest groups some conflict over goals is inevitable. This has been illustrated by many writers. Marris (1964) speaks of the goal conflict emerging from the separation of ownership and control. He found that while shareholders were concerned primarily about profitability, the professional managers acting as the directors of companies were more concerned with growth. In this instance profitability is a by-product, for it is growth which expands the director's sphere of influence and hence his personal power and reward. Despite such potential conflict between director and shareholder goals, some compromise is usually made by directors to protect their own position. Handy (1993) presents several examples of goal conflict, including that between the sales and production departments. The goals of the sales department are normally measured by volume turnover, while those of the production department are measured by cost-efficiency. We return to this particular problem in Chapter 6, when we depict the classic dilemma of the production department as that of satisfying the twin demands of customer satisfaction and operating efficiency.

In some cases such conflict can be seen to operate against the best interests of the organization. A study by Selznick (1949) of the Tennessee Valley Authority is viewed as a classic of its kind. An emerging organization, formed to solve the problems of irrigating and redeveloping a vast area in the Tennessee Valley, tackled its job through delegation and specialization. In this case, each specialist division within the organization (Selznick refers to these as sub-units) developed a greater commitment to its own sub-unit goals than those of the organization as a whole. This fragmented the total effort and resulted in groups devoting a great deal of their time to legitimizing their activities and competing for resources. This set up conflicts with other groups which further strengthened the resolve of each sub-unit to pursue its own goals. Selznick referred to this process as the 'bifurcation of interests'. Burns and Stalker (1966) noted how a similar conflict developed between the production and research and development departments in certain Scottish electronics firms with the subsequent decline in their competitive standing. In Pettigrew's (1973) study computer programmers saw their status threatened by an emerging group of systems analysts. In response they attempted to control information to preserve their exclusive position and prevent their work being downgraded.

In such cases, activities move away from dealing with customers or even coping with external changes in the market to focus on the resolution of internal tensions and management becomes the manage-

In 1991 London Zoo faced a financial crisis and closure was imminent. The surrounding debate between the owners, the managers and employees was a good illustration of goal conflict within a complex organization faced with considerable external problems.

London Zoo and its sister zoo, Whipsnade, are the property and responsibility of the Zoological Society of London, a body made up of fellows, elected on the basis of some special interest and expert knowledge in zoology and its related fields. The zoos had experienced financial problems for a number of years and in 1988 the Society commissioned a consultancy report. It recommended that the two zoos be run on a much more commercial basis and, following the publication of the report, the zoos were put under the control of a separate organization, Zoo Operations Ltd. A process of commercialization began which included a reduction in the number of animals, a marketing campaign to attract more visitors, the introduction of a more business-oriented approach and a number of organizational changes. Among these were wholesale changes in the terms and conditions of employees. Zoo staff were put on a consolidated pay scale and for the first time were faced with appraisal and performance related pay. At the same time the problems facing the zoo were cushioned somewhat by a Government backing of £10 million.

Despite the changes the recession in 1991 caused a decline in paying visitors and news of closure was leaked to the press. Paradoxically this led to a sharp increase in visitors to the zoo, perhaps sensing their last chance to see the animals. An appeal was launched and the management embarked on a number of fund-raising and cost-cutting exercises. A panda was borrowed from China in an attempt, amid much publicity, to mate London's own panda and a version of the popular TV programme, *Blind Date*, was used to gain maximum coverage. It became particularly important to focus on specific attractions since parts of the zoo had been closed as they were unsafe and policies to reduce the number of animals kept were well advanced. Almost each day saw more animals leave the zoo for other destinations or to be destroyed. This was a harrowing experience for most of the keepers who had built up a close relationship with their charges. At the same time staffing levels were being cut and employees were reduced by one-third. This necessitated jobs being combined, and keepers who were used to specializing in a particular area were asked to take on a range of tasks with different types of animals.

These changes highlighted a number of differences between various groups associated with the zoo. Goal conflict has never been far from the surface. As with any zoo there is a basic tension between those who see the zoo as a focus and means of academic research into zoological matters and those who see it primarily as a form of entertainment for the public. Some of the cruder attempts at commercialization were anathema to the former group.

In general the shift to a business management approach brought a number of tensions to the surface and several factions emerged. The members of the Zoological Society were one group, the management of the zoo another, and a third comprised those keepers and researchers who made up the majority of the zoo's employees. Within these groups there were differences. Some fellows saw commercialization as the only means of survival. Others, however, banded together as a 'Reform Group' opposed to blatant commercialism and questioned the policies of the zoo's management. There was a general debate about the role of zoos in society and the role governments might play. The £10 million grant was unusual for a UK government intent on creating a non-subsidized free-market society.

Despite this financial gesture many of the fellows were openly critical of the Government and cited a much greater financial backing given to zoos in other countries. There was a strong belief that no longer could zoos support themselves. The Reform Group formed a coalition with a group of employees who had established themselves as a 'Survival Group', and who were a useful source of information to the fellows on the daily events at the zoo. Within the employees, a number of different issues emerged. The primary concern of one group focused on changes in their terms of employment. Another group expressed the greatest concern for the loss of animals and the difficulties of providing adequate care for those remaining. Some researchers saw the crisis as an ideal opportunity to further their claim that greater attention should be paid to academic research and the furtherance of zoological knowledge.

The financial appeal and various marketing ploys were partially successful but the impact was essentially short-term and when, in 1992, the zoo made further losses and failed to achieve its targets for the number of visitors, closure seemed inevitable once again. The zoo was saved by a donation from the Emir of Kuwait as a gesture of gratitude to the British people for their part in the Gulf War. The publicity surrounding this donation and the plight of the zoo led to further donations and the short-term future seemed assured.

(*Sources*: *Personnel Management Plus*, July 1993; news reports of the day)

ment of internal coalitions. Case 3.2 illustrates issues of goal conflict in London Zoo that were brought to the surface at the time of financial crisis in the early 1990s. In many organizations conflict often remains hidden, emerging only when problems get out of hand. In most situations conflict can be contained and managed. A similar situation occurred within the BBC during the summer of 1993. Viewing figures revealed that BBC1 was achieving only 29% of the television audience against ITV's 41%. This created a much publicized debate about the future direction of BBC programming and there was a belief among senior managers at BBC1 that it was catering for an elite upper-income, middle-class audience and needed to widen its appeal. This debate led to further allegations of autocratic management and a stifling of creativity and positions were taken by different factions within the organization.

We can see that it is quite normal for multiple goals to exist in most organizations. Conflict does occur as can be seen by Case 3.2 and the illustrations above. However, not all conflict of this kind is necessarily a problem. It would appear to be limited by four factors.

- Most groups in an organization will agree to those goals formulated by senior management as a means of achieving their own goals. This is the result of the bargaining and negotiating process between interest groups.
- Most organization members would appear to accept the goals of top management with little question. This would seem to be an implied element of the employment contract.

- The dominant coalition normally sets up a series of controls to ensure compliance to their goals. Such controls have been alluded to earlier and include selection procedures, induction and training to ensure that rules are followed. In addition, management can use technological controls in the form of work design and job allocation, and financial controls in the form of budgets and reward systems. In such ways as these, the management of organizations ensure at least a minimum level of compliance with their chosen goals.

- In many firms senior management acknowledge that different groups may have their own goals which need to be satisfied. This is illustrated in Case 3.1.

In this section we have depicted the formation of goals as a complex process involving the resolution of external influences and internal politics. As such, the system is highly dynamic and changes in the goals will occur with changes in the external environment, such as market demand, technology and government policy, as well as changes that take place between interest groups within the organization. A change in ownership or top management may lead to a shift in emphasis of the firm's operations. The acquisition of the department store chain Debenhams by the Burton Group led to a change in operation as well as image. More franchises were awarded to established retailers to operate within each Debenhams store and there was considerable investment on internal refurbishment in all locations.

Goals are not formalized, meaningless statements but the products of a highly interactive and dynamic process. The changing of goals in the face of external and even internal changes is seen to be a prerequisite for the survival of the organization. Those managers that cling to inappropriate goals would appear to place their companies at risk. However, simply changing goals may be an inadequate response by itself, since the relationship between goals and performance often demands some consideration of the organization structure. It is to this we now turn.

---

| | |
|---|---|
| An organization structure is a grouping of activities and people to achieve the goals of the organization. Considerable variation is possible in the type of structure employed and the influences at work include technology, size, the nature of the environment, management strategy, the behaviour of interest groups, the firm's history and wider cultural factors. In general terms a particular structure emerges to maximize the opportunities and solve the problems created by these various influences. In practice however the evidence concerning the influence of structure and performance is very patchy indeed. | **KEY CONCEPT 3.2**<br>*Organization structure* |

## Structure

---

A dominant theme in our discussion of goals was that organizations are made up of different interest groups formed as coalitions. One of the factors which may facilitate or inhibit the way these groups pursue their goals and whether such goals may be achieved is the structure of the organization. In this section we will examine how structures develop, the variations that occur in structural type, and their impact on performance. You should note however that any discussion of structure is biased towards the large firm, and most of the studies in this area are of large corporations. This is inevitable in that structural problems tend to be associated with size and complexity. The balance is redressed later in this chapter when we devote an entire section to the problems of small businesses.

A structure is concerned with the grouping of activities in the most suitable manner to achieve the goals of the dominant coalition. It is concerned with the organization of work around roles, the grouping of these roles to form teams or departments, and the allocation of differential amounts of power and authority to the various roles. It is associated with job descriptions, mechanisms for coordination and control, and management information systems.

In much of the writing there is an implicit assumption that senior management seek a structural elegance for their organizations to enhance performance. This in turn assumes that managers have a choice and that structures can be deliberately created to affect overall performance. We will now examine those factors which can influence a firm's structure to determine the extent to which structures can be manipulated by management.

## The factors which influence structure

There are a number of factors which may influence the structure of an organization. We have identified them under six main headings, placed in no particular order of importance.

**Technology**   For some, technology is the most important, if not the sole, determinant of a firm's structure. This is part of the concept known as 'technological determinism'. Much of the work in this area is indebted to Joan Woodward's (1965) work on the impact of technology on 100 manufacturing firms in South-East Essex (also mentioned in Chapters 2 and 6). She and her research team found that differences in manufacturing, from small batch to mass production to process technology, resulted in corresponding differences in such factors as the extent of the management hierarchy, the proportion of management to other employees, the proportion of direct to indirect labour, and the number of subordinates controlled by any one manager (the span of control).

**Size**   Other researchers find size to be a more significant variable in influencing structure than is technology. This was a particular theme of a group of academics at Aston University in the 1960s and '70s (see, for example, Pugh *et al.*, 1969). As firms increase in size, additional problems are created in terms of coordination and control often necessitating structural changes. For example, as the business expands, the owner of a small business often faces increasing pressures on his or her time. No longer is he or she able to maintain a close control of operations, act as the major representative to customers, as well as managing administration and wages. In such cases some formalization and delegation is inevitable and a stage is reached when small businesses take their first steps towards bureaucratization. Such changes in structure with increasing size can be viewed in large as well as in small firms. We can see with Dow Corning in Case 3.3 that significant structural changes were made as the company expanded its product range and its markets. The way firms respond to size may vary resulting in different types of structure, which we identify in the next section. While there are obvious connections between size and structure, Child (1984a) points out that the complexity of an organization's operations may have a more significant impact on its structure than sheer size.

**CASE 3.3**
**Dow Corning**

Dow Corning was formed in 1942 from Dow Chemical and Corning Glass. The company operates in 32 different countries and is responsible for the manufacture of 1800 different products. The original focus of the firm was R&D, and the firm was highly centralized around technology and products. At this stage of its development the products were closely related and the firm operated under a traditional functional management structure.

By 1962 several changes had taken place. The company had grown, largely through product diversity, and central control of product development was no longer appropriate. In addition, there had been a change in top management and the new chief executive established five product divisions as profit centres, each with its own functional structures. The new structure was seen as successful in integrating the functions, and a contributory factor in the firm's continued growth and increased profitability.

Within a short time further international expansion brought its own problems. There was conflict between the demands of the home and foreign markets. Conflict also arose over the central supply of raw materials and the mechanisms for transfer pricing. The impact of an economic recession meant that profit levels fell. These problems were met by a further change in management along with a major structural change to a matrix organization.

The ensuing matrix comprised two major elements; specialist functions and ten business profit centres, newly created from the existing five divisions. Employees reported to a business centre manager and a functional vice-president. Each business centre comprised different product boards. Each product board was led by a particular functional manager and leadership tended to change with the product life cycle, from R&D at the early stages to marketing as the product move through each stage of the cycle.

Structures and processes were developed within the matrix to enhance coordination and deal with conflict. A great deal of attention was focused on modifying individual behaviour by such techniques as MBO and group goal setting and the firm was assisted in its search for goal congruence by having a management structure dominated by chemical engineers. As the businesses developed it became clear that the firm needed to rethink the basic components of its matrix structure. In addition to organization by function and by business product, there was also organization by geography, to satisfy the increasing international dimension of Dow's business. In part the focus on area management was made to solve a major problem attributed to the original matrix, that of building too many new plants and failing to capitalize upon economies of scale.

Problems with the matrix persisted. Area managers were seen to have too much power within the organization and were accused of empire-building, employees complained of too many bosses and the matrix created a cumbersome bureaucracy with a great deal of time consumed in meetings. Dow, unlike many other organizations, did not retreat from the matrix in the face of these problems. An expansion into the pharmaceuticals sector through a number of acquisitions meant that some form of flexible, semi-autonomous structure was required. Senior management decided to refocus the evolved matrix structure. A small team of senior executives were given the task of supervising all operations. They also had the responsibility of ensuring that only one of the three elements of function, business and geography took the lead in any venture, thus avoiding conflict and duplication of effort. In addition considerable attention was paid to employee communication, with the result that the matrix was viewed as a more open, less secretive form of organization structure.

(*Sources*: Galbraith and Nathanson, 1978; *The Economist*, August, 1988, pp. 61–2)

**Changes in the environment**   In the last chapter we saw how the contingency approach saw organizations as needing to adapt to their environment in order to survive. An important feature of that adaptation is structural. Burns and Stalker (1966) noted that technological and market changes in the post-war electronics industry were best served by a less bureaucratic, more flexible kind of organization. Such organic structures were an essential element in the firms' ability to cope with a highly changing environment, and firms which retained their traditional bureaucratic or mechanistic structures were much less successful. The IBM case at the end of this section illustrates the relationship between structure and a rapidly changing product market.

This theme of the structure fitting the dominant aspects of the firm's environment is the major plank in the work of Lawrence and Lorsch (1967). They believe that different tasks in the organization are confronted by different environmental problems and demands, differences which should be reflected in the structures of the departments carrying out those tasks. In their study of the plastics industry they found a highly uncertain technological environment which called for a flexible R&D function, while the demands imposed on the production department were more predictable, enabling a more traditional, bureaucratic structure to operate. The structural implications of Lawrence and Lorsch's analysis do not end with what they term the 'differentiation' of functions. In order to operate effectively all organizations so differentiated must establish integrative devices, which might include a committee structure or designing special coordinating roles.

An interesting illustration of a firm adapting to a predominant environmental condition is given by Child (1984a). He cites the example of the American multinational ITT operating in a highly volatile political environment in Chile in the 1970s. As part of its coping strategy, the firm set up a political intelligence unit.

**Strategy**   The influence of strategy on structure is related to the way management perceive their environment. A firm wishing to be a product leader in a technologically sophisticated product market will have a correspondingly large R&D department both in terms of investment and employees. A firm that places a great deal of emphasis on cost controls may have a larger than average accounting department.

The relationship of strategy to organizational structure owes much to the work of Alfred Chandler (1962, 1977). He based his first work around an in-depth case study of the development of four companies; DuPont, General Motors, Standard Oil and Sears Roebuck. His work, however, had a much broader perspective; that of charting the development of American capitalism and especially the role played by the professional manager. One of the major conclusions of his work is that structure is a product of managerial strategies. The relationship between the two is more complex than many summaries of Chandler acknowledge. He found that structure did not automatically follow strategy and that managements often needed a crisis before they would agree to structural change. This point emerges in Case 3.4 with IBM.

As might be expected of an economic historian, Chandler viewed the relationship between strategy and structure as dynamic and evolutionary. He identified several stages in the development of American capitalism. These were cycles of growth and consolidation, each with its own implications for the organizational structures of the emerging large corporations in his study. The growth of mass markets and the development of the techniques of mass production were accompanied by vertical integration to ensure the supply of materials and secure distribution channels, and horizontal integration through takeovers to maintain growth. Expansion brought its own problems of coordination and control and subsequent inefficiency. These were solved by the growth of professional management and the development of organizations structured around specialist functions, such as marketing and finance. As existing markets became saturated and the benefits accruing from organizational restructuring slowed down, new markets and products were vigorously pursued by overseas expansion and R&D respectively. Once again these developments brought their own problems of coordination and control. This time a new form of structure emerged. All four firms in Chandler's study had adopted a multidivisional structure by 1929, with DuPont and General Motors leading the way. The essential qualities of this structure will be identified in the following section.

Similar cycles of expansion and consolidation through structural change can be found in studies of British companies (see for example Channon, 1973). While such works offer strong evidence for the influence of strategy over structure, we have already noted the complex nature of the relationship. Chandler noted that the motivation for

**CASE 3.4**
**IBM**

In 1988 the senior management at IBM implemented significant structural changes, following the appointment of a new chairman in 1985. These changes were seen as a product of several interrelated factors not least of which was an unacceptable fall in profits since 1984.

Before 1988 the organization structure reflected a high degree of specialization between the various functional departments (known somewhat confusingly for our purposes as divisions). Clear distinctions were drawn between the technical division, which designed the computers, the manufacturing division, which made them, and the marketing division which was responsible for sales. In addition, IBM had no separate department concerned with software development. As a result of this type of structure management concluded that counter-productive internal conflicts were set up, new designs were delayed by as much as two years, and new models when they were introduced lacked supporting software, enabling competitors to increase their market share in key areas.

In a way IBM had been lulled by their dominant market position and early technical leadership in the field. The company firmly established its leading position throughout the 1960s and '70s. Current management thinking suggests that the company became complacent, highly bureaucratic, ultra-conservative and missed the essential entrepreneurial spirit associated with its early days.

While IBM still dominated the mainframe market, helped significantly by its US government contracts and supplies to many major companies throughout the world, it had not responded to important changes in other markets. The computer market has become technically very diverse and there have been many aggressive new entrants. Such new entrants have not been held back by a large bureaucracy, they have operated with flexible organization structures that have enabled them to respond more effectively to technological change and be sensitive to the needs of the customer. The resulting market has become highly fragmented and price-competitive. IBM mini-systems have been losing out to Digital and the personal computer market has been swamped by IBM compatibles like Arnstrad, selling at considerably cheaper prices and offering a more comprehensive range of software.

The structural response of IBM has been divisionalization and decentralization. Five divisions have been created; mainframes, mini-computers, personal computers, tele-communications, and new technology. Each division is autonomous, and is responsible for its own product design, manufacture, sales and ultimately profits.

(*Source*: John Cassidy and David Holmes, IBM spreads workload for quicker pace, *Sunday Times*, 14 February 1988)

structural change emerged not only from changes in strategy but that it needed the catalyst of an organizational crisis. We can see cases where structural change may be unnecessary or at least delayed by the sheer market power of the firm, as in the case of IBM. There may even be a case for arguing that structure can determine strategy. For example, once a company has adopted a multi-divisional structure, this could well give divisional managers the incentive, confidence and resources for even greater expansion. This interplay of strategy and structure reappears in Chapter 4 and is illustrated by changes in the US multi-national 3M depicted in Case 4.2.

Culture   The influence of culture on structure should not be underestimated. There is evidence that different structural forms are favoured in different countries. For example, American firms developed initially through the adoption of divisional structures, while in Britain we favoured the holding company (Channon, 1973). Firms in different countries often reflect different emphases, so it has been noted that while American firms stress the finance and marketing functions, those in Germany have a production orientation (Hayes and Wheelwright, 1984); industrial relations management plays a much more significant role in Britain than either of those two countries. Studies on such aspects as the shape and extent of the management hierarchy have also noted differences between countries (Brossard and Maurice, 1976; Trompenaars, 1993). For example the hierarchies in French firms tend to be steeper than those in the UK, and much steeper than those in Germany. Structure may also reflect specific organizational cultures; for example, those firms favouring the involvement of employees in decision-making may set up participative forums to facilitate this.

Interest groups   Although Chandler noted the resistance on the part of some managers to structural change, the whole issue of interest groups and organizational politics was largely overlooked. The preferences of the dominant coalition can exert considerable influence on the structure as can the demands of major stakeholders. Those firms where the owners play a major role in management tend to be highly centralized. In the public sector the pressure for accountability often results in elaborate financial control mechanisms and bureaucratic procedures. In some manufacturing firms the pressure from banks on lending may in times of recession lead to reductions in development activities, with a corresponding impact on the size of the R&D function.

   Cases 3.3, 3.4 and 4.2 all show structural changes following management changes. While size, market and other environmental influences inevitably played a major role in Dow Corning, IBM and 3M, the catalyst for new structures in all cases would seem to be changes at the top.

Two important points emerge from our consideration of the six influences above. First, there is considerable overlap between the various factors. For example, the structural changes of firms like Dupont and General Motors link technology, size and strategy; the different structural routes taken by firms in different countries are both a function of cultural differences and variations in environmental factors. In short, the structure of an organization can only be explained by reference to a number of interrelated factors. Once again this is amply illustrated in both the Dow Corning and IBM cases. Second, our analysis raises the issue of the extent of choice senior management have in determining the structure of their organization. Are structures creative innovations to implement changing strategies or are they the inevitable consequences of adaptation to prevailing influences? Such issues were raised in the shipping industry case in Chapter 1; structural changes were an important factor in the implementation of strategic change in a highly competitive environment, but they were also determined by technical innovations in such areas as cargo handling and telecommunications. In short the structure of the shipping companies would appear to be the result of both prevailing economic and technological conditions and management choice.

If managers do have a choice of structure for their organization, then it may include one of the following structural types.

### Types of structure

In this section we present a brief review of the major structural types and examine some alternative structural forms as well as cover, albeit briefly, the debate on the flexible firm. Very few organizations conform precisely to a particular type. In some organizations a particular kind of structure predominates, while others display a variety of types. We will explain the basic characteristic of each type and present in Figure 3.5 a summary statement of the supposed advantages and problems associated with each one. In this summary we group the divisional and holding company types together, since each represents a different method of achieving decentralization. As we mentioned earlier, structure does not emerge as an issue until a firm reaches a certain size. Many small firms have no apparent structure at all, beyond a centralized control system, but even this is not inevitable as in the case of partnerships between professional people. We identify five main types of organization structure.

**Functional**  The main criteria guiding this type of organization is functional specialization. As we can see from the illustration in Figure 3.1 employees performing related specialist tasks are grouped together under a single management structure. Most firms as they develop adopt this form of structure and it is especially suited to single product firms. The structure was widely used by British firms, even very large companies, up to the 1960s, but became less common in larger firms especially, as it was superseded by divisionalization (Channon, 1973).

| **KEY CONCEPT 3.3**<br>*The multidivisional*<br>*company* | A multidivisional company comprises a number of different business units which may pursue markedly different types of business activity. The various business units operate as profit-centres and are centrally coordinated by a corporate headquarters, which may also control certain central services such as research and development and finance. This kind of structure developed in the USA is response to business growth. In Britain many large, diverse organizations have tended to favour a somewhat looser holding company structure with possibly less central coordination of strategic planning. In reality there is much overlap between the two kinds of structure. |
| --- | --- |

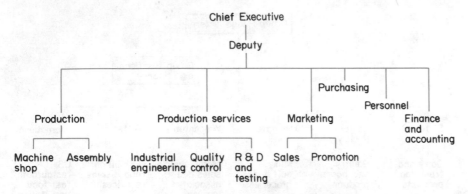

*Figure 3.1*   A functional structure: an engineering components business.

**Divisional**   The development of the divisional or, as it is sometimes called, the multi-divisional company is associated with market expansion and product diversification. In both these cases traditional functional structures showed themselves to be inadequate in coordinating and controlling the firm's activities. Divisionalization was a particularly American development and is associated with 'pioneer' companies like General Motors and DuPont in the 1920s and with the multinational expansion of American firms in the 1930s (Chandler, 1962).

An illustration of a divisional structure is shown in Figure 3.2. Under such an organization structure each division is self-contained and operates as a profit centre. Divisions can be grouped around products or markets or a combination of the two, as in the case of Ford. The activities of the various divisions are directed by a central headquarters unit who take a global view of corporate strategy. Other central activities might include R&D and purchasing, to benefit from economies of scale. The dual existence of divisional profit centres and central units is a source of tension for many firms operating this structure, especially in the allocation of the costs of these central units to the individual divisions. In one case, a divisionalized engineering firm operated a central foundry, which also had to act as a profit centre in its own right. As well as serving the needs of its own organization, the foundry, having spare capacity, was encouraged to seek contracts outside the firm. This set up two sorts of tension: first, the various divisions complained about having to pay the 'going rate' for foundry products, and second, the divisions always demanded priority over external contracts, which hampered the foundry from achieving its own profit objectives.

Once divisions have been established a decision still has to be made about grouping within each division. In some cases this is done along traditional functional lines, whereas in others staff are organized around products.

**The holding company**   This form of organization is associated with the growth of the firm by acquisitions and a high degree of product

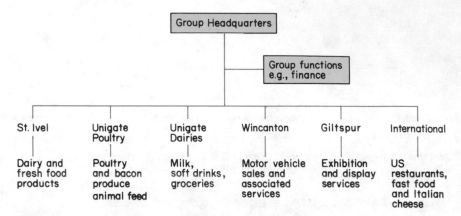

*Figure 3.2*   A divisional structure: Unigate – a divisionalized structure organized around product groupings. *Source*: *Company Reports and Accounts*, 1988.

diversification. It comprises, as we can see from the illustration in Figure 3.3, a group of independent companies controlled by a co-ordinating group usually made up of the chief executives of the constituent companies. At its extreme form, as exemplified by a company such as Lonhro, this structural type represents as much a form of ownership and investment as it does a kind of organization. Hanson Trust is one such company that has been subjected to considerable criticism for pursuing policies of short-term financial gain at the expense of company development through its selective policies of corporate acquisition and sales. Hanson's attempt to buy ICI in 1991 generated considerable speculation concerning major job losses and future investment in ICI. Amid growing opposition the takeover was eventually thwarted by the ICI board (a fuller account of this debate may be found in Adcroft *et al.*, 1991).

Holding companies can be highly diversified, as in the case of Trafalgar House, or built around loosely related products as with the TI Group. Ultramar on the other hand represents a holding company of highly related activities in oil and gas exploration and the production, shipping and refining of crude oil and petroleum products.

As we saw in the previous chapter, the holding company is the prevalent structural form for large Japanese companies. It has also been described as the peculiarly British route to divisionalization (Channon, 1973). Although there are similarities between divisional and holding company structures, Channon believed that the reluctance of British firms to adopt divisionalization was a contributory factor in their relative failure in competitive world economies; a case of structure influencing performance.

**The project team**   These comprise units specially created to cope with a highly unstable environment. In essence they are temporary structures formed around a particular task or problem and reflect technical expertise rather than any notion of management hierarchy. Such structures are commonly found in high-technology firms and some types of

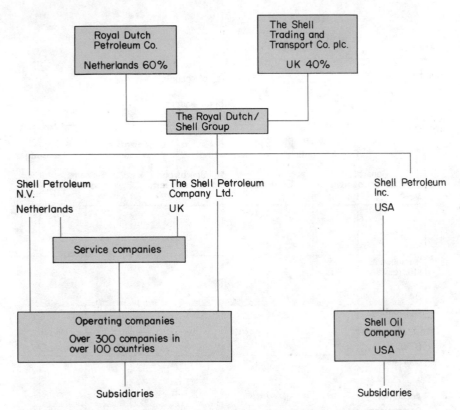

*Figure 3.3* A holding company: Royal Dutch Shell. *Source: Company Reports and Accounts*, 1988.

service organizations, especially consultancies. In advertising agencies, teams are usually created to deal with specific client accounts. In R&D departments the research work may be organized around several teams, each handling a different problem. In construction companies project teams may be created to deal with a particular job such as the building of a new office block. The membership of teams can be highly fluid; different specialists may be brought in at different times and one employee may be a member of several teams.

The approach reflects a close identification with the needs of the client and is an extension of the kind of client-based structure found in professional firms such as solicitors, accountants and the like. While focusing specifically on the needs of the client does have its advantages there can be some unnecessary duplication of resources and there can be scheduling and logistics problems. These become more severe as the organization gets larger and a stage may be reached where project teams need to be supported within a functional or divisional framework. The matrix structure was developed especially with such problems in mind and it is to this we now turn.

**The matrix** Essentially the matrix is an attempt to combine the best of all worlds; the customer-orientation of the project team, the economies

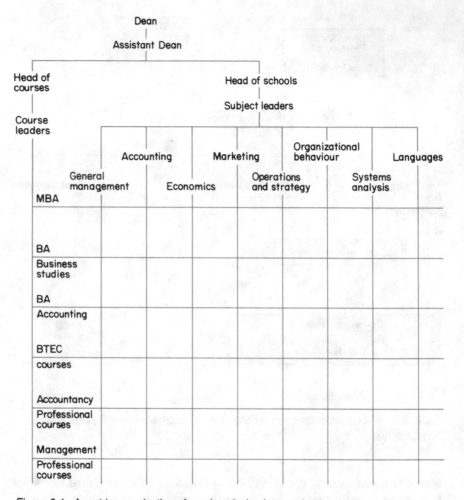

*Figure 3.4* A matrix organization of a university business school.

of scale and the specialist orientation of the functional organization, and the product or market focus of the divisional company. The matrix is an attempt to devise a structure that can effectively manage at least two different elements, be they size, products, markets or customers. The essence of the matrix is presented by the Dow Corning case; the work was controlled originally in two directions, by a functional specialism and by a product grouping, committees are set up to co-ordinate the two orientations, and attention is given to training the staff towards goal congruence. Further developments in the matrix at Dow added a third dimension to the structure, that of geography. The illutration of a matrix in a university business school is presented in Figure 3.4.

The matrix became very popular in the 1970s and owed much to the work of Lawrence and Lorsch (1967) and Galbraith (1971). It was embraced by companies such as Dow Corning (see the case later in the chapter), General Electric, Ciba Geigy and Citibank. The popularity

| ADVANTAGES | PROBLEMS |
|---|---|

### 1. Functional Organization

| | |
|---|---|
| ☐ Specialization. | ☐ Conflicting departmental objectives. |
| ☐ The logic of custom and practice. | ☐ Conflicting management values. |
| ☐ A clear chain of command. | ☐ A lack of coordination. |
| | ☐ A lack of consumer orientation. |

### 2. Divisional organization and Holding company

| | |
|---|---|
| ☐ The operation of businesses as profit centres. | ☐ Cooperation and interdependence. |
| ☐ The encouragement of entrepreneurship. | ☐ Accounting procedures, especially transfer pricing. |
| ☐ Reduces upward dependency on top management. | ☐ Increasing diversity of operations. |
| ☐ Economies of scale by centralization of common functions like R&D. | ☐ Overall management control. |

### 3. Project teams

| | |
|---|---|
| ☐ The ability to cope with an unstable environment. | ☐ A costly duplication of resources. |
| ☐ The use of individual expertise. | ☐ Scheduling. |
| ☐ The ability to cope with diverse problems. | ☐ The participants have no functional home. |
| ☐ Deal directly with the customer. | ☐ What happens when the project is finished? |

### 4. Matrix organization

| | |
|---|---|
| ☐ Emphasizes the strengths of the functional and project types. | ☐ Coordination and control. |
| ☐ Flexibility of labour. | ☐ A proliferation of committees and meetings. |
| ☐ The ability to transfer expertise where it is most needed. | ☐ Too many bosses. |
| ☐ Dual control via function and project. | ☐ Conflicting loyalties for staff. |
| ☐ Closeness to the customer. | ☐ Can be slow to adapt. |

*Figure 3.5* A summary of advantages and problems associated with different types of organization structure.

was short-lived and of all the structural types the matrix has attracted most criticism. In a later work Paul Lawrence referred to the matrix as an 'unnecessary complexity', which was only justified in certain situations (Davis and Lawrence, 1977, p. 21): first, if two or more of a firm's dimensions, like products and markets, were especially critical to its performance; second, if employees needed to carry out highly complex, interdependent tasks in an uncertain environment; third, if economies of scale were needed especially in the use of scarce or expensive resources. Unless such conditions are present then the matrix can cause more problems than it solves. Some of those problems are depicted in Case 3.3, as well as the organizational developments introduced by Dow to counteract such problems. Trompenaars (1993) has argued that the effectiveness of the matrix may be limited to specific cultures. Matrix organizations are not successful in Italy where, Trompenaars argues, bosses are seen as father figures. Since matrix organizations often require people to have two bosses, Italians find it difficult relating to two 'fathers'. It is interesting to note that at a time when most business organizations were finding the matrix wanting, it was emerging as perhaps the most popular structure in university business schools.

Students should always remember that the structural types identified above represent fairly broad categories. In reality a firm may display a mixture of structures. We have already seen how many divisionalized companies have functional specialisms within each division. In a functional organization we may find that different departments are organized along different lines; the operations department may well extend the functional structure, while the R&D staff may well be organized as project teams. New structural forms are emerging all the time, adapting the traditional approaches to suit their own needs. The Philips factory in South London was organized along functional lines but management redrew the organization chart to place the production function at the centre of a network of supporting activities, in an attempt to establish manufacture as the core activity.

## Alternative forms of organization structure

A currently popular concept is that of networking. This type of structure has been made possible by developments in computer technology whereby computer systems can interact. Such a system enables people to operate from home and has been heralded as the organization structure of the future. Networking has attracted considerable publicity both in academic journals and the popular press. This attention however tends to exaggerate the real extent of networking. Even in pioneer networkers such as Rank Xerox, those employees operating under this system are but a very small percentage of the total employed. Of course, a form of networking has been around for some time in certain types of manufacturing industry in the form of homeworking. In this case individuals or even families engage in simple assembly work (as with electrical components) or in such activities as dressmaking and alteration. Homeworking has become a way of life in some countries such as Japan and is a particularly low-cost form of labour.

While the publicity surrounding networking outstrips the reality, this is not the case for franchising, an emerging form of organizational structure akin to the holding company. Under a franchise agreement a parent company will assist in the start-up of a new business enterprise. The terms of that agreement usually involve an initial investment on the part of the franchisee and an undertaking to deal exclusively with the franchisor in the marketing of his products. The purchase of the franchisor's products invariably involves the payment of a mark-up in return for the advertising and promotional support of a larger company. A good illustration of franchising is presented by the fast-food industry, such as Kentucky Fried Chicken although there are more than 300 different franchise operations in Britain including such diverse operations as the British School of Motoring, drain clearance and wedding-dress hire. A recent growth in franchise operations has taken place in the financial service sector, as in the case of insurance broking. In this case the franchisee, instead of buying goods from the franchisor, buys access to a computer database. The main advantage to both parties in a franchise agreement is the spread of risk. As such it has become a popular form of small business venture.

The two illustrations of networking and franchising focus on criteria of flexibility and cost. These are two major considerations in the debate about the concept of the 'flexible firm' and about the relationship between structure and performance. We end this section on structure by examining these two issues.

## The flexible firm

The concept of the flexible firm emerged from work carried out by the Institute of Manpower Studies and associated largely with the writing of John Atkinson (his 1984 article offers an excellent summary). The main assumption is that new forms of organization are required as a strategic response to the combined effects of market stagnation, job losses, technological change, increased uncertainty, and reductions in the working week. The ideal strategic response to these forces involves some form of flexible manning. Atkinson identifies three types of flexibility.

- **Functional flexibility** is achieved when employees are able to perform a range of jobs and can move between them as the need arises. In many organizations this will see an end to demarcation between trades, the cause of many disputes and inefficiencies and lead to multi-skilling.
- **Numerical flexibility** is achieved through management's ability to make rapid alterations to the headcount of the firm to meet changes in demand. A growth in part-time and contract work was envisaged.
- **Financial flexibility** is required to reflect changes in the supply and demand of labour and to enhance the operation of functional and numerical flexibility. This can be achieved through the creation of differential rates of pay for full- and part-time workers and the use of incentives for workers to acquire more skills.

The ensuing 'flexible firm' will do much to break up traditional organization structures. For Atkinson, the key creation is that of the core and peripheral groups of employees. Core employees are those on permanent or long-term contracts and who hold the key skills in the organization. Accordingly they are well rewarded for their contribution. Peripheral workers comprise two groups. It is envisaged that there will be a group of full-time workers, who in general will be less skilled and not enjoy the security of the core employee. We identified a similar system as a feature of the Japanese labour market in Chapter 2. The second group of peripheral workers will comprise part-time and contract workers hired in direct proportion to the demand or to deal with non-core business, such as catering and cleaning.

A superficial analysis of many large firms in the UK will reveal elements of the Institute of Manpower Studies' model. Many private-, and in particular, public-sector organizations have increased the use of part-time and contract workers. Major manufacturing firms such as Ford have introduced policies towards multiskilling and the end to demarcation, as in the creation of maintenance jobs that bridge the mechanical and electrical divide.

The model has also attracted its critics. Pollert (1987), in particular, accuses Atkinson and his team of offering vague concepts and of producing a model that is not supported by current evidence. She argues that elements of the flexible firm model can be seen in many organizations, but they have been introduced as cost-cutting exercises rather than a strategic response to a changing market environment. This is particular true of local authorities and other public-sector organizations. She goes on to claim that many of the elements are far from new, citing multiskilling as a feature of 1960s productivity bargaining initiatives. In some industries, notably fast food, she cite core workers as anything but the skilled, highly paid élite of Atkinson's flexible firm. Finally she fears that the adoption of the flexible model could lead to more problems than it solves. Such problems as the growth of part-time employment have certainly attracted the interest of trade unions who view it as a part of the process of decreasing job security.

Clearly more evidence is required concerning the types and extent of flexibility and their relationship to overall management strategy.

## Structure and performance

We can see from Figure 3.5 and our discussion of the various structural types that some structures are more suited to some situations than others. Conversely a firm that adheres stubbornly to a structure that is totally inappropriate to the contingencies that it faces may be creating problems for itself. However, the evidence on these matters is far from convincing. The major difficulties in establishing a correlation between structure and performance would appear to be first, identifying appropriate measures of performance and second, proving causality. We can make some general points.

- Whatever the relationship between structure and performance, Johnson and Scholes (1993) point out that once a structure has been installed, it is often very difficult to change it. Equally, frequent structural changes could be damaging in terms of the disruption that takes place and the requirement on the part of staff to learn new systems.
- It is extremely doubtful whether structure alone can lead to improvements in performance. However sound the structure may be, it is unlikely that it can totally overcome problems created by staff

incompetence or even divisive internal politics. In some cases a high degree of specialization or divisionalization can lead to a worsening of relationships. We might even speculate that there is more evidence for suggesting that structure can affect performance in a negative way than there is for its having a positive impact. There is some evidence that structure in harness with other variables can lead to improvements in performance (Child, 1972). This point was taken up by Galbraith and Nathanson (1978), who argue that effective financial performance is obtained by achieving some kind of congruence between strategy, structure, processes, rewards and people.

- Child (1984) also points out that performance can influence structure, citing the example that more successful companies financially tend to have fewer cost controls. This fits in with the one of the key assumptions of our Business in Context model; that influences operate in more than one direction and while organizational factors such as structure can affect the outcome of a firm's activities, that outcome in turn affects the organization.

## Ownership

We might assume quite logically that ownership is an important variable in that the owners of a business will wish to determine the goals and the way that business operates. In support of our assumption we could cite illustrations of influential founders such as Henry Ford, Thomas J. Watson of IBM, and the Sainsbury family of supermarket fame. We could also refer to numerous cases of small firms where the owner, often single-handedly, controls the destiny of the business. In the case of the small firm the owners can be clearly defined and their impact easily assessed. Discovering who actually owns and controls businesses becomes much more difficult with large corporations like the major oil companies, or even an organization like British Airways, where privatization has been accompanied by widespread share issue, at least, in the first instance. It would appear that the greater the size of the organization and the greater the dispersal of share ownership then the more we can question our original assumptions and need to examine the relationship between the ownership and the control of businesses.

The degree of private and public ownership is another issue which holds significant interest for students of business in this country. Organizations that are wholly or partly state-owned, like the coal mines or the local hospital, raise important issues of management control and public accountability.

In this section we will focus on these two aspects of ownership and examine the implications for the way businesses operate. We deal first with the traditional debate surrounding ownership and control. Second, we examine the issue of the public ownership of organizations and the trend of privatization. The two elements were brought much closer together in the latter half of the 1980s in Britain. Traditional public-sector concerns such as hospitals and local authorities have been urged to take a more commercial approach. Since 1983, many organizations like British Telecom, Jaguar, British Aerospace, and utilities such as gas, electricity and water have passed from public to private ownership or to a mixture of public and private ownership. This has been accompanied by a massive increase in the proportion of the population owning shares and a highly dispersed ownership pattern for those concerns. It is this dispersal that is at the heart of the ownership and control debate.

## Ownership and control

The issue of ownership and control is one of continuing interest for academics, more especially among economists and sociologists. It is also a debate which raises significant questions for businesses in practice. How committed to the future of an enterprise are managers who have no stake in its ownership, or shareholders who have no interest beyond a return on investment? Are the resulting strategies in the best interests of all concerned; owners, managers, employees, the state, the public at large? How much freedom do managers have in developing business strategies?

The debate around these issues originates from the separation of ownership and control through the creation of the joint stock company and the subsequent dispersal of share ownership. With increased investment businesses grew in size and complexity and control by professional managers became a necessity. The complexity of such growing businesses led to a specialization within the management group and the separation of the firm into different specialist functions and activities. Bureaucratic rules and procedures were developed to coordinate and control such activities. Both the specialization and bureaucratization reinforced the control of the management group with a supposed weakening in the power of the owner to influence decisions. The owner's main source of control was through the possession of capital stock.

This phenomenon was highlighted in the seminal study of Berle and Means (1932) and developed in later work by Berle (1954). Berle and Means in a study of the 200 largest non-financial corporations in the USA classified the firms by their mode of control. They concluded that 44% of the firms were management controlled and that this trend was increasing. The Berle and Means study has been replicated in both the USA and Britain with similar results, although both the data and conclusions of such studies have been the subject of significant controversy (Scott, 1979 has a reasonable summary of these studies).

Berle and Means used their data to develop and support their own view of a 'managerial revolution'. To them management control was 'better' in that it resulted in more effective decisions both for the profitability of the firm and for the general good of society; it was more professional and more socially responsible. The concepts of a 'neutral technocracy' and a 'soulful corporation' have stemmed from such value assessments of management control. We can see a clear link between Berle and Means's notion of 'managerialism' and the earlier work of F. W. Taylor on 'scientific management' (published in 1947). For both Taylor and Berle and Means, management should use a professional approach based on the application of science to solve the problems facing the firm. According to Berle and Means, management control would be truly professional in that strategies would be guided more by scientific analysis and be more answerable to society than the potentially narrow self-interest of the owner-manager. This concept of a managerial revolution was popularly espoused by Burnham (1941), whose ideas have attracted perhaps more attention than his analysis deserves. Burnham, writing at the time of Roosevelt's 'New Deal' saw similarities in many nations through the increased state control of the economy. He believed that through this managers, as the controllers of capital, would be able to assume a powerful role in society and direct businesses to serve their own ends.

There is a tendency to view such debates as purely academic. This would be wrong since the questions that emerge are central to the way businesses operate and the control of organizations has implications not only for the survival and prosperity of the organization itself, but also for the people who work for it, firms who deal with it, and society at large. We therefore examine some key issues in the ownership and control debate and raise a number of questions around the conclusions drawn by Berle and Means.

- Do managers really have more power and control than shareholders? Even with a dispersal of share ownership shareholders' needs still have to be satisfied, which may place constraints on management decisions. There is always a danger that shareholders, in the face of what they perceive as unpopular management decisions will sell their shares creating instability in the firm's stock market position.

  In any case the distinction between managers and shareholders has become increasingly blurred. While in many companies there clearly has been a separation of ownership and control, there is an increasing tendency, especially in the larger firms, to offer senior management shares in the company as part of their annual remuneration deal. In this way, managers may well identify with shareholders' own aspirations. This argument has been extended by the Marxist analysis of ownership and control, which views shareholders and managers not as being separate but as different forms of the same animal; no real distinction is drawn between managers and capitalist owners. In addition to such arguments we can see that management freedom to make decisions is often held in check by banks, governments and trade unions. This complicates the ownership and control debate and we return to the role of the financial institutions later.

- In addition to the above arguments it has often been pointed out that many large and influential companies are both family owned and controlled and no separation has in fact occurred. In the retail trade in Britain such family-run businesses as Sainsbury, Asda and Dixons have grown and prospered in relatively recent times. Empirical work from the USA suggests that family ownership and control of major businesses is still a significant feature; Sheehan (1967) found that of the largest 500 American firms, 150 could be designated as having a significant family interest in terms of management and control.

- Has the ownership of shares really been dispersed? The data presented by Berle and Means (1932) showed that 86% of the largest 200 US companies had a minimum of 5000 shareholders, with 22% having over 50000. Putting such data in perspective Miliband (1969) cites evidence which reveals that in Britain in 1961 only 4% of the population owned shares and 1% of the population owned 81% of all shares. Others, notably Child (1969), interpret the evidence that while there may be some evidence of share dispersal, the majority of shareholders own relatively small numbers of shares and tend to be extremely passive. This can result in minority shareholders owning a substantial proportion of all shares with considerably more interest and potential influence in management decision-making. It is not just the dispersal of shares which should concern us, but the pattern of that dispersal.

  Most of these data are of course fairly old, and the entire pattern of share ownership, in Britain at least, has been confused by the large number of share issues in the 1980s and 1990s resulting from the government's policy of privatization. Many of the earlier share issues, such as British Telecom, were oversubscribed to a significant extent. While it is undeniable that large numbers have been brought into share ownership for the first time, it is however much too early to assess the situation. Many of those who have bought shares have done so with the prime intention of a quick sale for profit. This whole business has been summed up by the humorist Miles Kington as follows.

  > . . . the British public has learnt how to fill in forms they didn't quite understand, send them off at the last possible moment, receive negligible numbers of shares in public companies they are not interested in, flog them off immediately for a tiny profit.
  >
  > (*Independent*, 30 July 1987)

  The shares of such public sales may well find themselves consolidated among a much smaller group of traditional shareholders within a relatively short space of time.

- Are professional managers more effective and more socially responsible than the traditional owner-manager? Recent assessments of management in Britain have raised serious doubts about the competence of those managers. Degrees of social responsibility are particularly difficult to gauge. In any case there is some logic in suggesting that the career-motivated professional manager would show less, not more, paternalism towards staff and less concern for social issues in general than the traditional entrepreneur, who would often have strong connections with the local community.

The contemporary plausible interpretation of the ownership and control debate focuses on the role of financial institutions. We can always cite the case of small firms and even large corporations where owner control is the norm. However, in both Britain and America a substantial shareholding of many of the major firms has passed to the hands of financial institutions, including banks, insurance and pension companies (Scott, 1979 provides an excellent summary of the supporting evidence). Their presence changes the nature of the Berle and Means debate. There is an acknowledgement of a separation between shareholders and managers, but a serious challenge to the concept of the passive shareholder. Such financial intermediaries not only tend to hold a significant minority stockholding, which gives them both power and influence, but they also take an active interest in important strategic decisions. Their credibility with their current clients and their ability to attract future investors rests upon the ability of their investment managers to ensure that yields are both attractive and secure. The sale of large numbers of shares by a bank or pension fund could well undermine the confidence of the stock market in a particular firm. Scott (1979) argues that large financial investors have become the dominant form of strategic control in British companies. They possess the mechanisms to be well informed and the power to make their views known to management. They become particularly active in crises and may be instrumental in not just dictating the policy of top management, but determining the composition of that group.

The clear inference from such an examination of the stockholding role of financial institutions is that the envisaged separation of ownership and control has not taken place. However, as Scott points out, the influence of financial institutions on business is far from being just financial. He propounds the notion of a 'constellation of interests', whereby the representatives of financial institutions are elected or appointed to the boards of directors of those companies where they hold a substantial minority interest. The senior officials of a bank may each hold a number of such directorships, as do the senior officials of other financial institutions. A pattern is thus built up of interlocking directorships representing a very important network of information, which supersedes finance as an instrument of power. Such directors

---

**KEY CONCEPT 3.4**
*The public sector*

This is a broad term covering a range of organizations in both the manufacturing and service sectors. Despite the differences, public-sector organizations share many problems. These include the extent of State control over management decisions, the public accountability of management decisions, levels of government spending and conflict over goals. The Government in Britain since 1979 has attempted to solve such problems by taking organizations out of the public domain and establishing them as private enterprises.

will influence the recruitment of other directors and will inevitably favour those with access to vital information.

We can see that management decisions in a single firm may be influenced and even significantly constrained by directors representing the interests of other institutions altogether. A similar pattern of influence and constraint occurs in the management of public-sector organizations and it is to this we now turn.

## Management and control in the public sector

We often refer to the public sector as if it were a homogeneous group of organizations. This is highly misleading, for the public sector encompasses a wide range of institutions. At least three broad types may be identified. First, we have the nationalized industries; these are wholly owned and controlled by the state and include such organizations as the National Coal Board and the Post Office. Second, we have those companies which are controlled by the state acting as a majority shareholder and holding company; currently this operates through the British Technology Group (incorporating the National Enterprise Board). Both these types of enterprise have business objectives in that they sell their goods and services in the marketplace, in many cases with the profit motive in mind (although nationalized industries are theoretically bound by statute to break even). The third type of public-sector organization, such as the health, education and social services, offers its services to the population and is funded indirectly through the taxation system.

The rationale for a public sector can be explained in political, economic and social terms, although we can make a broad distinction here between the business and non-business institution. In terms of the provision for health, education, social services, and especially the police and armed forces, there is a broad consensus that public ownership and control is socially and indeed politically desirable, but even here there is fierce political debate on the extent of public provision in areas such as health and education. The major political contention concerns a public-sector business presence, brought sharply into focus by the privatization of many public-sector concerns in the 1980s. The commitment to public ownership has been a major ideological strand in the constitution of the Labour party enshrined in Clause 4. Indeed the nationalized industries have their goals defined by statute; to provide a specific service, to break even and to operate in the interests of employees and the public at large. Other arguments are made in support of the business public sector; that it supports the growth of other industries by providing such needs as energy; that it can both prevent and ease the decline of industries, significant either for the product or numbers employed or both, as in the case of British Leyland; that the state is in an ideal position to develop new technology. (For an illustration of this final point you are referred to the INMOS case in Chapter 5.)

Traditionally the public sector has always faced a number of serious problems arising from the tensions between public ownership, political control and day-to-day management. These tensions may be viewed in terms of goals and objectives, finance and control.

Despite the statutory responsibilities of nationalized industries, the goals of public-sector organizations have often been ill-defined and conflicting. For example, there was never a clear policy coordinating the activities of the coal, gas and electricity industries, when all three were under public ownership. Moreover, many public-sector operations have found conflict between the provision of a service and the necessity to break even, the railways being a good illustration. Such confusion over the goals led Sir Peter Parker to comment on his time as Head of British Rail,

> I'd never before been in a job where no-one could tell me what winning means.
>
> (quoted in Foy, 1983, p. 68)

The superordinate goal of the public sector to operate in the public interest is itself open to question. Who defines the public interest and is it possible to satisfy all elements of the public at the same time? The National Coal Board, British Steel and British Rail have suffered possibly the greatest losses of any public-sector industry, but would the public be best served by making reductions in the services they provide? In the 1990s the government clearly thought just that, with a radical pruning of the coal industry and the wholesale closure of collieries.

Financially the public sector operates under considerable constraints. Pricing policies are often dictated by government in attempts to tackle inflation, as under an incomes policy, or to direct consumption, as in the case of energy use. Public-sector enterprises often find investment difficult; they are often prevented from borrowing from the government to hold down the public-sector borrowing requirement (PSBR), and the sources of external funding are severely restricted. As we have seen, many public-sector enterprises are required only to break even, yet there remains a strong belief among senior management that the greater the profit, then the greater the freedom to operate free of government interference. Variations in profit margins have certainly led to inconsistencies in the treatment of public-sector concerns by successive governments, the relatively prosperous gas-supply industry enjoying considerably more policy-making freedom than the coal industry.

Excessive intervention has been a frequent complaint among public-sector managers. The very structure of the public sector demands answerability to different groups within government itself, to politicians, civil servants, appointed governing bodies, and to various consumer groups, all of whom may have differing expectations and impose conflicting demands upon management. The whole issue is invariably complicated by the organizational politics that develop in the relationship between the heads of public-sector organizations and their respective government masters.

The response to these problems by the Conservative Government since 1979 has been to embark upon a policy of privatization, deregulation and the introduction of a commercial approach in the public sector that remains. It is to these issues we now turn.

## Privatization

The privatization policy vigorously pursued by the Conservative Government has its roots, as we have indicated, in an ideological commitment to the free market, and a belief in the inherent inefficiency of the public sector. This has not only resulted in the selling of entire industries, but in the privatization of certain services within the public sector, such as the laundry in hospitals and rubbish collection in some local authorities. Could such a policy liberate management from excessive constraints on their freedom to manage as illustrated above?

We examine the case by looking at the development of the policy and its underlying rationale, before attempting some kind of evaluation.

In the first four years of the Government's reign following the 1979 election, no clear policy emerged beyond a support for the deregulation of certain services, such as public-transport bus provision and the sale of council houses to sitting tenants at favourable prices. The period 1983–9 was one of major activity with a mixed approach including share flotations, either in whole or part, and the selling of public companies either to their management or to the private sector. During this period such concerns as British Aerospace, Cable and Wireless, British Telecommunications, British Gas, British Airways, the British Airports Authority and British Petroleum either passed wholly or partly from public to private ownership. These were followed in the 1990s by the Electricity Boards, the Electricity Generating Industry and the Water Boards. The UK Government became a leading consultant in the process and its advice was eagerly sought by the French, Australian and Canadian governments embarking on similar policies.

The Government's opposition to the public sector and its belief in the private sector focuses on issues of efficiency and effectiveness, as well as control. Heald (1985) sensed that the pro-privatization lobby viewed the public-sector organization as inherently flawed, which no amount of attention paid to efficiency and control can cure. According to Heald, the privatization enthusiast's case rests upon two major assumptions. First, public-sector organizations are seen as less effective instruments of public policy than those of the private sector and second, the political objectives of public ownership are seen as less valid than the market criteria of private enterprise. The public sector was seen by the New Right Tories as group of organizations with confused goals and inefficient operations dogged by industrial-relations problems. The service they provided was considered poor, leaving its customers dissatisfied and creating a burden for the taxpayer.

The alternative, privatization, offered a number of advantages to different groups. It was envisaged that competition would be stimulated with an accompanying increase in efficiency and effectiveness. For the general public it was an opportunity to widen share ownership and to benefit from an improved service with a greater responsiveness to customer needs. For the newly privatized organizations there would be greatly increased opportunity for raising revenue which could be re-invested in the operation. It was assumed this would stimulate innovation to the benefit of all. For the government, public spending would be reduced and the sales would raise much needed revenue. Furthermore the policy was seen by some Conservatives as a further erosion of the power of trade unions and an ideological victory over the Labour Party opposition.

It is clear that share ownership has been broadened and the over-subscription of some issues indicates public support and some firms, notably British Aerospace and the National Freight Corporation, showed a marked increase in profits. Critics argue that the privatization of vast concerns such as British Telecommunications and British Gas seem not to have influenced the marketplace at all, but merely changed the ownership status of a monopoly. Further criticisms have been levelled against the pricing policies of newly privatized companies, the inadequate provision for regulating large monopolies and the short-term strategy of 'selling off the family silver'. More cynical critics have pointed to job losses and the large pay awards to those former heads of public corporations.

Almost certainly it is too early to assess fully the impact of such measures and there is considerable difficulty in disentangling the ideological, political and economic aspects of the argument. Apart from the social issues at stake there is at the moment mixed evidence to suggest that the private sector is any more or less efficient or effective than the public sector.

## Size

The influence of size as an organizational variable interacts across all levels of our Business in Context model. Many of the issues relating to size are dealt with elsewhere in this book and in this section we simply present a summary of those issues. We do however develop the concept further by examining the issues relating to small businesses.

We have already seen earlier in this chapter how size is an important determinant of structure. Hickson *et al.* (1969) noted that with increasing size the technological imperative gives way to the size imperative. Increasing formalization and bureaucratization are inevitable consequences of the growing firm, and the organization structure and management procedures are shaped by the need to coordinate and control large numbers of people. In our earlier discussion we saw how the growth of firms, especially through diversification, was an important element in companies such as General Motors adopting a divisional structure.

With size comes the development of specialist activities. In Chapter 8 we see how the development of personnel management as a specialist function is closely related to the increasing size of organizations. The employment of large numbers of people invariably calls for specialist expertise in the areas of recruitment, training, job evaluation, payment systems and industrial relations. In Chapter 5 we see a relationship between size and the R&D function. In this case it is not simply a matter of the numbers employed, but also a function of the need to maintain a powerful market position through investment in both product and process development and, of course, the ability to attract that investment.

Size is also related to dominance in the marketplace, as illustrated by the brewing industry in Britain. The industry is dominated by a handful of very large firms who maintain their market position not just by their ability to invest in product and process development, but also by the amount they are able to spend on nationwide advertising campaigns. Their position is further strengthened by their strategy of acquiring smaller independent breweries who find themselves unable to compete. The growth of lager sales at the expense of the traditional bitter beers has attracted the attention of the international brewing industry who are investing heavily in the British market. A similar pattern can be found in the record and music industry. By 1993, the industry was dominated by four companies controlling over 70% of the market. These were Warner, Thorn EMI, Sony and PolyGram. In almost every case they had grown by acquisition. A key element in concentration in the music industry has been the growth of sales in compact discs. Not only do these require considerable investment in technology for their manufacture, favouring the big firm, but also the public demand for reissues of old vinyl records in CD format has led to the larger firms buying up smaller independent producers to acquire their catalogues.

The big four record and CD producers dominate the sector, not just in terms of market share. There is a clear correlation in this industry between size and profitability. The biggest companies announce the biggest profit margins. There is a view that, in some industries, as with the illustration of the CD market, size is important. There is a considerable fear that the decline of the UK manufacturing industry in the 1980s has resulted in a lack of critical mass that is unable to compete in world terms. We have already discussed this issue in Chapter 2.

The ability of the large firm to dominate the marketplace is only part of its relationship with its environment. The size of a firm may be an important buffer in dealing with the demands imposed by its environment. We saw in Chapter 2 how the multinational corporation is able to dominate its environment, including influencing and in some cases overriding the policies of nation states. Size has also been a factor in attracting government support, not only in terms of R&D investment; the numbers employed by such firms as British Leyland have necessitated government rescue attempts during financial crises for political and social reasons as much as for economic ones. In the 1970s in particular, size was often a vital protection against enforced closure.

Size, structure and market position are themselves important variables in the determination of organization culture, which we deal with in the next section. At the micro-level there has been a great deal written about the impact of organizational size on the individual by focusing on the concepts of bureaucracy and alienation. Large organizations can undoubtedly present behavioural problems in terms of both management control and individual motivation. Such problems have been tackled by a range of devices including the creation of autonomous work groups in an attempt to break up the organization into more easily managed units. Despite such behavioural problems it should not be forgotten that, at the management level at least, many employees actively seek out large firms for the career opportunities they offer.

While there is considerable evidence supporting the dominant position of the large firm, the problem of control in particular questions whether large firms actually make the best use of their resources. The relationship between size and performance has been challenged by the small firms' lobby, elevated from a 'small is beautiful' campaign in the early 1970s to a near-political crusade for the future of Western capitalism in the 1980s. We now deal with the issues and arguments surrounding small firms.

## Small businesses

The small firm has played a key role in the development of the business enterprise, particularly in the nineteenth century when economic growth owed much to the activities of individual entrepreneurs. The role of the small firm was overtaken by the development of mass production, mass markets, and above all the creation of the joint stock company which created investment and effectively removed a major constraint to the growth of businesses. Throughout this century the focus has been on the increasing size of businesses and the market domination by big business and the multinationals in particular.

The watershed came in 1971 with the publication of the Report of the Committee of Inquiry on Small Firms, generally referred to as the Bolton Report, after the Committee's chairman. The Committee's investigation was born out of a concern that the small firms' sector was being neglected, but also out of a disillusionment and fear of the economic and social consequences of domination by big business. The conclusion of Bolton and his colleagues was that the small firms' sector in Britain was in decline, both in terms of it size and its contribution to the nation's economy and that the decline was more marked in the United Kingdom than in its major economic rivals. The report concluded that despite the decline the small firm sector 'remains one of substantial importance to the United Kingdom economy' and that 'the contribution of small businessmen to the vitality of society is inestimable' (Bolton, 1971, p. 342).

The Report's importance lay not just in its conclusions, but as the first serious and subsequently influential attempt to define the small firm and in its stimulus to later research, much of which takes Bolton as its base point. The stimulus of the 1970s became the academic growth area of the 1980s, with many business schools setting up special small firms' units, both for the purposes of academic research and to provide support for the regeneration of the small firms' sector. The stimulus was fuelled in the 1980s by a government increasingly determined to publicize the small business as the key element in the nation's economic revival. A report published in 1983 by a group of conservative MPs and researchers stated,

> A high small firms ratio is consistent with high levels of growth and output. The malaise of our small business sector is a symptom and a cause of our comparative decline as an industrial nation.
>
> (Bright *et al.*, 1983, p. 15)

Such statements were reinforced by a host of measures aimed at supporting the small businessman including special loans for business start-ups and special extension of welfare benefits to stimulate self-employment. In addition changes were made in the stock market through the creation of the Unlisted Securities Market whereby small firms could raise investment capital. The entrepreneur became the hero figure for the 1980s and people such as Clive Sinclair and Eddy Shah became household names. The rationale for government support was more than a belief in the economic importance of the small firm. At a time of high unemployment the small business start-up offered a practical, and to some, a highly attractive solution. Moreover it was a solution that was ideologically compatible with the Government's views on economic management, welfare, and self-help. It would be wrong of us to view the support of the small firm as the sole prerogative of the 'New Right' in British politics. Support for the small-firms sector has come from all sides of the political spectrum and it is one area where a Conservative government has met with agreement in many Labour controlled urban areas (with the notable exception of the now defunct Greater London Council, of which more later).

In this section we will look at the extent and nature of the small businesses in this country and assess their value, focusing particularly on the economic arguments for continued state support. Many of the points are illustrated in Case 3.5 which summarizes a study of several small firms in the Nottingham area.

## The extent of the small firms' sector

Any student of small businesses is immediately confronted with two problems. First there are serious difficulties in defining a small business. The Bolton Report's working definition included those firms employing fewer than 200 people. The Committee identified three primary characteristics of a small firm; these were having a small market share, being owner-managed and being independent of any larger concern. The Committee, while acknowledging the difficulties, recognized the need for a numerical definition of a small business, but also recognized that the criteria used for manufacturing (numbers employed) would be inappropriate for construction, where much smaller firms were the norm, and for retailing, where the totally different criterion of turnover was seen as more appropriate. Some kind

A survey was carried out of a hundred small firms in the Nottingham area. The firms were all wholly new businesses that had come into existence since 1977 and were independent, owner-managed and engaged predominantly in manufacturing. The main findings concerned the motivation behind setting up, the choice of product, the advice sought by small businessmen, and the labour costs involved.

The attraction of setting up in business was seen in terms of both pull and push factors, often operating together. The main push factors in order of significance were: redundancy; job insecurity and unemployment; disagreement at a previous firm; and the closure of a previous venture. The main pull factors in order of significance were; the desire for independence; the possession of specialist knowledge; the development of a product idea; and the incentive of financial reward.

The product chosen by the new company was invariably derived from the owner's previous experience, hobby or working skill. Seventy-eight per cent set up in businesses that were the same or similar to a previous employment and only 4% were classed as having innovated a new product or process. The advice available to small business concerns was seen to be not particularly helpful or attractive to the potential entrepreneur. Over 40% took no advice at all prior to starting up, and only 4% attended any type of training course. Labour costs were typified by the owners working long hours for little remuneration, especially in the first two years, and the relatively low wages accepted by employees. The labour-cost policy was related to a competitive pricing policy for market penetration.

The researchers conclude that such small firm growth in manufacturing is a response to economic recession and occurs in established industries with little contribution to product or process innovation and as such are unlikely to contribute towards economic recovery and growth. Moreover the pricing and wages policies of the new entrants is likely to have a depressing effect on the local economy by threatening the livelihood of established enterprises. As such, government policies aimed at increasing the number of small firms 'may simply be increasing the throughput of firms rather than the stock'.

(*Source*: Binks and Jennings, 1986)

**CASE 3.5**
*Small firms in the Nottingham area*

of quantitative definition is essential to the effective administration of government support and the law, small firms being exempt from certain aspects of employment law. The criteria used by Bolton are shown in Table 3.1.

Second, a difficulty arises in estimating the size of the small-business sector. Official statistics are incomplete as far as small firms are concerned. For example, the Census of Production excludes firms of less than 20 employees and has only limited data on those of less than 100 employees. In addition there is a marked preference on the part of some small businessmen to remain outside official statistics for the purposes of tax avoidance. It has been noted that this area of small business development, known as the 'Black Economy', has increased quite dramatically during the 1980s, with estimates of its contribution to the GDP as anything from 3% to almost 15% (Curran, 1986).

Because of these problems the estimates of the extent of small business activity and the contribution to the economy can vary considerably

**Table 3.1**    The Bolton Report definition of the small firm

| Industry | Statistical definition of small firms |
| --- | --- |
| Manufacturing | 200 employees or less |
| Retailing | Turnover £50 000 p.a. or less |
| Wholesale trades | Turnover £200 000 p.a. or less |
| Construction | 25 employees or less |
| Mining/Quarrying | 25 employees or less |
| Motor trades | Turnover £100 000 or less |
| Miscellaneous services | Turnover £50 000 or less |
| Road transport | 5 vehicles or less |
| Catering | All excluding multiples and brewery managed houses |

*Source*: *Bolton Report* 1.9, p. 3.

Nevertheless an attempt to summarize a review of the Bolton findings 15 years on, paints a much more optimistic picture than the original report. By 1986 it was estimated that 10% of the population worked for themselves and there was an increase in the number of small firms in all sectors, with the exception of retailing, where small businesses have declined. In addition, new types of small firm have emerged such as producer cooperatives and franchise operations (Curran, 1986). All these developments led Curran to conclude:

> the official data does indicate that, for a wide variety of small enterprise, there has been a remarkable increase since 1970 so that the overall total and proportion of small scale activity in the economy has increased.
> (Curran, 1986, p. 15)

Small businesses still predominate in the distribution, hotel and catering, repair and construction sectors, but between 1963 and 1980 there was a 25% increase in the numbers of small manufacturing concerns (Department of Employment, quoted in *New Society*, March 1986). The same source points to an increase in the numbers of ethnic minorities setting up small firms.

In addition to the increase in the number of firms, the survival chances of small firms appear to have improved. Although the problems of data accuracy are as acute here as elsewhere, estimates of the failure rate of business start-ups in the 1970s ranged from 50 to 75% within the first two years (Bannock, 1981). More recent and perhaps more reliable data suggest a figure of around 50% for the first two years, but that the chances of survival over ten years are 40–45% (Ganguly and Bannock, 1985). More significantly it has been found that the death rate of small firms actually slowed down during one of the worst periods of the recession in the early 1980s, although it is felt that business owners are intent on survival only in the absence of other opportunities (Stewart and Gallagher, 1985 have a fuller explanation). Other studies, however, remain more sceptical (Binks and Jennings, 1986, summarized in Case 3.5).

More recent international figures confirm the view that the small business start-up is still a risky venture. A survey of small firms across the world from 1980 to 1990 revealed that, on average, 50–60% of start-ups fail within the first five years. The same report highlighted that in some countries, notably Singapore, the failure rate was as high as 70% (El-Namaki, 1993).

However incomplete the database on small firms may be, there is considerable evidence that the United Kingdom has fewer self-employed than many other comparable industrial nations, and it has fewer small firms making far less of a contribution to the economy. The small-firms sector here is smaller than that in the United States and West Germany, and significantly smaller than that in Japan (Ganguly and Bannock, 1985).

## The value of small businesses

The value of small businesses may be viewed in terms of the benefits to the owners, their impact on economic growth, the number of jobs they provide, and their service to the consumer. We will deal with each of these aspects in turn.

In terms of the individual, the small firm offers a number of assumed advantages. A Gallup Poll finding in 1986 cited the desire to 'be your own boss' was the main motivation behind small business start-ups, and more significant than unemployment (*New Society*, March 1986). Certainly self-employment offers the individual far greater opportunities for control, and perhaps greater satisfaction through direct involvement, than working for someone else. The small business has for many been the pathway to real wealth, social mobility and perhaps political power in the local community. Some owners doubtless see their own business as a source of security for their family and as a kind of immortality via family succession. Against such values is the very real risk of failure, and serious financial loss for the owner and their family, and romantic tales of individualism, wealth and job satisfaction should be set alongside the long working week, the frustration and the stress that many small-business owners inevitably experience. The reality for many is that self-employment is less lucrative than working for someone else (*New Society*, March 1986), and those that are successful either become prime candidates for a takeover bid by a larger firm or fear a loss of control that inevitably comes with growth.

We have already noted that the Conservative Government of the 1980s saw the small firm as an essential ingredient of a healthy economy. The most obvious role for the small firm in this respect is to act as a 'seedbed' for future big business and in so doing secure the future of the economy. In addition, the small firm is seen as filling gaps in the marketplace by offering specialist products that would be uneconomic for the large firm to offer. More significantly the small firm is seen as a force for change by being inherently more flexible and innovative than the larger business. This image of the small firm was strengthened in the 1980s by the publicity given to the success and growth of certain small firms in the computer industry, although the majority of small businesses are decidedly 'low-' rather then 'high-' tech. In particular the small firm is seen as a useful vehicle in a recession; small firms are seen as price-takers and therefore offer no threat to inflation rates, and are able to plug the gaps left after larger firms have rationalized their operations. The rationalization of bus routes by the major companies, together with the government deregulation of bus services, paved the way for a number of smaller companies to enter the market, especially in rural areas and on the larger housing estates. These bus companies were able to operate routes that were uneconomic for the larger companies.

Many writers (for example, Scase and Goffee, 1980; Rainnie, 1985) are more sceptical of the economic contribution of the small-firms' sector, feeling that the small firm is exploited by big business and the main economic advantages of a small-business presence accrue to the larger company. Certainly large manufacturing concerns could not survive without the components supplied by a host of smaller companies, but this could be seen as a symbiotic rather than an exploitative relationship. However, we did see in our examination of Japan in the last chapter and the spread of Japanese-type subcontracting methods to this country that the purchasing power of the large firm can have a significant impact on the profit margins of smaller companies. Certainly there is evidence of larger firms taking over markets created by smaller companies when those markets prove successful, the activity of IBM in the personal computer market being a case in point.

There is an assumption that small firms are first to the marketplace because they are inherently more innovative. Supporters of this view cite inventions such as air-conditioning and cellophane that originated from individual entrepreneurs and that small businesses often emerge from ideas for new products or clever adaptations of existing products. Big business on the other hand is often accused of channelling R&D along predictable lines and being less cost-effective in its use of R&D expenditure. Apart from the difficulties of measuring such things, the evidence for these claims is very mixed (Rothwell and Zegveld, 1981 have a good summary of the research). More recent research suggests that even if small firms are inventive they often lack the development capital for successful innovation. (The distinction between invention and innovation is drawn more fully in Chapter 5.) Moreover there is evidence to suggest that a high proportion of small business start-ups do not involve new products but involve the owner in replicating his previous employment (Binks and Jennings, 1986). This trend becomes especially critical where buy-outs are concerned and may be a primary cause of small-business failure among buy-outs. In this case an ailing firm either sells out or divests part of its operation to a group of existing employees, usually management. Their experience and skills give them the optimism to continue operations in the same product market, perhaps ignoring the lack of demand or excessive competition operating in that same market, and they merely repeat the failure of the original firm.

There are obvious benefits of a thriving small-firms sector for the labour market. As we saw in Case 3.4, redundancy and unemployment are big push factors towards self-employment. Small firms have been started and operate successfully in growth areas of the economy such as computer software and consultancy and the service sector in general. Moreover, self-employment is a valuable source of work for those groups, such as ethnic minorities who are discriminated against in the labour market. In certain communities an overdependence on a few large firms for employment can have serious consequences when those firms close as the people of the Lancashire town of Skelmersdale found when Courtaulds decided to cease trading in the town. Under such circumstances a healthy small business presence may provide employment diversity and help counter the worst effects of mass redundancy. This view was taken by the government with the experience of mass redundancies at the nationalized British Steel Corporation in the Sheffield area. The company took advantage of tax advantages by providing venture capital to business start-ups in the area.

However, the small firm is hardly a great provider of employment. A study of the hi-tech industry, one of the flagships of the small-firms lobby, in the Cambridge area from 1971 to 1981 concluded that only 800 new jobs had been created during the entire period (Gould and Keeble, 1984). Rainnie (1985) points out that whatever new jobs are created, they can easily be overshadowed by job losses in a large organization and cites a report of 10 000 redundancies at Britain's largest computer firm, ICL, in 1984. Moreover we have already seen from the high proportion of start-up failures that small firms are a source of job losses too. Outside the arguments about the small firm as a source of employment, the Greater London Council was especially critical of the small firm as an employer citing exploitation through low wages, long hours and an absence of trade-union recognition as the main reason for their lack of support for small business development (GLC, 1983). This view of small firms was also taken by Scase and Goffee (1980) who saw their main contribution to employment as solving the problems as defined by employers. Obviously not all small firms exploit their workforce, and many employees prefer the informal working environment that the small firm can provide.

We have already seen in our example of the deregulation of the bus industry how the small firm can benefit the consumer by filling the gaps left by the larger company. There is also the argument that the smaller firm is also closer to its customers and can provide them with a more personalized, responsive and specialized service. There are certain highly specialized product markets, such as precision scientific instrumentation which tend to favour the smaller concern. Whether the smaller firm offers a 'better' service to the consumer is impossible to generalize or even judge. When buying expensive wine for keeping several years, a small specialist firm may be the most appropriate consumer choice, while a supermarket chain may offer the best value on less expensive purchases. The situation becomes particularly blurred when you consider that a number of larger firms of all types pay particular attention to customer sales and after-sales service. At a broader level a small firms' sector may be of considerable benefit to the consumer in challenging the power of monopolies.

## The small firm as a case for government support

We believe that the health of the economy requires the birth of new enterprises in substantial number and the growth of some to a position from which they are able to challenge and supplant the existing leaders of industry . . . We cannot assume that the ordinary working of market forces will necessarily preserve a small firm sector large enough to perform this function in the future.

(Bolton, 1971. 8.5, p. 85)

Bolton and his committee were clear that government support was necessary to secure the future of the small firm and hence the economy. In spite of its commitment to market forces the Conservative government of the 1980s revealed its support of the small business by a large number of different measures. In its annual reports on the small firms' sector the Government of the 1990s was still voicing its support and espousing many of the values of the small firm that we discussed in the last section. (The Small Firms in Britain Report, 1992 is a good illustration.) Despite this apparent attention, many critics still see a gap between government rhetoric and effective action.

One of the intentions in our analysis of small businesses was to look behind the current popular support for the small firms sector and attempt to challenge the view that the encouragement of small business development is a valid strategy for economic recovery and growth. It is indeed difficult to draw any firm conclusions at all, for despite the growth of research data and the space devoted to small businesses in the serious as well as the popular press, many difficulties remain.

Confusion still reigns over an agreed definition of what actually constitutes a small business and the evidence that we do possess is highly contradictory in its findings. The main danger is certainly one of politics and ideology, which are as much a part of the Conservative Government's support as the GLC's condemnation.

What we do find is that the small firm provides some jobs, offers some hope for the unemployed and meets the sub-contracting needs of big business. However there is very little evidence that a policy of support for the encouragement of small firms will either solve the problems of mass unemployment or result in substantial economic growth. Behind the rhetoric of politicians there is considerable criticism aimed at those very measures designed to support the small firm. The sheer number and complexity of such measures and the different sources of advice have been shown to be as confusing as they are helpful. Moreover the cost of government measures such as the Loans

Guarantee Scheme has proven much too expensive for many small firms. Outside the government schemes the banks appear keen to provide services for the small firm, but even here the picture must be seen in perspective. German banks on average lend twice as much for longer periods and at lower interest rates than their British counterparts (Bannock, 1981).

Bannock's vision of a healthy economic future involves small and large businesses in a kind of optimal balance, with small firms as the 'motivators of growth' and large firms as the 'consolidators and accelerators'. In this way the small firm may play a significant role in the recovery from recession. Others are less optimistic.

> the fashionable concern with the contribution of small enterprise to economic restructuring should not be allowed to obscure the dominating presence of the large enterprise.
>
> (Curran, 1986, p. 46)

Concern for the small firm may well be, like the interest in Japanese management, a fashion born out of recession. Certainly small business development is important in the future of any economy, but current political interest owes as much to ideology as it does to sound economic argument. For our purposes the case of the small firm is again an excellent illustration of the interplay between the various elements of our business in context model.

---

In general terms the culture of an organization refers to those factors which enable us to distinguish one organization from another and are the product of its history, management, operating environment, technology, goals and so on. More recently the notion of organizational culture has been used in a more positive way and a set of principles have been developed which mark out the culture of a successful company from that of an unsuccessful one. As with all such universal principles, such claims have aroused considerable debate.

**KEY CONCEPT 3.5**
*Organizational culture*

---

## Organizational culture

We have already encountered the concept of culture in our treatment of the environmental context of business in Chapter 2. Our emphasis there was on broad cultural distinctions between different groups of people, particularly in the comparisons of businesses in different countries. In this section we focus upon culture in a more localized setting, that of the organization itself. The goals, structure, patterns of ownership and size of an organization both reflect and are reflected in its culture. Other influences on the culture of an organization include its history and all those aspects we have identified as belonging to the environmental level of our Business in Context model. The importance of the organizational culture is that it sets the scene for the determination of strategy and hence the operational aspects of organizational life. The concept assumes therefore a central position in our model of business.

Interest in the workings of an organizational culture were heightened in the USA during the 1970s as American companies searching for a solution to the problems of the economic recession looked to the role models of Japanese firms and the more successful firms within their own country. In turn, academic research in business shifted its focus away from individual management techniques to examining the business as a complete entity and viewing the way people responded to their own organization. A more subjective view of organizations began to emerge. Some would differentiate between the term organizational culture and that of corporate culture, the latter sometimes being associated with specific management initiatives to achieve corporate ends. Increasingly, however, the two terms are used interchangeably, and this text is no exception.

In this section we will examine the precise nature of organizational or corporate culture, attempt a classification of different types, examine its relationship to the concept of the 'excellent company', and assess its value as a business tool. We will illustrate these points by reference to Hewlett-Packard, the American computer and electronic instrument firm, presented as Case 3.6.

---

**CASE 3.6**
*Hewlett-Packard*

Hewlett-Packard is an American multinational operating in most major countries of the world. It was founded in the late 1930s in Palo Alto, California by Bill Hewlett and Dave Packard, both of whom still have considerable influence on company philosophy. The firm operates in four main divisions each representing different product groupings. The divisions are: the Computer Systems Group, the Measurement Systems Group, the Medical Products group and the Analytical Instrumentation group.

The central element in all their activities is the 'HP Way', a set of beliefs, objectives and guiding principles, and described by Bill Hewlett as follows.

> the policies and actions that flow from the belief that men and women want to do a good job, a creative job, and that if they are provided with the proper environment they will do so. It is the tradition of treating every individual with respect and recognising personal achievements ... You can't describe it in numbers or statistics. In the last analysis it is a spirit, a point of view. There is a feeling that everyone is part of a team and that team is HP. As I said at the beginning it is an idea that is based on the individual. It exists because people have seen that it works, and they believe that this feeling makes HP what it is.
>
> (quoted in Peters and Waterman, 1982, p. 244)

The HP Way is probably best illustrated from a number of words and concepts extracted from Hewlett-Packard's own publications. These are love of the product, love of the customer, innovation, quality, open communication, commitment to people, trust, confidence, informality, teamwork, sharing, openness, autonomy, responsibility.

It is not just the communication of such sentiments that appears to be important in Hewlett-Packard but that such sentiments appear to be shared by a majority of employees and felt with a certain intensity.

The sentiments are reinforced by a series of processes and procedures which we identify below.

- Communication is the key underlying theme behind all activities in Hewlett-Packard and is an important ingredient of the company's attitude towards innovation and quality. Informal communication is encouraged between all employees of different levels and functions. The physical lay out of the offices and work stations has been deliberately created to encourage *ad hoc* meetings and brainstorming. The use of first names is almost obligatory and is the norm even in the West German operations, where employees are used to a much greater degree of formality in personal relationships. Management assists the informal processes by engaging in what Hewlett-Packard term MBWA ('management by wandering around'). At a more formal level there are frequent announcements to the workforce on such matters as company performance and all employees are given a written statement of the company goals, stressing as they do the contribution which individuals can make. The communication policy is assisted by the company's commitment to decentralization.

  An important aspect of communication in Hewlett Packard is the various stories and myths that are a continual feature of management training, retirement parties, company speeches and in-house journals. These stories generally tell of key moments in the company's history, or recount the exploits of the corporate heroes, usually Bill Hewlett and Dave Packard. These stories serve an important purpose of stressing a collective identity and underlining the goals of the founders.
- Quality, according to Peters and Waterman, is pursued with zealotry. The company certainly sees its prime objective as a commitment to the design, manufacture and marketing of high-quality goods. Commitment to quality is viewed as ongoing with continual product improvement as a major goal. All employees are involved in the definifion and monitoring of quality, a process reinforced by procedures such as MBWA and ceremonies to recognize, reward and publicize good work.
- Innovation, like quality, is regarded as the responsibility of all employees. Following the espousal to 'stick to the knitting' there is a clear commitment to products related to electrical engineering and the company's existing product portfolio. Openness is encouraged and prototypes are often left for other employees to test and criticize. Employees are free to take company equipment home with them. In relations with their customers the company is guided by yet another principle and mnemonic, that of LACE ('laboratory awareness of customer environment'). A central strategy in R&D is the design of products to customer specifications and the LACE programme gives customers the opportunity to make presentations to the company. Such procedures stress the strong emphasis on customer service.
- Personnel policies are carefully designed to reinforce the HP Way as well as ensuring that it works. Most HP employees have no requirement for clocking-on and many operate on flexible working hours. All employees attend a detailed induction programme with communication of the HP Way as a key ingredient. In terms of selection care is taken to select only those who meet the criteria of being high calibre and possessing flair, adaptability and openness. Most recruits are young. As we have seen, considerable attention is paid to the environment and the general well-being of employees is a major consideration.
- There is a somewhat traditional and conservative approach to finance and accounting. There is an emphasis on careful management of assets, self-financing investment, and minimal long-term borrowing

The overall impression is often that Hewlett-Packard is too good to be true.

We tried to remain sober, not to become fans. But it proved impossible.
(Peters and Waterman, 1982, p. 246)

Certainly on most measures of performance and employee satisfaction, Hewlett-Packard emerges as a highly successful company. A measure of the employees' commitment occurred in 1970 when in the middle of a recession and bad time for the company financially, a 10% pay cut was agreed rather than lay people off.

(*Sources*: Peters and Waterman, 1982; Beer *et al.*, 1985; Needle, 1984)

## The nature of organizational or corporate culture

Judging by the growing literature on the subject, corporate culture appears to have replaced Japanese management at the top of the management best-seller lists. If we add specific references on Total Quality Management (TQM), a technique which espouses a culture change approach to quality improvement, then we might assume that modern management is preoccupied with the notion of corporate culture.

Deal and Kennedy (1982) refer to corporate culture as the 'way we do things around here'. However, the concept appears to be used in two different ways as follows.

● First, it is used as a basic concept to understand social phenomena in organizations and to explain differences between companies, particularly those operating in the same product market. Pettigrew describes corporate culture as 'an amalgam of beliefs, ideology, language, ritual and myth' (Pettigrew, 1979, p. 572), which enables people to function in a given setting. That amalgam differs from one firm to the next as a result of the different forces operating upon them. Such forces have been listed by Handy (1993) as history and ownership, size, technology, goals and objectives, environment and people. The Business in Context model would be another appropriate model to analyse differences between companies.
● Second, it is used as a device by management to achieve certain strategic ends that could incorporate improved performance or the control of labour, or both. Management in several firms look to culture change, not only as a mechanism for greater profitability, but also as a mechanism for greater cooperation between management and worker and an end to industrial-relations conflict.

The main difference between the two treatments is the more specific context of the latter approach. This approach is typified by the work of such as Deal and Kennedy (1982) where organizational culture has the function of establishing values and creating a cohesive unit. There is a clear link between Deal and Kennedy's analysis and the notion of the 'excellent company' attributed to Peters and Waterman (1982). In this way the concept of organizational culture becomes a much more normative and prescriptive tool that can create and fashion increased productivity, profitability and compliance. Writers like Peters and Waterman and Ouchi believe they have discovered those elements of culture which contribute towards success in business which management can then develop in their own organizations.

In short, organizational culture is both a set of distinguishing features that mark off one organization from another, and more popularly used has become a set of universal principles guiding best practice. The concept has both descriptive and normative elements. A definition which can embrace both perspectives is offered by Gordan and Ditomaso,

> A pattern of shared and stable beliefs and values that are developed within a company across time.
>
> (Gordan and Ditomaso, 1992, p. 784)

## Types of corporate culture

A well-known classification of corporate culture has been offered by Handy (1993). A similar model has been developed by Trompenaars (1993), who feels that different types of corporate culture fit more easily with some types of national culture than others. We will use Handy's classification as a base and offer additional comments from Trompenaars as appropriate. The Handy approach would not be out of place in a discussion of organization structure. He identifies four types of culture as follows.

**Power culture**   Handy uses the analogy of a spider's web to depict a power culture. It is typified by an absence of bureaucracy and control is exercised from a central power base through key individuals. Such cultures are found in small entrepreneurial firms and certain smaller financial institutions. Power cultures are threatened by the increasing size of the firm and the death or departure of the central figure. Trompenaars refers to the power culture as the 'Family', with the head as a father figure achieving moral compliance from 'family' members. Such cultures are associated by Trompenaars with late industrialized nations such as Japan, Italy and Singapore. Firms in such countries are more comfortable with power cultures and find project teams and matrix management difficult, since, in such structures, employees must often divide their loyalty.

**Role culture**   Handy sees this as a Greek temple representative of a classic bureaucracy that acquires its strength through functions, specialities, rules and procedures. It is found in many organizations, more especially when economies of scale are important. A major drawback is its slowness in responding to change. Trompenaarrs's role culture is depicted by the 'Eiffel Tower'. It operates in most national cultures, but with different degrees of formality.

**Task culture**   Here the analogy used is that of a net, and task cultures are typified by matrix organizations. The focus is on getting the job done and such cultures are appropriate when flexibility and responsive-

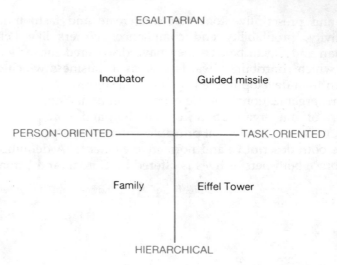

*Figure 3.6*  A typology of corporate culture. *Source*: Trompenaars (1993).

ness to market changes are needed. Task cultures are found in advertising agencies, research groups, and Grand Prix racing teams. The difficulties with task cultures are the same as those with matrix structures, discussed earlier in this chapter. Trompenaars refers to this culture as a 'Guided Missile'. He and his associates have devised a questionnaire to determine the kind of culture employees would favour. Most people, when given such a choice, opt for the 'Guided Missile', although the majority claim to be working in a role culture.

**Person culture**  Such cultures, viewed by Handy as clusters, focus on individuals. The main purpose of the organization is to satisfy the needs of individuals and the organization itself is secondary to individual self-fulfilment. A group medical practice or a barrister's chambers are examples of a person culture. Such a culture is attractive to many people who would like to operate as freeholders within the security of an organization. This is not always possible and conflict often arises when individuals attempt to operate according to a person culture within an organization that is essentially a role culture. A good illustration of this would be that of an academic focusing on goals of personal research within a university, increasingly operating as a classic role culture. Trompenaars refers to such cultures as 'Incubators'.

In Figure 3.6 we may view Trompenaars model of corporate culture. The model shows the importance of two sets of variables. The first relates to whether the culture is person- or task-oriented, and the second focuses on the extent to which the culture is hierarchical or egalitarian.

We noted in our introduction to this section that organization culture could be viewed descriptively or normatively. The models of Handy and Trompenaars are attempts to describe and analyse different cultural types. Such models are, however, simplistic and highly generalized.

Given the range and possible combination of different variables, as we have seen in the Business in Context model, it is very likely that far more than four cultural types can be identified. There is, however, a popular belief that there is an ideal type of culture that holds the key to improved corporate performance. It is to this notion we now turn.

## The concept of strong cultures

Strong cultures are associated with those organizations where the guiding values of top management are clear and consistent and are widely shared by the employees. Such cultures are typified by a set of strong values passed down by senior management. The values are strengthened by rituals which emphasize and reward appropriate behaviour and a cultural network, comprising a system of communication to spread the values and create corporate heroes. A feature of strong cultures is their association with hero figures, who exemplify the key values. Ray Kroc of McDonald's, Bill Hewlett and Dave Packard of Hewlett-Packard, and Anita Roddick of the Body Shop are examples of such corporate heroes.

The processes of creating such a 'positive' organizational culture would appear to operate as follows. The senior management of a company set goals and issue guidelines which promote strongly held shared values; there is normally an emphasis upon enthusiasm, diligence, loyalty and service to the customer. To ensure that such guidelines are passed on to all employees there is usually a high investment in the procedures of communication and integration. A number of techniques are commonly used to create and maintain a specific corporate culture. Some firms pay particular attention to the physical environment; the layout in Hewlett-Packard is designed to encourage communication and they try to maintain the same layout in all their establishments throughout the world; in IBM layout is equally important as is the use of a corporate colour, blue. The goals of the company are invariably written, explicit, communicated to all employees and tend to stress the contribution that employees can make to the firm. Heroes and myths play an important role in communicating the core values as illustrated by the 'Bill and Dave stories' in Case 3.6. The same role is ascribed to important rituals such as presentations to successful employees and social gatherings; in companies such as IBM, employees are encouraged to participate in out-of-work activities, with non-participation being frowned upon.

The culture is also strengthened by more formal procedures such as training and induction and the design of the organization structure. There is usually a deliberate attempt to create clearly defined autonomous units to enhance group identity and loyalty, together with an emphasis upon informality and avoidance of bureaucratic controls. In recruitment and selection procedures a great deal of care is usually taken to select only those individuals who would fit in with the prevailing culture.

At its most influential the corporate culture is seen as having replaced organized religion and the family as the most important focus in a person's life (Ray, 1986). In a recent television documentary about the establishment of the Japanese firm Komatsu in Britain, one of its senior Japanese employees listed his priorities in order as the firm, the state, and finally his family. Not surprisingly the Japanese firm is often held as the prime example of a strong corporate culture.

Those who subscribe to this view of organizations claim that firms which have such strong cultures are more successful than those that do not. This was the notion behind Peters and Waterman's study of 'Excellent Companies' and has been the subject of recent research. Unfortunately, much of the evidence remains inconclusive. For example, a study by Gordan and Ditomaso (1992) of 11 insurance companies over a six-year period found some correlation between the strength of a widely shared culture and short-term financial performance. The same study also pointed to the significant problems inherent in proving connections given the large number of variables involved. Nevertheless there is a belief that the ideas constitute a new management theory and a return to the universal principles approach which typified the earlier but essentially different theories of people such as Fayol and Taylor. The type of firms which embody such principles better than most are the so-called 'excellent companies'.

## The notion of the excellent company

Peters and Waterman (1982) may not be the only writers to attempt to identify the features of the excellent company (Ouchi attempted much the same a year earlier), but their attempt proved to be the most successful by far with their book *In Search of Excellence* selling several million copies since its publication in 1982 and arguably ranks alongside Taylor's *Scientific Management* as one of the most influential management texts of all time. Peters and Waterman carried out an investigation of 62 top performing American companies. Six measures of long-term productivity were devised and only those firms which ranked in the top 20 of their industry on four out of the six criteria were included in their in-depth study. Their final sample numbered 43 firms including IBM, Hewlett-Packard, Boeing, Digital, Caterpillar, Eastman Kodak, Walt Disney, and 3M. The sample was not intended to be representative of all types of firm and banks are notable by their exclusion.

In all eight attributes of excellence were identified. These were, using Peters and Waterman's own terminology, as follows:

- 'bias for action', being typified by clear objectives and a marked absence of committee procedures;
- 'closeness to the customer', typified by processes and procedures aimed at identifying and serving the customers' needs;
- 'autonomy and entrepreneurship', which are best achieved through the creation of small cohesive teams;
- 'productivity through people', with workforce involvement at all times;
- 'hands on; value driven', involving the fostering of a strong cor-

porate culture by top management who are seen to be in touch with all employees;

- **'stick to the knitting'**, which involves limiting activities to what the firm does best and avoiding diversification into unknown territory;
- **'simple form, lean staff'**, avoiding complex hierarchies and large administration sections;
- **'simultaneous loose-tight properties'**, which means that organization structure should display a combination of strong central direction with work-group autonomy.

Throughout their work Peters and Waterman stressed the importance of excellent companies socializing and integrating individuals into a clearly defined corporate culture. The firm becomes much more than a place of work,

> by offering meaning as well as money, the excellent companies give their employees a mission as well as a sense of feeling great.
>
> (Peters and Waterman, 1982, p. 323)

## How useful is organizational culture as a concept?

We need to distinguish between organizational culture as a means of differentiating between companies and organizational culture as a set of principles which shape 'excellent' companies.

The development of organizational culture as an analytical device leaves much to be desired. There are problems of defining the elements which comprise organizational culture, and, in a review of the literature, Hofstede (1986) is disappointed by the apparent lack of empirical research. Until we develop some systematic measures of organizational concept then its utility as an analytical tool must be limited. Even then, culture is much more complex than many credit. It is dynamic, in that the behaviour and expressed feelings of staff can modify a culture over time. Many organizations are also multicultural. Furthermore it is very difficult to observe and measure something that is implicit, informal and very often invisible. Given such problems it is difficult to prove consistent links between culture and performance, let alone understand how such a relationship operates.

The major controversy concerns the concept as a set of principles to guide 'good' management practice. Advocates argue that they have analysed successful companies and found links between organizational culture and performance. There are a number of difficulties with this approach which we identify below.

- Several writers feel that the importance of culture has been overstated. Carroll (1983) considers that the important effects of technology, market dominance, the influence of the state and the control of critical raw materials have all been ignored in the analysis. Dawson (1986) takes this a stage further. She feels that what people such as Peters and Waterman have uncovered is not a set of universal principles of management, but strategies that only work in certain types of company. She writes,

> Their 'slim consensual organizations' of the future are probably applicable to firms employing professionals and technicians from the primary labour market in the development and operation of new technology or highly fashionable products and processes. They may however be less successful in other technological, product and labour market conditions.
>
> (Dawon, 1986, p. 137)

- It is interesting to speculate whether the kind of processes and procedures illustrated in our Hewlett-Packard case would have any relevance for an inner-city local authority or the health service, or assist management in older industries such as British Steel. While strong cultures may be feasible in organizations such as hospitals or universities where shared goals are common, problems can and do arise when such institutions attempt to modify those goals. In addition, there are undoubted limitations of imposing or changing a culture in certain types of work, as with boring or unglamorous jobs, and with certain types of worker, such as contract staff or part-timers.

- Anthony (1990) feels that there is a misguided assumption that organizational cultures are relatively easy to change. Such assumptions are often held by managers, who see culture change as the panacea for all the ills facing their companies. Since cultures are built upon deep-rooted values developed over time, it is not surprising that exhortations to change the culture never progress beyond the exhortation stage. Given this difficulty it is hardly surprising that the focus is often upon behaviour change, rather than value change. In a study of culture change in British Airways there was evidence that cabin crew had changed their behaviour, but it was equally clear that they have not taken on board changed values and attitudes (Höpfl *et al.*, 1992). In such circumstances staff are acting roles.

- The focus of research has been on 'excellent' companies. Child (1984a) speculates what would happen if the very same attributes were found in less than excellent companies. There has been little or no comparison with the cultural characteristics of poor performers. In fact, immediately following Peters and Waterman's study, three of their excellent companies, including Texas Instruments and National Semiconductors, suffered serious setbacks in their performance and there was evidence of a reversion to more bureaucratic types of control.

- The above paragraphs may be summed up by the difficulty of proving a relationship between the features of excellence and company performance. More significantly, we could argue that the features displayed by these excellent companies are a direct result rather than a cause of company performance. It is much easier to gain employee consensus and focus on customer needs when profits are healthy.

- Situations might be envisaged where a strong commitment to a corporate culture could lead to resistance to change, when major reorganization is called for in response to market, technological or other changes. If all employees are selected in the same image, where will the organizations find the 'deviants' to initiate change? This view would doubtless be challenged by representatives of such as Hewlett-Packard who would point to the emphasis placed in their organization on innovation. Moreover, given the commitment to corporate values in such 'value-driven' firms, change could well be initiated through a series of top management exhortations.

- The type of processes and procedures used by 'excellent' companies do have certain similarities with techniques of conditioning and even brainwashing and may be morally unacceptable to some. Nevertheless, while there are personality types who would find working for such companies difficult, there are countless others who enjoy their association with them.

- There may also be problems for managers. They may become so obsessed with the attempt to impose their values on the employees, that they become isolated and fail to know what is really happening. In addition, middle management can feel threatened in that their roles for directing and controlling are usurped by centralized control.

Despite such criticisms the development of an organization culture to enhance performance can be appealing to management and workforce alike. For management it is an important source of control through the moral involvement of the workforce (Ray, 1986). In this respect there is a similarity with the techniques associated with the 'human relations' and 'organizational development' schools of management thinking. Moreover the popularity of *In Search of Excellence* is in part testimony to the optimism it portrays and its morale-boosting effects on managers. As far as employees are concerned, they are given clear guidelines about the kind of behaviour expected of them, which has been estimated as saving up to two hours a day (Deal and Kennedy, 1982). In addition there is no doubt that many employees enjoy working in the deliberately created integrated atmospheres of the IBMs and the Hewlett-Packards, and successful, 'excellent' companies do tend to pay well!

## Summary

In this chapter we focused our attention on the organizational elements of business which we identified as goals, structure, ownership, size and organizational culture. As befits our model, all elements interact not just with each other but with aspects of the environment, business strategy and operations.

We view goals as the products of a highly interactive and dynamic process such that changing goals may well be a prerequisite for business survival. Goals give a sense of direction to a firm's activities and may be presented in a hierarchy involving a mission, objectives and strategies. The formulation of goals is closely related to the way power relations are worked out in organizations, and often involve highly political processes of influence, conflict and compromise between different interest groups. A number of goals may operate at any one time. These may conflict, but in general the goals of a business follow closely those of the dominant coalition.

The factors which influence **structure** are identified as technology, size, environmental changes, strategy, culture and the behaviour of interest groups. We identify various models of organizational structure including, functional, divisional and matrix, but acknowledge that very few firms confirm to such ideal types. Many firms have mixed structures and new variations are emerging all the time with recent attention being given to flexible structures. The relationship between structure and performance is of obvious interest to businessmen, but as yet the evidence is inconclusive.

**Ownership** is important because of its potential impact on the way businesses are managed. We examine this relationship by focusing on the traditional debate of ownership versus control and the freedom of managers to make decisions in the face of the growing influence of institutional shareholders and the power of interlocking directorships. The dilemmas that can arise in the relationship between ownership and control are examined with reference to the public sector, and, in particular, the growing trend in many countries of the privatization of public companies.

We examine the influence of **size** on such factors as structure, market power, relationship with the state, and the impact on the individual. The main focus of this section is the small firm. The case for government support of the small firm is examined in light of the potential contribution of small businesses to the economy and society. We conclude that the current enthusiasm for small firms owes more to ideology than it does to economic analysis.

**Organizational culture** is viewed as the product of goals, structure, ownership and size, as well as company history, technology, its product-market environment and several other variables as well. The sum total of those influences distinguish organizations from one another. The main argument surrounding organizational culture is that a particular culture can be created to enhance performance and the debate has focused on the notion of 'excellent' companies. Despite the enthusiasm for 'excellence', the research is inconclusive and culture may be less important than technology or the product-market.

## Further reading

C. Handy, *Understanding Organizations*, 4th edn (Penguin, 1993) and S. Dawson, *Analyzing Organizations*, 2nd edn (Macmillan, 1992) are good sources for many of the issues discussed in this chapter. A good insight into the complexities of goal formation may be found in R. M. Cyert and J. G. March, *A Behavioural Theory of the Firm* (Prentice Hall, 1963). Discussions and illustrations of structural considerations are probably best found in J. Child, *Organizations: A Guide to Problems and*

*Practice* (Harper & Row, 1984), and those students seeking an historical perspective are advised to look at A. D. Chandler, *Strategy and Structure: Chapters in the History of American Capitalism* (MIT Press, 1962). Probably the best summary of the ownership and control debate is offered by J. Child, *The Business Enterprise in Modern Industrial Society* (Collier-Macmillan, 1969) and a good review of the key studies as well as the role of financial institutions can be found in J. Scott, *Corporations, Classes and Capitalism* (Hutchinson, 1979). A more recent review of financial institutions is offered by P. Howells and K. Bain, *Financial Markets and Institutions* (Longman, 1990). An interesting perspective on privatization is offered by T. Clarke and C. Pitelis (eds), *The Political Economy of Privatization* (Routledge, 1993). A good summary of the current research and debates about the role of the small firm is found in K. Keasey and R. Watson, 'Small Firm Management: Ownership, Finance and Performance' (Blackwell, 1993), and in J. Stanworth and C. Gray, *Bolton 20 Years On: The Small Firm in the 1990s* (Paul Chapman Publishing, 1991). Keasey and Watson's book focuses more on financial aspects. Although published more than a decade ago, a good account of the problems facing small firms can be found in R. Scase and R. Goffee, *The Real World of the Small Business Owner* (Croom Helm, 1980). No examination of organizational culture would be complete without a look at T. J. Peters and R. J. Waterman, *In Search of Excellence: Lessons from America's Best Run Companies* (Harper & Row, 1982) and a more academic treatment is offered by the *Journal of Management Studies*, May 1986 which devotes a whole edition to this topic. A more contemporary source, including some interesting cases is C. Hampden-Turner, *Corporate Culture Management: From Virtuous to Vicious Circles* (Economist Books-Hutchinson, 1990).

## Discussion

1 Critically analyse the goals and statements presented in Case 3.1? What function do they serve?
2 How are goals formed and what are the major difficulties encountered in goal formulation and implementation? What do events at London Zoo, Case 3.2, tell us about this process?
3 Identify the various strategic, organizational and environmental factors which led to structural changes in Dow Corning and IBM as illustrated by Cases 3.3 and 3.4. What problems will the new organization structures solve, and what new problems may emerge?
4 What purposes do the various structural types identified in this chapter serve? What are the major influencing factors which may cause management to favour one structural type over another? Is the flexible firm a myth or reality?
5 How significant is the separation of ownership and control to the way businesses operate?
6 Examine the advantages and the prime beneficiaries of privatization

in the UK since 1980. To what extent will privatization solve the problems of managing public-sector organizations?

7 Examine the rationale behind the Government support for the small-firms sector. To what extent are small firms economically relevant today?

8 What is the relationship between the type of corporate culture envisaged by Deal and Kennedy and by Peters and Waterman and company performance in terms of profitability and job satisfaction? Can the internal culture of an organization act as a buffer against environmental influences?

9 What are the advantages and disadvantages of the Hewlett Packard style as illustrated in Case 3.6? What threats could challenge the effectiveness of such a style?

10 Examine the relationship between organizational culture and the other organizational variables of the Business in Context model.

# Management strategy

## 4

Management strategy as a linking process between environmental and organizational variables is a fundamental aspect of our Business in Context model. We are able to observe the functional operation of R&D, production, marketing, human resource management and finance and accounting only through their relevant management strategies. In our introduction to this book we highlighted the cases of the shipping industry and News International, both representative of the exercise of strategic options in the face of external and internal opportunities and constraints in the two industries concerned.

Management strategy contains a number of interrelated elements. First, it involves a consideration of environmental changes which bring about new opportunities and pose new threats. Second, it is concerned with the assessment of the internal strengths and weaknesses of the institution and in particular its ability to respond to those opportunities and threats. Third, management strategy is the product of a decision-making process influenced by the values, preferences and power of interested parties. Finally, management strategy is concerned with generating options and evaluating them. Management strategy is therefore an all-embracing term dealing with goals and objectives, the firm's environment, its resources and structure, the scope and nature of its activities and ultimately the behaviour of its members.

In this chapter we deal with all these elements. We begin by examining the nature of strategy, through the way strategy is formed. We refer to this as the strategic process. We then look at the different contexts in which strategic decisions are taken, and go on to identify the various environmental and organizational aspects of management strategy. We end the chapter by examining a number of common strategic options, and a brief look at the criteria for strategic choice.

We prefer to use the term 'management strategy' since most strategies in organizations originate from the management group. The concept crops up in many guises and is sometimes referred to as 'business policy', 'corporate strategy', 'corporate planning' and so on. Although attempts have been made to formulate distinctions between such terms, the general interchangeability of their use indicates a similarity in approach.

## The strategic process

An examination of how strategy is formed gives us useful insights into the nature of strategy itself. We identify five different approaches, which we have termed, rational, flexible, creative, behavioural, incremental and a sixth which suggests that some managers operate without a conscious strategy. We deal with each in turn.

**The rational approach** Strategy formulation is often portrayed as a scientific and highly rational process, assisted by a range of techniques such as technological forecasting, portfolio analysis, environmental impact analysis and sensitivity analysis. The rational approach owes much to the development of contingency theory. In Chapter 1 we noted that the contingency approach stressed the importance of a strategic fit between the firm and its environment. Analyses are made of a firm's environment to assess likely opportunities and threats, and of its internal resource position to identify strengths and weaknesses.

This process is sometimes referred to as SWOT analysis, a mnemonic for strengths, weaknesses, opportunities and threats. An illustration of the kind of analysis that can be made is offered in Figure 4.1. The approach is based upon the assumption that information is readily available to the strategist and an accurate assessment can be made of its likely impact on the firm. As we shall see later, this is not always the case and the entire process is subject to behavioural influences. The so-called rational techniques illustrated above have been criticized as 'pseudo-science'. Nonetheless this is the basic approach used by many texts (e.g. Ansoff, 1968; Glueck and Jauch, 1984).

In the 1960s and 1970s the emergence of an increasingly complex and turbulent business environment called for modifications in the rational approach.

| OPPORTUNITIES | THREATS |
|---|---|
| Promotion to other divisions.<br>Increased revenue from success in cup competitions.<br>Sale of town-centre site and redevelopment on the outskirts.<br>Development of a membership squash club and fitness centre attached to the ground.<br>Use of ground for other functions, e.g., rock concerts.<br>Development of retailing activities. | Seven other professional clubs operating in a twenty-five mile radius.<br>Rising costs of wages and transfer fees; bank interest charges; policing; equipment.<br>Local authority refusing planning permission.<br>Government proposals to introduce a compulsory membership scheme for attendance.<br>Best players will leave.<br>Competition for spectators' time and money from other sources e.g., cinema, DIY.<br>Increased levels of unemployment in the area. |
| The club owns its own ground and car-parks in a good town-centre site.<br>Good housekeeping and relatively low wages.<br>A hard core of 2000 loyal supporters.<br>A successful and well established youth development policy.<br>The image of a 'friendly' club with good connections in local industry. | Large bank overdraft.<br>Ground facilities in poor order, especially seating and toilets.<br>Insufficient funds to invest in higher wages and transfer fees.<br>A relatively small population to support so many clubs in close proximity.<br>Poor image compared to first division neighbours. |
| STRENGTHS | WEAKNESSES |

*Figure 4.1* An analysis of the strengths, weaknesses, opportunities and threats of Swot United, a Third Division football club.

**The flexible approach**   The complexity and volatility of the environment may mean that a detailed SWOT analysis is both difficult and inappropriate. The environment may be changing so rapidly that many of the historical and current data are meaningless. This kind of situation led the oil companies, like Shell, to adopt a different approach to strategy formulation known as 'scenario planning'. The approach recognizes that uncertainty can never be eliminated, but it can be reduced by plotting different scenarios, each responding to alternative visions of the future. Managements are therefore prepared for a number of possible changes that may occur.

**The creative approach**   This takes the flexible approach one step further by stressing the importance of imagination in the strategic process. The idea that such an approach to strategy formulation is actually better has been taken up by management writers in the 1980s. Peters and Waterman believe that the more formal approaches to strategy formulation with the emphasis on complex environmental and organizational analysis can lead to 'paralysis through analysis' (Peters and Waterman, 1982, p. 31). The resulting policies are often too conservative, insufficiently adventurous and positive, and ignore the human contribution. Their 'excellent' companies are typified by a strategic-planning approach which recognizes the values of the decision-makers as one of the driving forces giving the firm its competitive edge.

The more complex and changing the business environment and the more difficult the problems facing managers, then the more creative they need to be. Such situations have been termed 'messy problems'. These have serious implications for the firm involved, but the problems are difficult to identify, and information is incomplete or of dubious value to the strategist. It is thought that such situations are now commonplace in many organizations, calling for a greater creativity in strategy formulation (McCaskey, 1982 has a fuller discussion).

**The behavioural approach**   There is strong support for the view that strategy formulation is far from being a rational, logical process (Cyert and March, 1963 and Child, 1972). Instead, strategic choice is the product of the organization's dominant coalition, invariably senior management, and is based upon its values, ideologies and personalities, and upon the process of organization power and politics, The process invariably involves some negotiation between senior management and other groups. The most overt of these processes take place at shareholders' meetings and in collective bargaining with trade unions. However, the most significant negotiations generally take place between competing factions within management itself, over such issues as the allocation of scarce resources, and are consequently much more difficult to observe.

Behavioural analyses of the strategy formulation see management values and objectives as more than individual inputs to the planning process. They influence the way the environment is perceived and hence, the choice of opportunities and threats and the assessment of strengths and weaknesses.

**The incremental approach**   This sees strategy not as a carefully prepared plan with clear goals, but a process by which the organization gradually comes to terms with its environment. Limited objectives are constantly modified in the light of experience and through the process of negotiation between interested parties. As a consequence, strategies are continually being changed. The incremental approach has been put forward as a more realistic and more effective method of dealing with complex and changing situations. The concept originated from the work of Lindblom (1959) in an article appropriately titled 'The science of muddling through'. Although his work was mainly concerned with large public-sector organizations such as hospitals and universities, there are strong parallels with larger private-sector firms.

**An absence of strategy?**   Finally, we present the view that strategy formulation is not a conscious management activity. Strategy is not an issue when firms appear to be operating to the satisfaction of management. It becomes an issue only in times of crisis when any attempt at strategy formulation may be too little and too late. There may be several reasons for this. Management may be complacent and reluctant to rock the boat or they may have myopic vision and hence a limited view of alternatives (see Levitt, 1960, and a discussion of the concept of 'marketing myopia' in Chapter 7). It may be that managements are too distracted by the daily business of survival and see themselves too weighed down by resource constraints to contemplate strategic options.

The various approaches we have identified reveal a mixture of rational and non-rational approaches to the formulation of management strategy. Nevertheless, strategies are more than management hunches played out in an information vacuum. More likely, managements select that information that is appropriate for their purposes, and this invariably involves consideration of both environmental and organizational variables. Management values and organization politics are important not only in the choice of strategy but in the selection of information upon which that strategy is based. All six of the approaches we have identified may operate together in the same firm. The following illustration reveals this mixed approach to strategic decision-making.

One of the partners in a firm of solicitors is keen to establish a computerized client record and accounts system. He spends several months persuading his fellow partners that this may be a good idea. The process of persuasion is accompanied by a gathering of information to show the growth of the firm over the past few years and illustrations are well chosen to show the advantages of faster information retrieval and better management information on the current status of client accounts. Information is also collected on the type of hardware and software systems currently available and their price. Quotations are sought from a few computer firms with experience in servicing professional firms. The partners agree to go ahead with the project and a more recent convert to the idea, one of the senior partners, uses his influence to promote and eventually engage a firm of computer consultants. This firm has been set up by the brother of a senior partner in another law firm and he has successfully installed a system in that firm.

The above illustration reinforces the notion of strategy as both an intellectual exercise in information gathering and presentation and a political exercise involving values, power and influence. In this case the situation was a relatively straightforward investment decision with implications for office practice. Strategic decisions to enter a new product market or change radically the structure of the organization involve even greater complexities.

Apart from these six approaches, we can identify three broad planning styles: formalized planning, consultation and negotiation, and entrepreneurship (a similar model is offered by Mintzberg, 1973). In

| APPROACH | STYLE | | |
|---|---|---|---|
| | Formalized planning | Entrepreneurial | Negotiation and consultation |
| Rational | X | | |
| Flexible | X | X | |
| Creative | | X | X |
| Behavioural | | | X |
| Incremental | | | X |

*Figure 4.2* Approaches and styles of management strategy.

Figure 4.2 we show how these different planning styles interact with the first five of the strategic approaches.

The suitability of a particular planning style may depend on the size and nature of the firm. For example, a formal planning system is more likely to be found in a large firm, smaller firms by their very nature will favour an entrepreneurial style, and a high degree of consultation will be found in larger public-sector organizations. Moreover, different styles may be appropriate for different functions. While formalized planning may be a key feature of production strategy, an R&D strategy may benefit more from an entrepreneurial approach. Where trade-union influence is considerable, management may need to proceed more through consultation.

Both the approaches and styles may change over time. A university which has operated through a mixture of an incremental approach and a consultative style may, when faced with the kind of threats identified in Case 4.3, need to operate in a much more entrepreneurial way. Indeed, at certain stages of their development, all organizations may require such entrepreneurial inputs to survive (Mintzberg, 1973). The role of the entrepreneur is usually associated with discussions of small businesses. It is our contention that entrepreneurial activity is equally important in large firms too, a theme we develop in Chapter 5.

## Strategic contexts

We have identified how managers may employ different approaches to the task of strategy formulation. In addition we can identify various contexts in which the strategic process operates.

First, strategy is not the sole preserve of the profit-making organization. All organizations have strategies, formalized to a greater or lesser extent. We can see strategies at work in such diverse organizations as businesses, schools, the police, charities, professional football clubs and the church. In recent years there has been a focus on management strategies in the public sector. The health service has actively recruited its area managers from industry and commerce in an attempt to introduce a more businesslike approach, including a greater emphasis on strategy formulation. In Case 4.3 we present the case of the new universities created out of the former polytechnics. For a number of years they have operated in a changing environment and have needed to formulate a different kind of strategy.

Second, we may differentiate between those strategies pertaining to entire industries, such as shipping or machine tools; strategies employed by firms operating in a number of different business markets, such as Unilever and General Motors; and strategies pertaining to those operating in a single or restricted product market. Cases 4.1 and 4.2 illustrate the strategic process at the level of an entire industry and within a multinational corporation respectively. The distinction is sometimes drawn between a 'corporate' and 'business' strategy. A corporate strategy is employed by those firms operating in a number of different businesses and focuses on issues relating to the overall business mix and helps identify the type of businesses management could pursue. A business strategy deals with a single business and concentrates on issues relating to successful competition. A multi-divisional firm like General Motors therefore operates both corporate and business strategies.

Third, we may identify strategies operating at different levels of the organization, from broad strategies at the top, moving through a series of successive stages towards strategies for specific functional areas like human resource management and marketing, and finally to individual targets and budgets.

## The uses and value of strategy

We can identify several reasons for management to engage in strategy formulation.

- Strategy assists in the formulation of goals and objectives and enables them to be modified in the light of information and experience.
- Strategy is a form of management control. It is a plan which guides behaviour along a predetermined route. At the operational level it results in budgets and targets.
- A clear strategy both assists in the process of allocating resources and may provide a rationale for that allocation so that it is perceived to be fair by organization members.
- It enables management to identify key strategic issues which the firm may face in the future and prepare appropriate action.
- Strategy performs a useful role in both guiding the action of the constituent parts of the organization as well as acting as an integrating mechanism ensuring units work together. The integrating power of strategy is a central feature of 'strong' corporate cultures as illustrated by firms such as IBM and Hewlett Packard.

**CASE 4.1**
***The machine-tool***
***industry***

The machine tool industry provides manufacturing firms with the means by which the products are made, including tools for such operations as metal cutting, stamping and drilling. Larger manufacturing companies with highly specialized machining needs, such as Austin Rover, will make some of their own tools, but most will buy from specialist machine tool manufacturers for at least some of their requirements. According to Hayes and Wheelwright (1984), a healthy machine-tool industry is an essential prerequisite for a successful manufacturing industry. It is only by using custom-designed tools that innovative products can be made, and only through such products can firms gain a competitive advantage.

The machine-tool industry in Britain has been in decline for a number of years. Its share of the world market fell by 50% from 1965 to 1982, while imports rose from 26% to 61% over the same period. A number of reasons have been forwarded to explain the decline. These are as follows:

- the general decline in manufacturing industry;
- the competitive threat posed by Japan and West Germany;
- a lack of graduate engineers in Britain;
- overdiversification resulting in short production runs;
- a general lack of automation and computer application;
- a vicious circle of decline resulting in a lack of investment;
- poor marketing;
- low volume production at high cost.

Several strategic options for the industry have been identified.

**Industry extinction**   This involves allowing the industry to die a natural death by starving it of investment and relying solely on imported machine tools. Such a strategy may be detrimental to manufacturing for the reasons outlined above.

**State intervention**   Attempts have been made at state intervention, including special provisions for the development of state-of-the-art tools in computer-aided design and manufacture and flexible manufacturing systems. Other measures have included attempts to encourage merger among smaller manufacturers to pool development ideas and achieve some economies of scale. The problems of state intervention lie in possible policy changes with shifts in political ideology and a danger of management complacency. The ultimate form of state intervention would be nationalization, a somewhat remote possibility in the current political climate. A suggestion has been made that the government imposes some form of import control. This could be a dangerous strategy in that other countries may retaliate, and despite its declining market share, British industry does depend on its exports. Furthermore import controls may speed up the process of Japanese machine-tool firms operating from British or other European bases.

**Rationalization**   Not surprisingly this is the most common strategy. The suitability of such a strategy would seem to depend on a number of mergers also taking place. This may achieve some kind of product standardization, longer production runs and subsequent cost reductions. The still declining market suggests that this strategy is not working, and it may be a route to eventual extinction.

**Foreign investment**   This is already occurring in that British firms are being bought by USA and Japanese interests. Investment would only be attractive in the case of highly specialized firms with attractive market niches or to get around the kind of import controls suggested in the second option.

Licensing   Under this arrangement British firms would manufacture products designed by firms in other countries. The current success of the Japanese machine-tool industry supported by a large manufacturing base, would make the Japanese attractive partners in such joint venturing. It is not clear what the Japanese would gain from the licensing arrangement beyond a fee for British firms manufacturing Japanese patented products. Licensing can be valuable if it generates innovation on the part of the licensee. The Japanese however are very restrictive on what they will allow licensees to do, and this may well preclude innovation.

(*Source*: Eilon, 1985; Lane, 1985)

---

**CASE 4.2**
***Minnesota Mining and Manufacturing (3M)***

The Minnesota Mining and Manufacturing Company, better known as 3M operates in 30 different countries producing around 50 000 different products using many different technologies. By most definitions it is regarded as a very successful company. It is truly multinational and multi-divisional, although the company was relatively slow to diversify both internationally and in terms of its product range.

The company was founded in 1902 to mine corundum, but quickly switched its attention to the manufacture of sandpaper, its only product for 21 years. In 1923 the company developed masking tape for paint shops in the car industry and this was followed by domestic adhesive tape and other tape products, such as sound recording tape. Tape products account for some 17% of output, but the company also produces office and photographic equipment, pharmaceuticals and chemicals. Only in 1951 did the company set up operations outside the USA, which remains its biggest market.

It fitted Peters and Waterman's model of an excellent company along several dimensions. First, it was a highly innovative company supported by a corporate goal that 25% of annual sales should come from products developed in the last five years, and a senior management dominated by scientists who encouraged R&D staff to follow through their own ideas. Second, the company was committed to high-quality goods designed to fulfil customers' requirements. Third, a considerable emphasis was placed upon communication throughout the company and management processes were dominated by a network of meetings; in Peters and Waterman's terms it was a 'loose, consensual organization'. Finally 3M was based around a strong central culture based on a traditional USA Midwest work ethic. Wherever they operated, small-town locations were favoured as best embodying the core values and management recruited staff who best fitted the culture.

In best Peters and Waterman tradition the company had no complex planning mechanisms. By 1980 the firm was undergoing change. The firm had grown considerably in a short period, especially in terms of overseas expansion. A new chairman was appointed and there was a belief that the company had become too committed to short-term goals. In particular the environment in which the firm was operating was changing in a number of different ways, which included an increased variability in interest rates, high rates of inflation in some operating countries, shorter life cycles for some products, scarcer and more expensive resources, and a declining demand in its traditional markets of office products and magnetic tape.

A major discontinuity was occurring involving changed senior personnel and both organizational growth and an increasingly threatening environment. The priorities identified by management were as follows:

● an even greater effort to be expended on product innovation;
● an improved control and coordination of the firm's global resources;
● a greater concern for the future by establishing a more comprehensive approach to long-term planning.

It was decided that new arrangements for strategic planning would accompany a major structural reorganization. This is shown in Figure 4.6.

The main elements of the new system may be identified as follows.

● It is an attempt to build upon the existing loose consensus by emphasizing the exchange of information and ideas, but facilitating this by more formalized systems. A database was set up to generate information about the company. In particular managers were encouraged to analyse and discuss the strategic options pursued in other parts of the company. This enabled managers to learn from the actions of others as well as being an excellent method for training new managers.

● A new formalized planning system was introduced whereby global strategies were worked out by the SBCs, the SPC and top management and individual business strategies were worked out by each division using the global strategy as a template. The division was able to set realistic performance measures based on detailed knowledge of its own product market.

● The SBCs acted as centres for the generating of ideas by integrating information and ideas from each of the operating divisions. It was hoped that some form of

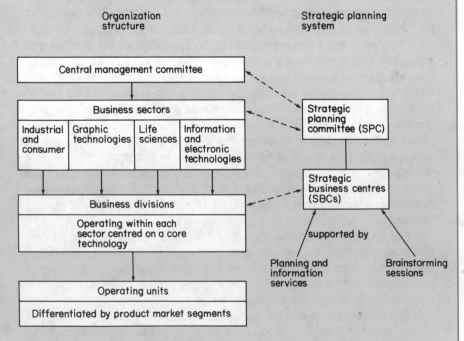

*Figure 4.6*   3M's new organization structure and planning system (Case 4.2). *Source*: Kennedy (1988).

synergy of ideas would take place. The SBCs focused specifically on product development issues. The generation of ideas was supported by an annual event, during which each operating unit must submit plans outlining where it will be in 15 years' time. This event acted as a forum for creativity outside the normal planning framework and deliberately adventurous ideas were encouraged. In addition to these systems the firm holds regular brainstorming sessions throughout the year.

Since the new system has been introduced there has been greater international activity, and an expansion of R&D work in Japan and Europe through the establishment of new laboratories and joint ventures with universities. Several unproductive businesses have been sold and the company attempted to establish a higher international profile through corporate advertising and the sponsorship of the 1988 Olympics. The new arrangements have also attracted some internal criticism on the basis that while the company has a greater knowledge of and direction over its existing businesses, no significant new ideas have been generated.

(*Source*: Peters and Waterman, 1982; Kennedy, 1988)

**CASE 4.3**
*The new British universities*

Between 1989 and 1992 the British higher-education sector comprising the polytechnics and colleges of higher education experienced a number of significant changes, brought about as the result of government education policy and accompanying legislation. First, all such colleges achieved corporate status, disassociating them from the control of local authorities and causing significant changes in the way they were funded and managed. Second, the Government abolished the division between the old university sector and the polytechnics by granting the latter, along with some of the colleges of higher education, university status and with it, the power to award degrees. The third change concerned the creation of the Higher Education Funding Council (HEFC), a new body responsible for both funding and quality control.

The environment in which the colleges operate is also changing. A declining population of school-leavers will affect traditional patterns of student recruitment, but the effect is likely to be uneven as some courses such as law and business studies continue to grow in popularity, while others such as some engineering courses decline. However, the proposed decline in the numbers of school-leavers has been more than offset by the rapid expansion of numbers to such an extent that target enrolment for the year 2000 was achieved by 1993. Much of that expansion has occurred in the former polytechnic sector. At the same time continued government pressure to hold down public-sector expenditure has resulted, in some cases, in reductions in staffing and the resourcing of such as libraries, setting up conflict with the increased demand from larger numbers of students. Since the majority of courses in the former polytechnics are vocationally oriented they need to respond to such changes in business as the use of new technology, and the creation of the European market in 1992, and may well require extra resources to meet the challenge. Many of the new universities are unsure about their new role. Do they continue with a strategy of pursuing different types of courses to the old university sector or do they attempt to compete on similar terms? In addition, a Government decision to alter the structure of funding by reducing student fees has added to the tensions

The new universities therefore face a rapidly changing environment. Many have responded by creating new administrative posts in finance and marketing to meet the new challenges. Most have placed an emphasis on income generation through the winning of research grants, hiring out staff as consultants, and setting up courses to bring in extra fees. For example, the government policy of charging full cost fees for overseas students has resulted in many universities, old as well as new, seeing such groups as an important source of income and actively searching new overseas markets. Some colleges have established special units to maximize opportunities in these areas. More attention is being paid to the marketing of courses and the attraction of students from non-traditional sources, especially mature students, to achieve expansion targets and to counteract the impact of falling school rolls. Some see their futures in becoming like the older traditional universities and have invested in research activity and used this as the single most important criterion in the recruitment of new staff.

While the environment may be similar for all new universities, there is considerable variation in the way each is responding. Colleges differ in their financial position, their resources, their own particular areas of excellence, and their perceived attractiveness to potential students, to businesses and to their central government paymasters. This may cause some to seek greater strength through merger and others to consider their portfolio of courses to build on strengths and eliminate weaknesses. The route that each goes down will inevitably be decided by a mixture of careful analysis, inspirational management, ideology, value judgement, pressure brought by interested parties and good fortune.

- Leading on from that, strategy formulation can be an important element in the process of social change. Strategic objectives are achieved by changing the behaviour of employees. This is the essence of organizational development programmes used by such companies as Shell and part of the current vogue for the creation of a strong corporate culture.
- The formulation of strategy is seen as a useful training ground for the development of future managers.

We have already questioned the extent to which formalized strategy is used by firms. An even more important consideration is the extent to which the existence of a formalized strategy contributes to organizational success. Studies suggest that those companies using some form of strategic planning process perform better than those who do not and where data are available they tend to show that the introduction of strategic planning methods leads to improvements in performance. (A good summary of a number of studies in this area is presented in Hofer and Schendel, 1978, ch. 1.)

The difficulty with such claims and indeed such studies is the problem of isolating and measuring the effect of strategic planning on performance, be it return on investment, market share or some other criterion. A firm's financial and market performance, even over time, may be influenced by so many variables outside the control of management that causal links between strategy and performance may be difficult to show.

Furthermore, the relationship is complicated in that performance may well influence strategy rather than the other way around. A firm which has been highly profitable may well be stimulated into seeking new investment opportunities either through new product development or acquisition. Conversely a firm incurring significant losses may well be limited in its strategic options and may well have them determined by people external to the firm such as bank managers or appointees of the Official Receiver. In this case the firm's performance is the reason for pursuing a divestment strategy, involving the closure or sale of the least profitable parts.

## The environmental aspects of strategy

In the last section we suggested that it was often difficult to establish a clear link between strategy and performance because of the great number of influences at work. Much of that complexity may be attributed to the firm's environment.

The firm's environment is of course a key aspect of our Business in Context model. In Chapter 1 we introduced the notion of contingency theory and the belief that a firm's performance was dependent upon its achieving a strategic fit between itself and the environment in which it operates. In Chapter 2 we identified, with the use of selected examples, significant aspects of the business environment. We noted how these aspects influenced and in turn were influenced by businesses. We further suggested that these elements not only interact with business but with each other, resulting, for most firms, in an environment that was highly complex and changing. In this and the previous chapter we have already noted how that complexity is further complicated by the values of decision-makers and the internal structures and politics of organizations. The strategist's task of making sense of the environment is therefore a very difficult assignment.

We can identify two aspects of the environment which may influence strategy. First, there are those issues which affect all firms operating in a given business environment. These are many of the issues we raised in Chapter 2 and may include the state of the economy, the nature of the labour force, changing technology, government policy and social and cultural influences. We call this the 'general environment'. Second, there are those factors which have direct bearing on the firm's competitive position, which we will call 'the immediate competitive environment'. An analysis of both these environments will enable management to arrive at some assessment of the major opportunities and threats facing the organization.

### The general environment

An analysis of a firm's general environment is sometimes known as environmental scanning, and usually comprises some sort of assessment of the key environmental influences, how they interact with the firm and with each other and how they change over time. There are many difficulties with such an analysis. Some managers tackle the sheer complexity of the environment by generating masses of information, not all of which is relevant and not all of which is accurate. The use of computers has increased the capacity for information handling and in some firms, managers can be submerged in a sea of data, most of which have only marginal relevance to their needs. At the other extreme there are some who either ignore the environment completely or who have a very blinkered perception of the firm's relationship to it. In such a situation key trends can be missed, and the firm either cedes opportunities to its competitors or is unprepared for changes when they occur.

Our analysis of the general environment is based on a model which classifies the environment as: simple and static; dynamic; and complex (Johnson and Scholes, 1984). We deal with each in turn.

**A simple and static environment**  Firms operating in a relatively simple and static environment can generally rely on management strategies that are based on historical data. Customer needs and hence sales forecasting can generally be predicted from past records. A company producing fireworks knows precisely that demand will peak dramatically prior to 5 November and will have a good idea of the size of that demand. However there is a danger that managers become complacent and the survival of the business may be jeopardized by sudden and unexpected changes as with a change in the law making the sale of certain types of firework illegal.

**A dynamic environment**  A dynamic environment changes quickly and frequently. Managers operating in this environment generally need to be sensitive to the environment and predict those changes that are likely to occur. The home-computer market has been particularly dynamic. Those firms, such as Amstrad, that have been sensitive to, and even helped create, changing consumer needs, have outperformed others, such as Sinclair, who, though first to the market, failed to maintain the required product development. Businesses which fail in dynamic environments are generally those where managements have failed to see the changes which are occurring or are either unable or unwilling to take appropriate action.

The case of professional soccer in England and Wales is one where an entire industry has lost ground to a variety of competitors for its customers' time and money, and the general trend towards declining attendance and hence revenue now seems irreversible. The result is that most of the 92 professional clubs suffer operating losses each year. There are many contributory factors, but the main one is that the clubs have underestimated the changing needs of the market and offer a product, particularly the facilities at grounds, which is largely unacceptable to an increasingly sophisticated clientèle. The problem has been compounded by a government, and often the media, which see soccer as the focus for violent, anti-social behaviour. Such problems have, in part, been tackled by the creation of an élite premier league and a Government Report which has insisted upon sweeping improvements in ground safety. For the smaller, non-élite clubs, attendances are likely to fall even further and so limit necessary investment.

Such environments require entrepreneurs who perhaps have the vision to spot opportunities and the motivation to pursue them. They are also suited to more creative approaches to strategy. However, there may be a danger that management could respond unnecessarily to changes in a dynamic environment. For example, some firms, when threatened by new entrants offering much cheaper products in the same market, respond by launching a cheaper version of their own product. This not only shows a lack of faith in the quality of the firm's original product, but it will inevitably take sales away from that product and have a potentially damaging effect on the firm's reputation.

**A complex environment** This is one in which different demands are placed upon different aspects of the firm's operation. A firm producing a range of different products for different markets could be said to be operating in a complex environment. Most firms in such situations reflect this complexity in their organization structures. We saw in the last chapter how the development of the multi-divisional firm was a direct response to the problems faced by emerging multinational corporations like General Motors in the 1920s. The problem facing firms in a complex environment is the extent to which the complexity needs to be accommodated by organizational changes. The TI Group, which operates in a number of different product markets attempted to reduce the demands placed upon it in a difficult economic environment by selling some of its individual divisions, including Raleigh bicycles.

In the case of dynamic and complex environments a firm faces a number of interconnected problems related to the degree of change, the speed of change, the complexity of its environment and the corresponding complexity of the organization. Managers tend to seek to reduce such uncertainty as much as they can by a variety of measures.

First, the uncertainty may be reduced by collecting relevant information. We have already noted the problems associated with collecting accurate information and with information overload. Second, as we saw in Chapter 2, managers will attempt to influence and control the environment. This can be done by a variety of measures such as technological innovation, forming coalitions with other organizations, political lobbying, acquiring raw material suppliers or retail outlets, stockpiling materials and equipment, training staff in rare skills, and so on. Third, new structures and procedures such as planning and forecasting may be set up to cope with uncertainty. There are, however, dangers with setting up new structures. A common reaction to developments in computer technology has been the establishment of a specialist computing department within the organization. The establishment of such specialist units can create its own problems of co-operation and integration which override the benefits of specialization

*Figure 4.3*   The model of competitive rivalry. *Source*: Porter (1980).

in the first place. (Selznick, 1949 and Pettigrew, 1973 have two good case illustrations.)

## The immediate competitive environment

We will attempt to locate a business in its immediate competitive environment using the model devised by Porter (1980) as shown in Figure 4.3. Porter has identified four forces which have immediate bearing on a firm's competitive position. We explain and illustrate these forces in turn.

**The threat of potential entrants**   The threat of entry is related to the ease with which a new business can establish itself in the same product market. The relative ease with which new restaurants emerge in a large urban area like London, suggests that the threat to existing restaurateurs is very real. However the ease of entry means increased competition and can result in a highly volatile market, to which the death rate of new restaurants will testify.

The threat posed by potential entrants is reduced if there are barriers to entry. These can operate in a number of different ways. Equipment and associated capital requirements place heavy burdens on investment and firms may have to withstand considerable unit-cost disadvantages initially. Such difficulties would be presented to firms attempting to enter mass car production or oil refining. It would be difficult for newcomers to achieve sufficient economies of scale to recover their outlay in a reasonable time.

These difficulties can be increased where access to raw materials is an additional problem. In some types of industry breaking into a market is difficult due to the considerable customer loyalty to existing products and brands. A soft drinks manufacturer attempting to launch a 'cola' type product would have considerable difficulty persuading the market to switch from Coca-Cola or Pepsi-Cola. In the industrial components industry getting customers to switch may pose the additional difficulties of part compatibility. Such barriers may be further compounded by the difficulty of obtaining access to channels of distribution. Our soft drinks manufacturer may have considerable difficulty persuading the major supermarket chains to stock their products. Patents held by existing manufacturers can pose a significant obstacle to those wishing to enter the market with imitative products.

The patents on the drugs Librium and Valium owned by Hoffman-La-Roche have enabled the firm to establish a monopoly position in the tranquillizer market. Similarly, patents held by Polaroid posed difficulties for firms such as Kodak to enter the instant camera market. In a more general way the operating experience gained by existing firms over a number of years can place the newcomer at a significant disadvantage.

Apart from the threat of new entrants, competitive rivalry can be heightened among existing competitors if the general growth rate of the industry is slow and if there are many firms of similar size with a relatively undifferentiated product range.

We should not forget that there are barriers to exit as well as barriers to entry. A large manufacturing company with considerable operating losses, but with many employees and a significant investment in plant and machinery, will undoubtedly face pressures to stay in business. Such pressures will be related to the extent of the firm's assets which may not be recoverable if the firm closes. This fear of lost investment may only be one factor. Senior management may be particularly attached to the company, emotionally as well as financially, and place a high value on its survival, despite market and financial evidence to the contrary. Pressures will undoubtedly come from the local community and, in the case of some firms, from the national government, fearing the effect of closure on local and national economies and on levels of unemployment. In the case of some firms such as British Leyland and Rolls-Royce in the 1970s, government pressure was accompanied by significant government investment to ensure the survival of these companies. Barriers to exit operate in small firms as well, where there is likely to be an even greater ego involvement on the part of the owner managers and a subsequent reluctance to accept forced closure in the face of market forces.

**The threat of substitution**  Substitution occurs where a consumer is able to replace your product with a different type of product performing the same service or satisfying similar needs. The cotton textile industry in Britain was not only threatened by new entrants from cheap labour economies but also by the development of substitute products in the form of man-made fibres. We have already identified some of the threats facing the professional football industry. A major threat has been the growth of substitute activities such as sport on television, passive rather than active participation in sport, and the growing popularity of DIY.

**The bargaining power of buyers**  Buyer power increases where there are a large number of firms offering the same or substitute products, especially where there is little or no cost involved for the buyer in switching from one supplier to another. A restaurateur in Central London faces considerable competition from the large number of other restaurants operating in that area, as well as other attractions competing for the potential client's disposable income. In such situations the product/market strategy of the restaurant becomes of utmost importance. Such strategies will include considerations of product differentiation and quality, market segmentation, price and promotion (Chapter 7 has a fuller account of these strategies). In the industrial components industry, particularly where specialist components are involved, then the relationship may be different. There may well have been a mutual accommodation of product changes over a number of years and such a strong relationship forged that the cost of switching would be high. Components suppliers often invest time and energy building up such relationships with customers. In such situations a threat still exists if the customer firm's acquisition strategy takes in a similar components supplier.

The buyer–supplier relationship is highly complex and involves most facets of our Business in Context model. The complexity of the technology plays a major part as does the competitiveness of the market. We saw in our discussion of Japanese management in Chapter 2 that a mix of cultural and economic factors was also significant. As part of their normal business strategy, Japanese industrial firms operating in Britain rely heavily upon subcontractors to supply components, and tend to build up close relationships with these suppliers. With British government backing, Japanese manufacturing companies have tended to locate in areas of low economic activity. This automatically places such firms in a strong bargaining position with respect to the local components industry.

The power of a buyer generally increases the more he or she buys. This power can be exercised in the demand for discounts or the expectation of preferential treatment in the supply of goods. A factor to consider here is the relative size of the two parties. Buyer power normally only exists if the volume purchased forms a high proportion of the selling company's total sales. The larger supermarket chains have considerable buyer power, particularly over such as the smaller food suppliers. Smaller foodstores have attempted to secure greater buyer power by banding together for bulk purchases, as with associations like Spar, Mace and VG.

**The bargaining power of suppliers**   Our illustration of the bargaining power of buyers in the industrial components industry works equally well for suppliers. In this and other cases supplier power is stronger where the component is highly specialized and few suppliers exist. Supplier power is also strong where the cost to the buyer of switching allegiance would include major product adaptations. A computer manufacturer can gain additional market power where it develops popular software that can only be used on its own machines. A large firm that has no central policy for the purchase of computer hardware and software may see the benefits of having a single operating system when it finds that much of its existing equipment is incompatible.

Most firms act as both suppliers and buyers and the bargaining power can be a two-edged weapon. A restaurant operating in an affluent area where there are no other restaurants probably does not face strong bargaining power from its customers and therefore maintains a strong competitive position. However if there are equally few suppliers of meat, fish and other foodstuffs then these firms have supplier power over the restaurant.

The use that managements can make of Porter's model is to establish a position for their firms in the market to maximize defences against competitive forces and where possible turn them to best advantage. Porter identifies three generic strategies of particular advantage in this respect. These are product differentiation, market segmentation and seeking to obtain the lowest costs. A further explanation of these strategies may be found in Chapters 6 and 7.

The strength of a model like Porter's is that it focuses on the immediate operating environment of the business and avoids prescription by enabling management to examine the forces acting upon their firm. The analysis does however depend upon a level of knowledge about a competitor which may just not be available.

## Environmental threats and opportunities

An assessment of the general environment and the firm's immediate competitive position should enable management to identify the major threats and opportunities facing the firm. In Table 4.1 we present an illustrative list of the of environmental opportunities and threats using the elements of the Business in Context model. This is usually the first stage in selecting appropriate strategic options. For a firm like Orlake Records (Case 6.1), producing gramophone records in a declining market, or a restaurateur opening in Central London, the threats and opportunities may be very clear. However, we can identify several complicating factors.

- A threat to one part of an organization may represent an opportunity to another. Thus in the 1970s when the post and telecommunications service in Britain were part of the same organization, a postal workers' strike led to increased revenue through telephone calls. The closure of some courses in a university due to falling student demand may divert resources to other areas.
- Defending yourself against a threat or capitalizing upon an opportunity is a function of both the firm's standing in its environment and its internal resource position. Survival in a declining market may be easier if you have a large market share to begin with and raising finance to invest in new products is often easier for larger established firms than the small business. Small firms often face the particular dilemma of spotting a market opportunity but lacking the resources to take full advantage. Laker Airways was relatively successful at breaking into the charter airline market by offering cheaper flights than those currently available. As the firm expanded by introducing flights to the USA it faced direct

**Table 4.1** Examples of environmental opportunity and constraints using the Business in Context model, as they affect a small manufacturing firm

| Aspect of the environment | Opportunity | Constraint |
|---|---|---|
| Economy | Growth in the market and demand for the product. | Increased foreign competition with rising interest rates at home and an unfavourable foreign exchange rate. |
| State | Tax concessions for small manufacturing firms. | New laws on safety and design necessitating a costly product modification. |
| Technology | Making more effective use of the computer system for administrative and financial control and information. | The high cost of new manufacturing technology to meet increased demand. |
| Labour | Local supply exceeds demand and there is a regular supply of part-timers and contract workers. | A shortage of workers in certain key skills and the relatively high wage demands of those workers. |
| Culture | A traditional small-firm community with a tradition for hard work and company loyalty. | An influx of newcomers to the area from declining industries with a long history of management–worker mistrust. |

competition with the larger state-financed airlines. Laker was ultimately unable to compete with the larger firms, who adopted price-cutting tactics, and the company overreached itself financially through the purchase of a large number of new aircraft in anticipation of increased revenue from the new routes.

- Managements differ in their ability to identify opportunities and threats. The management of a firm doing particularly well in a declining market may ignore the longer-term implications of their position. Even when opportunities and threats have been identified, managements may differ as to their relative importance and may develop different perspectives, based perhaps on their attitudes to risk. Careful analyses of market opportunities may come to nought in the face of a preference for inaction rather than entrepreneurial risk-taking.

Failure to take action in the light of environmental change is one form of management myopia. Perceiving the environment as presenting more of a constraint than it needs is another.

We can therefore see that the perception of an opportunity or threat is a highly subjective process. It is partly for this reason that strategy formulation is as much a behavioural and political process as it is analytical. There is another important point. We have tended to focus on the environment as offering the management decision-maker opportunities or constraints. A major contention in this book is that the manager can influence and shape the environment. This means more than simply recognizing that big business can dominate. There is increasing recognition that creativity in strategy formulation is the ingredient for giving firms a competitive edge (McCaskey, 1982; Earl, 1984). It is not simply the analysis of the environment that provides the answer but the ability of managers to see more in that environment than their competitors and in so doing create their own opportunities.

## The organizational aspects of strategy

In this section we will explore the relationship between management strategy and the organizational aspects of our model, and focus on particular issues of resource assessment such as portfolio analysis. Organizational analysis is traditionally an integral part of strategy formulation and serves two related purposes for management.

- Some kind of resource profile is needed to establish whether the various opportunities, threats, and management expectations can be met by the organization in its present state. A knowledge of the resources an organization possesses, and what can be done with them, is a prerequisite for determining future plans and establishes whether a gap exists between what management would like to do and what they can do. This is sometimes referred to as 'gap analysis'. For example, the management of a manufacturing firm would need to know if it could accept and meet a new, large order using its existing product range and its existing machine and labour capacity. The gap analysis will identify for management those resource aspects which may be lacking and which will have to be rectified if opportunities are to be realized or threats are to be successfully fought off. The completion of new orders by our manufacturing firm may be dependent upon product modification, the purchasing of new equipment and the hiring of new staff. This in turn may involve the raising of new loans from the bank and setting up programmes for the recruitment and training of staff. Expansion of this nature has further implications for the size of the supervisory and maintenance teams.
- An internal analysis will enable management to assess the attractiveness of the organization, its activities and its products in its current markets and assess their potential for future investment. This is the particular contribution of portfolio analysis.

A rather narrow, traditional view of strategic planning sees strategy as the result of environmental analysis and the organization factors are seen either to facilitate or inhibit the chosen strategy. Such a view runs counter to the major contention of our Business in Context model, which sees all elements as interacting with one another. Organizational changes are brought about by changes in strategy, but strategic changes are also the product of aspects of the organization. We have already noted in Chapter 3 that it is possible for structure to influence strategy. We can also see that expansion plans will undoubtedly build on strengths, a case of the firm focusing strategy around a key resource, such as the skills of a particular group. We deal with more general issues of strategy and organization before turning to the more practical questions of resource analysis and portfolio analysis.

## The interaction of strategy and organization

All the organizational elements of our model, goals, ownership, structure, size and culture interact will the process of strategy formulation.

We have already seen how the goals of an enterprise set targets for strategy to follow. We have also emphasized the behavioural nature of this process in that both goal and strategy formulation are the products of management values, and the processes of organizational power and politics, which have a major influence upon management decision-making.

The process of goal setting and strategy formulation is greatly influenced by ownership variables. A group of professional accountants in partnership may each have their own views about the growth of the firm, the recruitment and training of new staff and so on. In a partnership these views are generally resolved by discussion or through the dominance of a particular partner. Our discussion of ownership and control in Chapter 3 showed that for larger companies with diffuse share ownership and professional managers, strategy formulation was more complex and often dependent upon the influence of some shareholder groups. There are numerous illustrations where small business owners may deliberately resist growth strategies in order to retain personal control over the firm. However, the reverse is also true in that strategies involving merger and acquisition have a significant impact upon patterns of ownership and control. Managers may actively pursue acquisitions which give them more power and enhance their own career aspirations.

We noted in the previous chapter that, according to Chandler (1962), structure followed strategy, and this was a dominant feature in the expansion of American multinationals and in particular the development of multi-divisional structures. We also suggested that strategy can be influenced by structure. For example, a company with a large and active R&D department would almost certainly pursue vigorous strategies of new product development. The 3M case in this chapter shows how top management were concerned that their existing procedures for strategy formulation were inadequate and set about creating a new structure precisely to give the firm a new strategic impetus. At the operational level the organization structure can facilitate or inhibit strategy formulation and implementation.

Two aspects appear to be important here; the authority structure of the firm and the procedures for making decisions. Burns and Stalker (1966) studied the post-war electronics industry and saw differences in the strategic responses of firms to changing market conditions. Those firms which had responded most effectively to changed market demand were firms typified by a more flexible, open structure, which they termed organic. The firms which struggled in the changed environment and failed to adapt were by contrast more bureaucratic, with often lengthy and inappropriate procedures for making decisions, and where structural divisions between departments inhibited cooperation. Organizations, particularly those in the public sector, which rely heavily on committees for the formulation of important decisions, may find the process too cumbersome when a quick strategic response is needed. In a similar way participation, which can facilitate employee motivation and commitment, may inhibit decision-making through the inherent slowness of the procedure.

The authority structure of a firm usually determines the person or group with the ultimate responsibility for strategic choice. A study of how strategies were formed in five companies, including Cadbury Schweppes and Manganese Bronze, concluded, not surprisingly, that strategy was decided by a small group at the top of the hierarchy. What interested the researchers was the part played by entrepreneurship, even in large organizations, and that strategy was greatly influenced by the individuality and personality of the senior executives (Minkes and Nuttall, 1985).

Such considerations of structure are inevitably linked to size. In very large organizations strategy formulation may be cumbersome because of the reasons given above. There is also a danger that strategy can become fragmented through the diverse nature of operations and locations. It was these conditions which led 3M to reconsider its procedure for strategy formulation as illustrated in Case 4.2. Another handicap of large size involves the control of a strategy once it is formulated. The larger the organization then the more filters there are to interpret and perhaps distort a central strategy.

We have already discovered that an important element in the core management strategies of firms such as IBM and Hewlett Packard is the creation of an organizational culture, with an emphasis upon shared values. We have stressed the importance of management values in both formulating and evaluating strategy. In this case the creation of a value system to embrace the entire organization is seen by some to be more significant than strategy itself. We have already noted how traditional approaches to strategy have been downgraded by such as Peters and Waterman (1982). Nevertheless, the care with which such firms as Hewlett Packard embark upon staff recruitment, selection and training to develop such shared values (Case 3.6) would indicate the influence of a very distinctive strategy indeed. The culture of a particular organization may act as a constraint against strategy implementation. For example, strong trade-union organization may resist management's proposals to sell off part of the organization in an attempt to safeguard the jobs of its members.

## Resource analysis

At the beginning of this section we explained the importance of the current resource position to the formulation of management strategy. A manager needs to know what resources the organization possesses, how those resources are used and how they are controlled. The analysis will cover physical resources such as land, plant and machinery; financial resources; and human resources. In the case of the last category some analysis of the skill mix is important.

For example, the staff running a business course at a university may wish to change the curriculum to give much greater time and emphasis to computing. An analysis of the current position may reveal a shortage of available personal computers and terminals, a shortage of funds to increase the provision, and staff with insufficient skills and experience to teach this subject. Even if funds could be diverted or revenue raised from running extra courses, there may be physical constraints on the establishment of new computer laboratories. In addition, recruitment of appropriate staff may be difficult, so the management may need to seek substitute skills from its existing workforce. In this case an analysis of the resources may reveal that achieving the goal of increased provision by expansion is not possible. Consequently the utilization of the existing provision needs to be examined to reveal the existence of slack and to see what could be achieved using the existing resources.

In many firms resource analysis is accompanied by the use of a variety of accounting ratios such as return on capital employed, profitability and so on. Different ratios have more relevance at different stages of the firm's development than at others, so that while profitability may be appropriate for established firms, productivity and sales may be more useful for newly established companies and cash flows may be more significant when firms are in decline.

The value of resource analysis lies not only in assessing the viability of a particular strategic proposal, but also in assessing the ability of the organization to adapt to change. Can the firm deal with changes in demand or can it withstand a price war with its competitors? Has it the financial backing to invest in new technology? Is the age profile of its staff sufficiently balanced to ensure succession? Many such questions deal with issues of resource balance. We now turn to the question of maintaining an appropriate balance in terms of products and markets.

## Portfolio analysis

Portfolio analysis is a technique normally associated with those firms operating in a number of different businesses and markets, as is the case with the larger multinational corporations. It may also be applied to those firms who operate in the same market with a number of different products. The technique enables management to assess the attractiveness of its businesses and products in their current markets and assist decisions on the direction of future investment. Through

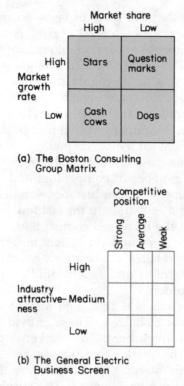

(a) The Boston Consulting Group Matrix

(b) The General Electric Business Screen

*Figure 4.4*   Illustrations of portfolio analysis. *Source*: Hofer and Schendel (1978).

such an analysis the manager may reach conclusions on the particular mix of products and markets, the growth and profit potential of those products and markets and the level of risk involved with each one. As a result, a clearer idea emerges regarding priorities for corporate effort and resource allocation.

There are several models which may be used in portfolio analysis and two are illustrated in Figure 4.4. The most famous portfolio technique is the matrix developed by the Boston Consulting Group (BCG). This was specifically designed to analyse individual businesses in a company with a range of different business interests. The matrix enables the analyst to plot the position of that business (or product) with reference to the growth of the market and the company's share of that market. We can see from Figure 4.4 that the matrix has been divided into four sectors, each with different product/market characteristics. The products located within these sectors have been labelled 'question marks', 'stars', 'cash cows' and 'dogs' respectively. We will deal with the characteristics of each.

- 'Question marks' represent products which have a low market share in a market of high growth. The market offers clear potential but the firm invariably needs significant financial and other resource inputs to compete. This may involve product modification, increasing output capacity, increasing promotional activity, recruiting extra staff and raising the level of bank borrowing. Investing in question marks carries a high level of risk, as can be seen through the British Government's excursion into microchip development by funding the firm INMOS (Case 5.2). The gains may be significant but the market tends to be highly competitive and the costs of improving market position are invariably high.

- 'Stars' are those products that have achieved a high share of a still expanding market. A company with a number or even one of such 'stars' is generally envied by its competitors. Nevertheless, the cost of maintaining this position is usually high. A growing market tends to attract a number of competitors and 'stars' usually need continuing investment in product development and promotion. The personal computer market in the last few years has maintained a high growth but the increased competition, particularly in terms of product development and price, has meant that several of its 'stars' have risen and fallen in a relatively short time. Other markets where 'stars' have risen and fallen rapidly include cameras and video cassette recorders.

- 'Cash cows' are products with a high market share but for which market growth has stabilized. These provide the firm with its greatest return on investment. The market is generally much less competitive and the market position is generally less costly to maintain than with 'stars'. Overall costs are generally lower and economies of scale can be achieved. The surplus funds generated by the 'cash cows' can be used to provide funds for the development of 'question marks' and the maintenance of 'stars'. The Volkswagen Golf has maintained its position as the best-selling car in Europe for many years and was the 'cash-cow' that enabled the company to develop a new luxury sports model, the Corrado, and thus break into new markets.

- 'Dogs' are products with the poorest profile on the matrix. Such products tend to be a drain on resources and can be candidates for being dropped altogether or being sold off. This was the reason behind the TI Group's sale of Raleigh Bicycles to Derby International. 'Dogs' are not necessarily worthless. Product ranges and indeed entire companies can be revitalized by perhaps a change of management and some fresh ideas. A 'dog' to one company may experience a new lease of life when sold to another. For example, a highly diversified company may find itself unable to devote sufficient attention to those products which are more peripheral to its central activities, as in the case of a manufacturing firm with a subsidiary whose primary activity is property development. The property business could be enhanced if it were sold to a firm specializing in that area.

The BCG matrix implies that management should seek to establish a balanced portfolio and carries with it a notion of progression. It assumes that 'question marks' should become 'stars' which will eventually turn into 'cash cows' to fund the next generation of developing product/ markets. Plotting a firm's products in this way may be a useful guide to

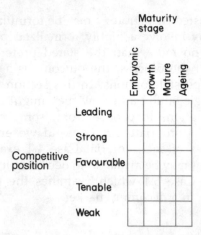

*Figure 4.5* 3M product and market portfolio matrix – this matrix is used to analyse both products and markets. *Source*: Kennedy (1988).

acquisition and divestment strategy. These options will be discussed in the next section.

The BCG matrix is not without its critics. Much of the criticism is concerned with the imprecise nature of the four categories. For example, 'stars' can differ considerable in their rate of growth and size of market share and the positioning of some products may be an inaccurate reflection of their value, simply because the category may be too broad. Mercedes-Benz have a low share of the total car market, but a high share of the luxury car market (Hofer and Schendel, 1978). In this case a number of matrices will have to be plotted to represent the different market segments. More complex matrices have been developed so that products can be plotted more usefully. An illustration of the General Electric Business Screen is shown alongside the BCG matrix in Figure 4.4. In this case the concept of industry attractiveness is used instead of market growth and nine categories have been identified to achieve greater accuracy.

In spite of the problems of plotting and measurement, such methods of portfolio analysis are of use both in planning future product/market strategy but they also raise important questions about how business interests are handled. We have already seen that by analysing a 'dog', changes may be possible to improve its position. One company to make use of this type of analysis is 3M. They have developed a matrix to analyse both products and markets, as illustrated in Figure 4.5. The management of 3M is concerned that each of its products and markets are capable of being maintained or improved. It was this method of analysis which led the company to sell off its photocopying equipment business (Kennedy, 1988).

## Strategic options

So far in this chapter we have discussed the various components of strategic analysis; the environment, resources and dominant values.

We have also suggested that strategy may be formulated by a variety of methods which may involve a highly formalized planning procedure or may simply be no more than the stated preferences of the chief executive. Whatever the process, the outcome is a particular strategic option or range of possible options. In this section we have identified four types of strategic option and how they might be achieved. When there are several options to choose from, some criterion is needed to select the most appropriate strategy and we end this chapter by identifying examples of such criteria. Case 4.1 examines the type of strategic options that may be available to declining industry and should be compared with Case 6.1 which examines the types of strategies employed by a firm in a declining market.

## Types of strategic option

There is an assumption in many management texts that the super-ordinate goal of most businesses is survival and this may only be achieved by pursuing strategies of growth. While it is difficult to argue against the first assumption, it is clear that not all businesses pursue growth strategies, and for those like the British steel and coalmining industries drastic contraction may be the only chance of survival. Our four strategies depict different approaches to growth and contraction. These options are not discrete categories and in some cases, especially between the first two, the distinction can be blurred.

**Diversification strategies**   Diversification is undoubtedly the most radical growth strategy open to management in that it represents a deliberate attempt to change the nature of the business. We can identify two types of diversification, related and unrelated. Related diversification can be further classified into backward, forward and horizontal integration.

   **Related diversification** occurs when the new business is related in some way to the old one. Several firms have sought to gain greater control over the source of raw materials or the supply of components by some form of backward integration. As we saw in Chapter 2, the larger Japanese manufacturing firms depend on a network of subcontractors for the supply of components. In many cases the larger company has a controlling financial interest in the supplier. In the restaurant business it is becoming more common for some restaurant owners to grow their own herbs and perhaps their own vegetables, or bake their own bread, to ensure both the quantity and the quality of the supply. This also provides the restaurant with an additional promotional strategy. Forward integration occurs when producers diversify to control the onward processes of delivering their goods to the consumer, as in the case of a manufacturer setting up a transport or retail operation or a group of actors leasing a theatre to stage their own work. British Rail has always been a major source of transport for Post Office letters and parcels.

   In recent years British Rail have extended their own delivery service,

Red Star, which has taken business away from the Post Office by offering a speedier and guaranteed delivery service. Together, backward and forward integration are known as vertical integration. Horizontal integration occurs when the product range is extended to incorporate similar items, as with the case of a firm supplying fitted kitchens diversifying its operation to include fitted bathrooms and bedrooms as well. Laura Ashley began by selling furniture fabrics, moved into dress fabrics and eventually diversified into selling dresses themselves. Horizontal integration may be a valuable way of using a firm's spare resources or capacity. The fibreglass operations of Pilkington Glass found that the waste created in cutting standard widths of fibreglass could be put to good use through the setting up of another operation which compressed the material into insulating bricks, thereby creating a different but related product. Case 6.1 shows how a record company has used related diversification into specialized products as a major strategy of survival in a declining market.

**Unrelated diversification** occurs when management expand their business into a totally different product market. Marks & Spencer have ventured into the selling of financial services, a totally different operation from their core business of clothes and food retailing. Many diversified companies have a mixture of both related and unrelated products. The London Rubber Company main product range of contraceptives has been augmented by a range of surgical and household rubber gloves, but the company also produces soap and cough medicine. As with many forms of classification the difference between related and unrelated diversification is often a matter of degree. The 3M case in this chapter is a good illustration of both types. The company switched from the mining of corundum (an abrasive) to the manufacture of sandpaper (using abrasives as a raw material). The company then began producing masking tape which led to the related products of adhesive tape and all other kinds of tape product.

The concept often associated with unrelated diversification is synergy. This refers to the collective influence of the various activities of the company producing an overall effect that is greater than the sum of the parts. Synergy is often cited as a major benefit of diversification although its impact is often difficult to identify and measure.

We have seen how diversification can provide managers with greater control over supplies and distribution and exploit resources. A highly diversified firm may also be one where risks are spread across a range of products and markets. The motives for diversification may be complex and may include the desire of senior management to extend their power and influence as the firm grows larger. In the USA, the diversification of many companies into totally different areas of business was a direct response to anti-trust laws which put severe restrictions on the creation of monopolies. There are problems with diversification strategies. A highly diversified company often presents special problems of communication and control and resources may be duplicated. It is for this reason that many diversified companies have adopted a structure involving a mixture of autonomous units sharing some central services, such as R&D. (A fuller discussion of structural devices may be found in Chapter 3.)

Many of the illustrations of diversification presented above represent activities which have grown out of the firm's existing business. Firms may also add new products and markets through acquisition. This has the advantage of being a much faster method of diversification than internal development. The company is gaining an 'off-the-peg' business with the experience, knowledge, resources and markets already in existence. Much has been written about acquisitions and mergers and such activity presents consistently good copy for the financial journalists, particularly when it is accompanied by accusations of insider dealing on the stock market.

The evidence suggests that acquisitions and mergers tend to occur in cycles (Channon, 1973). Another cycle appeared in the mid to late 1980s, especially among firms in the retail and the food and drink industries. Why such cycles occur has not been fully explained and may represent yet another business fashion. The overwhelming evidence is that acquisitions are rarely successful. In their study, Peters and Waterman (1982) cite the case of ITT and the difficulties the firm encountered when it diversified out of telephones by acquiring banking and hotel interests. They claim that synergy rarely happens through acquisition, and the whole exercise takes up a disproportionate amount of management time and effort. As befits two proponents of firms adopting a strong central image and consensus culture, Peters and Waterman see great difficulties in achieving a cultural fit between two different enterprises and advise managers to 'stick to the knitting'.

Other research echoes Peters and Waterman's concern and tends to warn against unrestrained diversification. A study of 200 companies in the USA from 1949 to 1969 concluded that the poorest performers were those operating in a number of unrelated businesses and those that had attempted vertical integration. The best performers were those that had diversified only in related areas around a set of core activities and skills (Rumelt, 1974). It is interesting to note that while vertical integration is a complementary extension of a firm's core activities, it often requires totally different skills from that core activity. For example, a successful manufacturer of domestic electric appliances may turn out to be a very poor retailer and provider of repair services.

**Strategies to change the competitive position of an existing business**   Whereas diversification and rationalization represent fundamental changes in the nature of a firm's business, strategies in this category attempt to improve the market position of the existing range of products and services. There are a number of strategic options available:

- new product development (Chapter 5);
- improved market penetration by deploying the various elements of the marketing mix, such as promotion or price strategies (Chapter 7);
- seeking new markets by aiming the product at new market segments or by export (Chapter 7);

- improving the quality of the product or service (Chapter 6);
- seeking cost reductions through an improved utilization of resources such as improvements in productivity (Chapter 6).

Many of these strategies are related. A firm which wishes to move 'up market' and aim its product at a more quality-conscious but less price-sensitive consumer group may need to accompany product changes with an intensive promotion campaign. We pursue this theme in more detail in our discussion of marketing strategies in Chapter 7.

Attempts to change the competitive position of the business can be made through acquisitions which improve the product range and gain access to new markets. Such strategies carry the same advantages and disadvantages outlined above. A growing type of competitive strategy involves franchising ('Structure' in Chapter 3). Through franchising its products or services to individual small businesses, a firm can reach a wider market, and, at the same time, spread the risk of that expansion.

All five options of improving the competitive position of the firm by focusing on existing products and services can be achieved by internal change strategies. Expansion into new markets may be accompanied by increased promotional and sales activity in that area. However, the more successful change strategies take time and involve more than simply exercising another strategic option. Moves to effect changes in product quality and productivity may involve industrial relations strategies (Chapter 8), and attempts to change the organizational culture (Chapter 3).

**Deleting operations** The decisions to cut back and/or sell off part of the operations of a firm is referred to as rationalization or divestment. At its ultimate level this will include liquidation and closure. Such strategies can pose enormous difficulties for the firm involved. The cutting back of activities such as R&D and training to achieve short-term savings may have damaging long-term repercussions. Reducing product lines and services may alienate customers. Cutbacks and closures are generally vigorously opposed by trade unions. The National Coal Board's plans in 1984 to close the Cortonwood Colliery in Yorkshire precipitated one of the longest and bitterest disputes in the history of the industry. On a more general level, rationalization strategies may cause a lowering of employee morale to such a level that existing operations are endangered.

Nevertheless, for some firms, rationalization is the only viable option and may, as successful management buy-outs have shown, offer a new lease of life to part of an organization. In 1981, the shoe manufacturer Norvic was forced to go into liquidation, and one of its subsidiaries, the Mansfield Shoe Company, was faced with closure and most of its workforce were made redundant. The Mansfield subsidiary was saved by a management buy-out which raised extra capital from local industry and from employees exchanging their redundancy payments for shares in the new company. Freed from the financial burden of helping to support an ailing parent company, the newly formed organization found new markets and became reasonably successful, expanding its operations by acquisitions in other parts of the country.

**Consolidation**   A consolidation strategy involves the firm operating in the same product market at existing levels. It is however far from a 'do-nothing' strategy. Even to stand still firms must keep pace with their competitors. This may involve all the kinds of strategies outlined above, and will certainly involve considerations of product development, quality improvement, marketing and cost reduction.

## Strategic choice

Faced with a number of strategic options a manager must make a choice. We have already indicated that the process involves consideration of a number of factors which we may summarize as follows:

- an analysis of environmental threats and opportunities;
- an analysis of company resources;
- the stated objectives of the company and those of the management team;
- the values and preferences of management decision-makers;
- the realities of organizational politics.

Johnson and Scholes (1984) use a checklist for the evaluation of strategic options. This involves testing various options for their suitability, feasibility and acceptability. The suitability of a strategy would include such considerations as its ability to tackle major problems, improve competitive standing, exploit strengths and the extent to which it meets corporate objectives. The feasibility of a strategy is the extent to which that strategy can be achieved given the financial, physical and human resource base of the company. Even if a strategy is both suitable and feasible it must still be acceptable to various interested parties, such as management, employees, shareholders and customers. Shareholders may be particularly sensitive to strategies of acquisition. The ultimate acceptance of a particular strategy might depend on the attitude of senior management to risk.

The Strategic Planning Institute in Britain and the USA offers assistance in strategic choice by identifying those strategies most likely to result in increased profit levels. They have set up a scheme known as PIMS (Profit Impact of Market Strategies). In essence PIMS is really a huge database generated by those companies participating in the scheme. A record is kept of strategic options and their links to profit levels. Firms participating in the scheme have access to the data generated by other companies and may therefore learn from their successes and failures. Analysis of the information to date suggests a positive relationship between profitability and market share, but a negative relationship between profitability and the intensity of investment. Surprisingly the PIMS data have uncovered that investment is not such a safe option as many assume. Intense investment usually occurs in highly competitive businesses and companies tend to engage in damaging price wars or find that excessive investment proves a barrier to exit (Beasley, 1985).

The way a strategic choice is made will depend very much on the power and authority structure of the organization. In some firms the strategy may be highly detailed with little scope for interpretation by functional managers. In other firms a great deal of freedom is given to functional management to develop appropriate strategies within broad guidelines. We deal with specific functional strategies in Chapters 5 to 9. A theme stressed throughout is that R&D, production, marketing, personnel and financial strategies should achieve a high level of internal consistency, irrespective of where in the firm the strategy was formulated.

## Summary

In this chapter we have portrayed the formulation of management strategy as a complex process involving the consideration of environmental and organizational factors as well as management values and organization politics. As a result the process is a mixture of rational techniques and subjective decision-making processes, including a consideration of management values and negotiations between interested parties.

We have identified a range of approaches and styles, which may operate at the same time, although at different stages of the firm's development one type of strategy may be more appropriate than another. The formulated strategy has several functions, not least of which is to anticipate the future by coordinating activities and focusing resources towards chosen objectives.

An analysis of the general environment and a focus on the immediate competitive environment will enable management to identify significant opportunities and threats, although how these are interpreted is a function of the values and creative ability of management. We identify four kinds of resource; product, physical, financial and people. All are important in enabling management to formulate strategy around the organization's strengths.

We examine four generic types of strategic option and suggest that each option should be assessed in terms of its suitability, its feasibility and its acceptability. The final criterion stresses the a central theme of this chapter; the importance of management values and organization politics in the strategic process.

## Further reading

G. Johnson and K. Scholes, *Exploring Corporate Strategy: Text and Cases*, 3rd edn (Prentice Hall, 1993) has emerged as the most popular British text by far. It offers a clear approach backed by good cases. At the time of writing a third edition has been produced, although several references in this text are taken from the first edition. An interesting approach is taken by J. Kay, *Foundations of Corporate Success: How Business Strategies Add Value* (OUP, 1993). Once again the text is rich in illustrative material. C. W. Hofer and D. Schendel, *Strategy Formulation: Analytical Concepts* (West Publishing, 1978) is an American text offering some useful research material. A book which examines a variety of approaches and styles used in management strategy as well as offering some good illustrations is A. L. Minkes, *The Entrepreneurial Manager* (Penguin, 1987). At a more specific level, a good analysis of the competitive environment is offered by M. E. Porter, *Competitive Strategy: Techniques for Analyzing Industries and Competitors* (Free Press, 1980). Some rate this as his best book. T. J. Peters and R. H. Waterman, *In Search of Excellence* (Harper & Row, 1982) offers good case illustrations, although as we note elsewhere in this book, the approach has its critics.

## Discussion

1   Examine the role of the scientific method in the process of strategy formulation. Is there a role for entrepreneurship and creativity?
2   What is the purpose of strategy and how might a particular strategy be evaluated?
3   Identify the major environmental opportunities and threats faced by a city centre restaurant, a large retail store, a high-street bank, a university, and a firm manufacturing television sets.
4   Using Porter's model identify the specific competitive forces operating in the five situations defined in the previous question.
5   In what ways can management use resource analysis and portfolio analysis to guide strategy? What are the major strengths and weaknesses of the models for portfolio analysis identified in this chapter?
6   Assess the relative contribution of environmental influences, resources and management behaviour to strategy formulation? In what situations may one of these influences predominate?
7   Make a critical analysis of the different approaches to diversification. In what situations would such strategies be appropriate?
8   With reference to Case 4.1, what strategic options would be most useful for the machine tool industry? What other strategic alternatives can be suggested?
9   Identify the environmental, organizational and management considerations which led 3M in Case 4.2 to rethink its planning procedure. What further threats might the company have to face?
10  Using Case 4.3 as a starting point, what strategic approaches, styles and options would best fit a new university for the late 1990s? What problems do you foresee with these approaches, styles and options?

# Innovation

## 5

> There can be little doubt that those activities which contribute to the efficient introduction and exploitation of new and improved processes and products are extremely important for the competitive performance and long term growth of any industrial economy.
>
> (Freeman, 1989, p. 199)

There is a strong and widely held belief that innovation is the key to economic growth for both national economies and individual firms. Undoubtedly, innovation is a key function of business since it is related to entrepreneurship, the driving force behind business growth and development. In this chapter we attempt a broad-based view of innovation. We will start by examining the differences between the related concepts of innovation, invention, research and development, design and entrepreneurship. We move on to examine the relationship between innovative business activity and the environmental aspects of our model, in particular its impact on economic growth, the role of governments in stimulating innovation and entrepreneurship, and especially differences in government policy and attitudes towards innovation in different nation states. Much of government policy focuses upon the encouragement of new technologies, yet it is our contention that the development and design of new products needs to be accompanied by corresponding developments in marketing.

In the latter part of this chapter we extend this view of innovation still further by examining how it operates within organizations, and in particular the relevance of organizational structure and culture to innovative activity. We end the chapter by focusing on a number of generic innovation strategies.

We can therefore see that innovation is not confined to the technological hardware of products and processes. We believe that successful product and process innovation invariably requires accompanying innovations in marketing and organization structure. These are sometimes referred to as administrative innovations as opposed to technical innovations of the product and process type. Research has pointed to the need to balance both technical and administrative innovation (Daft, 1982; Damanpour et al., 1989). The impact of technical change can be significantly lessened without accompanying changes in administration. For example, the adoption of an electronic mail system in a large organization is of little value unless staff are trained to use it.

There is a particularly close association between innovation and marketing. Peter Drucker sees these two activities as the basic functions of business, as he regards them as the only truly entrepreneurial functions (Drucker, 1968).

The link between innovation and entrepreneurship is important, since it establishes innovation as a function of all businesses. Many people associate innovation with the process of new product design in manufacturing industry. Yet, examples of innovation can be drawn from every conceivable organizational context. In the financial services industry, banking has been transformed by the introduction of automatic cash dispensers, giving the general public much greater access to their accounts. In an increasingly competitive market the banks have developed mortgage services and the building societies have begun to offer a range of services we normally associate with banks. In the entertainment industry, the innovation of multi-screen cinemas offers the public a wider choice and has contributed to significant increases in attendance and hence revenue. In the travel industry the booking of airline seats has been revolutionized by computerized booking systems with instant access. In education, innovations occur through the development of new courses or new methods of presenting those courses, such as distance learning. In most of the above cases the innovation is viewed as offering the adopter a competitive advantage.

What all these various forms of innovation have in common is the difficulty facing management in implementing such changes. These difficulties can include raising the necessary finance, ensuring that the firm is staffed by people with the required skills, being able to persuade the consumer to buy the new product or service, being able to deliver in sufficient quantity when demand is created, and invariably coping with the political processes within the organization which accompany any form of change. Factors which may add or detract from the difficulty involve the time-scale required for the change to take place and people to see the returns and the attitude of the people involved towards risk and their ability to cope with uncertainty. A major product change or the installation of new equipment can take five years and longer before the development costs are recovered, a reason why major innovations are apt to make both management and financial backers nervous. We examine the management and organization processes related to innovation later in the chapter. First, we make an attempt to sort out the various terms.

## Identifying the concepts

The terms 'invention', 'innovation', 'research and development', 'design' and 'entrepreneurship' are all used in a variety of contexts, often interchangeably. There is a further confusion in that while all are processes, 'research and development' or 'R&D' as it popularly known, is frequently used in an organizational context to identify a department whose primary objective is the creation and development of new products and new ways of making them. We will now look at the concepts themselves in a little more detail.

---

Innovation is the process through which new ideas and inventions become a business reality in the form of new products, processes, marketing strategies, and new methods of organization and management. Its importance to business survival and growth is acknowledged by many firms through the creation of special units such as research and development departments in manufacturing industry.

**KEY CONCEPT 5.1**
*Innovation*

---

## Invention and innovation

These terms are often confused, yet if we take Schumpeter's line there is a very clear distinction between them.

> As long as they are not carried into practice, inventions are economically irrelevant.
>
> (Schumpeter, 1961, p. 88)

Invention is the creation of something new, be it a new computer, a new method for painting cars, a new form of selling, a new university course, or a new form of organization structure. An invention becomes an innovation when the idea becomes a reality; when the new computer goes into manufacture and starts selling; when the new university course begins to recruit students.

This reinforces the notion that innovation operates in a variety of forms and in a variety of contexts. We are now able to distinguish three broad categories.

A distinction can be drawn between product innovation and process innovation. Product innovation is the development of a new product such as a new model of car, a new form of insurance policy, or a restaurant offering a new special vegetarian menu. Process innovation is concerned with how the product is made or delivered to the customer. The development of robots in manufacturing industry is a form of process innovation, as is a restaurant opening a self-service section in addition to an existing waiter service operation.

We have already noted that innovation may occur in every aspect of the organization's operations. We may therefore identify innovations in the selection and use of raw materials, in the way goods and services are produced, in the marketing activities and in the way the organization is structured and managed. For example, the introduction of work-group participation in management decision-making is a form of innovation, as are types of job enrichment to enhance worker motivation.

We can also make a distinction between basic innovations and innovations that are modifications and improvements on existing products

**Table 5.1** Different types of innovation

| Type of innovation | Extent of the innovation | |
|---|---|---|
| | Basic | Modification |
| Raw material | The use of plastic in place of glass in bottles. | Changing the components of the plastic in the bottles to make them tougher. |
| Product | The use of integrated circuits on microchips to replace transistors. | Employing electronic controls in a washing machine. |
| Process | Introducing robots to perform the welding operation in a car assembly plant. | Increasing the number of stages in a car painting process to gain a better finish. |
| Marketing | The opening of a high street shop by a mail order bookclub to widen sales. | Using television personalities instead of politicians in a televised political broadcast. |
| Organizational | Creating a matrix form of organization to replace the traditional arrangement based on specialist functions. | Creating a separate training function within the Personnel department. |

and processes. In fact the great majority of innovations are not major breakthroughs but modifications, often of a very minor nature. This incremental approach to innovation is pursued successfully by many Japanese companies and the reason why camera producers such as Minolta and Canon bring out a new model at regular intervals.

Illustrations of all these types of innovation are presented in Table 5.1.

In addition to the various types of innovation, we might add a fourth category. This has been termed 'pseudo-innovations' (Mensch, 1979). These are often introduced to revitalize a stagnant market, but in fact no real change has taken place. Such pseudo-innovations are often the product of marketing campaigns to change the fortunes of a flagging product. The product may be relaunched under a different brand name, repackaged to suggest product changes or advertised as containing a 'new improved formula' when no significant change has taken place. A case in this area is that of the washing powder Square Deal Surf. Its forerunner, Surf, was experiencing a declining market share in a market where every new product appeared to come with a new formula for washing whiter. The company aimed the product at a segment of the market that they had identified as 'anti-gimmick'. To emphasize this point they offered the product with a changed name, which suggested to consumers that they were getting a better deal than those offered by competitors. The change and repositioning of the product in the market was highly successful and sales increased. We deal with aspects of market segmentation and positioning in more detail in Chapter 7.

The case of Square Deal Surf illustrates the complexity of innovation. To Mensch it undoubtedly represents a pseudo-innovation in terms of product, yet the marketing strategy employed was highly innovative. Moreover not all innovations are visible. Where washing powders have radically changed their formula this is not instantly apparent to the consumer and the company relies upon its marketing effort to convey this information, reinforcing the importance of an integrated innovation and marketing strategy.

## Research, development and design

We can define research and development as the organization of innovation at the level of the firm. It is that activity of an organization that both seeks to satisfy a market need by developing new products and methods and find uses for scientific and technological inventions. This introduces to the concepts of demand pull innovation (fulfilling a market need) and technology push innovation (applying existing knowledge). R&D is clearly associated with science and technology, although the R&D function can be performed in all types of industry. We have seen that the process of new product development occurs in non-scientific and technical situations. In many organizations there is a group of people whose primary task is the generation of new business ideas, as in the case of television companies which have a department for new programme development.

In some industries, especially those involved in complex, competitive environments, R&D is a vital part of the business. Firms like IBM and Hewlett Packard in the computer industry, and Ciba Geigy, Bayer, and Glaxo in the pharmaceutical industry, have large teams of staff engaged exclusively in R&D work. The importance of R&D to Glaxo is shown in Case 5.1. In the case of Hewlett Packard, innovation is part of the organizational culture and is stressed as a responsibility of all employees (Case 3.5). The institutionalization of R&D can bring its own problems, which are raised when we look at organizational aspects later in the chapter.

The British pharmaceutical company Glaxo operates in a competitive world market where research plays a highly significant role both in terms of expenditure and in terms of the ever-present need to develop innovative products. Glaxo currently produces the world's best selling-drug, Zantac, a treatment for ulcers. However, the company did not emerge as a leading-edge researcher until the 1960s when the acquisition of a research-based operation led to the development of a successful drug for asthma sufferers. The company had developed in the early part of the century as a family business selling powdered milk for babies with a gradual extension into

**CASE 5.1**
*Glaxo*

products related to infant nutrition. The real point of entry into the drugs market came with the Second World War when the company began to produce penicillin.

The company is noted for its commitment to R&D. Between 1987 and 1992 more than 50% of capital spending went towards equipping research laboratories and for the financial period 1991–2 Glaxo spent £472 million on research. In the United Kingdom only ICI had a higher investment and Glaxo spent more than any of its UK rivals in the pharmaceutical industry. In 1992 a large new research complex was built at Stevenage to employ 1700 research scientists. In 1992, the Stevenage research laboratories was the largest investment project in the UK after the Channel Tunnel and Sizewell B.

The research arm of Glaxo is a separate company, Glaxo Group Research, with operations not just in the UK but also in the USA, Japan, Spain, France and Italy. Glaxo's R&D strategy includes a fairly ruthless approach to weeding out the potentially successful from the unsuccessful developments at a relative early stage and the marketing of innovative drugs at relatively high prices. There is a strong belief in different approaches to problem-solving and Glaxo not only attempts to capitalize upon cultural differences in the approach to research, but moves its researchers around the various locations. The organization of research is invariably flexible with the emphasis upon small teams feeding into project approval committees. There is a strong support of pure research and links with the university sector are seen as crucial. In 1992 the company supported University Chairs and projects to some £7 million. The location of its laboratory in North Carolina is in the 'research triangle' between three of the State's most prestigious universities and the Stevenage development resembles a university campus. Such a commitment to pure research underlines the long-term view of R&D strategy. This is inevitable in an industry where it is not uncommon for the development process to take between 10 and 15 years. An important feature here is the good relationship that the management of the company have deliberately fostered with City financial institutions.

While Glaxo produces the world's best-selling drug, its development owes much to initial work carried out by a British scientist, James Black whose findings were published in 1972. Black was working for the US firm Smithkline French, who were the first to the marketplace with their anti-ulcer drug Tagamet in 1978. The scientists at Glaxo were convinced that by reworking Black's studies they could develop their own superior product. An intensive research programme and product trial resulted in Zantac being lauched in 1981. The research and development period for Zantac was highly concentrated with a subsequent shortening of product lead time. Effective use was made of patent protection to differentiate the product from its main rival.

The success of Zantac as a product was invariably linked to its acceptance in the USA. Apart from it being the largest market for drugs there were fewer price controls than elsewhere and hence a greater potential for profits. Zantac was initially marketed in the USA by the Swiss company Hoffman LaRoche, well known in the American market through its own products, Librium and Valium, the world's biggest selling tranquillizers. Zantac was priced higher than Tagamet and it is widely acknowledged that the marketing campaign was aggressive. Not only were the superior claims of Zantac over Tagamet forcibly made, but Glaxo emphasized the negative side-effects of the rival drug. Subsequent pressure by the US regulatory body, the Food and Drug Administration, has resulted in Glaxo withdrawing some of the claims made concerning the superiority of Zantac. Nonetheless, Zantac took the US market from

Tagamet and is now the world's best-selling drug. The annual sales are estimated to be worth over £1.6 billion, representing some 40% of Glaxo sales.

In 1993 a new administration were elected to power in the USA. A key policy of the new administration is the reduction in health-care costs which are currently the highest of any nation. There is considerable pressure to reduce the costs for the elderly, who generally have inadequate insurance and must pay the full cost of treatment. There is also pressure to bring down health-insurances premiums and to reduce the cost of state-funded health care. A clear target is the drug companies who charge premium prices for their products and the US government have encouraged the purchase of cheaper generic drugs developed in lower cost labour markets such as Puerto Rico. The threat to Glaxo is obvious with so much of its sales reliant upon the performance of Zantac in the American market. Glaxo management feel that they have considerable strengths in their commitment to innovation to meet such threats. Furthermore they feel they have developed new opportunities in the launch of new drugs for migraine and asthma sufferers and to alleviate the side-effects of chemotherapy.

(*Sources*: Fagan, 1991; Connon, 1992; Kay, 1992; Buchan, 1993)

The British Government through the Innovation Advisory Board, part of the Department of Trade and Industry, now publishes league tables of R&D spending. Such information is now available for stock exchange listed companies as a requirement of SSAP 13 (Statement of Standard Accounting Practice). Table 5.2 comprises two tables revealing expenditure on R&D by companies in the United Kingdom and worldwide. The highest spending British company, ICI, ranks 35th in the world in terms of R&D spending.

R&D is an incremental process. We illustrate this by using as a framework the classification of R&D developed by Burns and Stalker (1966). Although their classification is biased towards technological industries it gives us further insights into the innovative process.

**Pure research**   This is concerned with advancing the state of knowledge in a particular field with little immediate concern for its commercial application. Very few firms engage directly in this kind of research, and on the whole it is generally left to the university sector. Business concerns are involved indirectly so far as some of them sponsor research activity in some universities.

**Basic research**   Here firms do get involved since this kind of research is directed at advancing the state of knowledge in a particular applied field with the very real hope that it will prove useful. The managements of these firms hope that such research will lead ultimately to those product and process innovations that will give the business its competitive edge. In some firms, like 3M, the active encouragement of staff to develop their own research projects is an important part of company policy, and many ideas generated from the staff's own programmes have been turned to profitable use by the company (Case 4.2). Other companies, like Glaxo, have a more organized approach to basic research (Case 5.1). Basic research is increasingly important in

**Table 5.2(a)**  Ranking of top 10 UK companies by R&D expenditure, 1991

|  | £000 |
| --- | --- |
| Imperial Chemical | 596 000 |
| Glaxo | 475 000 |
| Shell Transport & Trading | 472 000 |
| General Electric | 435 000 |
| SmithKline Beecham | 432 000 |
| Unilever | 426 000 |
| British Petroleum | 308 000 |
| British Aerospace | 263 000 |
| British Telecom | 243 000 |
| Wellcome | 229 700 |

**Table 5.2(b)**  International ranking of top 40 companies worldwide by R&D expenditure, 1991

|  | £000 |
| --- | --- |
| General Motors, USA | 3 153 398 |
| Daimler-Benz, Germany | 2 960 704 |
| Siemens, Germany | 2 781 321 |
| IBM, USA | 2 678 628 |
| Hitachi, Japan | 2 090 342 |
| Ford, USA | 1 996 786 |
| Toyota Motor, Japan | 1 831 735 |
| AT&T, USA | 1 667 916 |
| Matsushita Electric, Japan | 1 635 407 |
| Fujitsu, Japan | 1 404 996 |
| Toshiba, Japan | 1 273 584 |
| Philips, The Netherlands | 1 210 320 |
| NEC, Japan | 1 190 555 |
| NTT, Japan | 1 160 643 |
| Fiat, Italy | 1 046 633 |
| ABB, Switzerland | 1 034 279 |
| Hoechst, Germany | 1 011 101 |
| Nissan Motor, Japan | 1 001 064 |
| Bayer, Germany | 964 933 |
| Digital Equipment, USA | 883 438 |

**Table 5.2(b)** *Continued*

|  | £000 |
|---|---|
| VW, Germany | 881 057 |
| Sony, Japan | 876 621 |
| Alcatel-Alsthom, France | 838 699 |
| Honda, Japan | 826 577 |
| Eastman Kodak, USA | 800 214 |
| HP, USA | 783 610 |
| Boeing, USA | 758 971 |
| GE, USA | 750 937 |
| BASF, Germany | 727 013 |
| Du Pont, USA | 695 232 |
| Roche, Switzerland | 681 934 |
| Mitsubishi Electric, Japan | 680 523 |
| Dow Chemical, USA | 620 782 |
| United, Technologies, USA | 610 605 |
| ICI, UK | 596 000 |
| Motorola, USA | 577 932 |
| BCE, Canada | 562 716 |
| Rhone-Poulenc, France | 545 820 |
| Bristol Myers, USA | 531 869 |
| Merck, USA | 529 084 |

*Source*: *Independent*, 9 June 1992.

industries dealing with such as microelectronics, biotechnology and the development of new materials. There has been both an increase in such types of research as well as an increase in government support in the USA, Japan and Germany. In the United Kingdom, basic research, an area traditional strength is now in relative decline (Freeman, 1989).

**Industrial research**   Industrial research stands in relation to basic research as innovation does to invention. Industrial research attempts to transform pure and basic research into some form of profitable use.

**Development**   This takes research a stage further by translating the outcome of research into something more tangible. At this stage in the design of a new product, a prototype or a sample would be produced.

**Design**   This is the final stage in the R&D process which translates the development into the final product for the consumer. The design stage attempts to fuse certain elements which are referred to as the 'design mix'. These elements are effective operation, safety, easy maintenance, value for money and aesthetic considerations. These are all focused on satisfying customer needs.

The design aspect of research and development is an obvious area of overlap with both the production and marketing processes, to the extent that product design is seen as an essential element in both fields. Design and styling assume particular importance in industries such as car manufacture, where products are often sold as much on their appearance as their inherent product qualities. A firm like Bang and Olufsen produces televisions and hi-fi equipment to high technical specifications, yet its distinctiveness in the market place owes much more to its visual appeal. Making their products look very different from their competitors is a deliberate Bang and Olufsen strategy.

The British government targeted design for special consideration by businesses in 1985. Part of this targeting was an encouragement to schools and colleges to seek ways of incorporating design in the curriculum. A major concern has been the place of design in manufacturing industry. An underlying assumption behind such developments is undoubtedly the view that Britain as a manufacturing nation is falling behind its rivals, notably West Germany and Japan, in the perceived quality and desirability of its goods. We discuss the importance of quality in Chapter 6.

It is not only in manufacturing industry that design is important. A good illustration is presented by the clothing retail chain Burton at the beginning of the 1980s. The company had always been fairly successful catering for the needs of a middle-of-the-road male market segment. However the firm suffered a serious decline of its market share and profitability. The styling of their clothes had not kept pace with the needs of an increasingly fashion-conscious market, particularly those in the younger age group who spend a good proportion of their income on clothes. Moreover the image of their shops and store lay-out was decidedly old-fashioned and unappealing to the new consumer. As a result of a very detailed research programme to identify and meet the specific design needs of different consumer groups, the management introduced a completely new range of clothes to capture the growing market and invested in a modernization programme to give their stores a new image. This conscious effort in design management was held to be mainly responsible for the profit increase from £16.4 million in 1981 to £80.22 million in 1985.

| KEY CONCEPT 5.2 *Entrepreneurship* | The entrepreneur is responsible for creating new products, services and markets and the means through which these products are made, services produced, and markets reached. Entrepreneurs are often responsible for creating new forms of organization and new ways of managing people. The entrepreneur operates by introducing such changes directly and by having the ability to organize physical, financial, information and human resources to bring about innovation. |
| --- | --- |

## Entrepreneurship

We noted at the beginning of this chapter that the activities of the entrepreneur were crucial to the process of innovation. Innovation happens because the entrepreneur has initiated it, as illustrated by the work of Ronald Hickman and the 'Workmate' in Case 5.3. The entrepreneur creates new products, new markets, and new means through which products are made and markets reached, based around new forms of organization and new means of managing people. Entrepreneurs have therefore been key figures in business history.

The centrality of entrepreneurs to business development has led researchers to seek out those characteristics which make a successful entrepreneur. The research has shown that entrepreneurs are hard workers, risk-takers, outsiders, but, not surprisingly, no distinctive set of personality traits has emerged which adequately define entrepreneurs. Perhaps the most significant finding was that which suggested that successful entrepreneurs had a high need for achievement and a moderate need for power, while the less successful had a low need for achievement and a positively high or low need for power (McClelland, 1961). The message from this research is clear; entrepreneurs are achievers but those seeking entrepreneurial activity only as a means of achieving power over others are likely to fail.

For a time, the role of the entrepreneur in business was understated as the focus turned to the growth and activities of the large corporation. However, the entrepreneur re-emerged in the 1980s as a hero figure, when both the Government and the media highlighted the success of certain businesses when those around were failing. Success through a

---

The Inmos saga . . . provides 1980s evidence of Britain's still unbridged 'two cultures' gap, through politicians' ignorance of technology and technologists' naivety about politics.

(*Guardian*, 3 December 1985)

Inmos has been a hostage of political incompetence, City misunderstanding and corporate chaos.

(*Guardian*, 31 March 1987)

**CASE 5.2**
*Inmos*

In 1978 under a Labour government, the National Enterprise Board (NEB), in its role as an industrial holding company, invested £50 million in a newly formed company, INMOS, to develop, manufacture and market semi-conductors, popularly known as microchips. The company was formed by a small group of capitalist entrepreneurs, including an Englishman and two Americans, and was based originally in the USA. NEB accepted the proposals of the new company even though it had no product or even design for one at the time. The motivation behind the government's involvement was the desire for Britain to develop its own semi-conductor industry, not only because this was seen as a valuable and growing market, but also as part of a wider strategy for the development of the government-backed electronics industry, including such firms as Ferranti and ICL, an industry identified as central to the country's economic development through the 1980s. An important factor was the decision to join a race for the development of a new form of microchip, one which would perform the functions of several types of semi-conductors on a single chip. This creation of a 'mini-computer' on single chip was seen as the next development in 'Very Large Scale Integration' (VLSI) technology.

At the time, the semi-conductor market was dominated by the Americans with Texas Instruments leading the field. The Japanese however were launching a collaborative effort by leading companies to develop the next generation of VLSI. By contrast, European firms had a weak position in the market and prospects looked none too good. The management of INMOS decided that its main strategy was to push ahead and be the first company to produce the revolutionary chip, its particular version to be known as the Transputer. In the mean time it was decided to design and manufacture conventional semi-conductors and the company set up two production plants at Colorado Springs in the USA, designated the corporate headquarters and at Newport in Wales. The British operation was controlled from a research base in Bristol. INMOS saw its success in a highly volatile industry as being based upon, first, the development of an entirely new product acceptable to the majority of users as the best, and second on high-volume sales to offset the high development costs.

At the outset INMOS faced a number of difficulties. There was scepticism in the City, among the civil servants, from some trade unionists and from potential American customers wary of a state-controlled company. There was opposition from within the ranks of the Labour party, especially left-wing members who objected to the three founders acquiring such a large stake in the company and in particular to the large amounts of money being paid to the two Americans. More significantly several experts in the field felt that insufficient investment had been made given the nature of the company's strategy. Worse problems were to follow with the defeat of the Labour Government at the hands of the Conservatives in the 1979 election. The incoming Government were less than enthusiastic about INMOS, preferring to give support to those companies like ICL that were already established in their field. Moreover, there were proposals to limit the activities of NEB and an ideological commitment to privatization. This not only placed the future of INMOS in some doubt, but there were delays in necessary funding at a crucial time in the company's development.

In 1984, after investing an estimated £100 million into the company, the Government sold its interests to Thorn EMI for £95 million. This followed a well-established pattern in the microchip industry; that of small innovative companies being bought up by large multinational organizations. In Thorn's case it was seen in the City as a hasty acquisition, after the company had been refused in its attempts to merge with British Aerospace. The following year the microchip market suffered a downturn and INMOS was forced to cut back its activities by 20%, with lay-offs in both Britain and America. Later in 1985, Thorn EMI announced that it was looking for a development partner for INMOS, possibly from Japan and was willing to relinquish up to 49% of its shares.

There can be little doubt that the ideological and political differences, the selling of INMOS at a crucial stage in its development, and the continued uncertainty of its role within the Thorn EMI stable arrested the company's growth. However, the Transputer was developed successfully, it was ahead of its rivals and began to sell well. Thorn EMI did manage to sell INMOS, which is now part of the SGS-Thomson group.

(*Sources*: Stopford *et al.*, 1980, *Guardian*, 31.3.87. A much more detailed account can be found in McClean and Rowland (1985).)

CASE 5.3
*The Workmate*

In 1973 a Design Council Award was made to Ronald Hickman, the inventor of the 'Workmate'. This was only the third time such an award had been made for a tool. The 'Workmate' is a combination of a work bench, a sawing horse and a vice, but whose versatility as a tool is much greater than the sum of its parts. It is small, lightweight, and easily stored. The device is bought in great numbers by DIY enthusiasts, but also by professional carpenters and building firms.

Hickman, who had received only a high-school education and possessed no technical qualifications came to Britain in 1955, working first as a bookkeeper in a music store and then with Ford Motor Company in the styling department. By 1958 he had been doing freelance design work for Lotus cars and eventually joined them as a designer. He was entirely responsible for the Lotus Elan, and in five years had become the design director of the company. He reached the stage where the job was taking all his time, and in 1967 he left Lotus to form his own company Mate Tools.

The idea for the company arose during his time at Lotus. He had moved house and had invented a device to assist him in building fitted furniture to his own design. After various modifications the Workmate Mark 1 emerged, which he patented and sold through mail-order advertising in such magazines as *Do-it-yourself*, *Homemaker*, *Radio Times* and newspapers such as the *Daily Mail*. Sales started in 1968 and the product became an instant success. The demand for the product was greater than Mate Tools could satisfy. As a result several imitators appeared and Hickman began to look for a larger firm to take on manufacture and sales.

The patent protection saw off the imitators, sometimes after court action and damages awarded to Hickman. In 1972, Hickman granted Black & Decker an exclusive licence to manufacture the 'Workmate' which was now redesigned as Mark 2.

When the Mark 2 was launched in 1972 the demand was so great that all stocks were immediately exhausted. The Mark 1 had achieved an annual sales growth of 120% and under Black & Decker sales of the Mk2 were growing at over 138% per year. By 1976 over one million had been sold and by 1983 the product was being manufactured in Britain, France, Italy, Spain, Canada, Japan and Eire. Mate Tools still sold the 'Workmate' itself but bought them ready-made from Black & Decker.

(*Source*: Reports of Patent Cases, 1983)

general recession made household names of such as Alan Sugar at Amstrad, Anita Roddick at the Body Shop and Richard Branson at Virgin.

We see interest in entrepreneurship taking two directions.

First, the success of certain entrepreneurs to rise above the recession has prompted a government, already committed to a free market, to encourage even more entrepreneurial activity in the form of small business development. We deal at length with issues pertaining to small business development in Chapter 3. Suffice it to say here that not all small businesses are entrepreneurial, since many merely replicate existing forms of business. Becoming self-employed to run a newsagency business has little to do with innovation and entrepreneurship. Nonetheless people were encouraged to develop 'enterprise' as a route to prosperity both for themselves and the nation. The concept of 'enterprise culture' emerged as important government rhetoric supported by a number of significant policy changes to deregulate markets, reconstruct the public sector along business lines, influence curriculum in schools, and to remove impediments to enterprise. Such impediments were seen as an obstructive trade-union movement and a welfare state which was seen to offer little incentive for people to be self reliant. The Department of Trade and Industry was given the official slogan 'the Department of Enterprise'. Such policy changes are examined in more detail in Chapters 2 and 3.

Second, the focus upon small firms and the entrepreneur as a small businessperson has detracted from the importance of entrepreneurship in large businesses. In his study of General Motors, Sears, DuPont and Standard Oil, which we referred to in our discussion of structure in Chapter 3, Chandler stressed the importance for managers to be able to see beyond the daily problems of controlling a large corporation and develop new business ideas for the future. More attention is now being paid to the role of the entrepreneur in large firms. However, the qualities which give rise to a successful entrepreneur are not necessarily those of an 'organization person'. This may make entrepreneurs difficult to manage, an issue we discuss later in the chapter.

It is our view that all firms irrespective of size need the introduction of new ideas to survive. In Chapter 4 we introduced the concept of entrepreneurial decision-making as a type of strategy employed by all organizations at some stage. Whether innovation through entrepreneurship is most successful in a small or a large setting, or how it is best organized, are questions we leave to our discussion of organizational aspects. We turn now to environmental issues in innovation.

## The environmental aspects of innovation

Four aspects of our model are particularly significant here. We will look first of all at the relationship between innovation and the economy, which leads logically to a discussion on the role of the state in encouraging innovation. This in turn leads to the differences in the way nations approach innovation, which we examine by looking at cultural influences. There is a clear relationship between technology and innovation, which we acknowledge in our assessment of the contending influences of technological development and the marketplace. We will not discuss the relationship between innovation and the labour force here. It is an important relationship as the skills of the workforce and their attitude towards change, more especially changes in technology, are crucial to the successful implementation of innovation. These themes are developed in Chapters 2 and 8. A core element in all these discussions is the role of the economy, and the belief that innovation stimulates economic growth.

## The role of the economy

There have been many attempts to link innovation with economic growth. In general, innovation is perceived as the means through which economic regeneration occurs. As such it has held a particular fascination for those who see government investment in research and development as a positive strategy for tackling the problems of economic decline. More specifically economists have attempted to prove links between innovation and such factors as per capita growth and export competitiveness. In this section we will view briefly the general debate which sees innovation as the key mechanism in long-wave economic cycles and then examine attempts to identify more specific relationships.

## Innovation and long-wave cycles

The relationship between innovation and economic activity owes much to the work of the Russian economist Kondratieff. He put forward the view that economic activity exhibits regular long-term cycles of growth and depression, followed by a further period of growth and so on (Kondratieff, 1935). Each cycle is characterized by a particular form of economic activity; thus the period 1785 to 1842 was dominated by iron ore, coke and the cotton industry, whereas the following period to 1897 centred around the development of the railways. If we extend the cycles to the present day then we can see periods of economic activity based around electricity, chemicals and the automobile and more recently focusing upon aerospace, electronics and computers.

The explanation for the operation of these cycles has been taken up by a number of economists. For Schumpeter the key was innovation. Each phase of economic recovery can be attributed to clusters of innovations, enabling capitalism to evolve and usher in a new period of prosperity (Schumpeter, 1939). He thought that most innovations occurred when the economic climate appeared more favourable, thus acting as a stimulus for entrepreneurial activity. However, some believe that innovations only occur in the depths of depression, when profits are so low that entrepreneurs are stimulated into risk-taking ventures (Mensch, 1979).

The notion of economic cycles has generated considerable debate among economists and others, who, despite the absence of hard data have felt more than capable of contributing to the debate as to when the cycles begin, how long they last, and what the key innovations are. The problems with long waves are the task of identifying and dating the major innovations and the highly deterministic nature of cyclical activity, leaving some economists to view the theory as convenient rather than meaningful.

The belief that mankind is in the grip of mysterious forces which it is powerless to change recurs in periods of stress and difficulty.

(Brittan, 1983)

This may explain the resurgence of interest in long-wave theory in times of recession.

---

| | |
|---|---|
| **KEY CONCEPT 5.3**<br>*Innovation and*<br>*economic growth* | There is considerable debate concerning the relationship between innovation and economic growth at the level of both national economies and the firm. Several theories have been based around innovation as a prerequisite for economic growth and more especially its role in leading economies out of depression. Despite the plausibility of several of these claims it is difficult to measure the precise impact that innovation has upon the economy and establish clear causality. As with many aspects of business, the isolation of a single factor such as innovation can present a misleading view of the complex nature of business interactions. Nevertheless, the importance accorded by governments to innovation as the stimulus for economic growth has resulted in considerable state intervention in this area. |

---

## Innovation and specific measures of economic performance

A growing number of studies have been carried out in an attempt to provide hard data linking innovative activity and some measure of economic performance at both the level of national economies and the individual firm. Many of the studies highlight significant differences in measures of innovative activity between nations. We return to this theme when we discuss cultural and national differences later in the chapter. An indication of the types of study carried out is offered below.

- There is evidence to suggest that investments in R&D, particularly those relating to technical change, are the major cause of improvements in productivity and output. Some studies suggest that increasing the quantity of either capital equipment and or labour are by themselves insufficient for economies to grow and remain competitive and as much as a 90% improvement can be attributed to process innovations (Solow, 1957).
- Analysis of the performance of those companies that feature high on the DTI scoreboard (see Table 5.2) reveal that those companies with a high and rising investment in R&D perform better than those where R&D expenditure is falling. However, this is not always the case. General Motors was the world's biggest investor in R&D in 1992, spending £3.1 billion, yet, over the same period, made a loss and halved its dividend to shareholders. This illustrates the difficulty of examining R&D in isolation. R&D expenditure by General Motors may well have contributed to product and process improvements, but these could have been negated by other factors such as the depressed US car market or a lack of management strategy to capitalize upon the investment. Furthermore, the time horizon for the investment may be such that the pay-back will be at some time in the future.

- Tables 5.3–5.6 all pertain to patents. As with published expenditure, patents represent an easily measured output of R&D. Table 5.3 examines the number of patent applications per million population filed in the home country by eight manufacturing nations from 1979 to 1989. The same study revealed a correlation between patent applications and GDP and between patent applications and manufacturing output. The clear fact to emerge from the graph is the prolific patent behaviour of the Japanese. In 1989 the Japanese filed 2580 applications per million population, more than the rest put together and five times that of Germany.

- A correlation also exists between the number of registered patents and export performance. Between 1937 and 1975 West German patents registered in the USA outnumbered those from any other foreign country. During the same period West Germany was the leading exporter to the USA (Rothwell and Zegveld, 1981). Since 1975, the former West Germany has been replaced by Japan on both counts. In 1987, the top three companies receiving patents in the USA were all Japanese (Table 5.4). In fact, eight Japanese companies feature in the top twenty. Table 5.5 shows the US patents granted to automobile firms between 1986 and 1990. Once more the Japanese dominate despite General Motors showing a 50% increase on the previous four-year period and Chrysler a 100% increase on the same period. Both Volkswagen and BMW show a decline in patenting activity, although Table 5.6 shows the relative dominance of Germany among other European countries.

- This is some evidence to suggest that consumers appear willing to pay more for goods of superior technical quality. Once again West

**Table 5.3** Patent applications filed by residents in the National Patent Office per million population

| Year | Australia | Germany | France | Japan | Korea | Spain | UK | US |
|------|-----------|---------|--------|-------|-------|-------|-----|-----|
| 1979 | 327 | 502 | 211 | 1300 | 27 | 51 | 348 | 269 |
| 1980 | 448 | 466 | 204 | 1419 | 32 | 50 | 350 | 273 |
| 1981 | 425 | 484 | 202 | 1629 | 34 | 45 | 369 | 271 |
| 1982 | 435 | 497 | 196 | 1780 | 40 | 43 | 364 | 272 |
| 1983 | 451 | 515 | 204 | 1909 | 40 | 39 | 353 | 253 |
| 1984 | 461 | 532 | 206 | 2135 | 49 | 46 | 337 | 261 |
| 1985 | 415 | 528 | 218 | 2270 | 66 | 38 | 347 | 266 |
| 1986 | 361 | 527 | 219 | 2388 | 88 | 43 | 354 | 270 |
| 1987 | 400 | 517 | 228 | 2546 | 117 | 44 | 350 | 280 |
| 1988 | 370 | 519 | 222 | 2518 | 136 | 47 | 360 | 305 |
| 1989 | 407 | 503 | 224 | 2580 | 166 | 54 | 345 | 331 |

*Source*: Needle and Needle, 1991.

**Table 5.4**  Corporations receiving US patents by rank order

(a) 1987

| Rank | Corporation | No. of patents |
|------|-------------|----------------|
| 1 | Canon K.K. | 847 |
| 2 | Hitachi Ltd | 845 |
| 3 | Toshiba Corp. | 823 |
| 4 | General Electric Corp. | 779 |
| 5 | US Philips Corp. | 687 |
| 6 | Westinghouse Electric Corp. | 652 |
| 7 | IBM Corp. | 591 |
| 8 | Siemens A.G. | 539 |
| 9 | Mitsubishi Denki K.K. | 518 |
| 10 | RCA Corp. | 504 |
| 11 | Fuji Photo Film Co., Ltd | 494 |
| 12 | Dow Chemical Co. | 469 |
| 13 | E.I. du Pont de Nemours & Co. | 419 |
| 14 | Motorola, Inc. | 414 |
| 15 | AT&T Co. | 406 |
| 16 | Honda Motor Co., Ltd | 395 |
| 17 | NEC Corp. | 375 |
|  | Toyota Jidosha K.K. | 375 |
| 19 | Bayer A.G. | 371 |
| 20 | General Motors Corp. | 370 |

*Source*: Intellectual Property Owners Inc., March 1988.

(b) 1991

| Rank | Corporation | No. of patents |
|------|-------------|----------------|
| 1 | Toshiba | 1114 |
| 2 | Mitsubishi Denki | 936 |
| 3 | Hitachi | 927 |
| 4 | Eastman Kodak | 863 |
| 5 | Canon | 823 |
| 6 | General Electric | 809 |
| 7 | Fuji Photo | 731 |
| 8 | US Philips | 650 |
| 9 | Motorola | 613 |

*Source*: *Intellectual Property Newsletter* Volume 16 Issue No. 1, January 1993.

**Table 5.5**  US patents granted to automobile firms, 1986–90

| | |
|---|---|
| Toyota | 1218 |
| Honda | 1218 |
| Nissan | 1054 |
| General Motors | 993 |
| Mazda | 568 |
| Ford | 399 |
| Mercedes | 377 |
| Chrysler | 176 |
| Mitsubishi | 123 |
| VW | 97 |
| BMW | 62 |

*Source*: Narin (1993).

**Table 5.6**  US patents granted to European firms by country as a percentage of all European

| | *1963* | *1985* |
|---|---|---|
| Germany | 34 | 42 |
| UK | 26 | 16 |
| France | 12 | 15 |
| The rest | 28 | 27 |

*Source*: SPRU Database, quoted in Bowen *et al.* (1992).

Germany features, this time in comparison with Britain. Between 1971 and 1975 West Germany's share of exports to OECD countries was 22% compared to Britain's 10%, despite the fact that the unit value of West German exports was 40% greater (Rothwell and Zegveld, 1981). The assumption here is that investment in improving the quality of goods will pay back in the form of increased sales.

Despite the research findings and the persuasive pleas for investment in R&D, the links between innovation and economic performance remain speculative. One difficulty is our inability to measure innovation. Indicators that have been used, such as patents and the amount of money a firm has invested in its R&D activities, can at best be considered a rough guide. For example, a patent may be registered and then never used to produce anything of value; improvements in products and processes can originate as much from individual inventors and equipment users as they can from organized R&D departments.

We have already noted in the case of General Motors that significant expenditure is no guarantee of short-term financial success. More significantly the attempts to isolate innovation may give a false impression. The export success of 'upper range' West German cars such as Mercedes Benz and BMW may well be attributed to the technical superiority of the product when compared to other cars in the same range. Such an explanation fits the research findings identified above. There is another explanation. Both firms have been particularly active in carefully targeted advertising campaigns which not only stress the technical superiority of their product, but also attempt to give the product an image of exclusivity and high status. How much of their sales are attributable to technical innovation and how much to an effective advertising campaign? This illustration confirms the interrelationship of innovation and marketing that we identified earlier. It also emphasizes a key theme in this book; that business activities are interrelated and there are dangers in viewing one activity, such as innovation, in isolation.

Throughout this section we have made reference to the role of state intervention, and it is to this aspect we now turn our attention. We will view the role of governments in general terms and we then explore how governments in different countries operate with respect to the stimulation of innovation.

### The role of the state

In almost every country, the state has a significant involvement in innovation. Table 5.7 shows government-funded R&D as a percentage of GDP in six major countries. Three main reasons may be given as motivation for this involvement.

- Using the kind of economic evidence presented in the last section there would appear to be a clear belief that innovation and entrepreneurship are major factors in economic expansion and export competitiveness.
- We have already noted that investment in innovation is both long-term and high-risk. The mechanism of the free market may be inadequate in generating those basic innovations upon which economic expansion is based, hence the need for state subsidy when individual companies are reluctant to invest.
- Intervention is often necessary for political and strategic as well as for social reasons. In Britain and the USA defence spending forms a major part of all expenditure on innovation, as Table 5.7 shows. Many countries have seen space exploration as a goal of national importance and prestige, and the same could be said for the British and French governments' involvement with the development of the supersonic jet airliner, Concorde. Investment in the nuclear fuel industry is viewed by several governments as a desirable energy strategy.

**Table 5.7** Government-funded R&D as a percentage of GDP, 1988

|         | Total | Defence | Civil |
|---------|-------|---------|-------|
| UK      | 0.96  | 0.42    | 0.54  |
| France  | 1.37  | 0.51    | 0.86  |
| Germany | 1.05  | 0.13    | 0.92  |
| Italy   | 0.80  | 0.08    | 0.72  |
| Japan   | 0.47  | 0.02    | 0.45  |
| USA     | 1.23  | 0.83    | 0.40  |

*Source*: OECD Main Science and Technology Indicators, quoted in Bowen *et al.* (1992).

In the United Kingdom the state is involved in innovation in a number of different ways. It invests in R&D in individual firms, government research establishments and in universities. It has established the legal protection of inventions through the patent system. Various state departments are actively concerned in the stimulation of innovation; currently the Department of Trade and Industry proudly announces itself as 'The Department for Enterprise'. The state's financial support is clearly biased towards technological innovation in the manufacturing and defence industries but exhortations for innovation and enterprise are usually aimed at all firms in all sectors and we have already noted the state's commitment to the establishment of an 'enterprise culture'. Occasionally such exhortations are transformed into government policies and schemes, such as those aimed at innovation through small business development (Chapter 3).

The activities of the state in subsidizing, protecting and encouraging innovation provide an excellent illustration of the interrelationship between the state and business at a more general level. In this section, we attempt a classification of the types of intervention specifically concerned with innovation and examine the associated problems.

## Types of state intervention in innovation

We examine state intervention under six main headings; procurement, subsidies, education and training, patents and licensing, restrictive and enabling laws and, finally, import controls. These types of innovation occur even where the government has expressed its ideological opposition to interference in the workings of the free market.

**Procurement** The need of the state for certain products has stimulated research in many areas. UK private industry only funds a half of all R&D activity, but carries out over two-thirds, the difference being linked to government contracts (Bowen *et al.*, 1992). Defence work offers the clearest illustration with implications not only for the arma-ments industry itself, but also in electronics, computing and aerospace. Businesses in the USA have seen the armed forces as a very large and very stable market. There is a view that the goals of business and the military have become intertwined and form an important part of the image-building that goes on between ideologically opposed nations in a cold war (Galbraith, 1972). The significant political changes that have occurred in the former Soviet Union and Eastern Europe in general may alter this position. In Britain the needs of the National Health Service have stimulated developments in the pharmaceutical industry and in most nations the fear of disappearing natural resources has led to government-backed research to find synthetic materials.

**Subsidies**   Subsidies to individual firms occur in the form of invest-ments, grants and tax concessions. We have seen how special policies exist, such as those to encourage innovation through small firms. Most subsidies aim to support a particular form of research and develop-ment. For example, in 1981 the British Government made available £80 million to promote the use and awareness of information technology. This was deemed necessary as Britain was seen to be falling behind its major competitors.

The coordination of the UK policy of selective intervention has been placed in the hands of the British Technology Group. This body was set up in 1981 to incorporate both the National Research and Develop-ment Council and the National Enterprise Board. It seems clear that the Government wishes to align itself with more progressive industries and establish a more proactive role. The National Enterprise Board was often viewed as reactive and was all too often identified with policies to prop up ailing industries, as in the giving of financial support to British Leyland and Rolls Royce. The development of INMOS presented in Case 5.2 illustrates the role of British governments in subsidizing R&D and the dilemmas which often accompany it.

**Education and training**   There is an underlying assumption that state investment in education and pure science will have a significant impact in increasing the level of innovation and thus benefit both the economy and society. The relationship between primary research and the knowl-edge based activities of higher education institutions is supposedly one of the key features of the modern age. Galbraith observed of educators and scientists that they 'stand in relation to the industrial system much as did the banking and financial community in the early stages of industrial development'(Galbraith, 1972, p. 283).

There are certain well-publicized developments in both Britain and the USA that lend substance to the post-industrial society thesis. Develop-ments in 'Silicon Valley' in California and the growth of the science park around Cambridge in England all show the relationship between industrial research and major universities with a reputation for science. The growth of some American high-technology companies such as Hewlett-Packard in Palo Alto, California is clearly associated with this phenomenon, as is the development of a network of businesses in computing and related fields in the vicinity of Cambridge. We have noted in Case 5.1 that Glaxo chose to locate one of its USA research laboratories in the midst of universities in North Carolina. Such illustrations support the view that competitive endeavour among firms in close proximity to each other is a spur to economically successful innovations and that there is synergy to be gained both through such competition and through collaboration with the university sector.

In spite of such developments, British institutions of higher education are often subjected to financial stringencies as part of the Government's determination to reduce public expenditure. On the positive side this has, in many cases, pushed industry and universities much closer together. Some universities like Salford rely heavily on the outside funding of research by private companies, which has enabled many universities to generate income for re-investment. The critics of this type of development see a danger of weakening the primary research base and restricting university research to projects related to the very specific requirements of a limited number of companies. This could restrict opportunities for breakthroughs in basic technology considered essential for industrial regeneration.

The state sometimes intervenes in skills training and comparative research of training in Britain and Germany ascribes Germany's advantage in product and process innovation to its superior craft training schemes (Steedman and Wagner, 1987). Clearly a skilled workforce is one that can adapt readily to technical changes. Skills shortages in the United Kingdom may have been responsible for the relatively slow adoption of computerized aids to manufacturing, such as CNC machines. This aspect illustrates the interaction between innovation and the labour force in our model. Any innovation can only be effective if it is matched by a labour force having the requisite skills. The development of new processes may prove even more costly if they remain idle waiting the skills of the workforce to catch up, as Rolls Royce found to its cost in the early 1970s. The development of the high-performance jet engine, the RB 211, encountered many problems. Although the focus was upon the mounting costs of the project, costs which almost forced the company out of business, a contributory factor was the lack of expertise to overcome the many technical difficulties which arose at the development stage. In the 1970s many firms invested in computer hardware and software in the belief that this would change their business overnight. In some of these companies the systems were under-utilized, as insufficient consideration had been given to training the employees.

**Patents and licensing**   A patent is a legal device which enables the holder to maintain a monopoly in an invention for a stated period, which in Britain stands at 20 years. In exchange for granting this monopoly, the owner of the invention must make available its details to the general public. The patent system operates in almost every country in the world including the People's Republic of China. The stated benefits of such a system are, first, that it actively encourages new developments by offering protection to the patent-holder against others copying the invention. Second, by revealing the details of the invention, it encourages further inventions and innovative activity along similar lines. Third, it prevents the duplication of research, and fourth, it ensures that the benefits of research are passed on to society. A real benefit to the patent-holder is the opportunity to issue manufacturing licences, as illustrated in Case 5.3 by the licence bought by Black & Decker to manufacture and sell the 'Workmate'.

A firm holding a patent on a particular type of manufacturing process may allow another firm in the same business to use that process upon the payment of an agreed fee. In the case of major inventions this can be an important source of revenue for the patent holder. The revolutionary method for the production of glass, the 'Float Process', was developed by the St Helens firm of Pilkington Brothers Ltd in the early 1960s, since when licences have been granted to glass manufacturers all over the world enabling them to use the same process. Licensing is clearly a vital source of revenue for some companies. In 1991 Texas Instruments made $415 million from licensing its semiconductor patents, while in the same year its manufacturing activities made a loss of $203 million. In certain cases the law has had to intervene to enforce the issue of licences where it was felt that some companies were operating an unfair monopoly. This occurred in the case of Hoffman-La Roche, the Swiss pharmaceutical company. In 1971 the British Patent Comptroller ordered Hoffman-La Roche to grant licences to two British firms, Berk Pharmaceuticals and DDSA Ltd for the manufacture of the tranquillizers Librium and Valium. Despite frequent requests the Swiss drugs company had repeatedly refused manufacturing licences on the grounds of the safety standards of the finished product. However the British patent system held that the refusal to grant licences gave the Swiss company an unfair monopoly in the drugs industry (the Hoffman-La Roche case in Stopford *et al.*, 1980 has further details).

Since that time the law relating to licensing has been amended and compulsory licences may now only be issued in the case of the non-manufacture of the product by the patent holder or in cases where the product is not manufactured in this country. The main idea behind such laws is to stimulate the development and use of the invention in that country and hence assist local businesses.

Restrictive and enabling laws   Most countries possess laws which control manufacturing standards and relate to such aspects as safety and pollution. Not only do these laws ensure that innovations conform to certain standards, but they aim to encourage research into socially desirable end-products such as car engines with low fuel consumption or car exhaust systems which restrict pollution into the atmosphere. The ends are not only socially desirable but can have an effect on business performance as well. A firm which meets government standards of product quality enters the market place with additional competitive edge. As we see in Chapter 6, there is a growing trend in Britain for firms to show that they have met British Standards of quality assurance. There is a strong prediction that firms with strong policies on quality, like Marks & Spencer, will, in the future, only deal with suppliers that have met these standards.

Such regulations can benefit some firms but handicap others. The determination on the part of the 1993 USA Administration to reduce the health-care budget may pose a threat to Glaxo (Case 5.1), but may lead to the development of cheaper generic drugs. The use of restrictive laws has been greatest in the USA and there is a lobby which sees a danger that excessive government regulation may hold back technological innovation and hence the country's economic growth. However, as with the relationship between innovation and economic growth, there is a difficulty in establishing a direct causal link between such laws and innovative activity at the level of the firm. As an illustration, we can see that increases in the price of oil in 1973 resulted, in both Britain and the USA, in new laws relating to speed limits and exhaust emission. However, the ensuing trend in motor manufacture towards the design and manufacture of smaller cars would almost certainly have occurred in response to increased oil prices irrespective of any legislation.

**Import controls**   The theory here is that restriction on the imports from other countries will have a beneficial effect in stimulating research in the home country or intensifying the search for a substitute product or process. Import controls enforced by Japanese governments since the Second World War has often been cited as the major impetus to considerable innovations by Japanese businesses. The danger in such a strategy, however, is that other countries may well retaliate and impose their own restrictions. Concern about the trade imbalance between the USA and Japan, in favour of Japan, has resulted in presidential delegations to Tokyo and agreements on import quotas. The Americans themselves have in the past been fond of using import controls and the development of the synthetic fibre industry in the USA owes much to restrictions on the import of woollen products.

## Some problems with state intervention in innovation

We have seen that the main motive for state intervention to encourage and support innovative activity is the desire to improve economic performance. We have also seen the difficulties of showing a direct relationship between investment in innovation and economic growth, whether measured at national or organizational levels. There are other difficulties with the state's involvement and we identify these below.

An over-reliance upon state funding may have serious repercussions at times of reductions in government expenditure. It is noticeable from Table 5.7 that Japan, despite its commitment to innovation, has relatively low levels of government funded R&D, firms preferring to rely on generating their own investment income.

A major difficulty lies in the ability of government employees to make decisions in highly specialized technical and scientific areas, and decisions which are in the best interests of the business community as a whole. Government support may well be important in stimulating innovation but the critical skills and knowledge reside in the firms themselves or the higher-education sector. For intervention to be successful, extensive consultation is required and there needs to be freedom for individuals to pursue their own research goals, otherwise there is a danger that intervention can be misdirected. Several highly publicized government-backed ventures such as Concorde or gas-cooled nuclear reactors have not met with the success predicted for them as a result of these difficulties. In 1985, with much publicity, the US government launched its proposals for the Strategic Defence Initiative, a missile defence system in outer space. The initiative was to give a boost to the USA computer industry and, in Britain, firms and universities looked forward to lucrative research contracts. The project was officially cancelled in 1993, partly as a result of a changing world political scene, but mainly as a result of the impracticality of the project in the first place.

The issue of freedom raises the most fundamental questions of an ideological kind and is especially troubling for those governments committed to laissez-faire economic policies. As we saw in the INMOS case, the British Government was at the same time pursuing a policy of support through the British Technology Group, while planning to sell the company to the private sector. Such conflict of interests may well be detrimental to innovation since political considerations may come to dominate business development. Underpinning many of the difficulties outlined above is the view that governments have the power to constrain innovation and entrepreneurial activity by bureaucratic interference and restrictive legislation.

The direction of state intervention may raise conflicts within the agencies of the state as well as raising certain ethical issues. Proposals by one department such as the Department of Trade and Industry may be opposed by another, such as the Department of the Environment. For example, new developments in air travel, in particular the increased passenger carrying capacity of aircraft, have necessitated airport expansion. This can be of benefit to the local economy by stimulating the job market and offering opportunities for local businesses. The same proposals will almost certainly be opposed by local residents and environmentalists. Such debates have surrounded the siting of London's third airport and the expansion of the airport at Heathrow to incorporate a fourth terminal complex. An overemphasis on government defence contracts may result in a loss of competitiveness in civil markets. This is a criticism levelled at GEC and Plessey. In 1988, defence contracts accounted for 33% of GEC's overall turnover and 50% of its turnover in electronics. Despite increases in its own R&D investment GEC spends only one-sixth the amount on R&D than one of its main European rivals, Siemens (*Independent*, 9 June 1992).

Issues like these deal with aspects of business ethics and question the purpose, direction and outcomes of innovative activity. Kumar is especially sceptical and he sums up the whole argument most appropriately.

There are the familiar examples of the atomic bomb, other weapons of the biological and chemical kind, space exploration and large scale capital intensive technology with its propensity to pollute the environment and exhaust the world's supply of fossil fuels. Then there is the ingenious and expensive gadgetry of the mass consumer industry with its built-in principle of planned obsolescence and marginal technical improvements . . . medical research seems equally skewed in the direction of people with power to persuade and pay . . . and 99% of the knowledge effort of the industrial societies is devoted to the problems of the developed world.

(Kumar, 1978, p. 230)

## Cultural and national differences

So convinced have we become of the dependence of the total social, political and economic order on technical development that national output of scientific discoveries and the rate of technological advance have begun to appear as the ultimate criterion of culture and different political and social systems are compared as facilitators of this kind of achievement.

(Burns and Stalker, 1966, p. 19)

We have seen in the previous sections that the state in Britain has shown considerable interest in the innovative activity of private business. Nearly all governments in the major industrialized countries have attempted to influence the direction of innovation in some way. While there is a danger of creating cultural stereotypes and perpetuating myths, the response of different governments has varied and different areas have been targeted. Not only this, but investment in R&D has been taken as an indicator of a nation's economic health and future prosperity. We will explore both these issues.

Britain has always been typified as placing emphasis on basic research with its application in defence, nuclear energy and space research. The spin-offs have been few and limited to a small range of companies, but making little impact on the manufacture of commercial products. The USA too has been criticized for emphasizing big projects in defence and aerospace, usually with government backing, and consequently with a corresponding reluctance on the part of private companies to invest in their own long-term projects. France on the other hand is typified as giving strong central direction and significant financial support to private industry in a bid to achieve scientific and technological independence, by creating a domestic supplier in every major world industry. The Germans conform to a less directive model but give specific assistance to those areas where market success is guaranteed; a policy particularly successful in the machine-tool industry. In addition, we have already noted in Chapter 2 how much emphasis is placed in Germany upon supporting businesses through a national system of training, thus ensuring the workforce possesses the required skills both to enable them to develop and exploit innovations. These particular views of the UK, USA, France and Germany are reinforced by the data presented in Table 5.7.

When national myths and stereotypes are being voiced, the greatest number usually relate to Japan (see the section on Japanese management in Chapter 2). Japanese economic success has been linked to the import of key innovations and technologies from other industrialized nations, imperative for such a late industrial starter. The widespread belief soon developed that Japanese businesses could not innovate. While there is little doubt that Japan has gained from bought-in technology, there is also clear evidence that Japan is now probably the world's most innovative industrial nation (Table 5.4 supports this view). The Japanese have made significant advances in machine-tool technology and in particular in developments in automated plant and robotics, and in modifying existing technologies. While products such as the transistor and the video-cassette recorder were invented elsewhere, the Japanese have shown considerable innovation in commercializing such products.

Japan has more of its workforce engaged in industrial R&D than Britain, France or Germany (Peck and Goto, 1982). Japanese businesses spend five times the amount on R&D than their British counterparts (Bowen *et al.*, 1992). In addition to private investment, considerable assistance is offered by the Japanese Ministry of International Trade and Industry (MITI). MITI has been active in monitoring trends, in particular those pertaining to foreign investment. It has negotiated licences for Japanese companies and has acted as a channel through which the diffusion of innovation has occurred. At the same time the internal market has been jealously protected against incursions by foreign suppliers. The government role in R&D is thus far greater than Table 5.7 might suggest.

The two key strategies pursued by the Japanese are incrementalism and collaboration. The large number of patent applications by Japanese firms (Tables 5.3, 5.4 and 5.5) bear testimony to the importance Japanese firms place upon incremental developments. In terms of collaboration, MITI provided both encouragement and facilities to enable Japanese computer firms to engage in big budget research in the 1970s in areas such as VLSI (Very Large Systems Integration). Six of the largest computer companies were organized into two research associations to collaborate on new developments. The early focus of such collaborative ventures was the facilitation of access to existing research rather than the developments of new products. Firms collaborated in reverse engineering exercises to analyse the products of foreign competitors to determine how they were made. As the limits of such technological transfer were reached and as foreign firms became less inclined to license to Japanese firms, the focus of collaboration shifted to the development of entirely new products. While collaboration has been an undoubted feature of the Japanese approach to innovation, some research has suggested that the approach has not been without its problems. Mowery and Rosenberg (1989) suggest that some collaborative ventures between Japanese firms have been typified by a less than full disclosure by the participants and by some firms sending second-rate researchers. Additionally firms are less inclined to participate fully the closer the research is to the frontiers of technology.

An underlying theme in the comparative analysis of national attitudes to research and development is one developed in our earlier section on economic aspects of innovation: that trends in R&D investment are correlated with national economic growth. Underinvestment in R&D has been cited as the main reason for the decline in American competitiveness (Hayes and Wheelwright, 1984). A similar view can be taken of Britain. In comparison with other major industrial countries not only do we spend less on R&D as a proportion of GDP (see Table 5.7), but Britain is the only country to reduce expenditure since 1980 (*Sunday Times*, 16 February 1987). Similarly, the UK employs fewer research scientists as a proportion of its labour force than its main competitors. Furthermore, numbers of research scientists in the UK have fallen between 1981 and 1989 while numbers have increased in France, Italy and Japan (Freeman, 1989); 71% of German companies spend over 5% of their revenue on R&D, while the same can be said of only 28% of British companies (DTI Innovation Advisory Board 1990). The pattern of innovation among private-sector British firms is one of great concentration; 20 UK companies account for 64% of civil R&D and 50 companies account for 80% (*Independent on Sunday*, 30.6.91). As a comparison, while Glaxo in 1991 spent £12 740 per employee on R&D and ICI spent £4470, the Hanson corporation spent only £430. While we are not comparing firms operating in the same industry, this figure does show the wide difference, even among large firms, and indicates the concentration in certain types of industry.

The argument is admirably summed up by Freeman.

It is difficult to escape the conclusion that this represents a serious weakening of the long-term competitiveness of the UK economy during the 1980s.

(Freeman, 1989, p. 206)

One of the reasons offered for this poor performance is an over-emphasis on defence and prestige projects. However the main reason is probably a combination of high interest rates and the workings of a capital market which encourage short-term investment strategies. This is a theme we introduced in Chapter 2 and one to which we shall return at the end of this chapter. The implication is that Britain must step up expenditure on R&D not only to improve the nation's technical competitiveness, but also to generate more jobs in the manufacturing sector. This introduces a social as well as an economic objective for the investment in R&D.

While such comparative data and analyses are revealing, we repeat our caution, that it is difficult to show precise links between R&D expenditure, innovation and economic growth. Furthermore, while criticism is voiced at the British Government for pursuing an apparent selective policy, Japan is often held as a shining example for doing much the same thing.

Our discussion of cultural and national differences has focused almost exclusively on the role of technology. Differences exist in other forms of innovation too. While big business in America might fight shy of investment in R&D in favour of short-term profits, entrepreneurial activity is clearly a part of American life. This has its roots in the historical development of the USA and in particular the expansion from the Eastern seaboard. Individualism and enterprise have become key features of American culture, and probably explains why more people are engaged in self-employment as a proportion of the total population than any other industrialized nation. We should, however, treat such comparisons with caution since we have already noted that self-employment should not automatically be equated with innovation.

We return to the theme of technology, but the theme is used to further illustrate the interrelationship between innovation and marketing.

## Innovation and technology

There is an obvious relationship between technology and innovation. Numerous illustrations exist where developments in state-of-the-art technology result in business innovations and the development of new products and processes, the microchip being a good example. There are some, like Schumpeter, who see technical breakthroughs as the force which changes the whole nature of business, and the ability of firms to respond is crucial to their survival (Schumpeter, 1961). The emphasis on the role of technology is referred to as 'technology push'. There is an alternative view in which demand plays a leading role in determining the direction, extent and impact of inventions. While some industries undoubtedly have a richer knowledge base than others, notably chemicals and electronics, the profitability of the application of that knowledge was predominantly a question of demand. This process is referred to as 'demand pull' (Schmookler, 1966). Several attempts have been made to support the primacy of demand pull over technology push and vice versa and illustrations can be given on both sides. The development of synthetic fibres is clearly a case of demand pull, while the growth of the mass market in electronic calculators is clearly a case of the successful use of developments in integrated circuits and hence technology push.

In most instances the debate is highly simplistic. The growth of sales of the compact disc player is the product of both the application of laser technology to produce consumer goods (technology push) and a function of rising discretionary income and market segmentation (demand pull). The two forces would appear to operate side by side. The development and rapid expansion of 'International Direct Dialling' by British Telecom was a direct response to a growing market demand among the business community for telephone communication with overseas associates. Having developed the technology, British Telecom found that the resources were being under-utilized outside peak business periods. The company therefore launched a successful advertising campaign to increase private and domestic use of the available technology. The initial development was demand-led, while subsequent developments were clearly a case of technology leading the market,

### The Brownie 127 and the Canon Autofocus

**CASE 5.4**
*Innovation and
marketing – two cases*

Throughout the 1950s and 1960s one of the most popular cameras was the Brownie 127, made by Kodak, the British subsidiary of the American company. Its simplicity and ease of operation made it a market leader. The camera was produced from 1952 to 1964 and underwent just one model change involving a slight modification of the lens. A comparable camera today is the Canon Autofocus made by the Japanese company Canon. It has the ease of operation of the Brownie 127 but is much more complex technically. Introduced in 1979, there were five model changes in the first six years of its life. This was deemed necessary not only because of the rapid technological advances in electronics but also because of the intense competition among Japanese camera manufacturers, causing Canon alone to spend 10% of its turnover on R&D in 1985. The market expects regular product changes reflecting new developments in photographic technology and each new technical development, in the form of improved performance, styling and new features is eagerly paraded through advertising to give camera producers that significant edge over their rivals.

(*Source*: *Sunday Times*, 16.2.87)

### The 3M 'Post-it' notes

The R&D department of the American multinational 3M had developed a partially adhesive glue, but had found no commercially viable application for the development. The development waited five years until one of the team devised the idea that a notice-board coated with this adhesive would provide a much more convenient means of fixing and removing notices than the conventional drawing pin. This innovation was compatible with 3M's considerable interests in office equipment. The idea failed at the test-marketing stage. One of those responsible for the project then turned the idea around. The glue on the notice board was changed to glue on pieces of paper which could then be used on notice boards and other places where messages were fixed. The product was refined and the end result became the 'Post-it' note; a pad of readily detachable adhesive labels. Once again the marketing test failed, but it was thought that the product was not reaching the potential user. The company persevered and in a risky marketing venture introduced a mass trial of the product by giving away large numbers of pads to secretaries, typists, receptionists, bank clerks, and anyone else who might possibly use the product in the company's home town of Minneapolis-St Paul. The 'Post-it' notes soon became addictive and a massive local demand was created which soon spread both nationally and internationally.

(*Source*: Kennedy, 1988)

and a company anxious to obtain a healthy return on a not inconsiderable investment.

Another interesting example is provided by Case 5.4 concerning innovations in camera technology and the development of 'Post-it' adhesive notepads. Both illustrations reveal the close relationship between innovation and marketing. In the case of the Canon, technical

**CASE 5.5**
*Baystate Corporation*

Baystate Corporation is the third largest bank in Massachusetts. In 1974 it had the largest network of banks in the state with 173 locations and its financial performance was good. However, several problems were perceived:

- interest rates had fallen, and hence revenue;
- bad loans had increased;
- inflation had risen;
- competition had increased especially from smaller, independent banks offering interest on current accounts.

Most significantly the companies response to these threats was handicapped by its structure. Baystate Corporation was in fact a holding company of 12 different banks, all trading under different names. Attempts had been made to centralize operations with the introduction of a central computer. The individual banks had resisted any move towards a corporate identity and the issue had become one of intense political manoeuvring among senior management.

A new chief executive was appointed who supported the idea of the 12 banks operating in a coordinated fashion to compete more effectively. The vehicle chosen was 'electronic funds transfer'. This system had been in existence for a number of years and had operated mainly through cash dispensers. In 1974 it was not popular with account-holders who preferred personal service. Despite this, developments in electronic funds transfer, especially the 'Automatic Teller Machine' (ATM) offered Baystate an opportunity to unify operations. An account-holder would be able to gain access to that account through any one of the bank's 173 outlets at any time, for cash, or simply account information.

McKinsey's the management consultants were hired and initiated the following innovations.

- 'The Greater Boston Task Force', a group made up of the chief executives of the largest banks to study ideas for consolidating operations and marketing. This group was supplemented by specially selected staff members, picked out for their youth and their ability to generate bright ideas.
- The implementation of the ATM system in all banks to give the company a marketing edge on the independents and the savings banks.
- The selection of a new corporate name. 'Bay-Bank' was chosen and each of the constituent banks would now be called by this name, followed by their own, as in Bay-Bank Norfolk Trust.

(*Source*: McCaskey, 1982)

developments are used as a selling feature to give companies an edge over their rivals. For their part, consumers, through the media of persuasive advertising, have come to expect regular product changes which improve the performance or add on extra features to existing models. The 3M product would not have seen the light of day were it not for some lateral thinking on behalf of some staff, and the product would have failed but for an aggressive marketing effort and a persistent faith in the product.

We can see from these illustrations that the marketing function is both an important guide and support to the direction of innovation. Marketing activity helps in the selection of R&D projects by providing information on the probability of their commercial success. It then assists in persuading the consumer that change is desirable (Simmonds, 1986). EMI is a good example of a British firm that has been highly innovative but has lacked resources and, perhaps, has focused more on technological developments and less on market application to exploit its technological advantage. Glaxo, by comparison, has been ruthless in abandoning research on less promising products at a relatively early stage (Case 5.1).

We can see then that invention, innovation, research and development, manufacturing, and marketing have a complex relationship that is not always fully explored by those seeking to prove a correlation between innovation and economic growth. The illustration of the development of the railways in Britain is a good example of this complexity. In 1814 the technology for the development of the railways was available. However, it was several years before a number of factors converged. These were the technological know-how, the availability of cheap labour, an expanding export market, the need for rapid access to ports, a growing mobility among the middle classes, and the available investment from the profits of industrialization. In other words the innovation of the railways was a product of technology, market need, available capital, together with encouraging social and political conditions (Rothwell and Zegveld, 1981).

The picture becomes even more complex if we take organizational factors into consideration, and it is to these we now turn.

## Organizational aspects of innovation

When we examine innovation at the level of the individual organization, the most significant aspects to emerge are those of size, structure and organization culture. Ownership variables do not appear to be particularly significant, and despite the obvious interest of the state in the innovation process, there is certainly no evidence to suggest that innovation in publicly owned companies is any more significant than that in private firms. Indeed, critics of public ownership may well argue, citing the INMOS case as a good illustration, that political involvement slows down the process of innovation. We shall see that the question of goals is invariably tied up with issues of size, and we deal with these aspects together in our next section.

### Organizational size and goals

Not only does the impact of organizational size upon innovation present us with some rather conflicting evidence, but, in this country at least, public policy appears equally confused. From the 1970s onwards we may be forgiven for thinking that the attention of the policy makers has focused largely on small firms, possibly as a reaction to the merger activity of the previous decade. In practice however, R&D expenditure in Britain is concentrated in relatively few large firms. In 1978 five firms accounted for 41% of all expenditure on R&D and received 76% of all government R&D funding. We saw in the last section how this pattern has continued with 50 companies being responsible for 80% of all civil R&D. We will examine some of that evidence and attempt to show both the relationship of size with changing goals as well as illustrating the dynamic process of innovation at the level of the firm. However, we must remember the major difficulty in our assessment of innovation; that of measurement. While R&D expenditure is clearly some indication of innovative activity, firms can be highly innovative in their products, marketing and organization without having an organized R&D function.

There is a clear line of thinking going back through such writers as Galbraith to Schumpeter, which believes that developments in technology depend upon expensive research programmes of the kind that can only be found in the large corporation. Accordingly big firms are deemed to be best and monopolies even better. The complexities of modern technologies and the corresponding development costs set up irrevocable pressures towards the growing scale of organizations. Evidence in the 1960s was fairly clear in that large manufacturing firms spent proportionally more on R&D, had a larger share of innovation and were quicker to adopt new techniques of manufacturing (Mansfield, 1963). Findings such as these led to the assumption that R&D could only be economic once a certain size of firm had been reached. Certainly this line of thinking influenced British public policy in the 1960s with its encouragement of merger activity.

There can be little doubt that the large firm is able to invest in projects which carry a higher element of risk. Furthermore, the large firm has greater access to finance both from external sources and from the internal generation of funds. The Convair Division of the General Dynamics Corporation was able to ride a loss of $425 million on its production of jet aircraft because of the highly diversified nature of its operations (Galbraith, 1972). However, there are two pieces of evidence which appear to favour the smaller company.

- Small firms spend more on R&D as a proportion of total sales and employ proportionally more staff in R&D than the larger firms (Child, 1969); though this could be a case of economies of scale operating in favour of the larger firm, rather than any significant differences in their innovative capacities.
- Firms of less than 1000 employees account for more than 20% of innovations in Britain, far greater than their share of R&D investment, but less than their share of employment or net output (Pavitt, 1983).

Those who subscribe to the small-firms lobby would argue that the smaller company is much more adaptable, much closer to the consumer, and hence, the source of far more significant innovations than the big firm. We deal with such arguments in more detail in the section on small businesses in Chapter 3.

Jewkes has consistently championed the cause of the small inventor but found that size is a far less significant factor than the competitive nature of the market in which the firm operates (Jewkes *et al.*, 1970). We may conclude from this that highly innovative firms are more likely to be found in very competitive markets, as illustrated by the previously mentioned case of Canon cameras, and that this occurs irrespective of the size of the firm.

There are, however, important variations according to the nature of the sector in which the firm operates. Most innovations in the electrical, electronic, food, chemical and vehicle industries occur in large companies. In the case of mechanical engineering, instrumentation, leather and footwear, it is the smaller firm that tends to dominate (Pavitt, 1983). There is a danger with such analyses in that they confine innovation to products and processes. Significant innovations in such as retailing and financial services tend to be overlooked.

We may conclude from all this that there is no clear relationship between size and innovation, but we are able to make the following observations. The investment required in some types of innovation, and the need for high-volume production for a return on that investment, clearly operates in favour of large companies. A good example here would be the chemical and pharmaceutical industries. An influencing factor would seem to be the sector of operation. Some sectors, like chemicals, tend to be traditionally dominated by large companies, while in others, especially instrumentation, the small firm still plays a significant role. There are cases of breakthroughs being made by small firms in all sectors, but they may have to align themselves with larger companies to obtain the necessary development capital, production capacity, or access to markets, the 'Workmate', Case 5.3, being a good example. However, where markets are especially volatile, any firm, irrespective of size, may have to keep innovating to maintain market share. It is in such situations that entrepreneurial activity becomes most important.

The main difficulty with analyses of this nature is that they tend to view relationships at one point in time, when in reality the innovative process and the size of firms can be viewed as highly dynamic. Henry Ford produced five different engines in quick succession prior to the Model T in a relatively small, jobbing based organization. No product change then took place for 15 years, as the emphasis shifted to the development of mass production process technologies and incremental product improvements (Abernathy and Utterback, 1978).

Examinations of business histories show us that the most fundamental product innovations usually take place at a relatively early stage of a firm's development, when it is still relatively small. As the firm develops, more emphasis is placed on process innovations. A stage may well be reached where the growth of mass markets and the need for economies of scale in the production process mean that fundamental change is resisted as being too costly. In other words the goals of the company change over time with changes in size and the nature of the innovations. A longitudinal study of the development of Computer Aided Design (CAD) systems in manufacturing found that from 1969 to 1974 initial innovations took place in small computer software companies. From 1974 to 1980 the main developments were taking place in much larger companies. Either the original firms had expanded, or they had been bought out by firms such as General Electric, wishing to buy into the new technology. In both cases, size was seen as an important factor in the attraction of venture capital. From 1980 onwards, smaller firms once again entered the market, concentrating on the development of highly specialized CAD systems, with a limited field of application (Kaplinsky, 1983).

We have noted in this section the need for some small firms to align themselves to larger companies for access to development capital and markets. There are some larger firms who pursue a deliberate strategy of innovation through acquisition. This can be a useful strategy where the acquired firm operates in the same product market, but, as we saw in the last chapter, difficulties can arise where diversification is totally unrelated.

In recent years the phenomenon of corporate venturing has emerged. This involves a larger established business collaborating with a smaller, less established but entrepreneurial firm to exploit business opportunities. The large firm offers finance, management expertise, access to markets, an established financial control system, and perhaps the benefits of an established reputation. The entrepreneurial firm offers new ideas and perhaps a greater ability to respond to changing markets and technologies. The French-based multinational, Rhône-Poulenc invested in Calgene, a small American firm operating in the biotechnology market. The market was developing, but Calgene was in serious financial difficulty. Rhône-Poulenc's investment gave them instant access to a new technology and Calgene obtained much needed finance. The firm recovered, went public and provided Rhône-Poulenc with a tenfold return on its original investment (*Sunday Times*, 14 August 1988).

## Innovation and organization structure

> When novelty and unfamiliarity in both market situation and technical information become the accepted order of things, a fundamentally different kind of management system becomes appropriate from that which applies to a relatively stable commercial and technical environment.
>
> (Tom Burns, preface to 2nd edition of
> *The Management of Innovation*, Burns and Stalker, 1966, p. vii)

The starting point is appropriate, since it was Burns and Stalker's study of the post-war electronics industry, and in particular the failure of some of the Scottish firms in their study to set up effective research departments, that has been so influential, not only in the development of organization theory, but as a practical guide to innovative firms on the development of appropriate structures. In this section we will examine why such a 'fundamentally different kind of management system' is necessary, the problems encountered in setting up such a system, and the attempts that have been made to provide solutions to those problems. We illustrate the arguments by focusing on the R&D department in typically science-based industry. The same arguments apply for any group within an organization with the primary responsibility for initiating innovation. For example, in an advertising agency, tensions often arise between those staff who manage client accounts, and who have to adopt a business orientation, and those staff whose primary responsibility is the generation of creative ideas.

The R&D function and those connected with it have various claims for different treatment from the rest of the organization. There is a fundamental belief that the creativity inherent in the function requires its workers to communicate freely both within and outside the organization and to be free of the kind of bureaucratic controls to which other departments are subjected. The very nature of the work demands that there be flexibility as far as the allocation of priorities, patterns of working and normal management control systems are concerned. Specifically there is a demand for the relaxation of hierarchical controls and need to see investment in R&D as a long-term issue.

Those companies where innovation is a key activity have tended to respond by creating special R&D departments. The kind of problem that tends to arise most frequently is that this sets up a clash of cultures between R&D and the other departments. The need for flexibility as outlined above challenges the existing bureaucratic controls and with it, the existing power base. The old order with its allegiance to the organization and the status quo can be shaken by a group of scientists and technologists with their allegiance to a knowledge base whose source lies outside the organization. In such a situation it is often convenient for top management to isolate the R&D department both politically and sometimes geographically. In this way it presents less of a challenge to the status quo and can be conveniently amputated when costs need to be cut. It is not uncommon in times of economic recession for firms to cut back or close down altogether their R&D function. This sets up an interesting paradox between the need to reduce expenditure and the central role ascribed to innovation in economic recovery.

However it is often the scientists themselves who support this isolation within the organization. It absolves them of responsibility and gives them the kind of freedom they seek to pursue their own goals. This can involve role-playing to a widely held image of the eccentric scientist. As Burns and Stalker note,

> a reputation for eccentricity may be helpful not only in creating a complaisant attitude in industry towards the transgression of normal rules and towards a claim for privileges but also in furthering a career . . . also taken to imply in some degree abdication from claims to leadership in the general management of business concerns.
>
> (Burns and Stalker, 1966, p. 176)

The result for the organization is invariably a lack of coordination between R&D, and other activities like production and marketing, a situation which, as Burns and Stalker found, retarded the innovative process and was detrimental to the effective operation of the firm as a whole. A great deal of time can be wasted on internal politics and the situation can lead to a proliferation of committees and intermediaries to operate in a coordinating capacity, creating jobs like methods engineers.

In many ways, the R&D department needs to be different because its goals are different, the time horizon on which it is evaluated is different, and it has different needs with regard to the formality of its operations. An R&D department needs an informal structure because of the uncertain nature of its work and its need for a flexible response to both technological and market changes. Specialists may need to be brought in from outside, possibly on a temporary basis, decision-making and responsibility may have to be decentralized, and there will usually be a very loose specification of jobs and work procedures. Integration may be achieved through the management information system, by creating cross-functional teams, or by using some managers in special integrating roles.

There are dangers with this approach. Catering to the special demands of the R&D function can lead to the kind of isolation we have already discussed and the various attempts at integration can all too often result in paperwork jungles or the creation of supernumery roles whose sole reason for existence is to act as go-between. In his study of the management of innovation in eight different firms, Parker found that a great deal of attention had been paid to structural considerations, setting up departments, creating special teams, training and coordination. However he found this to be less important than an effective strategy for innovation, which he found to be lacking in most instances (Parker, 1982).

Nonetheless communication would appear to be a key issue. Multinationals which can draw effectively upon a worldwide network are generally more innovative than those who operate as separate national entities. As we saw in Chapter 2, many Japanese firms have built up close and effective relationships with their suppliers, which has led to new developments in both products and processes. In all firms a close relationship between R&D and marketing is essential to provide information which reduces uncertainty concerning the acceptability of innovative products.

Some believe that effectiveness is achieved through the organization of the firm around its dominant competitive issue. In this way, if innovation were identified as the priority then the firm should locate its centre of power and influence around that activity. Successful innovative firms not only see innovation as a priority but build an entire organization culture based on innovation. In the next section we reinforce this theme.

## The role of organization culture

In the previous section we dwelt at length on the structural issues pertaining to the operation of an R&D function. We have maintained throughout that innovation is not the sole prerogative of science-based manufacturing industry, nor does it depend on the existence of a formally established R&D department. We have already established that innovation applies to all forms of business, and many firms are entrepreneurial and innovative largely because it is seen as a responsibility of all staff irrespective of their function.

A culture of innovation may be built up in a variety of ways, such as through the recruitment of entrepreneurial staff, and by using training programmes to develop creative thinking. More significantly the lead normally comes through the activities and energy of senior management, and their creation of an organization to foster innovation. In the Hewlett Packard case and in our reference to excellent companies in Chapter 3 there would appear to be some correlation between the existence of a strong corporate culture and innovative activity. Ekvall (1991) reported on a research programme about creativity and found, not surprisingly, that creative organizations were typified by high trust, freedom, idea support, playfulness and risk taking. Such supportive climates are typical of Peters and Waterman's 'excellent companies'.

Deal and Kennedy's (1982) innovative organization of the future is highly decentralized, in which each member of staff is allowed to be his or her own entrepreneur. They refer to this as the 'atomized organization'. We came across a similar phenomenon when we discussed networking as a structural form in Chapter 3. For most organizations their vision is far in the distance or has only limited application. Nonetheless, effective changes in operation can be achieved using less revolutionary methods, as illustrated by Case 5.5 of the Baystate Banking Corporation, which successfully used the introduction of automatic teller machines as a catalyst in the creation of an organization with a much stronger central identity.

## Innovation and management strategies

Throughout this chapter we have seen that both management and representatives of governments have operated on the clear assumption that innovation is linked to increased productivity, market share and profitability, as well as being an indication of the state of a nation's economic health. A strong lobby exists for the promotion of an innovation strategy as the key to competitive advantage. Typical of the lobby is the stance taken by Hayes and Wheelwright. They maintain that firms must innovate to survive, since strategies which depend on imitation and following market trends will ultimately lead to a saturation of the market. While some firms will survive better than others by clever marketing strategies and introducing the kind of 'pseudo-innovations' we discussed at the beginning of the chapter, real growth is dependent upon the development of new products. An important feature of the Hayes and Wheelwright hypothesis, as far as manufacturing industry is concerned, is the primacy of individual machine-tool technology. Only through this will firms be able to manufacture products that are distinct from those of their competitors (Hayes and

Wheelwright, 1984). Clearly their hypothesis is biased towards manufacturing but has application for other sectors as well. We will return to this argument when we discuss manufacturing in the next chapter and refer you to Case 4.1, which deals with the decline in the British machine-tool industry.

In this section we will examine two types of innovation strategy, 'first to the market' and 'follower strategies'. Following our discussion of organization structure and culture we will revisit the concept of integrated strategies before closing the section with an examination of some constraints to innovation.

## Types of strategy

**'First to the market' strategy** According to Ansoff and Stewart (1967) organizations pursuing this type of strategy see research and development as a central part of their operation. There is a strong commitment to basic research, technical leadership and hence a willingness to take risks with comparatively large investments. Research tends to be close to the state of the art and the organization employs a high proportion of top-rate research scientists. There is considerable co-ordination between research, production and marketing and planning is usually long-range. The large pharmaceutical companies like Hoffman-LaRoche, Ciba-Geigy and Glaxo fit into this category. They use R&D and a 'first to the market' strategy as a deliberate attempt to dominate the market. As we see in Case 5.1, Glaxo employs large numbers of research scientists, has close links with universities in various parts of the world and successfully developed the anti-ulcer drug Zantac before its rivals, achieving a very large and very profitable market share.

Being first to the market gives a firm a number of distinct advantages. First, the firm can use the patent system to create a monopoly position and earn income from licensing activities, as we saw earlier with Texas Instruments. Second, those first to the market can control limited resources. The first development in a new beach resort can occupy the prime site and buy land when prices are relatively cheap. Those following, especially if the resort becomes fashionable and popular are faced with less desirable locations and higher prices. Third, those that are first can set the industry standards that others must follow as in the case of computer hardware and software. The battle for market share in the UK satellite TV industry was fought between Sky and BSB, with the two companies operating different systems. In some respects BSB operated a technically superior system, but being first enabled Sky to gain the largest market share. BSB experienced financial difficulties and were eventually taken over by Sky.

However, being first to patent the invention is insufficient in itself. Sony were not the first company to patent the Walkman, but were the first to produce it cheaply and market it effectively. Rank Xerox were first to the market with the photocopying machine and used the patent to create an effective monopoly but failed to compete with Canon and

Toshiba when they entered the market as followers. Being a follower can have advantages and it is to this we now turn.

**'Follower' strategies**  A variety of follower strategies can be identified. Some firms, such as Philips operating in the domestic electrical market, are highly innovative and take state-of-the-art technical knowledge invented elsewhere and use this to develop their own product range. Other firms in the same market, such as Hotpoint, will follow somewhat cautiously behind the state-of-the-art technology concentrating more on design modifications. In the two cases above, the companies possess R&D departments and, while not first to the market, are still concerned with innovation. By contrast there are some followers who have no R&D function as such. They exist largely on a strong manufacturing base and have the ability to copy others' products quickly and effectively. Successful firms of this type operate on low costs, have a comparatively low selling price and the ability to deliver on time. They rely on being highly competitive as opposed to innovative. Firms operating in this way do not tend to be household names.

Being a follower has its advantages. Goods can often be introduced more cheaply as high development costs do not have to be recouped. Those coming after can learn from the mistakes of the pioneers. For example, Boeing developed its highly profitable 707 range of aircraft by learning from the metal fatigue problems that dogged the early versions of the British Aircraft Corporation's Comet and, as a result, gained a much larger market share (Bowen and Ricketts, 1992). Coming second also means that a market is already established with support mechanisms such as knowledgable retailers, service and maintenance facilities and complementary products. In the computing area, later arrivals entered a market place where software standards were established and they could develop their products accordingly.

Follower strategies can be pursued in specific circumstances by otherwise highly innovative and well-known companies. We have noted already that when Rank Xerox's patent on the photocopier expired, several companies including Canon, Toshiba and Gestetner used the available technology to manufacture their own versions. Table 5.4 is some indication of the highly innovative nature of at least two of those companies. In many cases those coming second not only have the advantages highlighted above, but can also build upon their reputations in other fields. In the case of Canon and Toshiba they developed photocopiers that were not only cheaper, but more reliable as well. This in turn resulted in Rank Xerox rethinking its own strategy and led to a focus on quality and the development of 'total quality management' techniques in an attempt to recapture its former market position.

## Integrated strategies

Although innovation is a primary source of competitive advantage, it is usually an effective source only if it can be deployed in concert with some other sources of competitive advantage, or if it is at least supported by other strategic weapons.

(Kay, 1992, p. 127)

Our illustrations of the 'first to the market' and 'follower' strategies above suggest that the two are not mutually exclusive and that a firm can pursue different strategies in different product markets. The quote from Kay suggests that whatever strategy is pursued it is insufficient in itself without the support of the rest of the organization. This reinforces the theme raised in our earlier discussion of the relationship to innovation of organizational structure and organizational culture. We may conclude from the works of Kay, other authors and various case histories that the strategic implications for a firm wishing to be innovative are as follows.

- In general there needs to be a risk-taking ethos that is supported by top management. There ought to be a willingness to experiment and therefore a freedom to fail.
- This should be supported by the recruitment of people with creative talents and, where appropriate, with technical and scientific backgrounds.
- Recruitment policies need to be reinforced by training and development programmes which place emphasis on innovation and the acquisition of the required technical knowledge. Promotion strategies should include technical know-how and a commitment to innovation as key criteria.
- The exchange of ideas should be encouraged, not just within the firm, but especially for those operating in science-based industries, by fostering links with universities and other research establishments.
- Mechanisms can be set up which facilitate communication, such as suggestion schemes and more radical methods of employee participation, but more generally, innovation may be encouraged if the organization is flexible and decentralized.
- Whether a special R&D department is created or not, attention needs to be paid to integrating the function of innovation with the rest of the organization's activities. Kay (1993) goes further and speaks not only of the importance of integration within the firm, between departments, between management and labour but also between the firm and its suppliers and the firm and its customers. The close relationship between many Japanese manufacturing firms and their components suppliers illustrates this as does the policy of Hewlett Packard of consulting customers in the innovation new products (see the section on Japanese Management in Chapter 2 and the Hewlett Packard case in Chapter 3).

Probably the most significant feature to emerge from the points made above is the need to create a particular organization culture or climate that is supportive of innovation. This in turn needs to be supported by an environment where emphasis is placed on developing the skills of the workforce and where innovation is encouraged by banks and by effective political policies instead of rhetoric. The absence of these features present the innovative firm with considerable constraints.

## Constraints to effective innovation strategy

Despite the central role ascribed to innovation, there are constraints which may significantly limit its effectiveness. For any new idea there is a high probability of failure. If we add this to a tendency on the part of many managers to underestimate the costs involved, then it is easy to see why some companies have found innovation a particularly risky strategy. Lockheed and Rolls-Royce in the aerospace industry are good illustrations of this. This is compounded by yet another problem. Managers in many industries faced with the pressure for career development and pressures from shareholders for a generous dividend, may opt for safer short-term investments, which preclude more radical innovative strategies. Undoubtedly the problems associated with short-termism in general highlight the importance of a supportive financial system for effective innovation. The time lags between development and commercial exploitation can be highly variable, a process taking an estimated 22 years as far as television was concerned. In addition to all these problems, economic, social and political conditions may mitigate against effective innovation. We have already seen the importance of a skills infrastructure and supportive political policies. Objections by trade unions fearing losses in job security, either real or imagined, can set back the introduction of process innovations as we have seen in the newspaper industry (Chapter 1). High interest rates offered by banks as a result of high inflation can add to the reluctance on the part of managers to invest in new ventures.

Difficulties of the kind identified above have led to the preference of some firms to seek alternative strategies. A common alternative is the use of the patent and licensing system, identified earlier in this chapter. Instead of developing products and processes itself, a firm will manufacture a product or use a process that has been developed elsewhere, on the payment of a licence fee to the patent holder. This is not only a strategy for the avoidance of R&D costs, but can save a great deal of time in the development process by eliminating duplication of effort. The high cost of development in the electronics industry was considerably reduced for many firms, by using as their starting point the original patent for the transistor owned by the Bell Telephone Corporation. Licensing may not be totally passive and may in fact be a spur to modifications, resulting in a company developing its own innovations.

In addition to licensing, the costs of innovation may be reduced by undertaking joint development with another company, buying in specific research work as needed from a specialist research consultancy firm, or even through acquisition strategy. In this way a firm can add to its stable of new products, processes and patents by purchasing particularly innovative companies, operating in their chosen direction of diversification.

In discussing innovation strategies, students should always remember that the strategies are never as discrete as textbook models would like them to be. We have already noted that a firm can be first to the market place with some of its product range while following other firms in other types of product. A firm may well have a strong R&D department with a record of successful innovation. At the same time it could license developments from its competitors and even pursue an acquisition strategy of buying up certain highly specialized units.

What does appear to be important is an integrated strategy, a theme that appears central to the innovative process. A good idea may be wasted without corresponding policies in production and marketing, the respective themes of our next two chapters.

## Summary

Invention, innovation, research and development, design and entrepreneurship are all related concepts. For businesses it is the process of innovation that is the key concept, turning an invention into something profitable. Innovation can relate to products, processes, marketing and organization, and can range from the most fundamental to the most minor changes. Evidence suggests that the more successful innovations are those that are integrated, with product, process and organizational changes occurring together. Integration would appear to be an important theme in innovation.

We view innovation as the key to increased productivity, increased market share, and hence profitability and the firm's continued survival. The theme has been translated to the scale of national economies and we have seen how some regard innovation as the source of economic recovery out of a recession. These relationships are difficult to prove but there can be no denying that without innovation there can be no new products or processes.

The importance of innovation has been recognized by governments all over the world, although there are considerable variations in the extent and direction of intervention. Government support for innovation is seen not only for economic, but for political and social reasons too, although there can be significant ideological and practical difficulties in the state's involvement. All societies need to support innovation by ensuring that the workforce is educated and trained in the required skills.

There are clear links between innovation and technology, although in practice it is difficult to determine whether an innovation is a result of 'technology push' or 'demand pull'. Most important innovations in business are the product of a range of different factors. An understanding of the marketplace is particularly important and innovation and marketing are interrelated activities.

At the level of the individual firm there is no clear evidence linking the size of a company with its propensity and ability to innovate, although very expensive research tends to be concentrated in large companies. The sector in which the firm operates and the volatility of the market all interact with the size of establishment in a rather complex way. What is fairly clear is that firms with an R&D department have special problems in the integration of R&D with other activities and in particular, production and marketing. The most successfully innovative companies tend to be those that have paid attention to the creation of a particular organization culture and the encouragement to all staff to be creative.

Some firms clearly see themselves as technical and market leaders and invest a high proportion of their income in developing new ideas, products and processes. Other firms are more content to sit behind the field and rely upon minor developments or strategies of copying. There are a range of possible strategies that can be adopted either singly or together.

## Further reading

A recent approach to the economics of innovation, state involvement and, in particular, the links between innovation, corporate strategy and marketing can be found in A. Bowen and M. Ricketts (eds), *Stimulating Innovation in Industry: The Challenge for the United Kingdom*, London (Kogan Page/NEDO 1992). J. J. Van Duijn's *The Long Wave in Economic Life* (George Allen and Unwin, 1983) is particularly good on the economic aspects of innovation, more especially in an historic context. In the similar vein, but concerned more with the role of the state and offering a good overview of small firms and innovation, students should consult R. Rothwell and W. Zegveld's *Industrial Innovation and Public Policy* (Frances Pinter, 1981). The last two books are biased towards technological innovation. A broader based view of entrepreneurship may be found in most of the books written by Peter Drucker, especially P. Drucker, *Enterprise and Innovation* (Pan, 1986). The Open University text, J. Henry and D. Walker (eds), *Managing Innovation* (Sage, 1991) also offers a broad-based approach and provides a large number of interesting cases. Although the study is over 25 years old, there are neither few better nor more relevant books on the organization of innovation than T. Burns and G. M. Stalker's *The Management of Innovation* (Tavistock, 1966).

## Discussion

1 Which can have the greater impact on businesses; product or process innovations?
2 Examine the ways through which the state can subsidize, encourage and protect innovation in private firms. Why should the state get involved, and what difficulties arise with such involvement?
3 Assess the relationship between innovation and economic growth. Which criteria would you use to show such a relationship?

4   Select a range of consumer domestic products which illustrate the relationship between technology push and demand pull? Which of these two is the more significant?

5   What contribution can the size of the firm make to innovative activity?

6   Identify the major problems associated with the existence of a special function responsible for the initiation of new business ideas, such as an R&D department. What structural devices would you employ to reduce these problems?

7   Assess the innovation strategy alternatives for a manufacturer of consumer electrical goods, a major computer firm, a package holiday company, and a university.

8   To what extent is innovation the key to Glaxo's success (Case 5.1)? What do you see as the main opportunities and threats currently facing the company?

9   What can we learn from the INMOS case about state intervention in innovation? How could INMOS have been more effective?

10   What aspects of innovation do Cases 5.3, 5.4 and 5.5 reveal? What lessons do they contain for other companies?

# Production

## 6

The production function is concerned with the creation of the goods and services offered to consumers. In this chapter we use the term production in its widest context. We clearly associate production operations with manufacturing industry, but we can also see a production function operating in department stores, restaurants, banks, local government, schools and hospitals. If anything, in recent years, the concept has tended to focus on the non-manufacturing sector (e.g. Harris, 1989). The term operations is occasionally used to denote this broader approach, but since that concept has so many different connotations, we use the term production throughout. To reinforce this broad view of production, we will, where appropriate, cite illustrations from the non-manufacturing sector, and devote Case 6.2 to an examination of the production function in a firm of patent agents.

We begin by examining the central role played by production in all organizations and examine two specific aspects of that role; the design of production systems and the operation of those systems. For the purposes of this text we deal with the important function of purchasing in this chapter, under the heading of materials management. The production function is sometimes portrayed as the function that is most isolated from the environment in which it operates. We refute that idea and examine the relationship of production with its environment by looking at the influences of a changing economy and government policy towards manufacturing industry, factors pertaining to the labour force, the impact of technological developments and cultural differences in the way societies view and organize production. A particular reference will be made here to Japanese manufacturing industry. Our analysis of organizational aspects also explores cultural differences, but at the level of the firm and how they interact with the other variables of the Business in Context model, especially the role of organization size and structure. We close the chapter by exploring some common production strategies.

## A central function

The production function has a central role in most types of organization. According to some estimates it accounts for some 70 to 80% of a firm's assets, expenditure and people (Hill, 1991). In addition, it is central to the firm's success by providing what the customer requires either at a profit in a private company, or within budget in a non-profit organization. It is therefore concerned with issues that are crucial to the consumer, issues of quantity, quality, availability and price; and issues that are crucial to the management of an enterprise, issues of productivity and cost.

Despite its centrality it is often regarded as the 'cinderella' subject of management, and, certainly as far as production management in manufacturing is concerned, an area to be avoided by aspiring managers. As Wickham Skinner writes,

> Manufacturing is generally perceived in the wrong way at the top, managed in the wrong way at plant level, and taught the wrong way at business schools.
>
> (Skinner, 1969, p. 137)

There are signs that this view is being reappraised. The growth of the non-manufacturing sector has encouraged our rethinking of the production concept. Significant production problems exist in managing an airport as busy as Heathrow. Planes must take off and land safely and on time. In order for this to occur, key operations must be coordinated, including air traffic control, ground crews, baggage-handling, passport and customs, aircraft cleaning, refuelling and catering. Production problems also have to be faced in large hospitals with busy operating schedules. Operations must be carefully timed and scheduled, patients transferred to and from wards, equipment prepared and the various support systems from nursing to catering properly briefed. Production techniques, originally developed in manufacturing are now commonplace in non-manufacturing contexts, and senior staff in these organizations assume the role of coordinating production operations. It is the importance of the production function in solving this type of problem that led Drucker to define production as 'the application of logic to work' (Drucker, 1968, p. 122).

Furthermore, production management is making a comeback in manufacturing. The oil crisis of the 1970s, the rising cost of raw materials and labour, concern for the level of productivity, and the success of those countries with different approaches to manufacturing system design and management have all conspired to raise the level of interest in the production function in both the USA and Britain. There are signs that a former complacent attitude and a view of production management as simply a set of techniques is giving way to the elevation of production as the key management strategy, which, alongside innovation and marketing, can give firms a distinct competitive advantage, as well as making a significant contribution to export and the economy in general.

Despite the application of production techniques to manufacturing and non-manufacturing firms alike, some differences can be found. We examine these briefly before looking at the various elements which make up the production function.

## Some differences between manufacturing and non-manufacturing industries

Both these sectors are concerned with the production of goods and services, but differences do exist between different types of organization operating in the same sector. An oil refinery has little in common with a small business making hand-crafted furniture, yet both are lumped together as manufacturing concerns. By the same token, an organization like Barclays Bank would be classed together with a small hairdressing business, as non-manufacturing concerns. We can see that the differences within each of these sectors can be as significant as those between them. When we examine the organizational aspects of production later in this chapter, we make an attempt to classify different types of production system in each sector. At this stage, however, it is worth pointing out two major differences between manufacturing and nonmanufacturing.

- A major difference concerns the part played by the customer. In a non-manufacturing concern the customer is generally more of an active participant in the process. This is especially true in education and hospitals and those organizations offering a personal service, such as hairdressers, solicitors, financial advisers and counsellors. The interaction of the customer means that the process is often less predictable, and production systems correspondingly more complex.

- This unpredictability means that the production process is more difficult to control in the non-manufacturing sector. The degree of contact with the customer can affect the efficiency of the operation. For example, a doctor may not be able to plan her work as effectively as she would like due to the variability in the consulting needs of patients. Productivity therefore becomes more difficult to measure and quality becomes much more a matter of subjective assessment.

We examine the implications of these differences when we look at the various elements of the production process in the next two sections.

## Identifying the production function

We have seen that a production system exists to provide goods and services, which it does by transforming inputs into different kinds of

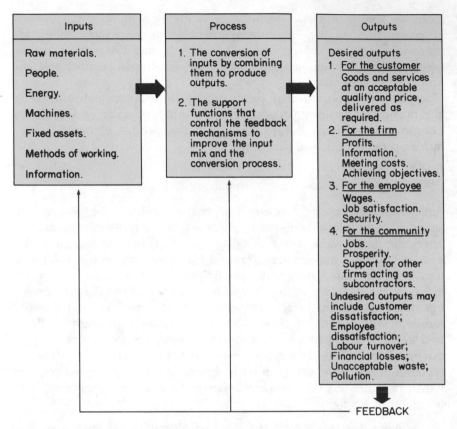

| Inputs | Process | Outputs |
|---|---|---|
| Raw materials.<br>People.<br>Energy.<br>Machines.<br>Fixed assets.<br>Methods of working.<br>Information. | 1. The conversion of inputs by combining them to produce outputs.<br><br>2. The support functions that control the feedback mechanisms to improve the input mix and the conversion process. | Desired outputs<br>1. <u>For the customer</u><br>Goods and services at an acceptable quality and price, delivered as required.<br>2. <u>For the firm</u><br>Profits.<br>Information.<br>Meeting costs.<br>Achieving objectives.<br>3. <u>For the employee</u><br>Wages.<br>Job satisfaction.<br>Security.<br>4. <u>For the community</u><br>Jobs.<br>Prosperity.<br>Support for other firms acting as subcontractors.<br>Undesired outputs may include Customer dissatisfaction; Employee dissatisfaction; Labour turnover; Financial losses; Unacceptable waste; Pollution. |

FEEDBACK

*Figure 6.1*   The production process as a system.

output. This represents a systems view of production, comprising inputs, process and outputs, which we illustrate in Figure 6.1. (See also the section on the systems approach in Chapter 1.)

We can see clearly from Figure 6.1 that the production function transforms the various resource inputs into the required goods and services. Three aspects of the model need further explanation.

- Not all the outputs of the system are necessarily desired outcomes. Waste, either in the form of substandard products or unused raw materials, can be a costly item in manufacturing and waste in the form of polluting chemicals can constitute an environmental hazard. Customer dissatisfaction can be an unintended output. The consequence of diners at a restaurant receiving bad service may well mean they decide never to return.
- The concept of environmental pollution introduces the notion that outputs of one system are invariably inputs to other systems. The manufactured outputs of a car components factory are clearly inputs to other firms. In the 1960s delays and industrial disputes in the car components industry caused production stoppages at the major car manufacturers and led them to rethink their purchasing strategies. Wages paid to workers will invariably be passed on to shops

and supermarkets, and also to such as building societies in the form of mortgage payments, which are then used to fund further investments.

- Outputs may also be considered as inputs to the same system. In this way, information gained during the production process can be used to improve the operation of the system, such as changing the supplier to improve the quality of parts and reduce the number of rejects. A large number of dissatisfied customers at a restaurant or a hairdressers is an indication that some element of the process needs attention. This is known as feedback. Another type of re-lationship can be built up between output and input when materials are recycled. In the manufacture of float glass at the Pilkington plant in St Helens, the smoothing of edges, the cutting of glass to size, and the generally fragile nature of the product, mean that there are always quantities of broken glass. While measures are taken to keep this waste to an acceptable minimun, it is broken up to form 'cullet', a vital raw material in glass production.

We can see from the systems model that production is a transformation process resulting in the creation of goods and services. This provides us with a means of classifying different types of production system. Wild has identified four types, each based predominantly on a different kind of transformation (Wild, 1985).

- A transformation in the form of raw materials or components is typified by manufacturing firms, but also by such as builders and landscape gardeners.
- A change in the nature of ownership is primarily the concern of suppliers, wholesalers and retailers.
- A change of place is the focus for transport systems such as road hauliers, postal services, or courier firms.
- A transformation in the state of the customer is the aim of service industries, so that insurance firms aim to make people more secure; building societies lend money for people to improve their standard of living; osteopaths aim to improve the physical well-being of their patients.

Many organizations operate all four types of transformation process. A typical manufacturing firm will not only make goods, but sell and transport them direct to the consumer or to an intermediary such as a wholesaler or retailer, and provide an after-sales service. We tend to think of restaurants as operating predominantly in the service sector, yet all restaurants have a manufacturing operation that transforms raw material foodstuffs into dishes for consumption. Retailers are not just concerned with ownership change but they are involved in place transformation too.

A good illustration of the interrelated nature of both production systems and the various types of transformation process can be found in the retail chain of Marks & Spencer whose primary product ranges are clothes and food and drink.

Marks & Spencer, one of the most successful retail chains in Britain, and with branches in Europe has vigorously pursued a policy of offering high-quality products at an acceptable price to a mass market. It relies on a high turnover of goods. An important output is therefore a high level of customer satisfaction, both with the product and the service. Three kinds of feedback are important to this process; the customer's willingness to make return visits to the store; the careful research of customer needs; and the shop policy of accepting returned goods, which may then be repackaged and resold. The pursuit of quality is reflected in store layout and staff selection and training, but most significantly in the choice of supplier. Marks & Spencer expects a high level of quality in the goods it buys to sell on. This has had a remarkable effect on the British textile industry. The policy of the company to buy British has meant that 90% of Marks & Spencer stock is British. It is by far the most important single buyer in the home textile market, taking 20% of the total British output. The demands for quality standards, good design and reliable delivery have led to improvements in the textile industry itself and enabled it to increase its competitiveness on a world scale, especially through the introduction of new technology. The relationship with suppliers, not only in clothing but in food and wine, becomes even more involved in that many of the products are sold under the store's own label, yet manufactured by independent producers. This is a good illustration of the fluidity of system boundaries as well as involving Marks & Spencer in the manufacturing process. However its major concern, retailing, is a good illustration of transformations taking place in ownership, place and the state of the consumer.

| | |
|---|---|
| **KEY CONCEPT 6.2**<br>*The conflicting objectives of the production system* | Within most production systems there is an inevitable tension between the needs of management to construct an efficient operating system which focuses upon minimizing costs and the needs of customers for goods and services which meet their specifications of design, cost and delivery. Many of the techniques used by management in production design, scheduling and control aim to resolve such potential conflict. In more recent years, the trend has been away from statistical techniques to focus on strategies which seek a greater compatibility between production and the other functional activities, especially marketing, and on the creation of more flexible operating systems. |

## Conflicting objectives and changing solutions

We have seen that our production system has a number of different objectives. These include production of a certain number of items at a certain level of quality; within a certain time period; within acceptable financial and social costs; at a price that will ensure sufficient sales and produce an acceptable return on investment; and with the flexibility to adjust to changing demands.

Consumers wish to purchase goods in the quantity and quality they require, receive them at the time they need them, and all at a price they deem reasonable. However, if we select an unframed painting at an art shop, we know that a hand-crafted frame in a special material will cost more than framing it ourselves using a ready-made frame, and that we may have to wait some time for the job to be done by an expert. Many consumers are willing to make trade-offs, to pay more for quality, to wait for made-to-measure items. Many are not and managers are left with the task of balancing a number of potentially conflicting objectives to achieve both customer satisfaction and the efficient utilization of resources. This is illustrated in Figure 6.2.

The main reason for conflict goes back to the interrelated nature of the production system as the following illustration shows. In an attempt to reduce costs, managers have a number of different options. They can cut back on raw material or staff, which may result in goods of lower quality and a generally poorer service; they can expect the workforce to increase productivity for the same reward; or they can gear up for higher productivity by ensuring long production runs in the case of manufacturing or reducing the time spent with clients in the case of the service industry. All these options give rise to potential conflicts. Goods of lower quality may not be acceptable to the consumer, unless the price is cut, thus negating the original cost-cutting exercise. The workers may resist attempts by management to increase the tempo of work. In manufacturing, the introduction of long production runs has a trade-off in the form of reduced flexibility and lack of choice for the consumer.

The production manager needs to balance the opposing forces which are the cause of such conflicts. The development of operational research during World War Two resulted in the post-war emphasis on the 'numerate manager', a concept which found a ready application in a range of production management techniques. These included value analysis, developments in work study, linear programming, network analysis, statistical quality control, and the emphasis on specific measures of efficiency such as machine utilization, work in progress, labour utilization and so on. Such techniques are used in the non-manufacturing sector as well, as the concepts of staff-student ratios and optimum class sizes in education will testify.

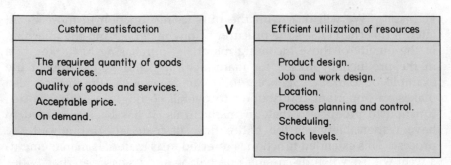

*Figure 6.2* The conflicting objectives of the production process.

Many of the techniques mentioned above are primarily concerned with efficiency. While efficiency is important, it can distort the system. In manufacturing, the achievement of long runs may be the most efficient use of materials, machines and labour, but it can frustrate some customers who may require a quick response to their order, and valuable customers may go elsewhere. A doctor faced with a waiting room full of patients may be more efficient by limiting consultation time, but with the attendant danger that a potentially serious problem could be overlooked. Efficiency is often the goal, when greater attention needs to be paid to effectiveness in the form of adaptation and flexibility.

As a result, the application of more complex quantitative techniques can produce a limited focus. In recent years attention has shifted to a greater emphasis on the management of the whole system and its relationshop with other systems. The production manager emerges as a mediator, coping with different demands both within the production system itself and between that and other systems. This role is sometimes termed boundary management. We develop these themes in more detail in our discussion of production strategies at the end of the chapter. In the mean time, we look a little more closely at the relationship between production and the other activities of the organization.

## The relationship between production and other functional areas

The centrality of the production function and the boundary role of the production manager brings into focus the relationship between the production function and the other functional areas. Examples of such relationships include the following.

**Innovation** As we saw in the previous chapter, innovation is at the heart of new product development with obvious implications for the production function. Production capabilities and capacities must be important considerations at the design and development stage. An innovative product design in manufacturing is no use if it cannot be made by the workforce within certain cost parameters. Similarly a new design for a business studies degree course must take into account the skills of the teachers and the capabilities of the students.

**Purchasing** We will deal with the purchasing function in more detail later in this chapter. As the procurer of raw materials and the guardian of the quality of those incoming materials, purchasing has a key role in the production process for manufacturing, and as we saw in the example of Marks & Spencer, for retailing as well. Purchasing also makes an important contribution to overall costing. So central is this function to production that, in many firms, it has been extended to have responsibility for the entire flow of materials throughout the process. This extended function is referred to as materials management, a term we use when discussing purchasing and its associated activities later in the chapter.

**Marketing** Information about consumer requirements is essential to those operating the production system. Production managers need to know the total demand for their product and when that demand is required. This will assist in the planning of production operations. Feedback from consumers on the utility of the product can assist both the R&D and production functions in the design and creation of future products. Holiday companies frequently ask clients to complete a questionnaire about every aspect of their holiday, not only as a public relations exercise, but to improve the product and the way it is delivered.

**Finance and accounting** The accounting function clearly interfaces with production in the development of production budgets and targets. In return, production information is essential to such decisions as pricing and wage determination. The accounting function will also play a major role in decisions to replace major items of capital equipment.

**Human resource management** This will assist in the recruitment, selection and training of production staff. Other key activities include industrial relations, the design of payment systems including incentives and the control of the safety, health and welfare of the workforce. Traditionally, industrial relations and wage incentives assume a significant role in manufacturing industry, but the role of staff selection and training are crucial to the success of those service industries with high levels of customer contact.

## The key activities of production management

In Figure 6.3 we offer a classification of the main activities of production managers. We draw a distinction between the design of the production system and the operation of that system. In this section we include a review of materials management.

### The design of production systems

**Product design** The two major decisions in product design concern first, the function and styling of the product and second, the range of products or degree of standardization to be offered. In manufacturing, decisions will also be made on the type of materials that are to be used. Design issues clearly interface with innovation (Chapter 5) and marketing (Chapter 7).

In recent years in manufacturing two systems have developed which focus upon the interface between design and production. These are CAD (computer-aided design) and CAM (computer-aided manufacture). Operating together these are known as CADCAM systems. CAD enables the designer through the use of computer graphics and computer memory to evaluate the consequences of various design alternatives. This has assisted in both the speed and the accuracy of the design stage. A linked CADCAM system has a memory bank of

---

System design
  Product design.
  Forecasting demand.
  Capacity planning.
  Equipment design.
  Work design.
  Location and site.
System operation
  Operations planning.
  Scheduling.
  Quantity control.
  Quality control.
  Technology control.
  Labour control.
  Cost control.
Materials management
  Purchasing.
  Inventory control.

---

*Figure 6.3* The activities of production management.

standard designs, and the appropriate machines and tools required for manufacture. In many industries this has assisted greatly in the development of modular production methods. A modular system exists where products are built up by the different combination of a family of standard items. In the car industry, for example, a great number of different models can be offered, yet all are based around different combinations of the same body shells, engines, gear boxes and so on.

Developments in modular systems can simplify the production process and represent a form of standardization. A lunchtime sandwich bar may appear to have a very large range of products, when in fact all are based on different combinations of a limited range of ingredients and all are made using similar production techiques. Many companies see standardization as an important means of cost reduction. A college offering a wide variety of evening courses, some of which are poorly subscribed, may decide to rationalize its operations around the most popular courses, reducing both staffing costs and overheads. For the manufacturer, standardization often means a better utilization of re-sources, such as longer production runs and the opportunity to obtain discounts on the purchasing of raw materials and components in bulk. For the consumer, however, it may mean less choice which may be acceptable if prices are reduced. One of the advantages of the modular system lies in the attempt to maximize both standardization and choice. This is the rationale behind the decision of many British universities to offer modular degree schemes. An important production decision is the extent of standardization that is both desirable and feasible.

**Forecasting demand and capacity planning** These two tasks form the basis of a series of decisions central to the production process, since it is here that the direction for the entire operation is set and resources are acquired and deployed. There is a particular need for market information and accurate predictions of demand. This is obviously much easier where goods are made to order, less so when goods are made to stock. In this case historical data are important, but even this may prove inadequate in a highly volatile market of changing demand and high levels of competition.

Even where demand can be forecast with some accuracy, capacity planning may not be straightforward. It can be especially sensitive to product and process innovation, and will be affected by decisions on the type of technology used, organization size and structure, the extent of subcontracting and policies concerning the intensity of labour, the size of the labour force and the hours of operation. Organizing the capacity to meet demand in some kind of sequence is known as scheduling, which we deal with under operations planning.

Capacity planning is especially difficult in service industries. In most instances, the product on offer cannot be stored when the capacity is not fully utilized, as with airline seats and perishable foods. The concern for unused capacity in the hotel industry has led some hoteliers in popular resorts to overbook rooms. This works well given the predicted number of cancellations, but can lead to holiday-makers not being accommodated in the hotel of their choice and their subsequent dissatisfaction. In some types of industry there are well-established peaks and troughs.

A number of strategies are used by service industries to reduce the difficulties imposed by capacity planning. A bus company or an airline will dictate demand and capacity by operating a fixed schedule, and in some cases insisting that passengers buy tickets beforehand. Extra capacity can be laid on in times of known high demand. Some services can operate a delayed delivery system to control demand and plan capacity. A garage will attempt to match the cars it accepts for servicing work with available equipment and labour and will delay bookings to times when capacity is available. The system can and does break down, through overbooking, staff absenteeism, and jobs taking longer than planned. In such situations the problem may be solved by overtime work, but this increases cost and any delay can impair the service the customer feels he is getting.

In the case of the bus company and the car service there is a certain flexibility in both equipment and manning levels. Such flexibility is not available in all situations. A telephone company must establish a capacity to cope with peak demand, which occurs during office hours. At other times the equipment is idle and represents a net cost to the company. In most countries, telephone companies attempt to smooth out demand through the use of cheaper rates for off-peak usage and frequent advertising campaigns to reinforce this in the public's mind.

There are instances where companies have used demand and capacity as a marketing strategy. Certain products have been known to develop a mystique, simply because they are not available. In the USA the demand for Coors beer was allowed to develop, through advertising and publicity, although there was insufficient capacity. The product developed a rarity value and cult status. When the company subsequently increased its productive capacity, a market had already been created. Some foreign car manufacturers, like BMW and Daimler Benz in Germany, deliberately limit the number of cars they release to Britain, thus keeping their product fairly exclusive and enabling them to maintain high prices.

**Equipment design**  Decisions here relate to the selection of the type of equipment to be used, how much of it is to be manufactured in-house, how much is to be bought in, and what equipment replacement strategies to adopt. There is a close relationship with product design, capacity planning, the nature and skills of the labour force and accounting procedures.

Key debates in this area concern the extent of automation and computerization, job security and job satisfaction. The choice of equipment will influence how the work is to be designed, which in turn will affect organization structure. We will return to these issues in our discussions of technology, labour and organization structure later in this chapter.

**Work design**  We are concerned here with two types of decision; the physical layout of the production system, and the design of individual jobs. Many of the issues pertinent to equipment design obtain here also and relate to the arrangement of equipment, work stations and people. The dominant considerations here are economic (meeting demand and keeping within cost constraints), technical (product design and utilizing available equipment), and behavioural (fulfilling the needs of both the consumer and the workforce).

Variations in these economic, technical and behavioural factors often result in different types of production system. We return to this theme when we offer a classification of production systems in the section dealing with organizational aspects of production. Work design is one way management attempts to satisfy those conflicting demands shown in Figure 6.2. The layout of a department store usually involves the grouping of like products to capitalize on staff expertise and meet customer expectations. The layout caters for both demand and buyer behaviour by locating fast-moving goods and those often bought on impulse on the ground floor. With goods such as furniture, the purchase is planned and deliberate and the store can afford to locate the furniture department on the upper floors. In a self-service cafeteria, the flowline of goods will correspond with the order in which people eat their meals.

The minimization of cost is a major management consideration and the technique used is known as work study, comprising method study and work measurement.

Method study is 'the systematic and critical examination of the ways of doing things in order to make improvements' (British Standard 3138). The approach taken is usually highly methodical with a set sequence involving a detailed analysis of the present method, the careful development and testing of new methods, the training of the workforce, the installation and regular testing of the new methods. The technique seeks to find more efficient and effective ways of doing work and as such, embraces equipment design and ergonomics as well as more subjective, psychological aspects of the person/job relationship.

Work measurement is 'the application of techniques designed to establish the time for a qualified worker to carry out a task at a defined level of performance' (British Standard 3138). The most common technique is time study, in which a trained observer times the job as it is being done, making adjustments for rest allowances and so on. Nowadays, work measurement is greatly assisted by the use of PMTS (predetermined motion time standards). Under this system, the work study engineer has a set of tables which list the times for a variety of motions that form the basis of most jobs. Work measurement can be done by simply piecing together the times of the constituent motions of the job.

Work study is useful in planning and scheduling, cost estimation, the determination of maintenance schedules, manpower planning and employee training, as well as forming the basis for most types of output related incentive schemes. The technique is applied to both manufacturing and non-manufacturing concerns. The standard method for administering drugs to hospital patients was changed as a result of work study. The old system involved drugs being kept in a locked drugs cupboard, and, for each patient, the nurse had to return to the cupboard, unlock it, and retrieve the appropriate drug. This involved most of the nurse's time in walking to and from the cupboard, and a safety risk if ever the cupboard were left unlocked. A new system was devised which is now standard practice in most hospitals. The drugs are kept in a mobile trolley which can be transported from patient to patient. On a more esoteric level, the change from overarm to underarm pitching in baseball to achieve greater speed and accuracy is attributed to the application of work study by Frederick Winslow Taylor!

**Locational decisions**   The location of the production system in manufacturing industry is usually based upon a variety of factors including the proximity to raw materials and power supply, to transport systems for supply and distribution, to a labour market possessing the required skills. Other considerations can include the level of local rates and taxes, the availability of government grants and even the relative cost of labour. The final point is very relevant to those multinationals who locate their labour-intensive operations where wages are lower (there is a discussion on multinationals in Chapter 2). One of the prime considerations of location is the attempt to minimize all costs, but less objective factors may operate. In the USA, there has been a shift of manufacturing industry from the North and North-east to the South and South-west. One of the motives for so doing is the relative lack of union organization in states such as Georgia, Arizona, Alabama, North and South Carolina. Whatever the real or imagined economic benefits of this to corporate executives, union avoidance would appear to be an important consideration in the location decision.

Location is an important consideration in the service industry, especially where customers are expected to travel to receive the service. The location of a hospital on the outskirts of a town may solve the land constraint problems of a central site, but the new site must be easily accessible by patients and visitors, otherwise it is failing in its service function. Similarly, large supermarkets located on the edge of towns must make the effort of travel worthwhile in terms of a wider range of produce at cheaper prices. An important consideration here is usually the availability of ample car-parking space. A professional practice such as the patent agency in Case 6.2 may need to balance the advantages of operating from a central London site, especially for client consultation and prestige purposes, against the rising costs. A compromise used by some professional firms is the retention of a limited presence in the centre of the city and a relocation for the majority of the operations on a cheaper site.

## The operation of production systems

We deal with two main aspects of operations management, operations planning and operations control.

**Operations planning**   The aim of operations planning is to ensure that sufficient goods or services are produced to meet demand. A basic consideration in manufacturing is whether goods are made to stock or to order. Ford Motor Company has a policy that all cars are ordered before manufacture. On the other hand Chrysler in the USA made various models which were then sold from stock. The fast-food chain McDonalds produces hamburgers to stock based on carefully prepared

---

| **CASE 6.1** **Orlake Records** | Orlake Records is a manufacturer of gramophone records in a declining market. From 1979 to 1986, the annual trade delivery of singles in the United Kingdom fell from 89.1 million to 67.4 million, and LPs from 74.5 to 52.3 million over the same period. Correspondingly trade delivery of cassettes rose from 23.5 million in 1979 to 69.6 million in 1986. By 1993 the compact disc industry had surpassed singles, LPs and tapes. Competition among gramophone manufacturers is high, not only in this country but internationally. In the period from 1982 to 1988, around 20 British manufacturers went out of business. |
|---|---|

The actual manufacture is the following stage from the recording studio. There the final tape is converted to a series of vibrations which cut grooves into a master disc, known as the lacquer master. Orlake takes this master and through an electroplating process, makes its own moulds to form the basis of record production. Several moulds may be required, depending on the number of presses to be used, the length of the run and the uncertain working life of each mould. The actual record is made by compression moulding which presses extruded plastic on to the mould on a specially designed machine. This takes around 22 seconds for a 12″ LP and 14 seconds for a 7″ record.

Record companies may use a number of manufacturers, particularly on high-selling items. Orlake manufactures for a range of different companies and as a competitive strategy attempts to meet customer needs at low cost, in as short a time as possible.

The variety of the work means that most production runs fall between 1000 and 5000 records, with occasional forays up to runs of 100 000, and some less than 1000. The firm uses two types of presses, fully automatic and manually operated. While Orlake is expanding the automated side of the business, certain products such as 'picture' discs and 'shape' discs can only be produced using manual machines. The nature of the business and Orlake's strategic response means that production planning and scheduling is carried out on a daily basis by the production manager in consultation with sales. Even then, schedules are regularly amended. The average turn around for orders is between two and five days.

Quality control was originally the responsibility of the production supervisor, but pressure of work often meant that minor faults were deliberately ignored. It is now a separate function and any conflict with production control is handled by the director. Quality control is particularly important when the master moulds are made and a strict procedure has been set up. At the pressing stage, one finished record in every 20 is checked visually; 90% of all faults can be spotted visually by a trained operator. In addition a particular pressing is checked audibly every hour. Before storage, a further one record in 40 is checked visually, a process that is repeated after nine hours have elapsed to allow the plastic to cool down. Faults found with the moulds can often be rectified manually. If a fault is discovered in a particular batch, then the whole batch is destroyed.

Orlake operates with a core staff of around 75 employees, supplemented by anything from 25 to 45 temporary workers. Female production workers operate three five-hour shifts, while the men operate in two eight-hour shifts. A night shift is worked in particularly busy periods.

The business is seasonal with a peak from October to December. Customers have been deliberately targeted so that the load can be spread more evenly; this strategy has been supplemented by discounts to some customers who place orders outside the busy periods. Orlake have done well in such a declining market, and have every intention of continuing to manufacture gramophone records, despite a further inevitable contraction of the market. Orlake's survival and success is a feature of several interrelated factors.

- The firm made no price increases for four years to 1988, and only minimal price increases since then. Any cost increase has been absorbed by increases in labour efficiency. The plant is 20% more efficient than in 1982. This has been achieved by a mixture of staff selection, reduction in administration, some automation and computerization.
- There are no job descriptions and the labour force is used interchangeably depending on customer requirements at any one time. Operators become packers and vice versa and both supervisors and management help out in the production and packing process.
- The firm has a strategy of fulfilling customer orders for any type of gramophone record in as short a time as possible. A reputation has been built up for low lead times and prompt delivery.
- A wide variety of specialist products are offered, such as picture discs, shaped discs, hologram discs, and artist interview discs for fan clubs etc. Orlake is the only company offering some of these products.

(*Sources*: Orlake Records, Dagenham, Essex; *BPI Year Book*, 1987)

**CASE 6.2**
*A patent agency*

A patent agency is a private firm offering a legal service to its clients to enable them to obtain patent protection for their inventions and innovations (Chapter 5 for a fuller discussion of the role of patents). A patent will protect an invention by giving a manufacturer a twenty years' monopoly for his product in this country. The patent agent also obtains for his client patents in other countries. In addition most patent agencies also deal with the protection of trademarks, registered designs, and offer advice on other related matters.

The process of obtaining a patent begins by the agent's taking instructions from the client. In this case the client may be an individual inventor, a company, the patent department in a firm, or a solicitor acting on behalf of a client. In the case of foreign companies wishing to apply for patents in the United Kingdom, the agent will normally deal with a patent agent from the client's own country. Acting on the instructions from the client, the patent agent prepares a patent application which includes a specification describing the invention. In the case of incoming applications from abroad, the foreign patent agent will normally provide this specification, but it will have to be reviewed in the light of UK practice and, where necessary, translated.

The patent application is then filed with the Patent Office, a government department, whose job is the careful scrutiny of patent applications and the granting of patents if they meet the necessary criteria. The application process is effectively a negotiation process between the Patent Office and the agent. The Patent Office normally initiates each stage of the process and sets a deadline for the agent to reply. Failure to respond in time will result in the entire process being terminated. This system also pertains for each of the countries where patent protection is sought. Success at each stage of the process ends with the granting of a patent.

It can be seen from this that the work of a patent agent involves the continuous meeting of deadlines. It is therefore essential for a patent agency to have appropriate support systems, often computerized, to ensure that individual patent agents are kept aware of approaching deadlines and that the necessary action is taken in time.

When a patent has been granted, renewal fees have to be paid periodically to maintain the patent in force. In most countries such fees are payable annually. A patent agency therefore needs a renewal system so that clients can be asked at each renewal if the fee is to be paid and so that any action can be taken in time. This is a high-volume, low-income operation which is generally undertaken by clerical staff, usually employing a computer. Some firms subcontract this task to another organization altogether, such as a specialist computer bureau.

demand forecasts. Hamburgers that are not then sold within a certain length of time are discarded. McDonalds claim that this system provides greater operating efficiency, and they still have the flexibility to produce goods to order when stocks are inadequate.

Operations planning overlaps with issues of capacity planning which we discussed earlier. In the service industry problems of manufacturing to stock or order reveal themselves in the provision of standardized or customized items. A hairdresser will offer a standardized service to all customers, such as haircut and wash, and a customized service in the form of styling. Restaurants often attempt to offer the best of both worlds. An 'à la carte' menu offers the consumer flexibility of choice, but within a limited range of dishes. In general terms the greater the choice then the greater the problems for the operations planner. The more dishes the chef must make to order, then the longer the potential delay for the customer and the greater the difficulty in serving a group of customers at the same time.

The problem highlighted above is one of scheduling. The aim of scheduling is to balance the costs of production against demands for goods and services; to ensure that demand is met in the most efficient way possible. This, of course, gives rise to the classic dilemma of production management as we saw in Figure 6.2. An important strategic consideration here is load-levelling, to ensure that the work is distributed as evenly as possible throughout the workforce, over the entire year, and making the most efficient use of available equipment. A whole series of theories and techniques have been developed to deal with such problems associated with the planning, scheduling and coordination of activities. These include queuing theory, linear programming and the more complex models of operational research.

The problem with all such techniques is that, while they can offer optimal solutions to the problems of production planning and scheduling, they cannot allow for all the constraints operating in a given situation, many of which cannot be measured and many of which are highly subjective. Increased demand for a particular product may, in some cases, only be met by overtime, and the increased labour costs have to be balanced against the extra revenue from the increased sales. In such cases it may be more profitable to refuse the order, unless it comes from a particularly valued customer. Alternative strategies here might include persuading the customer to accept a delay in delivery or subcontracting the work to another company. In the service industry, customer contact often makes scheduling difficult due to the variations in time demanded by each client. In some banks this kind of problem has been tackled by the introduction of 'automatic teller machines', and a division of labour into those staff dealing with standard transactions and those dealing with more complex enquiries.

Scheduling decisions can be highly sensitive and illustrate the relationship between the firm and the environment in which it operates; this is especially true of the public sector.

The provision and scheduling of the railways in this country was examined in the 1960s by a committee under the leadership of Lord Beeching. The resulting Beeching Plan meant that several lines were closed and certain towns were left with no railway provision whatsoever. This created widespread political and community opposition. The debate centred around the argument as to whether some public services should continue to operate at a considerable loss or be closed, thus saving the taxpayer money, but depriving some of them of a service they may need. Similar problems face bus companies in planning their routes, especially in less populated rural areas. Planning and scheduling problems are also highly contentious in the health services. Hospitals must schedule operations according to their available resources, which means that only a specific number of non-emergency operations can be budgeted in any one year, resulting in a build-up of waiting lists.

All these illustrations take production planning and scheduling out of the domain of programmed decisions and simplistic techniques and involve social, political and ethical considerations.

**Operations control**     There are various types of control used in any production system. We identify these various forms of control and the mechanisms through which they are achieved in Figure 6.4. As with all forms of control, those managing the system must determine the standards that are to operate. In some types of system such standards may be difficult to measure, for example the quality of education or social work. In other situations there may be conflict concerning the appropriateness of certain standards, for example, between marketing and production about delivery times; between management and unions over levels of productivity.

We can see from the five types of control identified in Figure 6.4 that there is considerable overlap. Labour control has a close relationship to quantity, quality and cost control; productivity is a function of quantity,

1. **Quantity Control**   This is sometimes known as production control and sometimes as progress chasing. It involves ensuring that the throughput of goods and services goes according to the planned schedule.
2. **Quality Control**   This ensures that the quality of the finished product or service meets the standards set in the design stage and also meets with the approval of the customer. In manufacturing it is closely linked with the quality of raw materials and hence the purchasing function. It can be particularly difficult in service industries where standards and expectations can be both subjective and highly variable. In all cases some form of inspection and sampling system have to be planned, although the extent and frequency of inspection will vary according to the type of product and the numbers produced (Case 6.1). In education, quality control is one of the remits of the government inspectorate who visit schools and colleges.
3. **Technology Control**   This refers to the maintenance of plant and equipment. Whilst considerations of maintenance are historically associated with manufacturing industry, the use of computers and various types of office equipment make this an issue in all types of organization. The basic problem is the determination of when a piece of equipment is in need of service. Many firms solve this by instituting a system of planned preventive maintenance. Developments in information technology have meant that, in some cases, visual warning systems can be installed. These operate as a function of the number of times a piece of equipment is switched on, its running time, how intensely it is used and so on. Such systems have been installed in some cars to indicate when a service is due. Some firms prefer to sub-contract their maintenance requirements by entering into service agreements with suppliers or by simply renting the equipment as in the case of photocopying machines. In cases such as these, maintenance is generally haphazard and often waits until a breakdown has occurred. At a certain stage in the lifespan of a piece of equipment a decision must be made concerning repair or replacement. In the case of such items as company cars, programmed replacement tends to be the norm.
4. **Labour Control**   Issues at stake here include the extent and style of supervision and the type of incentives used. Interest in more participative forms of management has resulted in more use being made of such techniques as quality circles and profit sharing.
5. **Cost Control**   There is a strong link here with the accounting function and budgeting. Cost control involves the collection and analysis of data on materials, operating, equipment and labour costs and comparisons made with some form of previously determined standard costing.

*Figure 6.4*   Types and mechanisms of production control.

labour and cost control. A key concern in most organizations today is quality. Many organizations have become so preoccupied with quality and a number of related techniques that we examine this phenomenon more closely in the next section.

With all types of control someone must decide upon the appropriate form of action when deviations from the standard occur. Various options are available as the following illustrations reveal. In the case of a bottling plant, the decision is fairly straightforward. Empty bottles are washed and then closely inspected prior to being filled; bottles that are cracked or chipped are broken up, bottles that are still dirty are sent through the washing process again. A clothing manufacturer making garments for a quality-conscious retail chain, like Marks & Spencer, has other options. It may be possible to sell elsewhere items which are not acceptable to the original client. Some manufacturers sell slightly imperfect goods to their own staff or to the public as 'seconds'. Such decisions get more complex in businesses such as a restaurant, where overall quality may not be judged until the meal has been eaten, and the only redress is in the form of compensation. Assessments, especially of quality, can be highly subjective and a potential source of conflict between producer and customer.

## Quality

From an analysis of management literature and the mission statements and internal publications of organizations, we might well conclude that organizational life in the 1990s is dominated by thoughts of quality. Notions of quality pervade all types of organizations. Universities, under new forms of government control, have fallen upon the concept of quality like converts to a new religion. In this section we will introduce the concept of quality and examine both government-led initiatives and the ideas behind 'Total Quality Management'.

The traditional view of a quality product is that it conforms to specification. This is a somewhat narrow approach to quality that has been superseded by a view which focuses much more on the perspective of the customer. In this way quality is seen in terms of fitness for purpose. This might entail appearance, safety, ease of use, customer support, as well as embracing issues such as availability, value for money, reputation, and the behaviour of staff with whom the customer has contact.

Quality has a number of associated costs identified as follows.

- **Failure costs** refer to those costs incurred when goods are found to be faulty, as with a battery that does not work or an airline meal that is not the one ordered by the passenger. In such cases the costs are those incurred by the company in scrap or replacement. However, other costs may be less easy to define, such as the customer's buying another brand of battery or changing airline for subsequent flights.

- **Appraisal costs** are those costs involved in the installation and operation of a quality control system. Such costs can include the time taken to complete paperwork systems and the employment of staff with specific responsibility for quality control.
- **Prevention costs** are those involved in the establishment of mechanisms which build quality procedures in all operations. An example of such costs would be those involved in the installation of systems to obtain British Standard 5750 or the similar international standard ISO 9000.

Increasing attention is being paid in many organizations to the notion of prevention. There is a widely held belief that engineering quality into both the product and the process is more effective than systems of detection and remedy. A distinction is often drawn between quality assurance, the embodiment of the former, and quality control, which typifies the latter approach. In Chapter 5 we have noted that quality can be used as a competitive weapon, a strategy successfully employed by many German companies, such as BMW and Daimler-Benz. Some customers are willing to pay more for goods of higher quality. However, higher quality goods need not necessarily be more expensive. A good quality assurance procedure may reduce wastage and save on quality control procedures. Deming (1986) goes further and argues that improved quality is a virtuous circle of lower costs, lower prices, increased market share and the provision of more jobs.

In Britain, the Government, mindful of the nation's declining position in world trade, has established measures in recognition of the role played by quality in international competition in both the manufacturing and service industries. The Government through the British Standards Institute (BSI) has defined quality assurance as an all-embracing concept involving all stages and all people in the production process. General guidance has been issued under British Standard 4891, urging companies to set quality objectives and establish programmes and procedures to see that such objectives are met. These measures have been strengthened by the establishment of British Standard 5750. The BSI will award this standard only to those companies who are able to show that quality is built into the production system at every stage of the operation, and whose employees display a genuine commitment to quality issues. The Government has stated its intention of giving contracts only to those firms who possess British Standard 5750 and the Department of Trade and Industry has published a register listing those companies that have been quality assessed. There are increasing signs that some industries will only buy goods and components from firms that have been quality assessed, and it is predicted that the future purchasing habits of the general consumer will be influenced by British Standard 5750.

In order to obtain British Standard 5750, firms must prepare a 'Quality Manual' which sets out policy and procedures on quality assurance. A key element of the policy is that companies must identify their own quality standards. There then follows an assessment process to review policy and procedures and to ensure that they are being carried out. Successful firms are awarded a certificate which gives them the right to incorporate the standard in their marketing literature. Maintenance of the award is dependent upon follow-up inspections, usually at annual intervals.

The process has been criticized for its cost, not just of the inspection process itself, but also of the time and expense involved in establishing acceptable quality assurance procedures. In some companies the quest for British Standard 5750 has resulted in the creation of vast quality bureaucracies and audit-proof paper trails. The notion of a firm setting its own standards has been attacked as subjective and misleading for the public.

We have already noted the tendency of some organizations to focus on the quality of their product and services as a key strategy and a key factor in the development of a corporate culture. Quality plays a key role in the so-called 'excellent' companies. We refer you to the relevant sections of Chapters 3 and 4 for a more detailed account of these strategic and cultural issues. Quality and corporate culture are inextricably entwined in the concept of 'Total Quality Management' (TQM).

## Total Quality Management

TQM is a strategic approach to quality which permeates the entire organization. As Hill writes,

> top management determines quality priorities, establishes the systems of quality management and the procedures to be followed, provides resources and leads by example.
>
> (Hill, 1991, p. 554)

The concept emerged from the work in statistical quality control at the Western Electric Hawthorne plant in the 1930s and was associated with the work of W. Edwards Deming and Joseph Juran (Binns, 1993). It was introduced to Japan by the Americans as the occupying force in the immediate post war era and found its greatest expression in Japanese manufacturing industry.

The essence of TQM incorporates the following.

- It is a top-down management philosophy that focuses on the needs of the customer.
- It comprises a quality plan which offers a structured, disciplined approach to quality and incorporates a number of tools and techniques. Particular emphasis is given to the collection and analysis of information and to employee training.
- It is culturally based with involvement as a core philosophy. TQM statements abound with references to teamwork and creative thinking.
- By focusing on the costs of poor quality, it saves money.
- It encompasses the notion of continuous improvement and, as such, it is essentially long-term.

Such elements are incorporated in the mission statement of Akzo Chemicals, a multinational employing two thousand people in the UK.

> The supply of quality products and services to meet both internal and external customer expectations and to promote the participation and development of all employees in the pursuit of continuous quality improvement.
>
> (Tayles and Woods, 1993, p. 3)

TQM as a concept has been subjected to a similar list of criticisms as those we presented in our discussion of organizational culture in Chapter 3. Like BS 5750 it has been associated with paperwork and bureaucracy which have stifled the very goals it seeks to achieve. Moreover, rather than a process of involvement, it is seen by some as an instrument of management control and domination. (Hill, 1991 and Binns, 1993 offer a good critique.)

---

**KEY CONCEPT 6.3**
*Materials management*

Materials management has become an important function in manufacturing industry and has superseded the more traditional activities of purchasing and stock control. It aims to improve organizational effectiveness through the planning, coordination and control of all materials and in so doing coordinates the activities of purchasing, progress chasing and stock control. Developments in materials management involve 'Just-In-Time' methods of production planning influenced significantly by Japanese management methods.

---

## Materials management

The purchasing function is part of a wider process that has been gaining in recognition and importance over the last few years. This is known as materials management, defined by the Institute of Purchasing and Supply as,

> the concept requiring an organizational structure which unifies into one functional responsibility the systematic planning and control of all materials from identification of the need through to delivery to the consumer. Materials management embraces planning, purchasing, production and inventory control, storage, materials handling and physical distribution. The objectives of materials management are to optimize performance in meeting agreed customer service requirements at the same time adding to the profitability by minimizing costs and making the best use of available resources.

The importance of materials management is twofold. First, from the perspective of this book, it illustrates, more than most activities, the interaction of the production function with its environment. The price and availability of goods is influenced by various environmental considerations, such as the economics of supply and demand. However, management will operate purchasing strategies in order to control supply and demand and hence the environment. Second, materials management can have a significant impact on a firm's costs and hence its profitability. While the 1960s focused on rising labour costs, the oil crisis of 1973, and subsequent rises in the cost of many materials and components, brought the precarious state of raw material supply into sharp relief. Even modest savings on the cost of raw materials, and greater care in the management of those materials as they pass through the organization, can have a greater impact on profit than increased sales revenue.

The key variables of purchasing are source, quantity, quality, time and price. We will examine each of these in turn.

Source   Management is faced with a number of decisions concerning the source of the firm's raw materials and components. The obvious strategy is one which maximizes the other four variables, obtaining supplies in the quantity and quality required, when they are needed, and at an acceptable price. In achieving these aims, managements must decide whether to produce their own materials and components or buy them from other manufacturers; and if the latter, whether to opt for a single supplier or buy from a number of different suppliers.

The 'make or buy' decision involves consideration of vertical integration, either through acquiring the raw material supplier or manufacturing your own components. This will give management greater control over the reliability of supplies, and may well add a new dimension to the firm as a supplier to others. There are considerable cost implications to such a strategy, which are not only financial. Consider the case of a firm that sets up its own foundry to manufacture its requirements for cast metal products. The foundry has to operate as a profit centre and since it operates in an area of declining demand contracts to do work for other firms. The foundry may be placed in a position of supplying major competitors as well as having a conflict of priorities over the respective demands of its own and other organizations. In more general terms we noted in Chapter 4 that acquisition through vertical integration may not be very successful due to the different nature of the industries involved.

A firm can build up a good relationship with a single supplier, but there may be greater security in using a variety of sources, especially where supplies are unreliable. We have already referred to the series of strikes in the car components industry in the 1960s which led to the closure of the major car manufacturers in this country and brought about a change in purchasing policy resulting in the use of a greater number of suppliers. Since the early 1980s a less volatile industrial-relations climate has seen a shift back to firms establishing close relationships with a limited number of suppliers.

The relationship between supplier and purchaser is often a question of relative power. We discuss this at length in Chapter 4 and you are referred specifically to Figure 4.3. If the purchaser is in a strong position compared to the suppliers then they may have to bid for the contract, enabling the buyer to obtain the most favourable deal. Such bidding and dealing introduce a highly sensitive variable to the purchasing function, so much so that it has been defined as 'a maelstrom of human relations' (Starr, 1972, p. 271).

The personal relationships between buyers and sellers are an important ingredient in purchasing. A purchasing manager with a supply problem may well be able to solve it by using his personal relationship with one of the suppliers. Time, effort and expenditure are regularly involved in building up such relationships. There are also cases where personal relationships have resulted in contracts being unfairly secured and even bribery used, as some legal cases over local authority building contracts will testify.

**Quantity**   The major purchasing decision here is how much to order at any one time. This is a function of cost, storage capacity, and the nature of the production system. The decision can be difficult. For example, a firm operating complex machinery on a continuous process basis may need to stock expensive replacement parts, even though they be needed only infrequently. A decision model has been developed, the Economic Order Quantity Model, which establishes a trade-off between the cost of acquisition and the cost of holding stock. Some firms have very precise stock and delivery requirements in an attempt to minimize material costs. This is illustrated by the 'Just-In-Time' method, ascribed to the Japanese and examined in the next section.

The greater the purchasing requirements then the greater the possibility of obtaining discounts. Some highly diverse organizations operate a central purchasing function to maximize such discounts. The needs of several London boroughs for certain goods is met by a central purchasing function.

**Quality**   The quality of incoming raw materials and components is a vital ingredient in the quality control function. The purchasing department or the materials manager is usually responsible for the acceptance sampling and inspection of incoming materials.

**Time and price**   The timing of a purchase is, like order quantity, a function of the needs of the production system, storage capacity and price. Certain commodities are particularly price sensitive and there can be significant speculation. In the 1970s the price of silver rose dramatically. This was particularly significant for the film-developing industry, which used silver as a major ingredient. Some companies refused to buy in a rising market, preferring to wait for what they saw as the inevitable fall. Some of those companies went out of business as their stocks ran out long before prices fell. Some firms, to offset the costs involved in stockholding, engage in hedging, a process of buying materials and stock at the current price for delivery at some future date. Other purchasing managers get involved with the futures market and options trading, although the speculative nature of some markets increases the risk in decision-making.

In our discussion of purchasing, we have made constant reference to the management of stock, sometimes referred to as inventory management. Stock is an expensive item and can account for 30% of a firm's total assets. Stock management therefore attempts to balance the needs of the production system against the cost of holding stock. It operates in three main areas; raw materials and components for product or process; the work in progress; and finished stock. Operating systems such as 'group technology' and materials strategies such as 'Just-In-Time' are attempts to minimize inventory and to hold down costs.

## Production and the environment

We began this chapter by challenging the notion that production could be buffered against environmental influences, and we have already seen several illustrations of how a production function interacts with its environment. All the environmental sections of our model relate in some way to the production function. In this section we will explore the more significant aspects of that relationship. We deal first with the interaction of production, the economy and the state with a focus on manufacturing industry. The theme of manufacturing also dominates the examination of production and technology, with an emphasis on new manufacturing techniques based on computerization. We look at the interaction of production and labour and close the section with an examination of production methods in different societies, with a focus on Japan.

### Production, the economy and the state

Until the 1980s, successive British governments recognized the economic importance of manufacturing through policies to encourage its growth, and through its attempts to regenerate flagging industries and firms. Since then, advocates of continued support of manufacturing industry have lost out to those who favour the operation of the free market. The somewhat spectacular decline of UK manufacturing industry is examined in more detail in Chapter 2, and the extent of that decline is shown Table 2.4.

The state is involved in the production function in a number of other ways. We saw in Chapter 5 how business operations can be affected by regulatory laws such as those relating to the purification of waste water or the emission of toxic waste as by-products of the manufacturing process. Earlier in this chapter we dealt with government attempts to improve the quality of goods and services by establishing national standards, and encouraging customers to deal only with firms which can operate to those standards. As part of its regional policy, successive governments have attempted to influence the location of both manufacturing and non-manufacturing industry. This has generally focused on measures to encourage firms to locate in areas of high unemployment by giving them generous grants and tax allowances

---

**KEY CONCEPT 6.4**
***New technology and
production***

Production systems, especially in manufacturing, have, in more recent times, changed significantly to take advantage of developments in new technology to enhance the effectiveness of the production process. Computers have been used extensively in product design and the operation and control of production systems. Machines that are used in this way are designated CNC machines (computerized numerical control). The concept of CAD/CAM (computer-aided design and computer-aided manufacture) is one which extends this application as a central feature in the production system as a whole. Robotics represents a specialized form of computer-controlled machine offering considerable flexibility to a production system, while the greatest flexibility is offered by a totally integrated, computer controlled production system known as FMS (flexible manufacturing system). While computers do play a significant role in modern manufacturing, the extent of their use, especially in the form of FMS is severely limited by their cost.

---

### Production and technology

> Advanced manufacturing technology in the 1980s exhibits some highly distinctive characteristics. The most important is the ability to manufacture a very wide range of component parts and assemblies in a highly flexible fashion. It is this flexibility which distinguishes today's advances from the automation of the 1950s and 1960s . . . Companies (and nations?) who do not succeed in implementing this technology stand to lose heavily – perhaps disappearing completely from the manufacturing scene.
>
> (Husband, 1984, p. 197)

We have seen the interaction of manufacturing industry and the economy in our discussion in Chapter 2. In the 1980s there emerged a widely held view that the recovery of British manufacturing industry in world terms depended upon the introduction of advanced engineering methods (Finniston, 1980).

In Chapter 2 we discussed also the influence of technology on the labour force and upon the way work is organized. We pick up those themes later in this chapter. In this section we will examine the impact on manufacturing of three major innovations in process technology; numerical control, robotics, and flexible manufacturing systems (FMS).

**Numerical control**   This is the basic concept underlying automated production systems. It occurs when machinery, tools and equipment come under the control of a digital computer, as in the case of the automatic positioning and direction of a drilling operation on an engine block. Strictly speaking, we should refer to this process as 'computerized numerical control' (CNC). The full extent of CNC can be seen in its application to flexible manufacturing systems. This type of system is an illustration of 'computer-aided manufacture', which we discussed earlier this chapter under the heading of production design. A big advantage of CNC is that it makes possible contour-controlled cutting operations. Such operations previously required the cutting machine to be reset several times.

**Robotics**   The nearest analogy to an industrial robot is the human arm, to which a variety of tools can be attached to perform a variety of jobs from metalwork to painting. The majority of industrial robots operate from a fixed position with the restricted movements defined by a computer program.

A study of robotics reveals an inconsistency between the image portrayed in the media and the actual use of industrial robots. Their use and capabilities are less than is normally supposed. Fifty per cent of all industrial robots are to be found in the automobile industry, where their use is generally confined to various types of welding operation and paint spraying (Williams *et al.*, 1987). The greatest number and concentration of industrial robots are found in Japan, where applications also tend to be more varied; for instance the electronics firm, Hitachi, has plans to robotize 60% of its production lines (Thackray, 1983). In this case robotics has been extended to perform the precision tasks of assembling electronic circuit boards.

Robots offer possibilities of continuous operation, improved quality and the liberation of human labour from repetitive, unhealthy and unpleasant tasks as with paint spraying. Very few robots, however, possess tactile or visual capabilities and while their potential impact on manufacturing systems will be considerable, for the present, the supposed flexibility they offer a production system has been exaggerated.

> Robots cannot be reprogrammed for new models by pressing a few buttons. That is a myth.
>
> (Williams *et al.*, 1987, p. 39)

The main handicap to the more extensive use of robotics in industry is cost, involving not just the cost of the actual robot, but the high costs of developing specific software and machine tools. This problem is heightened in times of economic recession or in cheap labour economies when a plentiful supply of cheap labour may lower the motivation for such an expensive investment.

**Flexible manufacturing systems**   A flexible manufacturing system (FMS) brings together the various elements of advanced manufacturing engineering to solve the problem of offering consumer choice and a quick response to market changes using a minimum of working capital. Potentially it offers manufacturing industry a solution to the kind of dilemmas outlined in Figure 6.2. An FMS usually embraces the following:

- equipment comprising NC machines, robots, and machine tools;
- an automatic transport system for moving tools and workpieces, as well as parts and raw materials;
- the whole system is computer-controlled with software for scheduling, tool selection, part selection, fault finding, machine breakdown detection and so on.

In a car plant an FMS would enable a range of different models to be built on the same production line, with the necessary tool changes being automatic, and the required parts being delivered automatically to work stations in the quantity and at the time they were required. A typical FMS would incorporate a multiple tool system, a CNC machine with the capability of performing a number of different machine-tool operations. For example, the drilling of a variety of different-sized holes in a single machine part could be achieved in a single sequence of operations. Prior to such multiple tool systems such jobs would require a number of different machines, and the consequent moving of work-pieces, or time-consuming changeover of machine tools.

The claimed advantages of such a system are many (see for example Piore and Sabel, 1984; and Ebel, 1985). The main ones are as follows:

- higher productivity would be achieved through the better utilization of plant, materials and labour;
- a greater number of product variants would be possible in smaller batches offering the consumer greater choice and potential satisfaction;
- reduced set-up times and consequently, shorter manufacturing lead times and a more flexible response to change;
- the need for less inventory at all stages of the production process; fewer parts, less work-in-process, and less finished stock;
- improved production and quality control.

A study of eight cases of FMS in Britain revealed that at constant sales level, a fourfold increase in plant investment resulted in higher productivity, a threefold reduction in inventory, and a threefold increase in profit. Further investment in plant together with an increase in sales had an even greater impact on profits (National Economic Development Office, 1985). While this case points the way for a rosy FMS future we must put such optimism in some kind of perspective.

The number of fully integrated FMSs was in 1985 estimated at no more than two hundred worldwide (Ebel, 1985). As with robotics the main drawback is the high initial cost of setting the system up. A 1986 survey found that 82% of all US, 46% of all European and 42% of all Japanese FMSs had cost over $3 million (United Nations, 1986). This would appear to limit their application to a small number of big firms able to carry such an investment. Where FMSs had been installed in the USA, their use tended to be restricted to products having relatively long runs, which suggests that their potential is not being fully exploited (Jaikumar, 1986).

Despite this potential for variety, the reality for many companies is that the pay-back on such substantial investments as CNC machines, industrial robots and FMS is only feasible on long runs. Automation paid off handsomely for Volkswagen because of the high volume production, whereas the relatively low volume of Austin-Rover's output meant that its automation turned out a poor investment (Williams *et al.*, 1987). Furthermore, as we found with robotics, only a limited range of product variety is feasible before costly programming and tooling changes are required. In any case the quest for product variety may well be a marketing myth. The continued manufacture of washing machines to the same basic design and the purchase of second cars and television sets would indicate that the consumers' need for repeat or supplementary purchases is greater than the need for variety.

Innovations in production technology undoubtedly carry the potential for a more effective and efficient production system. We have seen, however, that such enthusiasm must be tempered by the high cost and a recognition of the limitations of the new technology. Investment is no guarantee of business success and a focus on increasing market share may pay better dividends for many companies.

Further complications are caused by the impact of such developments on the labour force. The same technology that has the potential of eliminating the need for people to do noisy, dirty, dangerous work, that can improve working conditions, that offers interesting opportunities for restructuring the organization, also carries the very real threat of job displacement. It is to such issues that we now turn.

## Production and labour

The impact of the production system on the labour force and vice versa is such a complex and well-documented area that we can only hope to introduce some of the main issues here. These issues include the man–machine interface, training, industrial relations, the quality of working life, payment systems and the problems of introducing change. We will start here with F. W. Taylor's influence on the organization of production. We will identify some of the problems associated with 'Taylorism', particularly the deskilling hypothesis, and look at 'popular' solutions to those problems, notably job enrichment and autonomous work groups. We then examine the role of payment systems both as an incentive and as a production control device.

**Taylorism and deskilling**   The organization of labour in the production system is dominated by the work of F. W. Taylor and his treatise on 'Scientific Management' (Taylor, 1947). The thoughts attributed to the scientific management school represent an attempt to solve the problems of management incompetence. This was essentially a problem of control due to the growing size and complexity of organizations and the growth of trade unions. The main principle of scientific management draws a distinction between planning and doing, with management, as the planners, controlling every aspect of the work process. This involves the design of tasks and work measurement, the careful selection and training of the workforce, target setting and the design of payment systems. The application and in some cases misapplication of Taylor's ideas resulted in a tendency towards an extensive division of labour, work simplification and tight managerial control. Much of manufacturing industry and many of the larger production systems in non-manufacturing throughout the world exhibit elements of Taylorism, and the ideas of F. W. Taylor were popular not only among American capitalists but with Lenin and Mussolini.

Despite its widespread popularity, the scientific management approach has met with considerable criticism. Taylor's views have been labelled as authoritarian, subjective, unscientific and ultimately unfair. The main thrust of the attack is focused around the deskilling hypothesis encapsulated in the work of Braverman (1974). The extensive division of labour means that work becomes fragmented, the machine becomes more important than the worker, and control shifts from the skilled worker firmly into the hands of management, whose position is strengthened by their virtual monopoly of knowledge of the work process. Braverman saw scientific management as the essential control of labour in the production process. Deskilling occurs not only in manufacturing industry but in many service industries too, such as large banks and insurance companies. In such establishments work has been fragmented in much the same way as in manufacturing industry and both the discretion of individual employees and their contact with the public has been reduced by the operation of programmed decisions and standard letters using computer systems.

Criticisms of Taylor's approach tend to focus on managerial control, the reduction of man to the level of a machine, its crude economic approach and even the eccentricity of Taylor himself. More than most management writers, Taylor has been subjected to much hostile criticism which has tended to mask some of the more enlightened aspects of his thinking; his views on training and participation for example. Ultimately the widespread application of scientific management suggests that it offered solutions acceptable to many, even trade unions. Nevertheless attempts have been made to humanize the work environment, as a response either to Taylorism, his critics, or arising from other motivations. These attempts have focused on the problems brought about by deskilling.

**Solutions to the problems of deskilling** Several theories and techniques have been put forward to counteract the negative impact of deskilling on the individual worker, such as a lack of job satisfaction and alienation. These attempts include human relations management, job rotation, job enlargement, job enrichment, autonomous work groups, participation schemes and the current catch-all for many of these and similar approaches, the 'Quality of Working Life' movement. We will deal with just two of these, job enrichment and autonomous work groups.

Job enrichment owes much to the motivation theories of Herzberg (1968). It focuses on the content of jobs and attempts, by redesigning the work, to give workers more responsibility, more control, a greater sense of achievement and ultimately more satisfaction. Applications tend to be more successful among white-collar jobs (where there is more scope for change) and among those who actively seek more responsibility. However, successful application in terms of productivity and job satisfaction was found in a series of experiments with several types of employees at ICI in Britain (Paul and Robertson, 1970).

Autonomous work-groups have their origins in the notion of socio-technical systems and in particular in the work of the Tavistock Institute in Britain, although the application has tended to be given more scope in Scandinavia. The approaches vary, although in essence they involve the creation of an autonomous work-group which is given responsibility for the completion of a part of the operation. The manager thus freed from labour control operates more as a 'boundary manager', dealing with problems of the immediate environment. We will come back to this notion of the autonomous work-group in our discussion of 'group technology' in the next section.

As solutions to the problems of deskilling, both job enrichment and autonomous work-groups, like the other approaches mentioned, have been successful in certain situations but tend to operate under severe constraints and naturally have attracted their critics. A recurring theme in this criticism is that both approaches have been introduced to solve management problems of absenteeism, high labour turnover, low productivity and poor profit margins with job satisfaction for the individual as a subsidiary issue. In particular, writers such as Braverman see job enrichment as a reaffirmation of management control. The workforce is offered a palliative but the changes are carefully controlled by management. In most cases radical restructuring has not occurred and scientific management principles still dominate the production system.

**Payment systems**  An important aspect of the interaction of labour and production is the issue of pay. Pay acts as an incentive for the individual worker to participate in the production process and may also be used by management as a control device. These functions operate side by side. We saw in Figure 6.1 that labour is an input to the production system. The input is bought in and therefore represents a significant cost to the firm, which managements invariably attempt to control. The search for effective means of motivation and control has led to the design of a variety of payment systems.

In manufacturing industry the most common form of payment system is some form of payment by results. This usually operates in the form of a flat rate of pay supplemented by a bonus payment directly related to the output of the individual worker or group of workers. Payment by results takes many forms but each subscribes to the principle of extra payment for increased output subject to quality, wastage and machine utilization. Such incentive schemes tend to be most value in certain situations typified by the following conditions:

- in highly competitive markets, where output or a quick response to customer demands may be vital in establishing a competitive advantage;
- where the workplace is large and some form of impersonal control is needed;
- in firms with relatively high labour costs, where some control can be exerted by varying the work flow;
- where workers can control the pace of work either as individuals or members of a group;

- where opportunities for personal involvement with work is lacking and pay is the only motivator.

Many criticisms have been levelled at such methods, nevertheless, their persistence is a measure of their popularity, not just with management but with employees too. Furthermore, some form of payment by results operates in non-manufacturing firms, such as sales commission in retailing. In its crudest form, where payment is only made for work completed (known as piecework) it is the sole form of payment. This is also the case in some professions such as barrister and dentist.

The importance of pay in controlling and influencing production operations has been recognized by those seeking to change the culture of the organization to gain greater commitment from the workforce. The payment method associated with this is profit-sharing, a system whereby a proportion of pre-tax profits is shared out among the workforce. However, in Britain at least, profit-sharing is not widespread; employees see the relationship between effort and reward to be too remote, and, because of this, management see it as an ineffective control device. In those companies where commitment is a central feature of employment, as in IBM, employees receive an annual bonus based directly on their individual contribution to the organization as judged by management.

## Cultural influences and production

In Chapter 2 we examined the role of culture in business and examined the view that industry in general and manufacturing industry in particular was 'alien to the spirit and character of the English people' (quoted in Wiener, 1981, p. 113). As a consequence the core process, production has been especially neglected, and Britain has subsequently lost out in world trade to countries like Germany and Japan. Such views neglect to explain why the British were successful at manufacturing, even in relatively recent phases of its history, such as the 1950s. Instead, we look to other country's production systems for the secrets of their success. In Germany we are envious of their engineering technology, production planning systems and education and training. However, the greatest amount of attention has been reserved for Japan.

## Production systems in Japan

In Chapter 2 we spent some time looking at the phenomenon known as Japanese management. We referred to the increasingly popular view that sees Japanese economic and especially export success in terms of well-planned and executed methods of production management, especially in manufacturing industry. Three aspects of the process are singled out: an attention to detail, the importance of quality control, and a totally integrated production system from the delivery of materials and parts to the distribution of the final product. These are supported by a labour system which places emphasis on total flexibility and is marked by an absence of job descriptions. There are obvious similarities with Orlake Records, Case 6.1, which confirms the view offered in Chapter 2 that there is nothing specifically Japanese about Japanese production management. In this section we will view two aspects of the Japanese production system, 'Just-In-Time' and 'Quality circles'.

**Just-In-Time**   The origins of this system are ascribed to the Toyota car plant, although similar systems operate throughout Japan and are used by Japanese multinationals abroad, as well as spreading to other companies, notably Massey Ferguson, GKN, and Lucas in Britain.

Just-In-Time (JIT) aims to obtain the highest volume output at the lowest unit costs. The system is really a method of production control in which precise targets for subassembly are set based on the demands of final assembly. Because of this JIT is described as a 'pull-through' production system. Exact quantities are produced and specific requirements are placed on materials and parts suppliers, as well as each stage in the production process to deliver just in time for the next stage of operations. Materials intake, work in progress and goods dispatch are therefore kept to a minimum.

The claimed advantages for the system are that it smooths out the production flow and reduces all types of inventory levels and hence costs. By preventing production delays it enhances planning and enables the firm to meet its delivery deadlines. At the same time, it eliminates time wasted in waiting for components, as well as over-production.

The system has been viewed narrowly as an inventory control device. However, there are significant implications for the entire organization of production. JIT encourages a much closer relationship with suppliers and those able to meet the demands of the system are often offered high-volume contracts, sometimes as the sole supplier. This is a marked contrast to the kind of strategies used by some firms to guarantee consistent suppliers by using a number of competing components manufacturers. To obtain the maximum flexibility from JIT, it is often introduced with new multi-purpose machinery, enabling the firm to manufacture a wider range of product types in shorter runs. Most significantly, JIT demands cooperation from all stages of the production process and usually requires mechanisms for labour flexibility and teamwork, with implications for the organization structure.

At the Toyota factory, the system is controlled by an information system known as 'Kanban'. This is a system of cards which informs how much is to be produced by each process and the precise quantity each process should withdraw from the previous stage, which may be either another process, a materials store, or even a supplier. In Toyota, the Kanban system is extended to its subcontractors, who must conform to the precise delivery requirements of the parent factory.

While JIT and Kanban can strengthen the ties between company and supplier, as we saw in our earlier discussion, the system can place considerable pressure on subcontractors who are expected to be at the call of the parent company. The system can only work given the willingness of suppliers to participate. This situation has frustrated some Japanese companies operating in Britain and led to protracted negotiations with British supply companies, some of which find the demands placed upon them too great for the rewards involved.

Quality circles   While these are attributed to Japan, their pedigree dates back to production committees in First World War Britain and partici-pative management in the USA. Nonetheless it was in Japan where they spread in popularity from their inauguration in 1963. They com-prise small groups of employees who work together and who volunteer to meet regularly to solve job-related problems, especially to discuss ways of improving the production process and product quality. They are supervisor-led and have the authority to implement change.

Attempts to introduce them in other countries have met with mixed results (Bradley and Hill, 1983). Those that fail generally do so because of underlying distrust between management and worker and scepticism on the part of management. In Japan they thrive on more cooperative workplace relations, but more particularly, as in Germany, on an underlying ethos that stresses product quality. Toyota see quality as the responsibility of all workers and has even devised its own name for a system of autonomous defects control, which they term 'autonomation'.

The relative failure of the 'quality circle' idea in Britain does not imply a lack of interest in quality. As we have seen from our discussion of organizational culture (Chapter 3) and quality, earlier in this chapter, firms appear to be taking different routes to quality assurance. All the signs indicate that while the 'Quality circle' may be a passing fashion, JIT may well become the norm for manufacturing industry and the pattern of the future. In essence it focuses on the precise planning of production operations and, in so doing, provides guidelines for non-manufacturing as well as manufacturing.

## Lean production

The whole issue of Japanese production techniques has been elevated to celebrity status through the work of the International Motor Vehicle programme at MIT. This represents a detailed study of Japanese tech-niques focused on the decline of such American producers as General Motors relative to their Japanese competitors. In the best-selling book which emerged from the study, Womack *et al.* (1990) claim that the productivity in Japanese car plants is twice that of their American counterparts.

The set of techniques associated with this massive productivity advantage have been dubbed 'lean production'. The origins of this can be traced to Toyota and a diffusion process has been plotted which incorporated first Toyota's subcontractors, and subsequently the rest of the Japanese car industry. Lean production involves a flexible and multiskilled workforce using state-of-the art, flexible technology which incorporate JIT methods and facilitate both small batch sizes and rapid changeover. Lean production systems are typified by an absence of indirect workers, an absence of buffer stocks, and, through their built-in quality procedures, a marked lack of rework. The net result is the ability to produce both variety and quality at a cost that is substantially less than both those associated with small batch and mass production methods. As Womack *et al.* claim,

> (Lean production) . . . uses less of everything compared to mass production – half the human effort in the factory, half the manufacturing space, half the investment in tools, half the engineering hours to develop a new product in half the time.
>
> (Womack *et al.*, 1990, p. 13)

Such claims have been vigorously challenged by Williams and Haslam (1992a). They produce data which show that, Toyota apart, the margin of superiority of Japanese car manufacturers is small and, in some cases, bettered by European and US car manufacturers.

## Organizational aspects of production

The centrality of the production function to an organization means that more often than not, the nature of the organization is significantly influenced by the nature of the production process. In this section we will explore the interaction between the production function and the organizational elements of our model. After a brief review of organization size, we will devote this chapter to the interrelated elements of structure, goals and organizational culture.

### Production and organization size

The size of the firm, expressed both in terms of numbers employed and capital invested, has a close relationship with the production function. A firm dedicated to mass production is invariably large, both in terms of the number of employees and capital investment. A mass producer of motor cars, such as Ford or General Motors, will employ many thousands of workers at any one of their assembly plants throughout the world, as well as having a substantial investment in flow-line technology. As with most elements of the Business in Context model, the influence is two-way. The sheer size and complexity of the production process in a mass producer of automobiles will influence the size of the workforce and the capital employed. By the same token the size of the firm and its output requirements will determine the precise nature of the production system and in particular the production technology. For example, only the largest of firms with high outputs are able to invest in highly automated production systems at profit.

The relationship persists in other types of business too. The multi-national hamburger chain, McDonalds, which specializes in the mass production of a limited range of hamburgers, employs thousands in variety of outlets throughout the world. While McDonalds's investment in production technology may not be as high as a car manufacturer's, the cost of leasing prime sites in urban areas represents a considerable investment. The production technology employed in an oil refinery requires only a small proportion of labour to that employed in mass production technologies, yet the emphasis on sophisticated process technology means that capital investment is generally much higher. A very large insurance firm will almost certainly use a factory-style flow-line for the processing of the very large numbers of policies it has to handle.

The relationship between size and the production system reveals itself most clearly through the way the production process is organized and its impact upon organization structure.

## Production and organization structure

In Chapter 3, we introduced the popular claim that production technology and size have probably a greater influence on organization structure than any other variable. We argued then that the relationship also involved a number of other variables such as strategy, culture and the behaviour of interest groups. Nevertheless, since the production function represents the firm's central activity it would be somewhat surprising if the structure did not reflect both the technology and the strategies associated with producing the goods and services of the organization. There are clear overlaps with our discussion of structure in Chapter 3, and you are advised to refer to the relevant parts of that chapter.

We base our analysis in this section around the classification offered by Joan Woodward, to which we have referred in Chapters 2 and 3. She and her research team studied a large number of manufacturing firms in South-East Essex and identified three main types of production technology; unit and small batch, large batch and mass, and process production. The three types accounted for key variations in organization structure. Variations occurred in the number of levels in the hierarchy, the span of control of each manager, the nature of job descriptions, the degree of written communication and the extent of functional specialization (Woodward, 1965). For example, a small batch system is depicted by a more flexible structure than a mass production plant. The most important thing to Woodward was not simply the nature of these variances but that structural design should be matched to the nature of the prevailing technology. Woodward was thus one of the earliest exponents of contingency theory (explained in Chapter 1). For instance a small batch producer could only be successful if it adopted a flexible structure and that business failure could be attributed to a firm adopting a structure that was inappropriate to its production technology.

We will use a slightly expanded version of Woodward's classification to illustrate the relationship between the production system and organization structure. As we have mentioned, Woodward based her work on manufacturing industry, but the classification may be used to examine structural differences in other types of business as well.

**Project production**   This is a very specific kind of production system in which the entire production process is committed to the completion of a single task to customer requirements, as in the case of building a ship, fulfilling a major construction contract, developing computer software, or carrying out an extensive management consultancy exercise. The organization structure usually comprises a project team, specifically created for the project in question. In Case 5.5, the Baystate Bank created a project group to introduce automatic teller machines and integrate the work of several banks in the group. Upon completion of the project, the structure is usually disbanded. Many large construction companies use this arrangement within a broader matrix framework (Chapter 3 has a fuller discussion of matrix systems).

**Unit and small batch production**   Both project and small batch production can be classified as 'jobbing' operations. Whereas most projects are carried out on the customer's own site, small batch production is not. It may, like a project, comprise the production of a single item to customer specification. More often it represents the production of a small number of items. In manufacturing, the organization tends to be focused around a number of processes on general purpose machines, manned by skilled labour. The organization hierarchy tends to assume a somewhat flat shape. Examples of this type of organization would include an engineering company manufacturing precision parts for aeroplane engines, or a high-class restaurant serving a limited number of customers each night.

**Large batch and mass production**   In manufacturing, the move from small to large batch production usually involves a shift to assembly line methods. In most types of large batch production, equipment is specifically designed around a particular product or range of products and involves considerable machinery in the movement of goods and materials. At its most extreme, as in a car plant, this represents mass production on a grand scale, but most mass-market domestic products are made in this way. The typical mass production organization is labour-intensive, utilizing semi-skilled labour in repetitive jobs offering little discretion to individual workers. The system is highly bureaucratized with a correspondingly larger number of management levels, inspectors, progress chasers and the like than in small batch production. Firms that come into this category usually have a combination of production types. Components tend to be manufactured in large batches in a scaling-up of typical jobbing arrangements, whereas assembly tends to be carried out using a flow-line method.

Similar organization structures can be found in those service organizations catering for mass markets, such as a high-street bank, a bus company or a major airline.

**Process production**   At its most extreme, large batch production represents an almost continuous flow of materials through the process. With

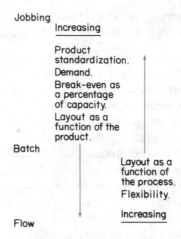

*Figure 6.5* Variations in production systems.

such industries as the manufacture of chemicals or the refining of oil, true process production emerges, comprising equipment specifically designed to handle large volumes. In such organizations, the workforce generally operates in small teams dealing with a particular aspect of the process, using cognitive rather than manual skills and having much more discretion than in assembly-line work. Consequently there tends to be less management engaged in quantity and quality control, and in most cases these functions are automated. Such organizations are typified by rather tall hierarchies, but this reflects complex grading systems more often than management control.

The changes that are typified by a shift from jobbing to process operations are summarized in Figure 6.5.

So far we have presented the classification of production systems as comprising four discrete types. In more recent years the search for increased flexibility of operations has resulted in more hybrid forms of organization. The goal of flexibility is uppermost in the development of group technology in manufacturing and associated developments in the use of autonomous work-groups.

**Group technology**   The idea of group technology emerged from the Soviet Union in the 1950s and refined in Germany, Britain and the USA. Its aim is to satisfy the consumer demand for flexibility, the management demand for increased efficiency, and the individual worker's need for greater involvement.

The first stage in setting up a group technology system is to group the manufacture of all similar components together. These are referred to as 'families' of components. Each component is made from start to finish by a small group of workers operating a range of machines in a flow-line arrangement. Workers are both mobile and flexible, moving from machine to machine according to the logic of the flow of production. A common form of organization is the autonomous work group, referred to in the previous section.

The claimed advantages of such a system are the speed by the reduction of the manufacturing cycle, with less queuing and work in progress. Flexibility is supposedly increased and operating costs reduced through less work in progress, reduced inventory and less scrap. Improved control is possible by giving the group responsibility for both production quality and the achievement of output targets, and there are resulting claims for increased job satisfaction.

A case quoted frequently in the literature is that of Serck-Audco Valves in Shropshire where claims were made that an introduction of group technology resulted, over a six-year period from 1961, in an increase of output per employee of 50%, a reduction in stock of 44%, a reduced manufacturing time from 12 to four weeks and an overall sales increase (presumably from improved delivery capability) of 32%. It was estimated that the capital investment involved was recouped four times over by the savings made on stock reduction alone (quoted in Williamson, 1972).

While cases such as Serck-Audco offer a glowing reference for the introduction of group technology, as with FMS we must be careful in our attribution of cause and effect in such instances. Dramatic sales increases following the introduction of a new method of production organization may be the cause of other factors such as an increased demand for the product, the closure of a major competitor, a change in product design, or even a new incentive scheme for sales staff. It is often difficult in such cases to isolate the required variables to make an accurate assessment. This frequently leads to controversy over the real impact of changes in production technology and organization.

The use of group technology and autonomous work-groups are means of achieving greater flexibility and the principles are transferable to other kinds of production system in the service sector. However, the systems may not work without the cooperation of both management and the workforce and may in fact be unnecessary in those businesses where flexibility is not a key issue.

## Organizational goals and culture

> Manufacturing organizations tend to attract the attention of general managers the way airlines do; one only notices them when they're late, when ticket prices rise, or when there's a crash.
>
> (Hayes and Schmenner, 1978, p. 105)

The implication behind this quotation is that management goals are rarely seen in terms of production; financial goals and marketing goals are much more common. We have already indicated elsewhere in this chapter that such a view may be changing. The attempts of many firms to focus on improved quality, often backed by government initiatives such as British Standard 5750, reveals an attempt to shift the culture of the organization around production issues. The Philips factory, manufacturing television sets at Croydon, attempted to reshape the prevailing organizational culture by redrawing the traditional organization chart to show production at the centre and all other functional areas being subsidiary to and either feeding into or out of production.

The notion of an organization culture based around production is the major theme in Hayes and Wheelwright's 1984 analysis of American manufacturing industry. They support the view that a strong manufacturing base is essential to a healthy economy and that a major handicap is often the attitude of management towards the production function. They see the prevailing culture of the typical American manufacturing firm being dominated by accounting and in particular the need for a quick return on investment. Managers are highly mobile and have little interest in developing the technical know-how essential for new product development and improving the manufacturing system before they move on to better their careers. Short-term profit is seen as a measure of success and there is inadequate investment in R&D and plant improvement. Portfolio management through the buying of other companies becomes the substitute for development. Instead of production the emphasis is placed on marketing as the key function to stimulate existing markets through advertising and re-packaged products.

The solution would appear to lie in a greater investment in innovation and, for manufacturing firms, a development of their own machine-tool industry. The development of dedicated machine tools is held to be essential to gain a competitive advantage in the product market. For many firms, this will require a change in the corporate culture which stresses technical competence as its key criterion. This is achieved by the selection and development of technically qualified managers, a much greater investment in technical training, and a much greater focus on quality by all employees.

The Hayes and Wheelwright hypothesis draws heavily upon comparisons with Germany and Japan. While the analysis is appealing, their views of both Germany and Japan are subjective and often idealized. Furthermore, we have already seen in the previous chapter that the relationship between innovation and economic growth are speculative. Nevertheless, accounts such as these emphasize the importance of production strategies and it is to these we now turn.

## Production strategies

We have already established in this chapter that production is the central function in all organizations. We have also noted that there is often a conflict between the two objectives of operating efficiency and achieving customer satisfaction. We can now restate those objectives in terms of a number of key strategic elements. These are costing and pricing, product quality, dependability, and product flexibility in terms of product range and volume.

These objectives have formed an underlying theme to most of this chapter. They also form the link between production and other functional areas. All the factors are dependent upon product design and development, which we dealt with in Chapter 5, and we shall see in the next chapter how such factors form the basis of marketing strategy. Achieving production objectives would be impossible without the necessary finance and accounting control mechanisms (Chapter 9), and without recruiting and training a workforce with the necessary skills (Chapter 8).

The specific contribution made by production strategy lies in the following:

- establishing the level of quality for the product or service;
- being responsible for the firm's capital assets and therefore having a major contribution to overall costs;
- establishing sufficient capacity to meet market demand.

An important element of this contribution is the manipulation of the various objectives established at the beginning of this section. While an ultimate aim might be to maximize the twin objectives of operating efficiency and customer satisfaction, we have already noted the difficulties of achieving this in practice. A more practical strategy may be the emphasis of certain characteristics to gain an increased competitive advantage over its rivals, a process we shall illustrate below.

Pricing strategies will be examined more thoroughly in the next chapter. The contribution of the production function to price lies in the cost of developing the product itself, any raw materials costs, and the cost of operating the production system. A firm may see low price as its key marketing strategy. If profit levels are to be maintained then the production system must be capable of delivering high volumes and there is a need to keep capital, labour and operating costs as low as possible. As we see in Case 6.3, one of Grundig's major strategies for improving its poor position in the 1980s was a focus on operating costs. There may be an important trade-off here with quality. A restaurant which attempts to reduce costs by buying cheaper raw materials, may find this not to the liking of its customers and may lose trade and ultimately its reputation.

We saw both in the last chapter and earlier in this one how product quality often gave firms the edge over cheaper versions of the same product and how some companies build their strategy around this. As we have just seen, this can be a costly strategy not only in terms of raw materials and product presentation, but also in terms of the need to employ skilled, trained staff, the need for establishing good-quality control mechanisms, and especially the need to keep improving and updating the product or service. For some firms, like Bang and Olufsen, this can be a successful strategy. For Grundig however, the advantages of a reputation for high-quality goods was eliminated by poor control over production operations (Case 6.3).

Dependability refers to the capability of the firm to deliver its goods or services to the customer's satisfaction, not just in terms of quality and price, but most importantly on time. This can be achieved by carrying large stocks, but this can be costly, as once again illustrated in the Grundig case. A more effective strategy may well involve investing in production systems to ensure effective scheduling and by paying

**CASE 6.3**
*Grundig*

Grundig is a German company with its main manufacturing operations in Nürnberg. It is a producer of high-quality televisions, video-cassette recorders, electronic office equipment and computer controls for CNC machines. It has a reputation for quality and precision which it uses as a marketing theme. It is currently owned by the Grundig family, the Dutch multinational, Philips, and by Swiss banking interests. No one group has overall control, the family still retaining 49% of shares.

The company is the market leader for television sets in Germany. However by 1984 Grundig was operating at an annual loss of DM 290 million. The reasons for the company's decline were several.

- In 1983 there were 500 different TV models in stock, some of which had not been made for five years. Stocks of all goods were operating at 28% of sales.
- Grundig had invested heavily in the Philips V2000 system of video recording, which proved a marketing failure. As a consequence there is still a large stock-holding of such recorders.
- The company had suffered badly in the video market at the hands of low-price Japanese competition.
- The family control of the company had been highly centralized, traditionally autocratic and somewhat idiosyncratic. Decisions were made that reflected the values of the chairman rather than reflected good business practice in those product markets. Consequently good advice from members of Grundig staff was ignored.

In 1984, faced with these problems and high operating losses, a new chief executive was installed, who came from Philips. The goals of the company under the new regime were to maintain product quality, but to reduce operating costs, to streamline production, and to establish greater control over supplies and stocks. This was achieved through a number of measures.

- The model range was reduced quite considerably.
- The company invested in a new automated production line for the manufacture of video cassette recorders, to produce high volume output at relatively low operating cost.
- The stocks were reduced to 19% of sales.
- Stocks of raw materials and work-in-progress were cut by 14%.
- Grundig attempted to rationalize its operations through a joint venture with Blaupunkt. Grundig would make televisions for Blaupunkt who would reciprocate by making car radios for Grundig.
- A much greater attention was paid to production planning, cost control and budgeting, as well as a more comprehensive effort to define market sectors.

The new strategies improved turnover per employee by 50%, although the revenue per product was relatively low due to price competition within the industry. The overall impact was measured by the transformation of an operating loss into a profit of DM 50 million by 1986.

(*Source*: A. Fisher, The pain of recreating a culture, *Financial Times*, 29 December 1986)

attention to employee pay and conditions to enhance motivation and reduce absenteeism and labour turnover.

The flexibility to alter products and meet volume demands with minimum lead time are often strategies for survival in highly competitive or, in the case of Orlake Records (Case 6.1), declining markets. Flexibility in terms of product type and volume does require a flexible and often multi-skilled labour force, as well as good relations with suppliers. While flexibility can be a distinct advantage, there may be just as great an advantage in going for a high in a single product market. This allows the firm to take advantage of the 'experience curve', which can result in a virtuous circle of expansion. An increased market share leads to greater experience in operating the production system resulting in lower costs. When these are passed on in the form of lower prices, the result is even greater market penetration. Such a virtuous circle can be enhanced by investment in production technology to reduce operating costs still further. This kind of strategy, while potentially successful in an expanding market, has severe limitations when the market is declining.

Managements need to decide the most appropriate strategy for their organization. It is possible for firms operating in the same industry to have significantly different strategies. Texas Instruments has traditionally opted for high-volume production, reasonable prices and high market share of calculators and measuring equipment. Hewlett-Packard on the other hand, operating in the same markets, has concentrated on low-volume, high-quality, innovative products.

Different strategies can even exist within the same organization. The Roux restaurant chain in London operates at the most expensive end of the market in its restaurant Le Gavroche, producing highly individual meals at high prices in luxury surroundings. Another of its restaurants, Gavvers, serves set meals at a fixed price and aims at value for money. At yet another restaurant, Rouxl Brittania, a high volume of pre-prepared vacuum-packed meals are cooked for a largely lunchtime clientèle from neighbouring offices. These different strategies mix all the elements we have identified above. In the case of the Roux organization there is a link in terms of staff development. The different strategies enable staff to be trained and developed in less exacting situations before the management has confidence in them operating at the highest level. Most airline companies operate a variety of services on the same route, first-class, business-class, economy, excursion, stand-by and so on. These are all priced according to the quality of service and the dependability and flexibility offered the customer.

The existence of a number of different pricing strategies for airline seats can be both confusing and annoying, especially when the variability is compounded by a number of market outlets all offering exactly the same product at different prices, which in turn reflect their own costs and profit goals. It is suggested that the most effective production strategy is one where there is a very clear focus. In manufacturing this has been referred to as 'the focused factory' (Skinner, 1974). It refers to a level of consistency both within the production strategy itself and between production and other strategies, thus reinforcing a dominant theme of this chapter and of this book.

## Summary

The production function is a transformation process which takes a variety of inputs such as materials and labour and turns them into goods and services. Viewed in this way the function operates in a variety of industries and settings and is not limited to manufacturing. The main activities of production management involve the design of a system to process inputs and setting up control devices to ensure effective operation. Materials management including purchasing is an important part of the process, especially in manufacturing industry.

A central problem in the management of production systems is the reconciliation of customer satisfaction with the efficient utilization of resources. Traditionally techniques of production management have emphasized efficiency. However there is a growing awareness of other elements, such as the flexibility to respond to changing market demand, and a need to focus on quality.

It is, however, misleading to see production solely in terms of responding to external forces. The function has a central position in nearly all types of organization. In manufacturing, an effective production function has a significant impact on the economy. Concern about deindustrialization has resulted in Britain's regional policy, as well as a growing interest in the way more successful economies view and operate their production systems. The centrality of the function means that it exerts considerable influence on organization structure, although the particular influence of production technology is quite complex.

Changes in technology have particular relevance for production systems, both in terms of product and process innovation. In manufacturing the current debate concerns the likely impact of 'new technology' on both the efficiency and effectiveness of production systems, with the cost of installing such systems as FMS a real constraint. For the labour force, production has considerable influence over employment patterns, wage levels, health and safety, and job satisfaction.

Production strategies are a core element of a firm's overall corporate strategy. The most successful production strategies would appear to be those which display a clear focus and are consistent with the strategies of the other functional areas.

## Further reading

Good basic texts are T. Hill, *Production and Operations Management: Text and Cases* (Prentice Hall, 1991) and T. Hill, *Manufacturing Strategy: The Strategic Management of the Manufacturing Function*, 2nd edn (Macmillan, 1993). R. Wild, *Essentials of Production and Operations Management* (Holt,

Rinehart & Winston, 1985) offers a perspective on production that is not confined to manufacturing industry, as does J. B. Dilworth, *Production and Operations Management: Manufacturing and Non-manufacturing* (Random House, 1986). Non-manufacturing contexts are viewed specifically in N. D. Harris, *Service Operations Management* (Cassell, 1989). An interesting and personal view looking at strategic, cultural, and comparative issues can be found in R. H. Hayes and S. C. Wheelwright, *Restoring Our Competitive Edge* (John Wiley, 1984). This book deals with manufacturing industry. J. Woodward, *Industrial Organization: Theory and Practice* (OUP, 1965), while dated, offers useful insights into the relationship between production and structure.

## Discussion

1  Examine the similarities and differences to be found in the production systems of manufacturing and non-manufacturing organizations. How do the production priorities differ in a firm producing television sets for a mass market to those of a large regional hospital?

2  Design a systems model for a firm like Marks & Spencer, which shows both the types of transformations that are taking place and the other systems with which the firm interacts. What are the key activities and key relationships?

3  What strategies can be employed to solve the conflicting objectives of operating efficiency and customer satisfaction?

4  What types of impact can product design have on the production process?

5  What are the key issue in the design and operation of a production system for a university? What are the key control issues?

6  Identify the operational aspects that influence scheduling in a restaurant, at an airport, and for a major national daily newspaper. What strategies and techniques would you employ to solve scheduling problems in these three situations?

7  Why is materials management an important aspect of manufacturing industry?

8  To what extent is the current focus on quality a vital concern to the management of the production process, or does it represent another passing fad?

9  How do you establish an organization culture which focuses on production? How would you involve the workforce more in the production process?

10  Examine the production strategies employed by Orlake Records and Grundig in Cases 6.1 and 6.3 respectively. What are the major influences which have shaped those strategies and what other strategies could the management have employed in the same situation? What do the cases tell us about the relationship between production and the other functional areas?

# 7 Marketing

In this chapter we will examine the nature of marketing as it applies to different types of organization. We will attempt to define marketing and chart the development of the marketing concept. The various elements of marketing, research, product, price, promotion, distribution and buyer behaviour will be analysed in turn, as will the key concepts of branding, the product life-cycle, and market segmentation. As in our treatment of all functional activities we will use the Business in Context model to look at the environmental, organizational and strategic aspects of marketing. In the two previous chapters we stressed the interface between innovation, production and marketing. This theme will be taken up in this chapter, particularly in the discussion of product development, the relationship of marketing with production technology, the place of marketing in the organization structure, and most significantly when we examine the design of marketing strategies.

Decisions in marketing generally focus on products and services, their prices, their promotion, and the means through which they are distributed. In most advanced industrial societies individuals are faced with a vast choice of such products and services, which can be acquired in a variety of ways, often at a range of prices. Advertising is a pervasive feature of modern life, often so glamorized by the media that the management decision to change its advertising agency is, for a firm like Guinness, a matter of high drama to be played out in the national press. For such reasons marketing, probably more than any other business activity, attracts strong positive and negative feelings. Many members of the public as well as many business-studies students associate careers in marketing with the glamour and fictional lifestyles of the people portrayed in advertisements. Such a view is misleading, for marketing is much more than advertising and the tasks can involve the much less glamorous work of collecting detailed market information and the problems of getting metal containers made in Mansfield to a customer's factory in Bromsgrove.

It is this high-profile nature of marketing that attracts its critics. Marketing is variously accused of creating (among other things) an excessively materialistic society, planned product obsolescence, the high-pressure selling of poor-quality products and the excessive political power of the multinational. Borrowing themes from Vance Packard, marketers are seen as 'The Hidden Persuaders' or 'The Waste Makers' or both. The marketers would counter this, listing their credits as the development and supply of products and services demanded by consumers, the provision of essential information for the shopper, and the use of marketing to create public awareness for such socially acceptable goals as improving a nation's health.

## Definitions and orientations

Marketing has been variously defined. It is seen as a management activity whereby suitable products are presented to the market in order to make a profit. It is portrayed as an interactive activity, an exchange process in which consumers play an important role, as illustrated by Kotler.

> Marketing is human activity directed at satisfying needs and wants through exchange processes.
>
> (Kotler, 1983, p. 6)

Another type of definition elevates marketing from both a management function and an exchange process to a philosophy to guide the entire business operation, as illustrated by Drucker.

> Marketing . . . is not a specialized activity at all. It encompasses the whole business. It is the whole business seen from the point of view of its final result, that is from the customer's point of view. Concern and responsibility for marketing must therefore permeate all areas of the enterprise.
>
> (Drucker, 1968, p. 54)

The different definitions of marketing reflect different approaches to the subject. Five such approaches are generally identified.

- The production orientation assumes that consumers will buy whatever is available and the emphasis should be on production and distribution. This approach to marketing works best when demand is greater than supply and goods and services are relatively easy to sell.
- The product orientation assumes that goods and services will sell themselves, usually because of inherent quality and performance characteristics, and that sales promotion is largely unnecessary. This approach also assumes that consumers are generally well informed.
- The selling orientation assumes that consumers will not buy sufficient goods and services unless they are persuaded to do so by advertising, sales promotion and incentives to the sales force. This approach is often necessary when supply outstrips demand, or in the case of what Kotler (1983) defines as 'unsought' goods, such as encyclopaedias, or with the promotion of political candidates.
- The true marketing orientation shifts the attention to the consumer. This approach involves the determination of consumer needs and

values and the design and supply of goods and services to satisfy them. The assumption here is that the consumer is sovereign.

● **Societal marketing** takes the previous orientation a stage further. The attention is still focused on the consumer's needs, but the assumption here is that those needs are satisfied in such a way as to enhance the well-being of the consumer and society as a whole; goods and services should be socially acceptable, non-harmful and non-polluting.

These five marketing concepts can be seen in operation across a variety of organizations and products. Precision engineering tools tend to sell on the reputation of the product, while certain double-glazing and kitchen installation firms use aggressive promotion and selling techniques. In some ways the five marketing concepts represent the historical development of marketing. The production concept is well illustrated by the expanding population and market in Victorian Britain, while the selling concept coincides with the development of mass production and the depression of the 1920s and 1930s, particularly in the USA. The elevation of the consumer is by contrast a relatively recent phenomenon, although we could argue that successful businesses have always practised a true marketing orientation. Certainly societal marketing can be traced to the greater social awareness of the 1960s and 1970s and the growth of consumer organizations.

If textbooks and professional journals are a reliable guide then the most popular view of marketing today as held by its practitioners is one which focuses on consumers and the determination and satisfaction of their needs. This view is not without its sceptics. J. K. Galbraith (1972) challenges the consumer-oriented marketing concept, which he calls the 'accepted sequence'. The growth of big business, the complexity of modern technologies and the correspondingly massive investments in product development have disenfranchised the consumer. 'The revised sequence' has taken over in which complex products, beyond the ken of the average consumer, are developed at great cost. The emphasis shifts from the satisfaction to the creation of consumer demand through investment in promotion to safeguard investments in product development.

A discussion which focuses entirely on individual consumers and manufactured products presents a somewhat restricted view of marketing. In the next section we examine the extent to which the marketing is applied in other contexts.

---

**KEY CONCEPT 7.1**
*The universality of marketing*

All organizations, be they public or private, manufacturing or service, large or small, have a need for marketing as a means of serving the needs of their consumer group. Marketing activity is not confined to products but can involve the marketing of services, places, people and ideas.

# Marketing in different contexts

Marketing as an activity is carried out in a variety of contexts. The most obvious context is of course the sale of manufactured goods to individual consumers as end-users. Marketing also occurs when a firm manufacturing petrol tanks deals with vehicle and lawnmower manufacturers and the like who use petrol tanks in their products; this is sometimes referred to as industrial or organizational marketing. Equally it is not only manufactured products which may be marketed, but services such as banking and management consultancy. Holiday resorts have always marketed themselves to attract tourists, but in recent years other places, such as Milton Keynes and Telford, have engaged in marketing to attract business development. In addition to the marketing of products and services, some firms actively promote themselves by presenting a corporate image to the public. Marketing is far from being the sole prerogative of profit-making organizations as governments, political parties and charities have discovered. We will deal with each of these aspects of marketing in turn.

## Organizational marketing

The concept of industrial marketing can be misleading since it implies the marketing of industrial components for the use in further manufacturing processes as in the case of our petrol tank. Organizational marketing is a more useful term since it can accurately embrace any marketing exchange between two or more organizations. Retail organizations like Marks & Spencer engage in marketing when they buy finished goods from a variety of different sources. In modern times the state has become a very powerful consumer and a very large market in its own right. The state can use this power for social and political ends, by awarding contracts to firms in economically depressed areas or by withdrawing contracts from those firms who do not adhere to government policy on something like wage levels. In general, organizational marketing differs from consumer marketing in a number of ways. Whereas consumers buy goods and services for a variety of reasons which may include less tangible considerations of status, industrial buyers tend to be more concerned with the utility of the product in their own process, as well as its contribution to their costs. Organizational buying is institutionalized and is often carried out by professionals using formalized procedures involving quotations and contracts and often as part of a close on-going relationship between buyer and seller. In the case of a firm such as Marks & Spencer, buyers will specify in detail quality levels and often how the product must be made. We saw this illustrated in Chapter 2 by the demands made by Japanese manufacturers on their components suppliers.

## The marketing of services

It is only recently that many service organizations have fully acknowledged the need to consider marketing in any serious way. The reluctance of the service industry to engage in marketing may be due to the relatively small size of many service operations, the intangible nature of many of their products, and, in the case of the professions, the constraints imposed by their own professional bodies. Significant changes have taken place. The service industry has grown and become fiercely competitive. The major banks facing competition from building societies and other financial institutions have invested heavily in advertising and other kinds of sales promotion. A student opening a bank account for the first time is wooed by a variety of offers such as free overdrafts and gifts. In addition the banks have been careful to target markets such as students, small businesses, and more recently those needing pensions, as well as extending their distribution network by re-introducing Saturday opening and installing automatic cash machines. Airline companies have decided to package their products in a much more tangible way; business travellers are now invited to buy British Airways' Club Class or Cathay Pacific's Marco Polo class and enjoy a number of distinctive product advantages. The lifting of advertising restrictions on the legal profession in Britain has led in some cases to vigorous promotion of price differentials on services such as conveyancing.

## The marketing of images

Organizations such as the Post Office, British Petroleum and ICI have spent heavily to convey a specific corporate image, which may well stress efficiency, experience, breadth of operations, company size, social responsibility or all of these characteristics. Theatrical agents have always existed to promote their clients, but the concept of marketing people has been extended to present any celebrity figure who may be 'packaged' to enhance their earning capacity through paid public appearances. The marketing of ideas has also grown in popularity. In 1987 the British government launched a major campaign to inform the population about AIDS, and anti-smoking campaigns by a number of different organizations are now commonplace.

The case of the Post Office represents another broadening of the marketing concept to incorporate the public sector and non-profit-making organizations such as charities. Political elections in Britain are now fought out by parties who invest heavily in marketing an image as well as an ideology. The Labour Party, conscious of a need to widen its appeal after three successive election defeats, targeted the young professional middle classes as future voters and tailored its appeal accordingly. Even this was not enough to win the 1992 election. The marketing of political parties presents an interesting combination of the marketing of organizational image, of ideas and of people.

Governments themselves use marketing. Between the financial years 1986–7 and 1987–8 there was an increase of 90% in government expenditure on marketing of all types and a 287% increase in advertising alone. In all £88 million was spent on press and television advertising. For the 'European Single Market 1992' campaign, the government allocated £6.7 million for television advertising and almost £4 million for other forms of advertising and promotion. Most government departments have large press and public relations offices; 60 PR staff are employed by the Department of Employment and 53 in the Northern Ireland office (*Independent*, 12 August 1988, *Sunday Times*, 4 September 1988).

The use of marketing by governments raises ethical issues. It invariably supports the particular ideology of the party in power, and may be abused by some individuals to promote their own political careers.

## Export marketing

This is often considered as a separate marketing context requiring adaptations of the product, its price and the way it is promoted to account for differences in cultural expectations or constraints imposed by the governments of nation states. Such differences have led many firms to appoint local agents in different countries to market their products or else engage in a joint venture with a local firm. The Danish brewery Carlsberg engages in such joint production ventures throughout the world either to ease the problems of distribution, to overcome government restrictions on the operation of foreign firms or both. Not all firms place such a distinction on international marketing. In Case 7.1 Woodville Polymer Engineering refuses to differentiate between home and export marketing as a deliberate strategy.

---

**CASE 7.1**
*Woodville Polymer Engineering*

This case looks at changes that occurred in the marketing strategy at Woodville in the mid 1970s and the factors that have influenced the development of the company since that time.

In the mid 1970s, Woodville Polymer Engineering (Woodville Rubbers as it was then known) was a producer of rubber components for the engineering industry, manufacturing such items as rubber seals for the automobile and domestic appliance industry. It was situated in Ross-on-Wye, but had a sister company operating as an autonomous unit in Swadlingcote. Both companies were owned by the American multinational Colt. The parent company's interest was solely financial and Woodville's operating decisions were its own.

The company had a reputation in the industry as being technically competent and as having good customer relations. A major strength was its staff, many of whom had previous experience in the engineering industry. Despite this apparently comfortable position, the management decided to adopt a more positive marketing strategy to strengthen their position as illustrated by the following actions.

- The company identified its business as engineering. They had never considered themselves as mere sellers of rubber to the engineering industry, but now they saw their role as making money for their customers. The later change of name identified them more closely with the industry they served.
- They set about building an even closer relationship with their customers. Production managers were encouraged to talk to customers about their requirements and in general products were tailored to customer needs. In one of the cases

where a customer (Skefko) was advised to modify its proposals to fit an existing Woodville product, the result was a considerable saving for the customer. Customers were encouraged to visit the plant and talk to staff. In general the entire operation was marketing-led and coordinated by sales engineers.

- Nine specific industrial markets were targeted. The nine were chosen for their growth potential and that in each market there were five firms or less who controlled 80% of the output. Potential customers were then checked out on financial and product viability. Where possible Woodville's sales engineers were recruited from the industry they served. The industries chosen included domestic appliances, water pump manufacturers, mining and reprographics.

- A special target was mass-production industries such as the domestic appliance and the motor industry. Woodville was aiming to have 50% of its business in this market, and recognized that a key factor would be the reliability of delivery to establish credibility as a relatively small operator in a large market. In addition, the company was developing work with the Ministry of Defence.

- As many of its customers operated internationally, Woodville drew no distinction between home and export orders.

The new philosophy was rewarded by increased profitability and in particular a 600% increase in exports from 1973 to 1976. By 1976 exports accounted for some 40% of business.

The position began to change after 1976. The effects of a worldwide recession began to have an impact in two directions. First, there was a dramatic slowdown in some of Woodville's main markets, especially the motor and domestic products industry. Second, the parent company, Colt, found itself considerably overstretched in the American market, used Woodville's financial surpluses to protect other ventures and consequently reduced investment in Woodville itself.

The result for Woodville was a fall in productivity, sales and profitability. The recession had also affected Woodville's competitors, except that they may have been better placed to keep up with technological developments in the industry. Nevertheless Woodville maintained its position as one of the top ten firms in its industry, perhaps a direct result of its marketing strategy.

By the mid 1980s Colt, intent on rationalization, saw Woodville as an offshore concern in a different business from its core activities. The firm was sold to the British-owned Doughty company for around £35 million and installed as part of the Doughty Polymer Group in 1987. By that time the company's profitability had fallen to around 8%, but this compared favourably with the Doughty Polymer Group's 5% return.

The company continues to pursue its marketing policy, and current growth areas include an extension of the reprographics business to include all kinds of paper-handling equipment and increased work with the MOD. Export business continues to be a major feature and at 50% is still growing.

(*Sources*: Rines, 1976; *Company Information*, 1988)

## The elements of marketing

We have already seen that the marketing concept focuses on the consumer and his needs. Marketing strategy is enshrined in the concept of

> The marketing mix generally refers to an overall marketing strategy which involves the manipulation of four key elements. These are decisions concerning the nature of the product and its design; decisions about price; decisions about sales promotion, advertising and customer awareness; and decisions concerning distribution. These four factors are popularly referred to as the 4 Ps; product, price, promotion and place. Two important aspects of this are not made explicit. These are market research and buyer behaviour. Decisions about the marketing mix cannot be made without researching the market in all its aspects and that includes a thorough understanding of buyer behaviour.

**KEY CONCEPT 7.2**
*The marketing mix*

the marketing mix, popularly referred to as the Four Ps – product, price, promotion and place. Consumers constitute an implicit rather than explicit element of the marketing mix, but we shall include them under the heading of buyer behaviour. In addition to these considerations an effective strategy requires information, usually through the process of market research. We are therefore able to identify six key elements of marketing; market research, product, price, promotion, place and buyer behaviour. The six elements will be treated as separate entities although in practice there is considerable overlap. The price of a product, especially when higher than comparable offerings, can be used as a product feature and even a method of promotion stressing the exclusivity of the offering; this in turn depends upon the consumer perceiving and acknowledging a relationship between price and quality. Packaging is a means of protecting the product, an important form of promotion, and a means of facilitating the distribution of the product. The concept of place is concerned with the way the product or service reaches the consumer; in some cases free delivery is presented as a feature of the product to mark it out from competitors. We reinforce these six elements by examining the important concepts of branding, segmentation and the product life cycle in the next section.

### Market research

Market research deals with the collection and analysis of information about the other five aspects of marketing. Four types of market research can be distinguished, although there is considerable overlap between them and most firms engage in all types.

● Management needs to possess accurate information about its current marketing activities. This will include the number and value of the sales of its current range of products and services, and its market share compared to its competitors. Such information can provide useful feedback on sales variations by region and also by salesman and may well provide the basis for implementing changes.

- Management needs to be aware of developments that are occurring in the marketplace which might have a direct or indirect bearing upon the business. This might include information on new products brought out by other companies, the relative prices of goods in shops, how competitors are promoting their products, or whether changes are taking place in the way consumers buy goods. This second activity is sometimes referred to as market intelligence for it enables management to build up a picture of the market in which they operate and chart the significant changes and trends so that strategies may be initiated and changed as appropriate.
- Market research involves feasibility testing to assess the market potential of a new product or service; to assess the consumer reaction to pricing policies or price changes; to assess the reaction of consumers to a particular advertisement and so on. When a company like Rowntree-Mackintosh launch a new chocolate bar, the product has invariably been tested on a wide range of people, and their reactions to appearance, taste, price, value for money, and sometimes the method of promotion carefully assessed. An essential element of feasibility research is an analysis of the market itself, especially its size and composition in terms of the age, sex and occupation.
- The fourth type of research is a mixture of the previous three in that it collects information to evaluate a product and the way it is priced, promoted and acquired by the consumer as an ongoing process after the initial launch.

Individual organizations, especially if they are large enough can do their own market research. However it has developed as a specialist activity over the last 25 years or so, and numerous agencies have arisen offering a variety of services. A firm like Audits of Great Britain, for example, operates multinationally and among its many services offered to clients provides regular television viewing figures so enabling firms to target and evaluate television advertising campaigns. Such firms provide their clients with regular market intelligence on market share and trends, tasks often beyond the resources of an individual company. Some market research agencies specialize by product or the type of service offered; some, for example, have built up reputations for consumer interviewing.

## The product

In our discussion of the different contexts of marketing we saw how the term 'product' has a wide connotation and may include manufactured goods, services, people, organizations, places and ideas. A product comprises a number of elements apart from its more obvious features. These can include a brand name, packaging, after-sales service, delivery, warranty and so on. Marketing needs to consider all these aspects of the product. Free delivery or extended guarantees may be seen as essential product characteristics by some consumers.

A product line is the total number of variations of the same basic product, differentiated by quality, cost or extra features. A car manufacturer will make several versions of the same basic model with variations in engine size, type of gearbox, paintwork and so on. The breadth of a product line is closely related to the degree of market segmentation, a concept we introduce in the next section.

A product mix is the total number of different products offered by the firm, sometimes referred to as the product portfolio. The size of a firm's product mix can have a significant impact on its profitability in that the effect of poor performers may be lessened by the income from better selling items. However, too broad a product mix can cause problems of control. In 1982 Guinness, with a large number of highly diverse activities, sold off forty of its subsidiaries to achieve a better control of its product portfolio (Earl, 1984).

Marketing considerations are an important input in the process of developing new products. We saw in Chapter 5 that new product development was not only potentially expensive, but also that the risk of failure was high. Extensive market research is needed concerning such aspects as the utility and acceptability of a new product's design, its target market and the likely acceptable price. An estimate may be made about likely future sales, which, when set alongside likely development costs, is essential in assessing the business viability of a new project.

We will return to consideration of the product in our discussion of branding, segmentation and the product life-cycle.

## Price

If marketing strategy were based entirely on the analysis of the neo-classical economists then price would be the most significant feature of that strategy and would be based on the concept of the price elasticity of demand. A product is price-elastic if changes in price influence changes in demand. All things being equal an increase in price will lead to a fall in demand and consequently a fall in revenue and vice versa. All things rarely are equal, and consumers can behave in an unpredictable manner. Many factors influence price and pricing strategy and operate at the environmental, organizational and strategic levels of our model. We deal with some of those factors under the following headings.

**Cost**   A business firm wishing to make a profit must use the cost of making a product or providing a service as an important base point in setting its prices. However, the sensitivity of most pricing decisions lies less in the cost of raw materials, labour, and the like than the understanding of those factors which may determine the extent of mark-up on the basic cost price. These include most of the factors identified below. An idea often propounded by neo-classical economists is that cost and therefore price are associated with the economies of scale and that volume production will lead to price reduction. While this may be true for some products there are many exceptions which challenge both the notion of economies of scale and the necessity of tying price to volume production. We return to these arguments in our discussion of the product life-cycle and marketing strategies.

**Consumer behaviour**    The price of a product may well be related to what a consumer can afford and to what he is prepared to pay. These in turn are related to income levels, the consumer's perceptions of quality and value for money, and the consumer's budget for a particular purchase. In purchasing a new camera for a special holiday or a new word-processor for the office of a small business, the consumer's own target price based on what he wants to pay may be the primary factor. The range of products considered will then be limited to those priced within a range around or below the target price. A manufacturer aiming at a particular target market may be best advised to discover the budgeting behaviour of those consumers before setting the price. One of the main functions of promotional activity is of course to influence the perceptions of the consumer. The brewing industry today in Britain has focused its attention on the lager market. Many brands are deliberately marketed as highly priced products offering the consumer 'real' quality. This strategy was successfully pursued by the brewers of Stella Artois to establish their product in a highly competitive market. Such strategies depend heavily on 'brand image' (discussed in the next section), fashion and social influences. The lager market is aimed at the young drinker and the social superiority of drinking a particular brand is stressed.

**Economic factors**    Price is related to the economy in a number of different ways, all of which have a potential impact on an organization's pricing policy. The affluence of consumers will have an obvious influence on their level of budgeting and regional variations may produce differential demand, especially for certain luxury items. The role of the state in managing the economy may affect both demand and prices. The control of interest rates will influence the extent of consumer credit and hence the size of an individual's budget, as will levels of taxation. During periods of high inflation the government may well introduce measures to control prices. A major influence on price for exporters is the currency exchange rate which fluctuates according to the state of the economy. In early 1985 the pound and the dollar approached parity which made many British goods highly attractive in the USA, giving firms such as Jaguar a significant boost to their profits through increased sales. As the dollar weakened against the pound British exports became less attractive and for 1987–8 Jaguar cars announced significantly reduced profit figures due in no small part to changes in the exchange rate. (Case 2.1 examines further implications of the exchange rate.) As a changing exchange rate brings prices of products more into line with competition from domestic suppliers or other country's imports then other criteria than price become more important. The relationship is far from simple and no matter how attractive the price of imported goods may be, it can be offset by delays in delivery, an inadequate distribution network, or a poor after-sales service.

**Competition**   Many firms price their products by reference to an existing market, basing their price around that offered by competitors for products of similar features and quality.

**Management goals**   The price of goods is often related to the extent to which managements wish to optimize profit. We saw in Chapter 3 that management goals rarely conform to simple economic models and are complicated by considerations of power, politics and personal preference. The desire of a group of managers for a larger market share for their products may result in a low price strategy to build up demand. In some firms price may be deliberately used as a promotion strategy to create an image of product quality in the eyes of the consumer.

**Organizational size**   The size of an organization may give it market power and the ability to manipulate market prices. This is especially true of oligopolies. The Swiss pharmaceutical firm Hoffman la Roche controlled by the 1970s around half of the world tranquillizer market, largely through its products Librium and Valium. This brought the firm to the attention of the Monopolies Commission, who, in 1971, accused the company's British subsidiary of exploiting the market against the public interest by charging excessive prices (Stopford *et al.*, 1980). A major supermarket chain such as Sainsbury or Tesco is able, because of its purchasing power and stock turnover, to insist on large price discounts from its suppliers.

We began our discussion of price by challenging the all-important view attributed to the price element in marketing by the neo-classical economists. A much more detailed account of the relationship between price and demand and, in particular, the limitations of the neo-classical approach may be found in the companion volume, *Economics in a Business Context* (Neale and Haslam, 1994). The role of price in marketing strategy is, as we have seen, highly complex. Nonetheless it is the only element of marketing strategy that generates income, all other items incurring cost. Pricing policy is therefore a vital strand of strategy, which because of the complexities involved is often difficult for management to judge. We return to such strategic considerations at the end of this chapter.

## Promotion

We can identify four types of promotion; advertising, sales promotion, personal selling and publicity. The significant growth of promotion as marketing activity is a function of the growth, complexity and competitiveness of markets and the developments of appropriate technology, as in the newspaper and television industries. It was not until 1896 that newspapers, following the leadership of the *Daily Mail*, recognized the value of advertising revenue to offset rising costs (Cannon, 1986)

All types of promotional activity use psychological theory and communication models of human behaviour, but the nature of the promotion used will depend on a number of factors, including the strategy of the organization, the available budget and the type of market. While television advertising may be an appropriate medium for the promotion of consumer goods such as chocolate bars, a specialist magazine may be preferred for promoting expensive camera equipment, and personal selling may be the best way to market industrial goods to other organizations. Some forms of promotion, such as television advertising, are obvious, while others, such as shop design, are less so. The Burton Group on taking over Debenhams invested heavily in redesigning the department store interiors to project a new image and attract different market segments.

Promotion like distribution often involves management working together with representatives of other organizations. Advertising, for example, may involve the marketing manager working closely with an agency as well as representatives of the media. We will return to these aspects when we discuss the organizational aspects of marketing and turn our attention, for the time being, to the various types of promotion.

**Advertising**    The management of advertising involves four major considerations: the design of the message, the selection of the media, the cost of both production and exposure and the evaluation of its effectiveness.

- **The design of the message** reflects the three functions of advertising. First, it operates to inform the consumer and may be useful in creating initial demand for a product or informing consumers about such things as price changes. Second, it operates to persuade the consumer to buy the advertiser's product rather than that of a rival. This form of promotion tends to focus on specific features which distinguish a product from its competitors, and by building up a brand image. The third function serves to remind the consumer of the product and encourage repeat purchases. Such promotion is not aimed solely at consumers, but also at wholesalers and retailers to give products shelf space. In general the nature of the message will vary in all these cases. For example, an advertisement which aims to change the buying habits of consumers will often use images with which the potential consumer identifies.
- Advertisers have a wide choice of **media** including national and local newspapers, magazines, cinema, television, radio, and posters. In recent years there has been considerable increase in the use of local independent radio and local newspapers no doubt reflecting the expansion of both types of media. The selection of appropriate media also involves questions of timing, and an advertising campaign may be carefully scheduled to use various forms of media either concurrently or consecutively to achieve maximum impact.
- **The cost of promotion** tends to vary with the media selected. In

1988 a full-page advertisement in one edition of the *Daily Telegraph* could cost around £26 500, while the same advertisement in a local paper could cost £2500; and between £14 000 and £26 000 would buy a 30 second television commercial slot in a single television area. The above costs are for exposure only and do not include the cost of producing the advertisement. Each of those prices may vary considerably with the demand for advertising, the positioning of the advertisement, and the extent to which special deals may be struck between the buyers and sellers of advertising space. The major problem with such expenditure is the degree of waste, since much advertising can be ignored by large sections of the population and the real impact is often difficult to evaluate. We will deal with the problems of evaluation in our discussion of marketing strategy.

**Sales promotion**  This incorporates a wide variety of different techniques including free samples, money-back coupons, trading stamps, contests and so on. Manufacturers promoting goods through the trade often provide attractive point-of-sale displays or product expertise in the form of a specialist salesperson. Firms such as Dunlopillo, Aristoc and many of the cosmetic manufacturers train and pay their own staff to operate in department stores. Exhibitions and trade fairs are popular ways of promoting goods both to the trade and to industry as a whole. Such forms of sales promotion apply to services as well as manufactured goods. British Rail has introduced several types of fare structure to attract off-peak users, and new restaurants often invite a specially targeted clientèle to a launch evening. The case of cheap rail fares illustrates the interaction between sales promotion and pricing strategies.

Sales promotion is sometimes referred to as 'below-the-line' advertising and is often underestimated in considerations of promotion. It is estimated that sales promotion comprises over 50% of all expenditure on promotion activity and has achieved a particularly rapid growth since the 1960s. The growth has been attributed to increasing rates of inflation and changes in management thinking. Rising inflation has made the consumer more conscious of special offers, while management have apparently grown sceptical of the effectiveness of advertising and believe there to be a much clearer and direct relationship between expenditure on sales promotion and sales figures themselves (Strang, 1976).

Case 7.3 offers two different illustrations of promotion campaigns. In the first, a travel offer by Hoover, the promotion was far more popular than envisaged by the company, resulting in significant financial losses and generating bad publicity. In the second, a use of cultural stereotypes by McDonalds in Singapore proved to be an outstanding financial success for the company.

**Personal selling**  This form of promotion is favoured by the sellers of industrial goods recognizing the importance of building up good personal relations between seller and buyer. However, the cost of employing a sales force to maintain regular contact with customers

**CASE 7.2**
*Austin Rover*

This case is set against the background of a declining British car industry and focuses on a single marketing strategy, the Customer Satisfaction Initiative, launched in 1988 by the Austin Rover company. In order to place the strategy in its true context, some background information is essential.

## The background

The Austin Rover Group was formed when the government-controlled British Leyland was broken up into different operating units. By far the largest of these was the volume cars division, producing automobiles for the mass market. This division became known as Austin Rover and the company inherited many of the policies and the problems of BL, which in turn had inherited them from its predecessor BLMC (although to avoid confusion the company will be referred to throughout as Austin Rover). The main problem was the British car industry itself and in particular Austin Rover's market share. In 1971 this stood at 40%. By 1984 it had fallen to 18%. Up to the mid 1970s the British market had been dominated by Austin Rover and Ford, but there were two major differences.

First, Austin Rover concentrated exclusively on the home market; the company had never enjoyed a major presence in Europe and both its dealership and distribution network were poor outside Britain. Ford, by contrast, was a multinational with a strong base in Europe, and in an ideal position to capitalize from the growing internationlism of car production, where different models for different markets were wholly or part manufactured in a particular country. Second, Austin Rover had the greater share of the private market while Ford dominated Fleet sales.

The oil price rises of the 1970s affected the car market worldwide and British producers in particular, as the government's deflationary measures led to reductions in demand. In addition the market in which Austin Rover operated had become more competitive. Ford decided to compete in the small-car market for the first time, launching its Fiesta range in 1976, and most significantly, the market share of imported cars had risen from 10% in 1969 to 35% in 1977. The major threat was seen as the Japanese car industry, which quickly gained a reputation for reliable, value-for-money, cars. Generally the imports had little effect on the fleet market where Ford maintained its position. In addition to these market changes, significant organizational changes were happening in Vauxhall and Ford, involving a greater integration with European operations.

The decline of Austin Rover during this period has been the subject of considerable debate. The trade unions were a popular scapegoat. Poor labour relations were a feature but other factors were more significant. The company had failed to capitalize upon its successes in the 1960s. There was a lack of investment in developing a viable product range and in modernizing the plant. The company became known for the poor quality of its products and unreliable distribution.

In the 1980s several changes took place at Austin Rover. A new product range was launched, backed up by considerable investment in new technology. A significant reorganization occurred involving considerable rationalization of both management and labour. The company began a joint venture with the Japanese firm Honda to produce the Triumph Acclaim and later, the Rover Sterling. New showrooms were opened in Europe and significant inroads were made into the Portuguese market.

The reorganization and investment in new technology improved the company's productivity, but given the size of the British and European car markets and Austin

Rover's market share, it was doubtful whether there would be sufficient pay-back in terms of volume sales. Export to Europe was still dogged by a traditional European reluctance to buy British cars and a poor dealership network; in volume terms the Portuguese market is marginal. The new model range received an unenthusiastic press and the cars were not seen as innovative. Moreover, traditional problems of reliability had not been solved. Warranty costs to Austin Rover were an average £79 per car, compared with £60 at Ford, £30 at Vauxhall, and £10 at Nissan. Most significantly the British market was shaken up by the re-emergence of Vauxhall as a major producer.

It is against this background that Austin Rover set about improving its market share by focusing on the service given to customers.

Since the Customer Satisfaction Initiative was launched, Austin Rover has undergone several changes in ownership. As the renamed Rover Group, the company was sold into private ownership to British Aerospace. Along the way the company strengthened its joint venture with Honda, with the Japanese company acquiring 25% interest. In early 1994, British Aerospace sold its controlling interest to the German firm BMW. This occurred amidst much debate concerning the sale of the only UK volume car producer to a foreign competitor.

## The Customer Satisfaction Initiative

This was introduced by the company in 1988 emphasizing the relationship between the dealerships and their customers. The aim was,

> to ensure the satisfaction of customers' total requirements by creating a process of continuing improvement . . . to be known as an organization that actually cares about its customers, and through its dealers provides a service which is second to none.

Six key initiatives were identified.

- Two types of franchise standards were set; minimum and enhanced operating standards. These were applied in four areas; environment and equipment, staff, systems and controls, and marketing. In all over 260 different elements were identified where minimum standards have to be attained. The ultimate aim was that all dealerships should reach enhanced operating standards over a period of time.
- Support programmes were set up by Austin Rover to assist dealerships in reaching the required standard in all areas of their operation.
- Every staff member needed to understand the customer satisfaction initative. This was achieved by:
  - each garage appointing a 'Customer Care Manager' with overall responsibility for the initiative;
  - holding training workshops for the executives and management in each dealership;
  - organizing launch evenings for each dealership at which all employees should attend;
  - organizing training days for all staff on a rota basis;
  - reinforcing the training by a system of distance learning packages.
- The company's residential training centre was relaunched as 'The Marketing Institute' to 'set new standards in dealer training'.

- Dealers were to be rewarded for excellence and increased effort. Managers were given targets based not on volume of sales or work, but on a 'Customer Satisfaction Index'. This comprised: the performance of staff against the standards, feedback from customers, participation and success in the distance learning programme, and quality sampling by Austin Rover personnel making anonymous visits and telephone enquiries. Points were awarded, dealer and individual league tables introduced and top performers rewarded by overseas trips. Those dealerships who failed to achieve the minimum standards had 1% of their dealer margins withheld. Those who achieve enhanced operating standards gained $\frac{1}{2}$% bonus.

- As part of an improved marketing effort, targeted direct mailing was introduced and a new 'lifestyle magazine' launched under the editorship of a well-known television personality and journalist.

(*Sources*: Marsden *et al.*, 1985; Williams, Williams and Haslam, 1987; Austin Rover Sales and Marketing, *Customer Satisfaction Initiative*, 1988)

| CASE 7.3 | **Hoover** |
| --- | --- |
| *Two sales promotions* | |

Hoover, part of the US Maytag group, operate in the highly competitive domestic products market. Hoover has been under pressure for some time and sought a plan to boost sales in the recession. This was particularly important, since most people only purchase a new domestic appliance, such as a vacuum cleaner or a washing machine, when the old one breaks down.

In the summer of 1992, Hoover executives launched a sales promotion in association with a travel firm, JSI. The offer was of two free airline tickets to one of six European destinations with the purchase of a Hoover product for £119 or more, the price of a vacuum cleaner. Hoover estimated that the offer would attract 50 000 new customers and in November and December of the same year, when sales usually fall, the offer was enlarged to offer free flights to a number of US destinations as well.

The process involved in obtaining the offer was complex. Purchasers had to make an application within 14 days and were then promised a registration form within 28 days. Provided the registration form was returned within a further 14 days, customers had up to 30 days to nominate their destinations and flight dates. Should these be unavailable, the company could nominate alternatives. Clearly, Hoover believed that the complexity of the application process would restrict the number of takers.

The promotion was successful in a spectacular fashion and sales were boosted far beyond the company's estimates. Rather than 50 000 as predicted, the offer was taken up by 200 000 with half requesting transatlantic flights. The majority of customers bought the cheapest vacuum cleaner under the terms of the offer.

Shops could not get enough stock and the Hoover production plants were placed on seven days a week operation, with the necessity of overtime payments and the hiring of extra staff to cope with the increased demand. The company were unable to cope with the applications for flights, and, in any case, insufficient flights were available. There were innumerable complaints of delay and of forms which did not arrive, cases were brought before the Trading Standards Office and Hoover received a particularly bad press. Many who received offers of flights found them wholly unacceptable, either in terms of destination and/or date of travel. Maytag, the parent company, were forced to send in an investigation team and the three executives responsible for the promotion were dismissed. Hoover had to spend an extra £20 million pounds acquiring flights, and some put the additional cost at nearer £40 million. Several thousand vacuum cleaners were being sold on the secondhand markets. Since the cheapest available transatlantic flight at the time of the offer was around £200 per person, the offer was viewed by most in terms of two flights for £119, with a free vacuum cleaner thrown in.

## McDonalds Kiasu Burger

Kiasu is a local Chinese dialect word in Singapore, which roughly translates as a 'fear of losing out'. The positive connotation of this word is generally associated with healthy competition and the need to be first. The negative attributes are associated with aversion to risk and even selfishness and cowardice. Kiasuism is a well-known concept in Singapore, and, since 1990, has been popularized through a comic-strip character, Mr Kiasu. The character was developed by four young Singaporeans and his adventures usually depict the worst elements of Kiasuism, such as gluttony and pushing to the front of queues. The comic strip developed cult status, but soon gained wider appeal and became a local craze. The comic-strip character was augmented by a range of Mr Kiasu merchandise, such as T-shirts.

McDonalds has 50 outlets in Singapore and is the nation's most popular fast-food outlet by a long margin. A decision was made to launch a new product in May 1993 using the concept of Mr Kiasu. The company developed a local product, the Kiasu Burger, described as 'an extra large chicken patty seasoned with extra spices, marinated in extra sauce, topped with fresh lettuce, all sandwiched in an extra-large sesame seed bun'. The product was sold at 2.90 Singapore dollars (about £1.25 at 1993 rates) and was cheaper than the rest of the McDonalds's hamburger range. The product was also introduced as part of a range of value-for-money meal combinations and purchasers of the Kiasu Burger were entitled to buy a Mr Kiasu figurine for 90 cents (about £0.40). Four types of figurine were offered, each bearing a typical Mr Kiasu slogan, such as 'Everything also I want!' and 'Everything also must grab!'. Such slogans poked fun, not only at Singaporean attitudes, but also at Singaporean slang English. The campaign was supported by television advertising featuring Mr Kiasu as a cartoon character for the first time.

Within two months of the launch, a million were sold and the Kiasu Burger itself had become a craze. Demand for the figurines was also high. At the end of July 1993, McDonalds launched a further promotion celebrating their success and congratulating their Singaporean customers for being able to laugh at themselves. For a limited period the company offered its Kiasu Burgers and figurines at half price.

means this can be a most expensive form of promotion. In recent years a much cheaper form of personal selling has developed especially among the manufacturers of double-glazing and fitted kitchens by employing part-time workers to contact potential consumers by telephone.

**Publicity** This can be an important form of promotion in that the credibility of products or services may be enhanced by linking them with news stories. Many newspapers now have specialist business features or even supplements and such stories can be an effective way of keeping a firm and its products in the public eye. Some of the larger firms institutionalize this function by employing a specialist public-relations department.

An examination of promotion raises many important issues. Advertising in particular has been challenged for developing an overly materialistic society, and the ethics of advertising goods such as cigarettes and alcohol have been questioned by a number of interest groups. The high cost of promotion sets up considerable barriers to the entry of new firms and may operate in favour of big business. Expenditure on promotion may be more effectively directed at product improvements or improving after-sales service. We return to these issues later in the chapter and continue our coverage of marketing elements by looking at the concept of place.

## Place

Place refers to the processes by which products and services reach the consumer and involves consideration of marketing channels and physical distribution. A marketing channel represents the flow of goods and services and may comprise several stages involving intermediaries such as transporters, agents, wholesalers and retailers.

Intermediaries play a number of different roles. They are usually able to distribute goods to customers in a more cost-effective way than the manufacturer is able to do, particularly where goods are mass produced and items are fast moving. For the first six months of 1988 the *Daily Mirror* sold an average of 3.1 million newspapers every day. This would be impossible without a complex and well organized network of transport, wholesalers and retailers to ensure that newspapers are available for readers each morning. In this case the intermediaries break down the number of newspapers into more easily managed batches and are geographically dispersed to ensure an effective delivery. Such wholesalers and retailers handle the other daily newspapers as well, and so facilitate the buying process by offering consumers choice. Manufacturers and consumers are therefore linked in a cost-effective network. The cost of a single newspaper establishing its own network would push up prices to many times their current value.

An intermediary is also an important source of market research and sales promotion since it stands in closer proximity to customers than the manufacturer. For the same reason intermediaries are often better placed to offer a comprehensive after sales service. Some intermediaries may offer limited processing facilities such as cutting glass or mixing paint to order. For the manufacturer the intermediary shares some of the risk by buying goods in bulk to sell on (some of which may not sell), and in so doing helps finance the manufacturer's operations.

Those manufacturers seeking greater control over the distribution process have tried to integrate vertically the marketing channel network. Perhaps the clearest example of this is franchising. We saw in Case 7.2 how Austin-Rover tried to impose improved standards of customer service upon its dealer network. However we have already noted in this chapter the power which can be wielded by big super-market chains over some manufacturers; a case of the marketing channel controlling the manufacturer.

Not all marketing channels involve intermediaries. In the case of in-dustrial goods it is more common for the manufacturer to deal directly with the purchaser, often by building up a relationship between the sales and purchasing departments in the respective organizations. As we saw in the discussion of materials management in Chapter 6 there is a growing tendency for very close relationships to be built up be-tween components suppliers and manufacturers, particularly with the introduction of 'Just-In-Time' production methods.

In all cases it is important that the marketing channel makes the goods and services accessible to those who seek them. The importance of accessibility varies with the nature of the product on offer and the needs and wants of consumers. It is important for a fast-food restaurant to be located near centres of population and to be sited so as to encourage casual callers; accessibility becomes less important for the prestigious restaurant rated by food guides, since customers will often be willing to travel several miles. Hospitals, too, especially those offer-ing casualty services, need to be located near to and be easily reached by the populations they serve.

## Buyer behaviour

An understanding of the needs, wants and behaviour of consumers are vital elements in designing a marketing strategy. Buyer behaviour involves considerations of why people buy and how they arrive at the decision to buy. Several writers have attempted to formulate theories of consumer behaviour so that marketers can predict the outcomes of various strategies (for example, Rogers, 1962; Nicosia, 1966; Howard and Sheth, 1969). As yet the predictive validity of such theories and models leaves much to be desired.

The weakness of such theories lies in the very complexity of buyer behaviour. We have seen how changes in the economy can affect consumer perceptions of their own purchasing power. In addition we can identify a number of psychological and sociological influences. These include perception, attitudes, patterns of learning, motivation, personality, social class, peer groups and culture. A knowledge of such factors is an important contribution to marketing strategy and may be used in the development of the marketing mix. Advertisers use these influences in a number of ways; by linking products to certain social groups with whom the consumer identifies; by using 'experts' to extol the virtues of particular brands in an attempt to influence the percep-tions and attitudes of the consumer.

Predicting buyer behaviour becomes particularly important with in-novations and is an important ingredient in decisions concerning new product development. Rogers (1962) attempted to differentiate people according to their response to innovative products and identified five types: innovators, early adopters, the early majority, the late majority and laggards. The innovators and early majority comprise an estimated 15% of the population and are important as opinion leaders in the diffusion of innovations. The implications for the marketer is to establish the characteristics of these groups and focus the marketing communication accordingly. The diffusion of new products is seen as a chain reaction of influence between pioneering consumers and the mass market. While Rogers found that early adopters tended to be younger, more affluent, more cosmopolitan than later adopters, such generalizations, like so many models, have foundered at the sheer complexity of buyer behaviour. For example, a consumer may be an early adopter of the latest in camera technology but particularly conservative where furniture, clothes or holidays are concerned. In this case we would need to identify the opinion leaders for each product group.

Considerations of buyer behaviour often focuses attention on specific target groups. These are referred to as market segments and we deal with the concept of segmentation in the next section. Not all product markets are highly differentiated. A product such as Coca-Cola is bought by the widest possible range of consumers.

The complexities of buyer behaviour has led some to conclude that consumer marketing is inherently more complex than is the case with industrial or organizational marketing. Such a perspective ignores the complexities in organizational marketing, which may be different to those in consumer marketing, but are just as real. These complexities include the nature of management values and organizational politics, and those involved in the relationship between the buyers and sellers of industrial goods.

## Branding, segmentation and the product life-cycle

These concepts deal with issues raised under the various headings of the marketing mix. We deal with them separately here because of their importance.

### Branding

Branding is the process through which the product is given a name to distinguish it from the range of other products on offer. The name can be given to a whole range of products, thus identifying them with a certain producer, as with Kelloggs, or be given to individual products even though they originate from the same stable. For example, the washing-powder market is dominated by two producers, Lever and Proctor & Gamble, yet each markets a range of washing powders under different brand names; in fact many believe them to be the products of a range of different companies. There may be several reasons why a firm is keen to differentiate a number of brands within the same product range; to appeal to different market segments or simply to capture those consumers who like to switch brands; to gain more exposure and shelf space in retail outlets; and, in the case of firms such as Proctor & Gamble, as a means of structuring the organization around brands to create healthy internal competition.

Apart from the brand name, a particular logo or mark may be used, and some manufacturers feel it important to create a brand style so that any one of their products from a given range is instantly recognizable. Alfred Sloan insisted to his design teams that all General Motors cars possessed the definitive 'GM look' (Sloan, 1986).

A relatively recent development in branding has been the growth of 'generic' or 'own' brands. These can be found especially in the major retail stores such as Sainsbury, Safeway and Tesco. A generic is a product that is sold under the brand name of the retailer and applies to all kinds of products. It may in fact be identical to a nationally known brand on the same shelf, but is generally sold at a cheaper price to appeal more to the price-conscious shopper. In some cases generics have acquired a brand image that goes beyond price and value for money to indicate real product quality. Marks & Spencer deliberately promote this image with their own generic name 'St Michael'.

The importance of branding for the marketer lies in the process of creating brand awareness, brand image and ultimately brand loyalty, thereby ensuring repeat purchases of the product. Branding is also useful in helping the consumer search for goods. The hope is that over time the consumer will develop value judgements about certain brands and use these as a basis for discriminating between products. In this way the brand becomes representative of a whole bundle of product attributes, such as quality or value for money and can be a vital element in the selling of products as symbols (Levy, 1959). In this way certain brands such as Martini are promoted as offering the potential consumer a lifestyle as well as a product.

The use of brand image and its variability is illustrated in a newspaper article by Terry Coleman (1988) on the selling of cars. The Audi 100 was launched in Britain under the Audi-Volkswagen brand, doubtless stressing the Volkswagen image of reliability. In the USA the same car with a few minor adjustments to the trim became the Audi 5000 and was sold as an Audi-Porsche, capitalizing on the latter's reputation for expensive, fashionable, high-performance cars, and appealing to the large American demand for sports cars. Coleman does note that the same car was sold in South Africa mainly as a taxi!

A successful brand image can be a great attribute to a company when launching new products, as they may well acquire the favourable attributes of other products belonging to the same brand. Branding is, however, valuable for all products, new or otherwise, in that it can add value to the product. It is for this reason that many firms protect their brand names by registering them as trademarks. The registration of a trademark enables its owner to use the law to prevent competitors from using the same or similar brand name or mark for the same type of product or service. This also protects the consumer from being deceived and confused about the origin of the goods.

Branding is not without its critics, who claim that it misleads consumers by drawing false distinctions between products and directing

**KEY CONCEPT 7.3**
*Segmentation*

Segmentation is the process through which the total market is broken down to create distinctive consumer groups. The criteria used to form such groups varies and may include geographical location, social class, occupation, sex, lifestyle, and so on. Once market segments have been identified then products can be developed which focus upon a particular group in an attempt to maximize both the marketing effort and the needs of consumers. Some firms specialize in catering for the needs of a particular segment only, while others produce a range of products each aimed at different segments of the same market. In this case, the branding of each product becomes especially important to distinguish it from the others. The process of broadening the segments to which a product might appeal or changing the market segment altogether, is known as repositioning.

investment away from product development and into packaging and promotion to maintain the myth of product differentiation. Branding is further attacked for its encouragement of status consciousness. For many teenagers a simple pair of training shoes will not suffice; they must be the brand favoured by their peer group at that particular time. It is not just the teenage market that is pursued by marketers promoting a particular brand image. Increasingly markets have become highly differentiated and branding can assist in the process of market segmentation. It is to this aspect we now turn.

## Segmentation

Segmentation occurs when the market is broken down along a number of different dimensions. Commonly used segments include geographical location, age groups, gender groups, income groups, social classes, and those groups that may be differentiated according to their lifestyle. Kotler defines a market segment as,

> consumers who respond in a similar way to a given set of marketing stimuli.
>
> (Kotler, 1983, p. 40)

Market segmentation and product differentiation go hand in hand in that products are designed, developed, promoted and even priced and distributed with a particular market segment in mind. True segmentation occurs when genuinely different products are made for the different market segments. The concept of segmentation is the essence of the marketing concept as identified at the beginning of the chapter; the production of goods and services to meet the specific needs of consumers.

Segmentation is an increasing feature of marketing, as the following illustration of the holiday industry will show. Many package-tour holiday companies originally promoted all their holidays in a single brochure, leaving the consumer to select the most appropriate holiday from the entire range offered. In 1989, Thomson Holidays produced around 15 different brochures each aimed at a different market. 'Freestyle' holidays were aimed at the 18–30 group, while 'Young at Heart' aimed for the older market. The main brochure 'Thomson Summer Sun' catered for the mass market, but the 'À la Carte' holidays aimed to capture those groups with a higher disposable income and a different life style. Lifestyle is also an important consideration in the 'Ski', 'Small and Friendly', 'Simply Greece' and 'Lakes and Mountains' holiday offerings. While few companies aim to match Thomson for product differentiation, others do target-specific markets, Bales for exclusive, long-distance holidays and Saga for holidays and cruises aimed at the older age groups.

Not all such product differentiation is motivated solely by the desire to cater for consumer needs. The growth of the winter holiday market may be related to affluence and changing lifestyles; it is also related to the hotel owner and tour operator's desire to utilize capacity all the year round. In some cases winter holidays are aggressively promoted and attractively priced to push up market demand. In this case some segments, such as the retired population, are especially singled out.

So far we have focused upon consumer goods, but segmentation is a feature of industrial goods as well. Many engineering companies in the components industry have successfully targeted specific groups and tailored their products accordingly. As we saw in Chapter 2, Japanese companies often forge very close relationships with their suppliers, although this is more a case of the segment defining the product rather than the manufacturer targeting a segment.

An important strategic decision in marketing is the determination of the most appropriate segments for the marketing effort. There would appear to be three broad options.

- Producing a single product or a small range of products for a single segment or limited range of segments.
- Producing many products serving many different market segments.
- Producing a single product for an undifferentiated mass market.

The choice will depend on a range of factors including whether the segment can be accurately identified, whether it is large enough to be profitable, whether it can be served within certain cost constraints, and of course, management goals.

Aiming for a limited market segment can be a highly successful strategy, as shown by such companies as Mothercare and those holiday companies such as Bales or Abercrombie and Kent, who provide more expensive holidays. Such a strategy can be restricting and once a certain market size and share have been reached the company may need new products and new markets to continue growing. Mothercare recognized this by extending its market to cater for older children as well as its original market of baby and maternity wear. Kuoni, in an attempt to capture a younger market, launched a group of holidays using cheaper accommodation and has made other attempts to widen its appeal.

A deliberate attempt to change its market segment was adopted as a survival strategy by the British motorcycle industry in the mid 1970s.

Faced with overwhelming competition from Japanese bikes the British industry continually retreated up market, ultimately to be defeated in that segment as well by the Japanese. The British manufacturers went for an inappropriate segmentation strategy and might have been more successful had they invested in the process technology to manufacture reliable, low-cost, mass-produced bikes (Earl, 1984). This interrelationship of marketing, product development and process technology recurs in our discussion of the product life-cycle and marketing strategy.

A differentiated product range serving different markets has long since been the strategy followed by the major car producers (Case 7.2). It is a strategy pursued by firms operating in the service industry too; building societies for instance offer a range of investment plans to suit the needs of different groups. Excessive segmentation can pose problems and it has been referred to as 'marketing mania' (Levitt, 1975). The development, production, promotion and administrative costs associated with product differentiation can render excessive segmentation an expensive strategy, particularly where minor product changes result in major process adjustments. Differentiation may be a strategy for survival in a declining market as shown by the Orlake Records case in Chapter 6, but the strategy may not always work. The willingness of the British textile and steel industries to take on any order, whatever its size led to dramatic cost increases and merely hastened the decline of those industries, when product concentration might have been a more appropriate strategy.

An important element of segmentation is positioning. This refers not only to choosing the correct market segment for your product, but also to finding the appropriate niche in that market, to differentiate it from its competitors on such matters as price and quality. Repositioning occurs when the same product is offered to a different group, either to combat falling sales or as a general growth strategy. This was successfully achieved by Guinness, who in the 1970s aimed their promotion at the younger drinker with highly successful results. Manikin cigars attempted the same ploy but were less than successful; the new target market found the cigar too strong for their taste, while the original market disliked the new style of promotion.

## The product life-cycle

The product life-cycle assumes that all products have limited lives during which they pass through a series of stages, all of which have implications for sales and profitability. The classic life-cycle is depicted by four phases as presented in Figure 7.1.

During the **introduction** phase sales are slow as both consumers and distributers become aware of the product and decide to adopt it. The cost of development and promotion are high and firms may suffer initial losses.

During the **growth** phase there is a rapid acceptance of the product and a dramatic increase in sales. This is generally sustained by improved distribution, product improvements, and even price reductions.

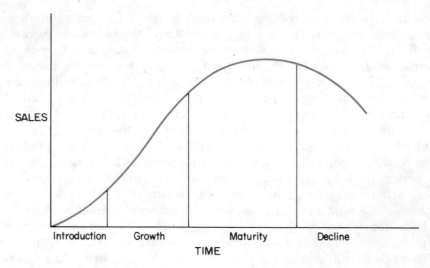

*Figure 7.1*  The product life-cycle.

There are normally high profits for pioneering firms but a growing market attracts competitors leading to brand differentiation. While the production learning curve may lead to a reduction in costs, the need to satisfy an expanding market can involve costly investment in new production processes. The end of this phase is marked by a high level of competition, recognized by Wasson (1978) as a separate phase which he termed 'competitive turbulence'.

As it becomes saturated the market reaches maturity. Sales and profits are still high but there tends to be considerable investment in maintaining sales. This is achieved through product changes, increased promotional activity and price-cutting. Products are sometimes relaunched at this stage, usually with new features, different packaging and often an attempt to create a new image. Firms seek to maintain brand loyalty at the same time as attempting to broaden the market by repositioning. At this stage the less competitive firms drop from the product market.

The decline phase is marked by a falling off in sales, and while some firms do well as others leave the market, survival is often dependent upon successful product diversification.

The product life-cycle can be useful as a framework for planning a marketing campaign over time and as an indication that marketing strategies need to be adjusted to match changes in the cycle. There is an implicit assumption in much of the writing that careful marketing policies can do much to slow down the cycle of decline, i.e. the cycle may be manipulated by the marketing mix. An understanding of the life-cycles of a range of products may be an important factor in determining the introduction of new products and ensuring that the product mix is well represented at the introductory, growth and maturity stages. A company has significant problems if its entire product range is in the decline phase at the same time.

The utility of the product life-cycle has been questioned on several counts. First, it is a gross simplification of the behaviour of markets and seems to ignore changes in the economy, the behaviour of competitors, the actions of governments and even dramatic swings in consumer fashion. Second, the cycle is highly variable for different products, in both the length of time it takes to reach the decline stage and the amount of time spent in each phase. The path for any product is extremely difficult to plot and the model is therefore a poor guide to marketing strategy. Third, even if we accept that the model is descriptive of a general process, it may be difficult to assess when a product has reached a particular stage. A temporary rise or fall in sales may be mistaken for a fundamental shift in the cycle, so that action is taken that is inappropriate at that time. Fourth, the model is criticized for ignoring the production implications of a changing market position.

Each stage of the product life-cycle has implications for the design of the product, the volume and variety of production, and the nature of the process. In this way the product life-cycle is related to a process life-cycle. The introductory stage of the product life-cycle is marked by a highly flexible production process. As markets reach their maximum potential the capacity can only be met by relatively inflexible mass production systems. The cost of such systems necessitates a high market demand and long production runs. There is a similarity here with the 'revised sequence' (Galbraith, 1972), discussed earlier in this chapter. In this situation marketing becomes production led rather than demand led. However, the relationship between the product and process life-cycles has been complicated by the introduction of flexible manufacturing systems (see the discussion of this in Chapter 6).

## The environmental aspects of marketing

Marketing, probably more than any other of the business functions we have dealt with, operates at the interface between the firm and its environment. We will see in this section how marketing activities are not only influenced by environmental factors, but that the management manipulation of the Four Ps represents a deliberate attempt to shape consumer behaviour and hence the market environment within which the firm operates. Marketing strategy is therefore a key element in the corporate strategy of any organization. We will view the relationship of marketing with the environment of the firm by looking in turn at the economy, the role of the state and consumer interest groups, technology, and finally cultural and social factors.

### Marketing and the economy

For some, marketing as a subject has emerged as a branch of applied economics, and economic theory is used as the basis for the development of marketing strategies. Marketing activity is influenced by economic factors in a number of different ways as the following illustrations reveal.

We have already seen how marketing is a very important feature in the strategies of those firms operating in the service sector. In this way major economic changes in the shift from manufacturing to service industry have brought about new directions in marketing. The entry of new firms into the marketplace, especially in the form of overseas competition, may necessitate a change in marketing strategy for existing firms to retain their market share. Changes in supply and demand reflecting changing levels of employment and income call for changes in marketing strategy. Falling demand may call for price reductions, attempts to broaden the market by appealing to new segments or diversifying into new areas of activity. In economically depressed areas attempts by the unemployed to set up shops are often doomed to failure owing to the low levels of demand in that area. Where demand is so low, then little in the way of marketing strategy can change the basic position. Changing rates of inflation together with the level of economic activity will affect savings and the availability of credit. Where price inflation rises at a faster rate than wage inflation, the demand for certain luxury goods may fall. Some firms combat this by offering favourable credit terms to customers in an attempt to boost sales.

These illustrations show how marketing strategy has often reacted to changes in the economy. However, many firms will attempt to manipulate the economy through its marketing activities. In Chapter 5 we examined the link between levels of investment in new product development and economic growth at both the level of the firm and nationally. We have seen that one of the functions of promotional activities is to persuade consumers and hence attempt to manipulate demand. We have noted several times in this book how very large companies, especially those operating multinationally, are able to manipulate markets to their advantage through product development, pricing and promotional strategies in such a way as to affect national economies.

While the relationship between marketing and the economy is significant, we saw in our discussion of price elasticity that economic theory has its limitations in our understanding of marketing behaviour, ignoring as it does a range of important cultural, social and psychological influences. Political and pressure group influences also play a part and it is to these we now turn.

## Marketing and the role of the state

The state represents a powerful presence in the marketplace as a dominant employer, supplier and purchaser. It has been estimated that well over one half of all commercial transactions in Britain involve the state directly (Cannon, 1986). We have already noted the increases in Government advertising expenditure. The state is involved in marketing in a number of different ways.

- The state provides information on Government policy.
- Advertising is often used to direct the behaviour of individuals as

in the case of health education or to encourage the unemployed to take advantage of training schemes.

- The pricing and promotional policies of state-controlled industries can be used to direct public expenditure and consumption, as in the case of energy. The potential for the government direction of markets in this way is considerable. In reality, particularly in the example of the energy industry, the actual control is often diluted through the absence of an effective coordinating policy.

- The state attempts to regulate the marketing activity of private firms in a number of different ways. Most of these measures are aimed at regulating free competition and protecting individual consumers and the environment.

- In terms of product development, the British Standards Institute (BSI) has devised technical standards to which products should comply to ensure minimum standards of quality, and to protect both the consumer and the environment against the potentially dangerous product.

- We have seen in Chapter 5 that the granting of patents gives inventors a monopoly to market their products in return for making their invention public. The aim of such legislation is both to reward and stimulate innovation.

- Through its law relating to monopolies and mergers the state attempts to define and prevent unfair competition.

- The abolition of resale price maintenance under the Resale Prices Act 1977 has loosened the control of major manufacturers over the marketplace and so protected the consumer from unfair business practices.

- The Trade Descriptions Act 1968–72 tackles the problems of deception in advertising and sales promotion.

- The Sale of Goods Act 1893 and the Supply of Goods (Implied Terms) Act 1972 set out the contractual rights of consumers on such issues as the return of goods and warranty.

- Many governments attempt to limit the advertising of certain types of products such as cigarettes and alcohol.

- Britain's membership of the EU means that firms are subject to a range of further regulations affecting firms and consumers alike, as with the pricing of agricultural produce or the description of products when promoting them for the European market.

| KEY CONCEPT 7.4 *Consumerism* | Consumerism has developed as a social movement to inform and assist consumer choice and to act as a pressure group to represent the interests of consumers. These interests are represented to organizations in an attempt to influence product design, price and distribution. Consumer interest groups also act as watchdogs to guard against unsafe products and dishonest producers. That consumers are now more aware and better informed is due largely to the activities of consumer groups and the publicity given to consumer matters over the last twenty or so years. |
|---|---|

The various measures outlined above are reinforced by a state bureaucracy. Many marketing issues are dealt with by the Department for Trade and Industry and government-backed offices such as the Office of Fair Trading and the Advertising Standards Authority. As we can see, many of the measures are aimed specifically at consumer protection and some of them are the direct consequence of consumer pressure groups. We now deal with such interest group activity under the heading of consumerism.

## Consumerism

The concept of consumerism has developed in the last 30 years around four tenets: the right of the consumer to be informed, the right to choose, the right of redress and the right of safety. If we accept that marketing is nothing more than the effective satisfaction of consumer needs and wants, then consumerism would in fact be synonymous with marketing and the presence of organized consumer groups would be no more than an important source of information and market research. The consumer movement has however developed as a political interest group to represent the rights of consumers largely because those rights are seen to be threatened by the marketing activity of many firms. It is interesting to see Baker (1991) deal with consumerism as 'marketing under attack'.

The crusades against dangerous products by people such as the American Ralph Nader; the growth and success in Britain of organizations such as the Consumers Association and the Campaign For Real Ale; magazines such as *What Car*; the popularity of consumer programmes on television and radio; all these have both focused the attention of the public on consumer affairs as well as feeding its need for information. Consumer information exists to satisfy a need, but like marketing promotion itself it has created an even greater need. Most national newspapers now give significant editorial space to consumer matters and concern themselves with a range of consumer issues, from testing new cars and bottles of wine, to offering advice on financial matters, to highlighting sharp practice in the business world.

As well as feeding off its own publicity and success, the growth of consumerism is often related to the factors identified below.

- The public needs protection against the effects of dangerous products. A series of articles in the trade press and newspapers in the 1970s in the USA focused the public's attention on the number of accidents involving Ford Pinto cars, all the result of the location of the petrol tank. The pressure was such that Ford withdrew the model.
- The public needs protection against the dishonest behaviour of some producers. The growth of fierce competition in home improvements has resulted in the Office of Fair Trading receiving a number of complaints about such firms misleading the public about the true cost of credit. The Financial Services Act 1987 emerged

partly to protect consumers by regulating those firms dealing with such matters as investment, insurance and pensions; several complaints had been received that investment returns were less than promised and costs were much higher than expected. Strict rules now operate for the promotion of investment and pension plans.

- The growth of pressure groups like the Campaign for Real Ale is a reaction to the monopoly power wielded by the main producers in a particular industry. The brewing industry was moving towards a market dominance by a handful of producers and the gradual elimination of beer brewed by traditional methods in favour of a product that was more easily stored and transported. The campaign not only brought pressure against the major producers to produce more 'real' ale but was successful, with the aid of considerable media coverage, in creating a much greater public demand for that product.

- Consumers themselves are better educated, more affluent and, largely because of the growth of the consumer press, more informed. The result has been increased expectations and demand for products of a higher quality. While this is probably true for all consumers, the growth of consumerism is undoubtedly a middle-class phenomenon, closely related to the degree of affluence of particular consumer groups.

As an interest group the consumer movement has been influential in broadening public awareness of consumer matters and bringing about a range of protective legislation. In many cases this has led to improved goods and services and more effective marketing. There are still those who feel that the consumer lobby needs to go much further to protect the rights of consumers, while others, particularly in business, may resent the influence of consumer groups on governments, fearing that excessive regulation may stifle innovation.

## Marketing and technology

These interact in three different ways. First, we have seen in Chapter 5 the process of product design and development and its protection through the patent system. We also noted that marketing was an essential vehicle for the information and promotion of new products and processes. Second, in our discussion of the product life-cycle we identified the clear relationship between process technology and levels of demand. It is no good management using product development, pricing and promotional strategies to increase demand if that demand cannot be met by the existing production system. Third, developments in technology have had significant impact upon the marketing process. Among the most obvious aids to marketing have been the developments that have taken place in mass distribution. A range of developments have taken place in retailing to simplify the process of purchase. The system of 'electronic funds transfer at the point of sale' (EFTPOS), may well, together with the credit card, obviate the need for cash. A wide range of goods may now be bought over the telephone using credit cards for payment, and some firms have set up computer databases of suppliers willing to offer such goods to consumers at highly competitive prices. We saw in Case 5.5 how the introduction of automatic teller machines was a key marketing strategy used by a banking group to fight off growing competition.

## The role of cultural and social influences in marketing

In our discussion of segmentation we suggested that markets were increasingly segmented and the marketing effort was correspondingly targeted at specific groups. Invariably the basis for such segmentation is social and cultural. Differences within societies and between culturally distinctive groups has resulted in different patterns of product adoption. The popularity of a product among one social group is no guarantee that it will appeal to another, totally different group; for example, devising a marketing campaign to find a mass market for snails may well prove difficult in Britain and the USA! Yet marketing is more than a product of social and cultural factors; managers often use such factors in promotion. Using the aspiration of one group in society to acquire the lifestyle of another group is a commom theme in advertising. The growth of the teenage market is both a reflection of changing social values and a deliberate creation by producers actively seeking new business opportunities. As with other aspects of our model the influences are invariably two-way with marketing acting as both a product and a cause of social change. Several social and cultural factors illustrate our point.

Changing demographic patterns relating to age, sex, location and naturally incomes may have a profound effect upon marketing. An ageing population in many Western industrial societies has opened up new marketing opportunities in such industries as tourism and in general focused the attention of marketers towards a sector they had previously seldom considered. Geographical shifts in population may have a considerable impact upon consumer demand and property prices. In the 1980s rising property prices in London and the South-East of England had a knock-on effect on the property market of surrounding areas. This manifested itself in changes in the types of new property being built, the prices of those and existing dwellings and the way the property was promoted by estate agents. Small terraced housing in areas within commuting distance of London became desirable cottage residences to tempt the buyer with dreams of country living. Such changes also have an impact on the marketing of public transport systems.

Values and attitudes are important influences on the marketing process. Core cultural values such as family life and concern for children are constantly used in advertising, and marketers take care not to transgress such social mores. An interesting variation to this is shown in Case 7.3. In 1993, McDonalds in Singapore launched a new product, the Kiasu Burger. Both the naming of the product and the accompanying promotion made fun of certain aspects of Singapore culture. Reference groups such as experts, peers, social classes and those groups portraying a desired lifestyle are frequently used in marketing communication as mechanisms of attitude change.

Advertising in particular uses and builds upon social attitudes as the following two examples show. Ford in the USA sells its German built Lincoln-Mercury Scorpio as 'imported from Germany for select dealers', while Austin-Rover's television advertisement to launch the Rover 800 'Fastback' shows the car as a product of British technology being driven by German businessmen. Both promotions are using the widely held belief that the Germans develop superior technical products. The Americans use this value directly in their advertising. Austin-Rover on the other hand appear to be promoting the superiority of British technology, yet the promotion is based on the credibility of German technical know-how and the use of Germans as 'expert witnesses'.

Such cultural stereotyping has benefited the Germans considerably as exporters of manufactured goods and they have been especially successful with more technical products such as machine-tools. Japan on the other hand had to overcome damaging negative stereotyping, which saw its exported goods in the 1920s and 1930s as cheap, imitative products (Wilkinson, 1983). The cultural stereotyping extends to the role of marketing itself and the emphasis placed on different elements of the marketing mix. The Germans are noted for their emphasis on product development and careful targeting, while the Americans are noted for their emphasis on promotional activities and selling.

As with all such stereotyping the differences that exist within a country are often greater than those between countries. The last point does however raise the issue of the role of marketing within the overall strategy of the firm and in the next secton we explore the organizational relationships of the marketing function.

## The organizational aspects of marketing

We have already dealt with several organizational issues elsewhere in this chapter. In examining the different orientations to marketing we saw how the marketing goals have developed over time and how much they vary between organizations. Several references have been made to the impact of organizational size on marketing. We have noted that increasing size has led to increasing specialization within the marketing function and how the costs associated with the various marketing activities have acted as barriers to entry, favouring big business in the achievement of market dominance. As we noted in Chapter 3, there is increasing recognition that so-called 'excellent' companies are built around clearly defined cultures. An important element of such organizational cultures is a close identification with the needs of the customer. In the Austin-Rover case (7.2) we show how the company has attempted to change its culture and image by involving all personnel in the marketing effort.

In this section we will focus on structural issues pertaining to marketing, dealing first with the way the function is organized and second with the relationships between the marketing personnel and those representing other functional areas.

## The organization of marketing

Marketing was initially viewed as being synonymous with sales. With the growth of the firm and the development of its markets came the problems of organizing the sales force, often achieved by creating sales territories operating under a hierarchy of district and regional managers. The need for improved market research and sales promotion created research and advertising units as sub-divisions of the sales department.

The growth of increasingly complex markets, the emergence of large organizations, and changing attitudes by management towards consumers, all called for corresponding developments in the functional organization of business activities. Marketing emerged as a function in its own right, with the previously dominant sales department as a subsidiary activity. The marketing effort now spawned further specialisms in advertising, sales promotion and market research, and some marketing departments also assumed responsibility for new product development. In the larger organizations, marketing management became the coordination of a range of specialist marketing activities.

This functional organization of marketing mirrored functional developments occurring elsewhere in the firm, but some companies were experimenting with other forms of organizational structure. As we saw in Chapter 3 in our discussion of structure, divisionalization occurred because some firms such as General Motors found it most appropriate to organize around products or markets. The marketing efforts in many organizations went down the same route.

In the 1920s Proctor & Gamble developed the concept of product management. Under this arrangement the firm is organized around its products and each brand or group of brands has its own manager. Such a structural arrangement may be necessary where product knowledge is highly technical, or where the firm is dealing in totally different product markets. The benefits which may be gained by management from such an arrangement include an increased knowledge of the product market and an ability to respond quickly to changing market demands. A healthy internal competition can be built up, leading to increased sales. Furthermore, product management has often been a good training ground for aspiring senior managers as it interfaces with most aspects of the firm's operation. The customer gains by dealing with people who have real product knowledge. Product and brand management can be costly ways of organizing the marketing effort. Specialist activities such as advertising may be unnecessarily duplicated, or else product managers may lack expertise in the more specialized areas of marketing. In firms where every brand has its own manager there may be overstaffing of management at the lower and middle levels, with the ensuing problems of career progression.

An alternative structural arrangement would be to specialize around different markets. The markets may be differentiated geographically, by industry, or even by customer. In consumer marketing some form of geographical specialization is a fairly traditional approach; sales forces have tended towards regional organization for ease of administration and control and television advertising is invariably regional. It is in the marketing to organizations, with the prospect of high-volume, high-value orders that specialization by industry or by customer is regarded as a factor in increasing sales. The Xerox Information Systems Group switched from selling by product to selling by industry, and organized its marketing efforts accordingly. The advantages of this approach lie in building up a close relationship with individual customers and gaining insights into their operations (Hanan, 1974). Some firms operating in the computer market, like IBM and Digital, offer a consultancy service to potential customers; this leads to improvements in the customer's own operating systems and potentially more sales for the computer company. Gaining experience of the customers' operating problems and their marketing environment is often invaluable to the process of developing new products. Such a structure would seem most appropriate where the market is becoming increasingly competitive and there are long-term advantages to be gained from building up such close relationships with customers.

As we saw in Chapter 3, organization structures rarely conform to ideal models. Many firms have marketing departments which display elements of all the structural variations identified above. A system of brand management can be backed up by a centralized research or advertising function. The marketing effort can be organized according to different industrial markets but may be further differentiated according to product. The system is further complicated in that marketing departments frequently use agencies external to the firm. The last 30 years has seen the growth of advertising agencies. Some like Saatchi & Saatchi have achieved a very high public profile as the creators of the Conservative Party's early successful election campaigns. Specialist agencies also operate in market research and sales promotion. The advantages of using agencies lie in their ability to stand back and offer an independent assessment of the firm's marketing activities, to offer specialist expertise which the company may not possess and act as a source of fresh ideas.

Dealing with outside agencies can be a costly exercise and may be a potential source of conflict. In fact, any structural differentiation within the marketing function itself may set up internal conflicts. Brand differentiation and management may create competition but that same competition has the potential for unhealthy conflict. Tensions can exist between marketing management who direct operations and the sales force who must carry them out. Much wider tensions can exist in the relationship between marketing and the other functional areas and it is to this we now turn.

## Marketing and the other functions

Turner (1971), writing about the rise of Donald Stokes in the British Leyland hierarchy, identified his influence in changing the orientation of the then Bus and Truck division from production to sales. He paints a picture of Stokes as essentially a salesman who sometimes promised orders the manufacturing departments could not meet. Turner notes that this made him very unpopular with the production managers and set up tensions between them.

The Stokes case is probably fairly typical of the kind of conflict which can occur when two different orientations have to come together. Probably the most comprehensive treatment of the conflict between marketing and manufacturing is offered by Shapiro (1977). He identifies several areas where the priorities of the two departments may differ as illustrated in Table 7.1, and a similar version of the same problem may be found in Figure 6.2.

Shapiro felt that the need for cooperation was greatest among the manufacturers of industrial components and he identifies a number of reasons for such conflict.

**Table 7.1** An illustration of the potential conflicts between the marketing and production functions

| Issue | Stereotype marketing response | Stereotype production response |
|---|---|---|
| Capacity | We never have enough when we need it. | Market forecasts must be more accurate. |
| Scheduling | We need greater flexibility, faster change times, and a quicker response to changing market demands. | Change is disruptive and should be minimized. |
| Product line | A varied product line is essential for customer satisfaction. | Variety means short uneconomic runs. |
| New products | These are essential for the firm's survival. | There are too many minor design changes. Too much change is costly. |
| Warranty and aftersales | Costs involved in this must be reduced. It is the responsibility of production quality control. | Consumers use products in the wrong way. Much warranty work can be avoided. |
| Distribution | We never have enough stocks. | Stocks must always be kept at a minimum. |
| Quality | Customers should be able to get quality products at a reasonable cost. | Quality and low cost are incompatible. |

*Source*: adapted from Shapiro, 1977.

- The two functions are evaluated according to different criteria. Marketing personnel are rewarded for achieving a high sales turn-over and a high market share, while the primary orientation of manufacturing is towards the achievement of minimum cost and a smooth operation flow. The marketing staff are encouraged to create change by developing new opportunities while the production staff tend to resist it since it increases costs.
- It is often difficult for the two types of personnel to cooperate since they operate in different cultures. The marketers often deal with rather vague concepts like customer preferences while production staff deal with information that is generally quantifiable. Moreover the orientation of marketing is essentially to customer groups outside the organization, while the production orientation is predominantly internal.

Shapiro acknowledges that all such conflict is not necessarily dysfunctional; persuading customers to adopt standardized parts may enable the firm to offer a better service as well as reducing costs. Where conflict is disruptive it may be tackled in a number of different ways. Management might consider different reward criteria; marketing staff could be rewarded for accurate forecasts rather than meeting some artificially contrived quota and production staff rewarded for meeting delivery times. Conflict may also be avoided by encouraging more interaction and mixed career paths.

Such tensions may be found in many firms, but for others, such as Woodville Polymer Engineering described in Case 7.1, the cooperation and harmony between manufacturing and marketing is the essence of the company's success. In addition, the type of tensions identified by Shapiro are complicated by a range of factors such as the size and history of the firm, the nature of the process technology, and economic changes affecting demand. All these may aggravate or minimize the conflicts. The developments in flexible manufacturing systems identified in Chapter 6 have gone a long way towards easing some of the tensions, although the use of FMS is limited to a small number of firms.

We have concentrated on the relationship between marketing and manufacturing, but similar tensions may occur with other functions; with R&D over product design or with accounting over methods of payment. Nor are such conflicts the sole property of the marketing department. We have already identified the type of conflict that can emerge between the R&D and manufacturing functions and in the next chapter we see the traditional antagonisms that occur between the personnel department and line management. Such conflicts are the inevitable consequence of organizational size and managerial specialization. They may however be minimized by strategies focusing on coordination. We introduced such notions in Chapter 4 and develop them as far as marketing is concerned in the next section.

# The strategic aspects of marketing

The process of developing a marketing strategy bears a striking resemblance to the process of developing a firm's corporate strategy, underlining the centrality of marketing to the firm's planning process. Opportunities are analysed, target markets selected, market-share objectives are set and the particular marketing mix is developed. The marketing mix is central to the whole process since it identifies and guides the strategic options. Strategic considerations in marketing therefore embrace all of the factors we have discussed in this chapter. We will use the four elements of the mix to examine the various strands of marketing strategy. Finally we examine how these various elements may be combined and stress the integrated nature of marketing and the other functional strategies.

## Product strategy

> The historic fate of one growth industry after another has been its suicidal product provincialism.
>
> (Levitt, 1960, p. 34)

References have been made to product strategy in our discussion of innovation and production in the previous two chapters, as well as earlier in this chapter. Levitt's quote from his highly influential article 'Marketing myopia' is a plea to management for a marketing-led product development strategy. Most industries, he feels, restrict themselves by defining their businesses too narrowly, largely because they are product-oriented rather than customer-oriented. He cites the case of the decline of the US railway business which identified itself too rigidly with railways rather than the transport needs of its customers and lost ground to the airline and car industries.

Following the market in this way may be desirable but depends upon the firm's possessing the appropriate financial resources and skills. A firm's competitive edge may lie in the production of highly specialised goods and skills and resources may not be easily transferred. In such cases survival may depend upon acquisition or merger.

In general terms a product strategy needs to consider the type and range of products on offer, the style and quality of those products, the use of brand names and packaging, and the nature of the services that are offered with the product, such as warranty and after-sales care. We saw in our discussion of the product life-cycle that product market planning needs careful consideration of the production process.

## Pricing strategy

We have already discussed the various constituents that determine the price of a product, and singly or together these form the basis of pricing strategy. 'Cost-plus' pricing consists of a standard mark-up after all costs have been taken into consideration. 'Target profit' pricing involves establishing the price in accordance with projected demand, using some form of break-even analysis. In this way a book can be priced according to two criteria; the minimum sales required to cover production costs and the required profit margins based on estimated sales figures.

Both the 'cost-plus' and 'target profit' methods are based on the assumptions that prices are related solely to cost and demand. As we saw earlier, this is too simplistic a view. The pricing strategy needs to take account of factors external to the firm, in particular prices charged by the competition and the perceived value of the product by the consumer. In the former case there is a tendency for firms operating in the same product market to adopt a going rate, although, as we shall see later, more aggressive tactics can be pursued by firms breaking into new markets. By contrast to the going rate, pricing goods according to their perceived value can lead to considerable variation. Such a strategy is based on the customer's assumption that 'he is getting what he pays for' and he relates price to quality and hence to the cost of producing the goods or services. However a high price can be used to denote exclusivity and so attract a particular market segment. Of course, management may simply be pricing goods to see what the market will stand, but such a strategy may encourage new entrants with more cheaply priced products.

All these factors come together in the pricing strategies relating to new products. The simplest method may well be to price goods by comparison to the nearest equivalents, roughly in accordance with the going-rate method. However, two general strategies have been identified, skimming and penetration.

Skimming occurs when the initial price is high. This tends to occur where the price elasticity of demand is low and the barriers to entry are high. The product must appeal to a market segment where price is not an important consideration. This will generally be a high-income group of market leaders, but it may comprise, for products such as cameras and hi-fi equipment, the lower income 'enthusiast'. The price will offset the high development cost for this type of product and so ease the firm's cash-flow. A skimming strategy is usually accompanied by extensive promotional activity, particularly in up-market and specialist magazines. Once a reputation and a market have been established there may be a reduction in price to broaden the market, using the original purchasers as important opinion leaders. Price reductions may also be necessary to maintain a market share as competitors arrive on the scene. Several products have been priced in this way. Both the video cassette recorder and the compact disc player entered the market at high prices, with considerable price reductions as the market expanded and the competition increased.

A penetration strategy involves setting a low price to attract a mass market at the outset. Such a strategy is used where demand is price-sensitive and where economies of scale can be gained by mass production. Penetration is usually associated with competitive markets. However, the strategy can be used to discourage competition by raising the barriers of entry, since those entering the market must be certain of high sales to offset development costs. Such a strategy has been used by many firms. Texas Instruments dominated the American hand-held calculator market in this way and in 1988 Amstrad attempted to dominate the business market for personal computers by selling at 50% less than its rival, Apricot.

We can see that the pricing decision needs to take account of a range of interconnected factors. Additional complexities can and do exist. The same product may be differentially priced for number of reasons. It may be discounted for bulk purchase or to specific groups such as senior citizens and students. The same cinema seat may be differentially priced for different performances to even out demand and particularly to attract customers to less popular showings earlier in the week. The price may be a function of the number and type of distribution channels. Imported goods may be more expensive because they pass through more intermediaries, and products are generally more expensive in a prestigious store. Such variations can be confusing and lead to customer complaints, as some airline companies have found. The price of the same seat on the same flight may vary considerably, depending upon when and where the ticket has been bought. Tickets bought well in advance and those bought on a stand-by basis are much cheaper, as are those obtained from discount agencies and 'bucket shops'.

A further complexity is that the pricing strategy generally changes over the life of a product as a function of demand, market share, and changes in the economy. Price cuts may be introduced to regenerate a product nearing the end of its life-cycle or to beat off competition, and price rises may be needed to keep pace with inflation.

## Promotion strategy

Earlier we identified the three main functions of a promotion strategy; to inform, to persuade, and to remind. We also suggested that effective strategy was dependent upon selecting the most appropriate message and media for the product and target market. Two important decisions remain: how much to spend and how to gauge whether a campaign has been effective or not.

It is clear to management that a promotion strategy must be affordable, yet setting an appropriate budget is far from easy. In addition to the notion of affordability, three common methods are identified by marketing texts (Lancaster and Massingham, 1992; Kotler, 1993). The 'percentage-of-sales' method sets the budget according to the previous year's sales figures or is based on sales forecasts. The inherent flaw in such a strategy is that promotion is a function of sales rather than vice-versa; nevertheless such a method is simple and may appeal to the cautious decision-maker. The 'competitive-parity' method pegs promotional expenditure to that of the major competitors in proportion to the market share. The 'objective-and-task' method has probably the most rational appeal in that specific targets are set and the budget apportioned accordingly. Such a method enables the results of the expenditure to be assessed against the objectives.

In most organizations the marketing manager has to operate from a budget allocated as the result of some complex decision-making process involving all managers in all functional areas. Dhalla (1978) accuses many managers of short-sightedness in setting the promotional budget. He feels that promotion should be treated as a capital investment and not, as in most cases, as an operating cost.

Promotion may be evaluated on three levels. The first consideration is that the particular advertisement or sales promotion has been seen and by how many and what type of people. The second consideration is that the public and in particular the target market are aware of the product and its attributes. The final and most important consideration is that the promotion results in the desired action on the part of the target market. In the case of consumer products then the ultimate test lies in the number of sales, whereas a government campaign to reduce drinking and driving will have to be measured by the number of convictions.

The evaluation of a promotion campaign is especially difficult for a two main reasons. First, a decision has to be made about the time-scale for such an evaluation. Is the impact of an advertisement to be measured over a week, a month, several months or longer? Second, it may not be possible to isolate the impact of a promotional campaign from the influence of other variables such as changes in the economy, the behaviour of competitors, changes in social behaviour and so on. Accurate evaluation under such conditions may require extensive econometric models or a level of experimentation not feasible in most organizations. Few firms have done as DuPont and tested advertising expenditure in their paint market by varying the amounts in different parts of the same territory to assess the impact on sales. They discovered that the effect of the heaviest expenditure was weakest in areas where they had a high market share. Perhaps this is a pointer to the diminishing returns of advertising expenditure (case quoted in Buzzell, 1964).

Not all promotion activity has the strategic intention of increasing demand for products as the following case illustrates. In 1987 Burroughs Wellcome had developed a drug that had been successful in trials in slowing down the effect of the AIDS virus for some people. The company was concerned that the launch would be accompanied by media exaggeration and many would be misled into thinking that a cure had been found. The product was launched simultaneously, in open forums at major hotels in several American cities. In each case the launch was linked by television to a panel of medical experts and questions were encouraged. Such a promotion served to limit demand for the drug specifically to those cases who could benefit the most.

## Distribution strategy

Distribution strategy is concerned with such issues as the type and number of channels, the location of those channels and how they might be controlled. Stock policy is an important consideration here and incentives in the form of discounts may be required to persuade intermediaries such as warehouses to hold stock.

As we can see from Austin Rover in Case 7.2, an effective distribution strategy is essential if a firm wishes to expand in new or existing markets.

## An integrated marketing strategy

Integration can occur along three different dimensions: within each component of the mix; between the various elements of the mix; and between marketing and the other functional strategies. We will deal with each in turn.

- The various activities and strategies associated with each component of the mix should work together. For example, effective promotion is generally achieved through a campaign in which press and television advertising and sales promotion are carefully coordinated to achieve the maximum impact upon the consumer.
- The elements of the mix should work together. Price reductions are often accompanied by a promotion campaign and both need the reinforcement of sufficient stocks and effective distribution in anticipation of increased demand. Improvements in product quality necessitating increases in price need to be sensitively handled in promotion.
- The effective integration of marketing with the other functional strategies, especially those of innovation and production is considered essential to the firm acquiring a competitive advantage. An effective product portfolio should be built around the skills and other resources of the organization. A business school which attempts to offer courses in international business but lacks staff with the necessary expertise may attract a poor reputation and see support for all its courses suffer as a result. Some see this integration of functional strategies as an iterative process, requiring the constant monitoring of markets, products, processes and technology, and the firm working these elements around its chosen field of distinctive competence (Skinner, 1974).

# Summary

Marketing involves the understanding of customer needs and behaviour and the researching of markets for the effective development, pricing, promotion, and distribution of goods and services. These activities operate in a number of different consumer and organizational contexts and can incorporate the marketing of people, places, company image, and ideas as well as goods and services.

The product, price, promotion and distribution elements of marketing are known as the marketing mix. There is a growing trend for firms to segment the markets in which they operate calling for variations in the marketing mix for each target market.

Marketing operates at the interface between the organization and its environment, and changes in the economy, state regulation, technology and social trends all call for changes in marketing strategy. Marketing managers use their knowledge of the environment, especially of those social and cultural influences which shape behaviour in an attempt to manipulate demand for their product. In recent years marketing activities have been significantly affected by consumerism and Britain's membership of the EC.

The development of an effective marketing strategy depends upon an understanding of the workings of the marketplace, of customer needs and the appropriate mix for the market segment and prevailing environmental conditions. The implementation of that strategy depends upon the integration of marketing with the other functional specialisms.

## Further reading

The text which has dominated reading lists in business schools for many years is either P. Kotler, *Marketing Management: Analysis, Planning, Implementation and Control*, 8th edn (Prentice-Hall International, 1993) or P. Kotler, *Principles of Marketing*, 3rd edn (Prentice-Hall International, 1993). Much of the same information appears in both books. (Please note that in this chapter references are made to the 2nd edition of Kotler's *Principles* text). Two books aimed more at the British market are M. J. Baker, *Marketing*, 5th edn (Macmillan, 1991) and G. Lancaster and L. Massingham, *Essentials of Marketing*, 2nd edn (McGraw Hill, 1992). All these books deal with most of the issues in this chapter. Some excellent cases of marketing, particularly in terms of its interaction with the environment are found in A. Palmer and I. Worthington, *The Business and Marketing Environment* (McGraw-Hill, 1992). An excellent treatment of the marketing/manufacturing interface is offered by R. H. Hayes and S. C. Wheelwright, *Restoring Our Competitive Edge* (John Wiley, 1984) and T. Levitt, *The Marketing Imagination* (Free Press, 1986) offers some interesting essays.

## Discussion

1　Assess Drucker's claim that marketing is not a specialized activity since it encompasses all the activities of the firm.
2　How far and in what industries do the five orientations to marketing operate today?
3　Critically analyse Galbraith's assertion that consumer oriented marketing has been replaced by the 'revised sequence'.
4　For what reasons do governments engage in marketing? Does this raise any ethical problems?
5　What type of market research information would you need in the following situations: a holiday company offering a new resort location; a manufacturer developing a new motor for domestic

appliances; a restaurant owner planning a more expensive menu?

6   What factors would you consider to determine the price of the following: a new high performance sports car; a new breakfast cereal; a management consultancy contract?

7   Why does market segmentation occur and what are its drawbacks for management and the consumer?

8   How useful is the product life-cycle concept to management?

9   To what extent is a marketing manager able to change the environment in which the firm operates?

10  What are the essential ingredients of an effective marketing strategy?

11  Taking the Woodville and Austin Rover cases in turn, assess the marketing strategy in the context of the firm's organizational and external environment.

12  Can the criticisms levelled against marketing be balanced by the social benefits it provides?

# 8  Human resource management

To use a marketing analogy, personnel management has been re-launched. In organizations, management circles, job advertisements, textbooks, and even in the title of this chapter, the term Human Resource Management is superseding the former title of personnel management. The process has been taking place over the last decade to the accompaniment of 'Japanese management', 'corporate culture', 'quality of working life' and 'TQM', all to a greater or lesser extent displaying a certain similarity of approach.

Human Resource Management or, as it is more commonly known, HRM came to prominence in the 1980s and was defined in a seminal text as,

> Human resource management (HRM) involves all management decisions and actions that affect the nature of the relationship between the organization and its employees – its human resources.
>
> (Beer *et al.*, 1984, p. 1)

Most traditionally minded personnel managers would see nothing in that definition to imply that HRM is emerging as a radically different form of personnel management. Indeed, in this chapter we tend to use the two terms, HRM and personnel interchangeably unless otherwise stated. The heading of the chapter simply acknowledges a growing tendency. Nevertheless the issue has generated a substantial debate. As David Guest explains:

> To managers it seemed to offer an attractive alternative to the jaded image of personnel management and the dated rhetoric of traditional industrial relations . . . among academics, it offered new hope for those who had begun to despair of the long term potential of industrial relations and personnel management as important academic subjects.
>
> (Guest, 1990, p. 377)

In this chapter we will examine the extent to which HRM has supplanted traditional personnel management by comparing more traditional approaches to the new style HRM. Whichever term is preferred the activities involved illustrate well the workings of the Business in Context model. The growth of personnel management as a specialist activity has been influenced by a number of key environmental variables, in particular the intervention of the state through an increasingly complex system of employment law, the workings of the labour market, the strength of trade unions, the state of the economy and changes in the competitive environment. In addition to these environmental factors, the role and status of personnel managers themselves have had a significant influence on the scope and effectiveness of personnel strategies. These same factors are associated with the development of HRM.

We will deal with those environmental, organizational and strategic issues after we have examined the comparison between traditional approaches to personnel and HRM.

## Identifying personnel/HRM

### Traditional approaches to personnel

In this section we will attempt to define more traditional approaches to personnel and the activities most commonly associated with it. This will serve as a useful comparison with the supposedly different approach taken by HRM.

There would appear to be as many definitions of personnel management as there are books on the subject. This is hardly surprising, for, as we have noted, the activities are highly dependent upon the context in which they operate. For example, a discussion of personnel management in Britain would place greater emphasis upon industrial relations, than it would in the USA, where trade unions play much less of a role and collective action is rarer. Despite these variations, a useful starting point is the definition offered by the Institute of Personnel Management.

> Personnel management is a responsibility of all those who manage people as well as being a description of the work of those who are employed as specialists. It is that part of management which is concerned with people at work and with their relationships within an enterprise. It applies not only to industry and commerce but to all fields of employment. Personnel management aims to achieve both efficiency and justice, neither of which can be pursued successfully without the other. It seems to bring together and develop into an effective organization the men and women who make up the enterprise, enabling each to make his own best contribution to its success, both as an individual and as a member of a working group. It seeks to provide fair terms and conditions of employment and satisfying work for those employed.
>
> (IPM, 1963)

If we ignore the somewhat idealistic stance and the absence of precisely defined tasks and duties, the definition stresses the dual goals of serving the needs of employees and the organization. It also serves the useful purpose of distinguishing between a business function and a departmental presence within an organization. Many students of business conclude mistakenly that all businesses conform to textbook models, relating as they do to fairly large-scale organizations differentiated into specialist departments.

Daniel and Millward (1983) estimated that if all firms, including small businesses, were considered, then 75% of companies would have no specialist personnel manager, the function being performed by a manager who deals with personnel matters alongside other duties. For example, in many professional partnerships, such as solicitors or accountants, one of the senior partners is usually given responsibility for personnel, but would view their main role as that of a solicitor or an accountant. Some smaller firms may operate the personnel function through a one-person-secretary-cum-records department. The absence of a personnel specialist may even be deliberate policy. Hewlett-Packard, the American multinational, did not introduce a personnel department until staffing levels had reached 1200, its founders preferring personnel matters to be the responsibility of all managers (Beer *et al.*, 1985).

In Table 8.1 We present a detailed list of the various activities associated with personnel management. These activities may be categorized as people processing and industrial relations (see Key Concepts 8.1 and 8.2). The division of the personnel function along these lines can be seen particularly in large, unionized firms, such as Ford, where industrial relations plays a particularly prominent role.

All firms will have a need for some of these activities, in that management, for example, must conform to the prevailing employment laws and operate some system for paying employees. At some stage all firms will have need for the recruitment and selection of new staff or the reallocation of existing staff. The extent and formalization of these activities depends very much on the size of the labour force, the extent of trade-union membership, and whether or not the firm has a

| **KEY CONCEPT 8.1** *People processing* | People processing relates to those activities of personnel management to do with the acquisition, development, motivation and control of individuals at work. It includes the various activities associated with recruitment, selection, training, appraisal, pay administration and welfare. |
| --- | --- |

| **KEY CONCEPT 8.2** *Industrial relations* | Industrial relations is concerned with the relations between employers and their representatives and employees and their representatives over such matters as work practices, pay, conditions, job security and forthcoming changes. The relationship involves elements of negotiation and bargaining, which in practice are usually dealt with by management on one hand and trade union representatives on the other. The importance of industrial relations to the general conduct of business is acknowledged by the State in most countries and a corresponding development has taken place in laws covering employer and employee rights and laws governing the conduct of collective bargaining. The conduct of industrial relations is influenced significantly by the general state of the economy and the ideology of the interested parties. |
| --- | --- |

specialist personnel department, as well as other influences raised in the next two sections.

The activities identified in Table 8.1 may be performed in a variety of ways.

- They may be performed by a personnel specialist or a general manager with responsibility for personnel matters, or by individual managers themselves acting alone.
- In some cases personnel specialists operate only in an advisory capacity to other managers. Members of the personnel department will advise on the setting up of personnel systems which will be operated by other managers. Examples of this could include the establishment of a job evaluation and grading system of criteria for promotion.
- In many cases, the personnel specialists act in conjunction with other managers, as for example in interviewing candidates for a vacancy, or designing and implementing a training programme for a sales department.
- In all kinds of organizations there is increasing use made of personnel consultants, particularly in the fields of recruitment and training. In this case the personnel specialist operates as a hirer, coordinator and manager of the consultant's activities.

As we have seen, in smaller firms, the activities tend to be carried out by all managers, and no specialist operates. In larger firms with formalized procedures a mixture of all four methods occurs. A personnel manager may advise the sales manager on the type of person he or she is seeking to fill a vacancy and may assist in the drafting of the job advertisement. A number of candidates may be interviewed by the personnel manager alone and a short-list drawn up for a second interview at which the sales manager will take a leading role. The use of consultants is appropriate for small firms where specialist personnel inputs are an intermittent requirement. In larger firms consultants are seen as a more cost-effective method of delivering certain personnel services than bearing the cost of maintaining a large internal personnel department.

## Human resource management

The broad definition of HRM offered at the beginning of this chapter gives little hint of what activities comprise and what makes it particularly different from our traditional view of personnel management. Over the last five years the HRM concept has spawned a vast literature offering a range of varying perspectives. However, there is some measure of agreement that HRM involves a focus on:

- treating employees as individuals, but, at the same time, developing mechanisms to integrate individuals into teams;
- the careful selection, training and development of core staff;
- reward systems that stress individual performance and commitment and which are linked to employee appraisal and development;

**Table 8.1**  The activities of personnel management

| Activity | What it involves |
| --- | --- |
| Manpower planning and control | The analysis of a company's manpower needs in light of its current manpower resources and the nature of the labour market. Such planning lays the foundation for policies related to recruitment, selection, training, pay and so on. |
| Recruitment | The first stage usually involves a detailed job analysis followed by the selection of the most appropriate method of recruitment, be it the use of government job centres, using specialist recruitment consultants or placing advertisements in newspapers. Decisions made here aim to attract a field of suitable candidates. |
| Selection | The use of one or more of a variety of techniques including application forms, interviewing and tests to select the most appropriate person from a field of candidates. The interview tends to be the most favoured method of selection. Decisions are usually made against some general or specific criteria relating to the type of candidate required. |
| Training and management development | This involves the analysis of the type of training required and the people to be trained, followed by the selection of the most appropriate method. This can range from simple on–the–job instruction to sending people on specific courses. In many firms the training and development of managers is seen as a special case involving long–term planning and consideration for individual career development. |
| Appraisal | This is a contentious issue in personnel and sometimes resisted by Trade Unions. It involves the setting up of formal systems to assess the contribution of individuals to the organization. The system is often designed by personnel specialists but administered by all managers. |
| Pay administration | This is a complex area involving decisions about the rate of pay (often involving negotiation with Trade Unions), about the way pay is differentially distributed (using some form of job evaluation or individual merit rating), and about the viability of one of a variety of payment schemes such as flat rate payment, payment by results, profit-sharing and so on. Decisions made in this area have broadened to include the number and range of fringe benefits such as pensions, company cars, cheap mortgages and the like. |

**Table 8.1** *Continued*

| Activity | What it involves |
|---|---|
| Job and organizational design | In some cases personnel managers contribute to decisions about how jobs are to be carried out and how the organization is to be structured. This may involve the design and administration of programmes such as job enrichment, organizational development or the quality of working life. |
| Collective bargaining | Personnel management are invariably involved in the preparation of the employer's case and usually in the negotiations with employee representatives. Once collective agreements have been made, it is usually the job of the personnel manager to apply such agreements and deal with the outcomes. |
| Grievance and disputes handling | Related to the above, the personnel manager is usually in the front line in dealing with situations arising from individual or collective grievances. In larger firms specific procedures are laid down, but in all cases there is an expectation of the personnel manager to solve disputes as and when they arise. |
| Legal advice | With developments in employment law (outlined in the next section) many personnel managers are seen as the resident expert in legal matters pertaining to employment and act as a guide to other managers. |
| Employee communications and counselling | The personnel specialist is often given responsibility for communicating general information to the workforce as well as administering specific programmes for employee participation such as suggestion schemes. Some firms go further and involve the personnel manager in employee advice and counselling. |
| Personnel information and records | The need for personnel records has increased as firms have grown in size. Such records, kept by the personnel department, are often an important source of information upon which personnel decisions are based. |

- communication networks and the involvement of employees, preferably as individuals, but allowing for trade-union involvement as well;
- emphasizing a culture which stresses commitment to organizational goals, quality, and flexibility. In many cases it is recognized that this will involve a culture change, more especially in those organizations typified by confrontational industrial relations;
- the integration, not only of all personnel-related policies as a

**KEY CONCEPT 8.3**
*Human resource management*

Human resource management is replacing personnel management as the term to define the former personnel function. There is considerable debate as to whether it represents a distinctly different type of function from its predecessor. In some cases the name has changed, but the function remains the same. Advocates of HRM as a new function stress its focus on the individual, particularly in terms of reward, and an emphasis on selection training appraisal and communication networks. HRM is usually associated with the creation of a strong corporate culture with an emphasis on commitment. HRM is inevitably portrayed as having a strategic and integrated focus.

meaningful whole, but also of these policies within the overall strategy of the enterprise;

● business values as an overriding consideration.

The analysis of such core characteristics of HRM has led some writers, notably Storey (1989), to see two strands emerging. One is defined as 'hard' HRM with a focus on business values and management strategy. The other is defined as 'soft' HRM, focusing as it does upon the selection, development and the reward of people.

Many of the core characteristics of HRM are incorporated in Figure 8.1.

We have commented already on the relevance of the strategic, organizational and environmental contexts in shaping personnel/HRM activities. It is to a convergence of recent changes in those contexts that we must look to explain the emergence of HRM as a concept in its own right.

Significant changes in the competitive environment of most companies have placed greater emphasis on the need to innovate, the need to improve the quality of their goods and services and above all the need to be more cost-effective in their use of labour. This in turn has resulted in many of those companies re-examining the way they select, train, use and reward employees.

A significant aspect of this new competition has emerged from Japan,

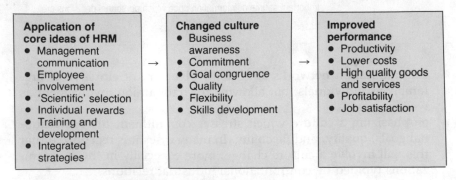

*Figure 8.1* The human resource management process.

whose management practices, as we saw in Chapter 2, have been envied by managers in the West. It is no coincidence that many features of HRM can be likened to Japanese employment relations practices. Changes in technology have added to the demand to use employees more flexibly than hitherto.

It is not just Japan that offers suitable HRM models. In Chapter 3 we examined the influential movement that emerged from the USA built around the concept of corporate culture and the notion that 'excellent' companies serve as models for others to follow. Many of the companies defined by Peters and Waterman (1982) as 'excellent' operate HRM policies. IBM is such a company and aspects of its HRM policy may be found in Case 8.1. The coming together of an increasingly competitive environment and the availability of such corporate models led a group of academics at the Harvard Business School to establish HRM as a core subject on the MBA programme, based on the premise that human resources are a key area in the search for competitive advantage (Beer *et al.*, 1984, 1985). They gained inspiration not only from non-union companies such as IBM, but observed changes in more traditional unionized environments. In General Motors, for example, management worked closely with the Union of Auto Workers in setting up HRM style practices at the Cadillac plant at Livonia, and in all its plants attempted to change management–worker relations from low to high trust and seek productivity gains through workforce cooperation and commitment.

In Britain and the USA the industrial relations climate had also altered as a result of economic and political changes. A series of recessions had weakened the bargaining power of trade unions and unemployment in those industrial sectors that were former union strongholds had led to a decline in trade-union membership. (Further analysis of these changes is offered elsewhere in this chapter and in Chapter 2.) In both countries, but more especially in Britain, the politics of government shifted to the right. The rhetoric of the 'New Right' revolved around concepts such as the free market, the freedom of the individual, and the enterprise culture. The climate was therefore suitable for those managements seeking alternative models of employment relations.

Another reason for the growth of interest in HRM lies in the relationship between personnel specialists and other managers in the organization. This is a theme which re-emerges when we examine the organizational environment of HRM later in the chapter. The lack of access to strategic decision-making and low status felt by many personnel practitioners may well have created a receptive environment for HRM to flourish, with its promise of a high-level strategic approach. To other managers who saw the policies of traditional personnel management as inadequate and inappropriate for entry into the 1990s, HRM may have offered a favourable alternative.

We will now examine the extent to which these changes have resulted in HRM emerging as something distinctively different from personnel management and the extent to which the practice of HRM matches its rhetoric.

**CASE 8.1**
*IBM's personnel
policies*

IBM is the world's largest and most successful computer manufacturer. It has been established in Britain since 1951 and is a market leader in most of its product ranges. There are no unions at IBM and the company has never experienced a strike and until 1991 has not had to lay people off. Paradoxically, many of its current employment and personnel practices were developed during the depression in the USA and many were ahead of their time. The company scrapped payment-by-results methods for its manufacturing employees in 1936, treating all employees as salaried staff and in effect offering them lifetime employment. Around the same time the company introduced job enlargement and flexible working and embarked on a programme of involving all employees in the design of new products. Employee training has always been a major feature of the company. IBM is often cited as a model for human resource management practice and one that others would do well to emulate.

In Britain the company expanded rapidly in the 1960s and was still growing in the 1980s. Only 27% of employees work in manufacturing, the majority operating in marketing and technical services. Pay is high compared with other firms and labour turnover is exceptionally low, operating at around 2%. A feature that has always intrigued British commentators is the absence of a trade union. The management claim that the employees have no need for a union nor do they want one. This is supported by an ACAS survey in 1977 which discovered that only 4.9% of employees wanted a union and 91% claimed they would refuse to join if a union were introduced.

A trade union would certainly contradict the stated corporate commitment to individualism. Additionally it is claimed that a union is not needed since the company offers terms and conditions far in excess of those usually demanded by trade unions. The key features of the employment practices would seem to be the following:

- a fairly sophisticated system of manpower planning, employee recruitment and training;
- lifetime employment for all employees with the expectation that employees will change jobs as and when required;
- single status for all employees in terms of canteens, facilities, and fringe benefits; the only exceptions are overtime payment for manufacturing workers and company cars for some senior management and some sales staff;
- salaries are determined centrally, usually by making a favourable comparison with other firms; the exercise is carried out annually to ensure pay rates keep ahead of those in other companies; once established, increases are always based on merit and determined through a management-by-objectives type appraisal scheme;
- training is emphasized, with management receiving an average of 40 days' training a year (40 times the national average); much of the training focuses upon human resource management;
- an opinion survey of all staff is held every two years, to ascertain attitudes towards such factors as working practices, pay and conditions, and personnel practices; the response rates are very high;
- emphasis is placed upon managers sorting out their own problems; a centralized personnel function operates a 'hands-off' policy; the company prefers to leave personnel matters to individual managers, especially grievance handling;
- the company operates two formalized communication procedures; a 'Speak-Up' system encourages employees to raise business-related problems, while an

'Open-Door' system allows employees to appeal against decisions taken by their own managers.

IBM would seem to operate a successful employment relations policy that is well-liked by its employees. The company expects a great deal of its employees, but offers them secure jobs at relatively high rates of pay. The policy has been criticized on a number of counts. The company has been accused of being anti-union and ensuring that unions never become established. While the firm operates a philosophy which stresses individuality as part of its commitment to entrepreneurship, individuals are nevertheless expected to conform to IBM norms of behaviour, even to participating in out-of-work company social events and activities. The company has also been accused of operating a recruitment policy which ensures that only those committed to the IBM way will be selected. In general, sceptics have attempted to label IBM as running an oppressive system, which is only possible in the rarefied environment of a successful hi-tech company. However, any firm which has developed such a strong corporate culture leaves itself open to attack by those who see it as too good to be true.

By 1991 IBM was facing a different kind of attack. The computer market had become even more competitive, both in terms of the number of firms competing and in terms of customers expecting much more for their money. Faced with an unprecedented fall in profits IBM confronted its own lifetime employment policies by embarking on a strategy of cutting labour costs. This needed to be done quickly as the impact of the recession accelerated, not only in the UK but in IBM worldwide. Given the low labour turnover and the absence of opportunity to transfer employees to other IBM operations, the Company introduced a programme of voluntary redundancy. The Company offered an attractive package, amounting to an average two years' salary per employee with support mechanisms such as advice on job-seeking, personal finance as well as general counselling. In addition, time off was freely given for job interviews and those employees with company cars were allowed to buy them at favourable terms.

From the Company's point of view, it was important to ensure that they did not lose key employees and management constructed manpower planning models to determine target groups and target areas of operation. Use was made of the Company's internal communication system to explain the need for the strategy, to encourage volunteers and to prepare those the Company considered ineligible. Use was made of briefing groups, information releases, information packs and one-day briefing sessions. In addition, employees had access to individual advice. The result of the exercise was a reduction in headcount of 15% of which only 2.3% represented 'normal' turnover. The reduction exceeded the Company's expectations. A positive outcome was that some employees used the opportunity to establish their own business out of their IBM activities. The Company actively encouraged this and gave assistance, reflected in a reduced redundancy package. The companies that were established in this way initially sold back their services to IBM. However, there were cases of dissatisfaction where some employees were prevented from taking advantage of the offer.

Some would advocate that IBM not only have a successful personnel system but that their model made it possible to carry out a relatively trouble-free programme of voluntary redundancy. The reality is probably that IBM have developed a system which works for itself and which seems to operate in both the interests of the Company and its employees. The employment relations policies are probably far more sophisticated than in most unionized companies. The extent to which it offers other companies a model to follow may well be limited by the ability of their management to carry such policies through effectively in non-IBM setting. For IBM itself, the redundancy programme struck at the heart of one of its key human resource policies. The resilience of those policies will lie in the continued commitment of retained employees in an increasingly competitive environment, and in particular the management of those employees aggrieved by the redundancy policy itself.

(*Sources*: Drucker, 1968; Bassett, 1986; Peach, 1992)

## The differences between HRM and traditional personnel management

In examining whether there has been a shift away from traditional personnel practices to a more strategically oriented HRM three positions emerge.

- There are those who see HRM as a radical departure, offering personnel managers a new strategic role and de-emphasizing industrial relations as a major activity.
- Others see little more than a title change and feel that HRM is really personnel management in a new guise, embodying as it does what is viewed as 'good' personnel practice.
- Those subscribing to a middle if somewhat cautious position recognize that changes have taken place in such areas as labour flexibility, employee involvement, appraisal and training. Furthermore they see some attempts by British firms to blend HRM with traditional industrial relations. However, they view the changes as yet as neither significant nor widespread (Storey, 1992).

Legge (1989), while arguing considerable similarity between what both personnel management and HRM set out to achieve, sees in HRM some important differences. First, she views HRM as being much more about management. Personnel is no longer about the treatment of the shop floor, but there has been a switch of emphasis to focus on issues of management development and management teambuilding. Furthermore HRM is the prerogative of senior management whereas personnel management was viewed as an activity to be carried out by more junior managers. Second, she argues that HRM has elevated human resource issues to a position of key strategic importance. Third, she sees that HRM is about organizational culture and culture change in a way that personnel never was. Finally she and others sense a major difference in the language of HRM, which borrows heavily from the rhetoric of the 'New Right'.

The different positions and perspectives offered above have presented researchers with a number of hypotheses to test and there has been no shortage of research activity into the changing role of personnel. Major studies have been established at the London School of Economics, Warwick University and at Cranfield; the latter examining HRM practices across Europe. (Good summaries of this and other

British Airways was formed in 1972 through a merger between BEA and BOAC. It possessed a very extensive route network, an exceptionally good safety record, and, in Heathrow, an enviable operating base within easy reach of London. Its first decade of operation was typified by a number of problems and in 1982 the company reported losses of £100 million. The problems were overmanning, a lack of operating efficiency compared with its major competitors, a series of industrial disputes and a particularly bad image with the travelling public. Part of the problem was attributed to a highly bureaucratic organization structure and decision-making process, typical of many nationalized industries. In British Airways' case the problem was compounded by a hierarchical structure that reflected the armed forces rather than a business operating in a fast-changing environment. By the 1980s the airline business was more competitive than ever and new entrants such as Virgin had quickly developed favourable reputations based upon low price and quality service. By 1983 the Government had announced its intentions to denationalize the airline and the recently appointed chairman and chief executive were given a clear message that the company had to be made commercially viable.

The workforce was cut by some 20 000 and certain routes were withdrawn. A much greater attention was paid to marketing, and organizational changes were made including a reduction in hierarchical levels and a de-emphasis of status differences and job titles. In 1983 the company launched its major culture change initiative which used as its focus customer care. This was based upon research carried out on effective behaviour in the caring professions and the experience of SAS (Scandinavian Airlines) in implementing a similar programme. British Airways enlisted the help of the same consultants as those involved in the SAS project.

Two major training initiatives were launched. The 'Putting People First' campaign was aimed, initially, at those employees in direct contact with the general public, such as check-in staff and cabin crew, although it was extended to other groups as well. The 'Managing People First' campaign was aimed primarily at middle and senior management. Both campaigns were based on customer perceptions that portrayed British Airways as bureaucratic and saw its staff, while competent, as aloof and uncaring. The assumptions upon which the campaigns were launched were that people perform best when given the maximum support by their peers and, most importantly, by their supervisors, and when given maximum discretion in solving problems. Human Resources staff were given training in organization change by the consultants and much of the responsibility for personnel issues was passed to line management.

'Putting People First' training confronted staff in groups with the negative image of British Airways held by its customers and encouraged employees to suggest ways of changing it. Role-playing was also used, through which staff were encouraged to use their own initiatives to resolve customer problems such as flight delays and lost luggage. Presentations were given of what various people and groups in the organization did on a daily basis in an attempt to break down barriers and build a greater sense of identity. An important part of the process was the involvement of the chief executive, Colin Marshall, who was present for at least part of the training sessions. An important outcome of the sessions was the creation of 'Customer First Teams', a variation of the quality circle concept.

'Managing People First' was a five-day residential programme for managers. The programme comprised three elements: the encouragement to managers to adopt a

**CASE 8.2**
*British Airways*

more visible, open and dynamic style; the coaching, training and supporting of subordinates; and an attempt to get managers to link the goals of their part of the operations with overall corporate objectives. As part of the latter process managers were encouraged to develop their ideal of the company's mission. At the same time a management appraisal scheme was launched and tied in to an individual reward system with both performance related pay and share options.

In 1988 profits of £320 million were reported by British Airways. Customer feedback was favourable and the airline received several awards for its customer service in the business press. The feedback from employees on their perception of the company was equally encouraging. Measured in terms of profitability, customer and employee satisfaction, the change appears to have worked. As with all major changes there were conflicts, notably between maintaining customer care and cutting costs at the same time, a clear case of 'soft' v. 'hard' HRM. Some commentators see that problems still exist in the form of an insecure middle management, too much functional specialization and an overemphasis at the top on acquisitions and takeovers. Others believe these to be relatively understandable but minor issues in a major culture change, successfully tested by a further series of job losses as a result of the recession and the Gulf War in the 1990s.

(*Sources*: Bruce, 1987; Hampden-Turner, 1990; Höpfl *et al.*, 1992; Kay 1993)

research can be found in Guest 1990, 1991; Brewster and Bournois, 1991; and Storey, 1992.)

Clearly there are companies which conform to the classic characteristics of HRM. In this league are firms such as IBM, Hewlett-Packard and British firms such as Marks & Spencer and British Airways. For example we see in Case 8.2 how British Airways invested heavily in a massive training programme to change the culture of its organization towards a greater emphasis on customer care. However, most of these classic companies were known for their sophisticated approaches to personnel long before HRM emerged. Indeed we might argue that HRM is a product of such companies and hence they cannot be offered as evidence of an HRM revolution.

Many of the techniques associated with HRM, such as employee involvement, quality circles, increased flexibility, psychological selection testing, appraisal, new forms of individualized payment systems and various methods of culture change, have been introduced in a number of companies. However, there is little evidence of any grand design and in many instances the techniques have been introduced in a piecemeal fashion or even in isolation. Some firms have experienced mixed results. Ford UK achieved a measure of flexibility in its assembly-line operations through the reduction in demarcation and by redefining jobs to the extent of reducing 500 differently defined assembly jobs to just 50 (McKinlay and Starkey, 1992). The same company, however, failed in its attempt to persuade the unions to accept both quality circles and a formalized system of employee involvement, the latter having enjoyed a measure of success in Ford USA.

For the United Kingdom, at least, the research is sanguine about there being a significant shift from personnel to HRM. The focus has been on the extent to which HRM practices occur and has hardly begun to explore the extent to which such practices result in the kinds of favourable outcomes envisaged for the firm and its employees. The evidence does point to differences in application and this will be discussed in the next section when we explore environmental influences.

Despite the lack of hard evidence the language of HRM has clearly infiltrated personnel practice. Examination of job advertisements in the IPM's own journal for March 1993 reveals that of the 77 positions advertised only 26% have HRM in their job title. Of the other advertisements 36% have personnel management in their job title and the remaining 38% refer to a specialism within personnel, the large majority being training and development. However, closer examination of the non-HRM titled jobs reveals that a good proportion make some reference to HRM. For example, an advertisement for the job of personnel manager is subtitled 'managing the change from personnel to HRM' and several of the training vacancies emphasise development and culture change. An interesting fact to emerge is that the title HRM tends to be reserved for the higher status, more highly paid positions. We will return to this issue when discussing the organizational context of HRM. The journal from which the recruitment information is taken is still called *Personnel Management* but with the added subtitle of 'the magazine for human resource professionals'.

In recent publications, the IPM too appear to be shifting their ground. A statement by a group of senior personnel practitioners endorsed by the IPM states,

> Personnel is an important part of the management process and not an exclusive function. It is an enabling activity with responsibilities for core organizational values in relation to people.
>
> (Personnel Standards Lead Body, 1993, p. 1)

The core strategies identified in the same document clearly owe considerable allegiance to developments in HRM. The extent to which this is a product of strategic innovation or opportunism in the light of environmental changes is a theme which recurs in the final section of this chapter. We now turn to examine the environmental context of personnel/HRM.

## The environmental aspects of personnel

In the previous section we examined the emergence of HRM and associated this with certain environmental changes, such as increasing competition and the weakened position of trade unions. In fact, the development of personnel management as a specialist function in organizations owes much to the influence of external events. The growth of markets and the creation of the joint stock company led to increases in the size of the firm with a corresponding demand for recruitment, training and some centralized payment administration system. The growth of trade unions, especially in Britain, created the need for industrial relations specialists among management. The impact of two world wars created problems for the labour supply and a corresponding attention being paid to training methods and employee consultation. Full employment in the 1960s once again focused the attention on labour shortages and methods used to tackle them, such as the retraining of existing staff and active recruitment from other companies. In the 1970s the focus turned to state intervention and the problems created by new technology, while the 1980s brought us HRM and the transplantation of practices from other countries. We can see that all five environmental aspects of our model interact in some significant way with the personnel/HRM function. We deal with each one in turn.

## The role of the state

The state operating through government policies and the legal system has had considerable influence of the personnel function in three major areas; through legislation; through manpower policies concerned with the supply of labour and education and training; and through third-party intervention.

**Employment legislation**   Employment legislation is concerned with the rights and obligations of employers and employees and the conduct of industrial relations. The growth in employment law in the 1960s and 1970s and the 1980s laws governing the conduct of industrial relations have had a significant impact on the work of personnel. In Figure 8.2 we show the growth of employment legislation since 1960 by listing the major Acts of Parliament. A good summary of recent legislation, with an emphasis on industrial relations, may be found in Kessler and Bayliss (1992b).

---

Factories Act 1961
Contract of Employment Act 1963, 1972
The Industrial Training Act 1965
Race Relations Act 1968, 1976
Equal Pay Act 1970
Industrial Relations Act 1971
Employment and Training Act 1973
Health and Safety at Work Act 1974
Trade Union and Labour Relations Act 1974, 1976
Sex Discrimination Act 1975, 1986
Employment Protection Act 1975
Employment Protection (Consolidation) Act 1978
Empolyment Act 1980
Employment Act 1982
Trade Union Act 1984
Employment Act 1988
Wages Act 1986
Employment Act 1989
Employment Act 1990

---

*Figure 8.2*  Major employment law since 1960.

Many of the laws have had a direct impact upon the day-to-day work of personnel managers. The Industrial Training Act 1964, with its introduction of the levy-grant system for approved training, resulted in the expansion of training programmes. Recruitment advertisements must be carefully drafted so as not to contravene race and sex discrimination legislation. The Arbitration, Conciliation and Advisory Service (ACAS) set up by the Employment Protection Act 1975 has had a significant impact on the conduct of industrial relations. Several of the laws have set up a judicial system of Industrial Tribunals as in the case of redundancy and unfair dismissals cases. The preparation of such cases on behalf of the employer is often done by a personnel/HRM specialist. Despite the growth in the tribunal and the number of cases petitioned, only a small percentage reach the final stages. Most cases are dealt with through a variety of conciliation procedures, sometimes involving ACAS (described later in this section), but almost inevitably involving a personnel manager. The expansion of employment law has been an important causal factor in the increased number of personnel specialists. For example, the Industrial Training Act 1964 required firms to pay a government levy which could only be reclaimed upon the satisfactory completion of an approved training programme. In many firms this resulted in the establishment of training departments staffed by specialist training officers.

Some commentators see the expansion of labour law as a vehicle for the increased status of personnel managers (for example, Legge 1978). This has been reinforced by studies of the role of the personnel manager following the introduction of industrial relations legislation of the 1980s (Millward and Stevens, 1986; Millward *et al.*, 1992). Managers faced with a complex array of new legal provisions seek expert advice and often turn to the personnel specialist as their source. However, not all such legislation had had the impact predicted. The Industrial Relations Act 1971 attracted much media attention and was elevated to the status of a political *cause célèbre*. In reality its provisions were dismissed by some managers as much as they were by the trade-union movement, its measures were largely ignored and its impact lessened long before its repeal in 1974.

In the 1980s industrial relations entered a new phase and legislation came to the forefront. There is clear indication that this aspect of personnel management has been politicized as never before. In the main, the Labour Party, with its traditional allegiances to the trade-union movement, has introduced legislation which has tended to establish and further the rights of individual workers. The Conservative Party on the other hand has been more concerned with establishing laws which control the internal affairs of trade unions and which attempt to regulate collective bargaining. As new laws have been introduced and repealed by successive governments, personnel managers have had to respond and amend policies accordingly. The politicization of personnel management is seen most clearly in the public sector where, for example in the 1980s and the 1990s, trade unions in coal mining and the health service took stands against government policy on such issues as pit and hospital closures, on pay restraints and attempts to reduce public spending in general. This has clearly placed personnel management in those industries in a political arena where consultation and collective bargaining with trade unions has considerable political implications.

The legislation of the 1980s was based on the assumption that trade-union power needed to be curbed, that individuals should be free to choose whether they join a union and that the general public needed protection against the damaging affects of strikes and other forms of industrial action. The series of five Employment Acts from 1980 to 1990 represent a cumulative strengthening of the law relating to industrial relations and deregulation at the workplace. Together with the Trade Union Act of 1984 they have built up a collection of laws that have affected the conduct of industrial relations in the following ways.

- Trade unions as organizations are now responsible for the actions of their members. If, during a strike, damage is caused to property, then the union may be held responsible. Previously trade unions were immune and only individuals could be sued.
- A much tighter legal definition of a strike has been formulated. A strike can only take place if it relates wholly or mainly to industrial matters such as pay and conditions and can only occur between an employee and his or her direct employer. This has effectively ruled out any form of political strike and any form of secondary action, such as a sympathy strike to further the cause of a group of workers at another plant. In addition a strike can only be called following a properly conducted secret ballot.
- Senior trade union officials, including those in non-voting and presidential positions must now present themselves for re-election every five years by secret ballot. The Government clearly felt that trade-union leaders should be more accountable not only to their members but to the public at large.
- The concept of accountability has been extended to include legal restrictions on the closed shop. A ballot must be held by the unions wishing to operate a closed shop and support must be obtained from 80% of the membership. By giving individuals the right to opt out, the 1988 Act made the closed shop unworkable and the 1990 Act banned the pre-entry closed shop altogether.
- The laws relating to the closed shop strengthen the rights of the individual to belong or not to belong to a trade union. Individuals were also given rights protecting them against union disciplinary action. However, employers were given the right to dismiss selectively any worker participating in unlawful industrial action.
- There has been a deregulation of the restrictions imposed upon the conditions of employment of women and young persons.

Other provisions in this legislation include restrictions on picketing and the introduction of a compulsory ballot to test union member's support for contributions to a political fund. In general the legislation appears to favour ballots over other forms of voting on the basis of their alleged democratic superiority.

The 1980s legislation represented a major shift in the government's attitude towards industrial relations. The impact of the legislation has been difficult to assess. From 1979 to 1989 there was a 50% reduction in registered closed shops, although this may be as mush a factor of the loss of employment in manufacturing as a direct result of the legislation (Edwards *et al.*, 1992). Certainly the anticipated conflict over union electoral and political fund issues did not materialize and nearly all unions appear to be operating this aspect of the legislation willingly.

Much media attention has been directed towards the impact of the legislation on strikes. Mercury, the communications company, successfully took legal action against the Post Office Engineering Union when they refused to join up the British Telecom network to the Mercury system. Mercury had acquired the right to operate an independent telephone service under the Government's liberalization and privatization policy. The union claimed that its refusal to work and eventual strike action was to protect jobs in British Telecom. The court ruled that the action was primarily an opposition to government policy, hence political and therefore illegal. The laws have also been used to the benefit of Eddy Shah in extending his newspaper empire in the North West. He took the National Graphical Association to court to prevent its blockading a non-union printing plant. He succeeded in winning his case and in gaining significant damages from the union. As we saw in Chapter 1, the law played a significant role in the 1986 New International dispute as it did in the 1988 Seamans' dispute with the P&O ferry company.

Many of the court actions have involved smaller employers who have probably most to lose from a dispute. It was Mercury and not British Telecom that took action against British Telecom's workers. Many larger companies are loath to use the courts for fear of alienating their workforce. Contrary to the image of industrial relations portrayed in the popular press, management and workforce, indeed management and unions, in most firms, have reasonably good relations, which recourse to law may damage. Nonetheless the legislation of the 1980s has changed significantly the nature of collective bargaining and consequently the work of personnel specialists. There has been a marked reduction in the number of recorded disputes in British industry. This could be related to changes in the law. It could also be related to economic conditions which we will discuss later. In some cases it is clear that changes in legislation have been accompanied by deliberate attempts on the part of management to change the employment relations culture of the enterprise. In part this is an attempt to replace traditional adversarial bargaining with a more cooperative approach. This theme recurs in our discussion of labour matters later in this section and when we discuss personnel strategies at the end of the chapter. Whatever the direct impact of legislation on industrial disputes it is clear that the threat of law 'has caused unions to be more circumspect in their behaviour' (Edwards *et al.*, 1992, p. 17).

**Manpower policies** There have been attempts by successive governments to achieve a stable balance between supply and demand in the labour market through a series of manpower policies. For 20 years after the end of the Second World War unemployment remained below 2% and the major concern was the development of mechanisms to improve the supply of skilled labour. Certainly since 1852 governments have been consistent in their criticism of the quantity and quality of training in British industry. A Government White Paper in 1962 linked the inadequacy of training in British industry to the nation's economic problems and the result was the Industrial Training Act 1964 referred to earlier. Its impact was immediate with a dramatic increase in levels of training. Training Boards were set up for each industry and several innovations were introduced. The Engineering Industry Training Board radically restructured its apprenticeship scheme to produce trainees with more flexible skills in a shorter time. Skills shortages, however, have persisted to dog British industry.

Despite the continuing skills shortages in some areas the focus shifted to introducing measures to combat the problem of rising unemployment. Such measures have tended to fall into two categories; those aiming to increase the demand for labour and those aimed at reducing the total supply. Schemes to increase the demand for labour have included wages subsidies, job creation, community enterprise programmes and the youth training scheme. Measures to reduce the labour supply have included early retirement, job release, temporary short-time working and job splitting.

Government training programmes have been introduced to tackle both the problems of skills shortages and unemployment. The Youth Training Scheme and its predecessor, the Youth Opportunities Programme, have been in operation since 1982 and in 1987 the Job Training Scheme was introduced for long-term unemployed adults. Since the mid-1980s the Government has also attempted to influence both the content and values of school education, based on comparative information which shows British workers to be less educated, less qualified and receive less training than those in countries with whom we are in direct economic competition. This has resulted in the Training and Vocational Education Initiative (TVEI) and the attempt to secure a series of national standards and certification in education and skills development through the National Council for Vocational Qualifications (NCVQ). In more general terms the Government has attempted to foster not only vocational skills but also a business culture among the population through the introduction of a National Curriculum for primary schoolchildren.

The extent to which such initiatives have been successful in raising levels of training is debatable. Some firms use such schemes as the YTS as sources of cheap labour and relatively few trainees obtain permanent employment. If the Government saw the Youth Training Scheme as an attempt to introduce to Britain a German-style apprenticeship training programme, then it has largely failed. The unions remain sceptical, fearing such schemes will disrupt traditional patterns of recruitment and dilute skills. A big obstacle to the government's attempts to raise the profile of training lies with business itself. Many firms tend to see training as a cost rather than an investment, and a cost that can easily be cut in the pursuit of short-term goals.

**Third party intervention**   Governments have always been willing to inter-vene in those industrial disputes they see as damaging to the nation's economy. The government currently funds the Arbitration, Conciliation and Advisory Service (ACAS), set up in 1974 and given statutory rights under the Employment Protection Act 1975. ACAS consists of a full-time Chairman and nine part-time members made up of equal parts of TUC nominees, CBI nominees and academics. It is staffed by civil servants. Its functions include the following:

- bringing the two sides of an industrial dispute together so that agreement may be reached (conciliation);
- bringing the two sides together but making recommendations for an agreement (mediation);
- making a decision on behalf of the two sides but with their agree-ment (arbitration);
- carrying out an investigation into a major dispute and making recommendations to guide future action (inquiry);
- establishing codes of practice for the conduct of industrial relations.

ACAS is therefore a state mechanism which attempts to influence the conduct of industrial relations without either party having recourse to the use of law.

## The role of the economy

In the 1960s and 1970s there was an unprecedented increase in those involved in personnel work. Membership of the Institute of Personnel Management increased from 4308 members in 1959 to over 10 000 in 1969. It then doubled its membership to 20 194 by 1979. As a rough guide, it is estimated that members of the Institute represent half those involved in personnel.

While we have attributed part of the growth to developments in legislation, there is a clear correlation between personnel management and the state of the economy. In the two decades of full employment prior to the early 1970s considerable emphasis was placed on recruit-ment, selection, training and payment systems, to overcome labour shortages and to assist in the substitution and retention of skilled labour. During the same period the increased bargaining power of the trade-union movement, especially at workplace level, resulted in in-creases in shopfloor collective bargaining and hence an increased work-load for the personnel manager.

Traditional activities of personnel management such as recruitment and training are clearly related to full employment economies. The continued growth of personnel throughout the 1970s is harder to re-concile with the economic expansion argument since it was a period of slow-down and considerable economic problems. However, if we see the growth of the personnel function as a reactive process where organizational responses lag behind the real stimulus, then the growth of the 1970s may be seen as a response to problems first recognized in the late 1950s and early 1960s. Its impact upon personnel management organization extended well into the 1970s.

Given the hypothesis that economic growth and full employment lead to a thriving and active personnel function, then the reverse hypothesis might also be true; that an economic recession will reduce not only the need for recruitment selection and training, but that the negotiating power of trade unions will be impaired, resulting in a reduction of the extent and frequency of collective bargaining negotiations.

The evidence, however, paints a different picture. A study of personnel during a particularly severe recession 1980–2 reported that personnel managers had survived better than most other management groups. New opportunities to demonstrate competence had been created in redundancy management and in achieving lower wage settlements in a generally peaceful industrial relations climate (Guest, 1982). Although the economy picked up in the latter part of the 1980s a further recession occurred at the beginning of the 1990s. Despite these fluctuations, personnel management, as measured by Institute membership, appeared to flourish. By 1993, membership had risen to just over 30 000 with a further 20 000 registered as student members. There could be several explanations for the durability of personnel. As we saw in Chapter 2, structural changes in the economy were especially severe upon traditional manufacturing. Personnel managers clearly suffered job losses in manufacturing, but there has been a growth of opportunities in other sectors, notably the service sector and newer high-tech industries. There has also been an influx of foreign multinationals, many of whom display more sophisticated human resource strategies than their British counterparts. In addition to such changes, new types of employment have emerged with an emphasis on flexibility, bringing with it a demand for training and the management of part-time and contract workers.

In one area, industrial relations, there has been reduction in the traditional activities of collective bargaining and dispute management. Unions are weaker, disputes fewer and settlements tend to be speedier. Nevertheless, where bargaining is still the norm, there has been a decentralization of activities placing more and not less emphasis on the role of workplace industrial relations managers. We have already seen how HRM offers the personnel function new strategic directions and that the British experience is one where HRM is not incompatible with trade-union negotiation. This is amply illustrated at Perkins Diesels (Case 8.2) with the negotiation of new work practices. The Perkins case is also a good example of the work of personnel specialists during a recession.

Economic factors have clearly shaped personnel strategies and these will be examined in the final section in this chapter. In all cases, however, economic influences must be seen in conjunction with the role of the state, the power of trade unions, management ideology and the organization structure. This reinforces the idea that the elements of our model cannot be viewed in isolation.

## Personnel management and the labour force

From our brief review of traditional personnel activities in Table 8.1 we can see that the personnel function interacts with the labour force in two ways. It deals with individuals in the labour market through the activities of manpower planning, recruitment, selection, training and by administering payment and other reward and control systems. Second, it deals with the organized labour force through the mechanisms of joint consultation, collective bargaining and conflict management. We have already referred to these two activities in terms of people processing and industrial relations management. Even with the coming of HRM we may still regard these as the core work of the personnel/HRM function. As we noted in the first section of this chapter, the difference between traditional personnel and HRM is largely one of emphasis. We examine the interaction between the personnel function and the labour force by examining these two aspects of personnel work.

**People processing** Operating within a given labour market, the personnel manager will attempt to fulfil the organization's demand for labour. This will be achieved mainly through the processes of recruitment, selection and training, often within the framework of a manpower plan. In some cases the labour market will act as a total constraint to the extent that severe labour shortages in a given area may cause management to rethink its plans. In other cases the labour market operates as a partial constraint, and attempts will be made to entice workers away from existing jobs by offering them attractive pay packages and opportunities for career development. This can cause high levels of mobility among certain groups with scarce skills in an otherwise depressed labour market. In other cases the firm attempts to change the composition of the labour market, meeting labour shortages by training substitute labour or by attracting certain groups back to work, such as married women with children, by providing working conditions compatible with school hours. The increased use of flexible employment practices has been one of the reasons for the proportion of women in the workforce to rise from 33% in 1951 to 48% in 1990 (Edwards *et al.*, 1992).

The student relying on textbooks may be forgiven for the assumption that personnel management is an exercise in scientific management. This exercise is a matching process between the labour market and the needs of the organization employing a variety of scientifically based techniques of selection, training and employee motivation and retention. The student is confronted by a vast literature expounding such theories and offering a variety of such techniques. However, part of this literature has concentrated upon a critique of these same theories, analyses and techniques, often labelling them as intuitive and subjective. A good illustration of this is to be found in the process of employee selection.

Personnel management textbooks see selection in terms of a matching process between the candidate and the job description. The decision to employ or reject a candidate is ultimately the prerogative of line management, but the administration of the process tends to be carried out by personnel specialists applying scientific principles of structured interviewing and psychological testing.

In most cases there will be a job description resulting from a job analysis. The process of creating a job description will generate criteria against which job candidates will be judged. Managers will use such information to build up stereotypes of 'ideal' candidates. However, the job description could well be dated and in any case, the manager is just as likely to establish criteria based upon his or her own prejudices.

The most popular form of selection method is the interview. Management literature abounds with advice for the would-be interviewer, but such advice owes more to general experience and deductive reasoning than it does to empirical research. There is considerable evidence that the interview is a relatively poor selection device and is particularly poor in terms of cost-effectiveness to the company. However, it is retained because no better method has yet been devised and because it allows management to exercise judgement in the selection process.

If we view other areas of personnel processing we will find much the same story. Attempts by personnel managers to use 'scientific techniques' often adapted from the behaviourial sciences have met with mixed results. This is true of a range of techniques incorporating the use of psychological tests, in selection and placement, appraisal schemes, approaches to training and devising methods of payment to increase worker motivation.

The major problems with using such techniques in people processing are reliability and validity. Reliability refers to the extent to which a measure of consistency can be achieved, as for example in getting interviewers to behave in a similar fashion and ask candidates similar questions. Validity refers to the extent to which a technique used in personnel has some practical value for the organization. Does a selection interview actually discriminate between suitable and unsuitable candidates? Will a training programme lead to improved worker performance?

Because of such problems, personnel managers have difficulty in proving that the work they do contributes in a measurable way to the effectiveness of the organization. For example, the results of a management development programme may not be apparent for a number of years, if at all, and many of the managers may have left the organization by that time. The difficulty of personnel proving its worth is a theme developed when we examine the relationship between personnel management and an organization's goals later in this chapter. It is not surprising that many personnel managers feel safer dealing with the day-to-day firefighting of industrial relations problems than devising policies and procedures where the outcome is uncertain. It is to industrial relations that we next turn our attention.

## Industrial relations management

We can identify four major activities associated with industrial relations management.

**The recognition of trade unions**   This involves both the recognition of the employee right to organize and the recognition of the union right to represent employees in such matters as wage negotiation. In some industries recognition has been slow. The recognition of the National Union of Bank Employees by the major clearing banks was only achieved in 1967 after considerable disruption and eventual strike action. In other cases management will positively encourage their employees to join trade unions since they view a healthy union membership as contributing to the stability of workplace relations. This acceptance and encouragement has been a major factor in trade-union growth and consequently the development of the personnel function. In recent years there have been new variations on the theme of recognition.

A key approach in companies such as IBM (as illustrated in Case 8.1), Hewlett-Packard and Marks & Spencer is the development of employment relations strategies that do not involve trade unions. The growth of Japanese firms in Britain and their preference for company unions has led to the establishment of single union agreements being made in companies such as Nissan (Case 2.3) and Sanyo. Under such agreements management will allow only one trade union to represent all employees in the workforce. This has caused considerable consternation in the trade-union movement, but agreements have been reached between Nissan and the Amalgamated Union of Engineering Workers (AUEW). The News International case (Chapter 1) is an interesting one. A single union deal was originally agreed between the management and the EETPU (the electricians' union). Subsequently the union has been de-recognized for bargaining purposes. Such de-recognition has been widely predicted in the face of weakened unions and alternative HRM strategies. The evidence suggests otherwise with management in unionized firms still prepared to enter into collective bargaining negotiations, perhaps encouraged by their relative increase in power.

**Collective bargaining**   As we can see in Table 8.1, this involves management and unions in the negotiation of wages and conditions. The growth of localized bargaining in the 1950s and 1960s widened both the role of personnel managers and shop stewards as actual negotiators. There is every indication that decentralization has increased in the late 1980s and early 1990s. The activities of personnel management in collective bargaining include research, assisting in policy formulation, negotiation and in general developing a climate to assist the bargaining process by encouraging inter-union cooperation and minimizing areas of avoidable conflict. In addition personnel managers provide information and facilities for shop stewards, in accordance with the Industry Act 1975 and the Employment Protection Act 1975.

Both management and unions have resisted the introduction of legally binding contracts as the outcome of collective bargaining. However, the changing climate of single union agreements has been accompanied by an increase in contractual bargaining.

**Disputes and grievance procedure**  The process of collective bargaining inevitably involves a degree of conflict. Many firms operate a disputes procedure to resolve such conflicts. In most cases the formalization and complexity of the disputes procedure is directly related to the size of the firm. A breakdown in negotiation can result in a strike, although the occurrence of these is rare, contrary to popular opinion. Most disputes procedures have provisions for third-party intervention, such as the use of ACAS.

Those firms who favour single union agreements, such as Nissan, tend also to favour a new approach to disputes procedure. This new approach usually includes the following.

- a 'legally binding contract';
- a 'peace' clause whereby the employees agree not to strike and the employers agree not to lock workers out for the duration of the contract and while the new contract is renegotiated;
- an agreement on pendulum arbitration, whereby the arbitrator must opt for one side or the other.

Such provisions limit the use of the strike weapon to an irrevocable breakdown in the negotiation of a new contract, and a recourse to pendulum arbitration is an attempt to avoid unwanted compromise. Much has been written about such measures, but there is little indication that they will represent a popular model for industrial relations management.

**Administering procedures relating to employee participation**  These can involve a sophisticated arrangement of works councils and employee committees, as employed by the John Lewis partnership. For many firms, however, it involves no more than the administration of an employee suggestion scheme. As we saw in the first section of this chapter, HRM favours employee involvement over collective bargaining. This has led to a renewed interest in forms of participation such as works councils and briefing groups.

In 1980 a survey of personnel management in manufacturing industry and the health service found that those working in personnel regarded industrial relations as their most important activity. In a private-sector manufacturing concern, four of the seven most commonly performed tasks involved industrial relations and included, giving advice to managers on their legal obligations as employers, operating discipline, grievance and disputes procedures, taking part in negotiations and acting as the industrial-relations specialist at the workplace (Guest and Horwood, 1980).

Since then of course, as we have noted, personnel management has been undergoing shifts in emphasis. This is especially true for industrial relations, although we should be cautious about the speed and extent of that change. There may be a number of possible models of operating industrial relations at the level of the firm. We will view these when we discuss personnel strategies at the end of this chapter.

## Personnel management and technology

In Chapter 2 we examined the impact of technology and in particular technical change on jobs. We deal with two areas of significance to personnel/HRM; training and industrial relations, although the type of technology and changes in technology have implications for recruitment, selection and payment systems as well.

Technical change invariably results in a mismatch between the needs of the firm and the skills of the workforce. For example, there are more jobs in Scotland in micro-electronics than in coal and iron and steel, its more traditional industrial base. Some firms tackle the mismatch by the use of outside contractors, but longer-term cost-effectiveness will probably lie in developing training programmes. Such training focuses not only on the development of 'hi-tech' skills but upon general workforce orientation towards using new technology, as in using computer terminals to input data and upon more general management training. The creation of a more flexible workforce has been identified as a training priority for many organizations.

The commonly accepted view of the impact of technical change on industrial relations, doubtless fuelled by media coverage of events at places such as Wapping (Chapter 1), is that it created problems, largely because trade unions resist change. This resistance is inevitably linked to fears over job losses, deskilling and increased management control. It was such issues that concerned the Fleet Street printworkers for several years in their opposition to photocomposition.

However, certain factors may temper this perspective. The TUC has adopted a stated policy of influencing the direction of new technology to maximize its benefits and minimize its costs. A survey by Daniel (1987) concluded that the reaction of most workers to technical change has been favourable. He found that technical change was equated with investment and optimism, and was often seen as a route to better jobs and higher wages.

There is however general agreement that in many companies the level of consultation over technical change issues is low. This was a major cause of the failure of the TUC's attempt to introduce 'New Technology Agreements' in the 1980s and a major cause of problems in general.

The nature of the technology offers some groups of workers more bargaining power than others because they operate and control key technologies. This power has an impact on the negotiating process. A number of disputes in the 1970s in British Leyland were centred on the toolroom, where stoppages involving relatively small numbers of the total workforce caused the entire operation to cease since those who manufacture the tools for a particular industry are central to the entire operation. Mineworkers have traditionally used their position as the providers of an essential fuel supply as a strong bargaining weapon. In their disputes of 1972 and 1974 the National Union of Mineworkers used an overtime ban as a tactical weapon to reduce coal stocks in the power stations before calling for an 'all-out' strike. The resulting power cuts and their impact on the rest of industry was a significant influence in the collective bargaining process. Not all workers enjoy bargaining power as a result of controlling key technologies. The postal workers in their dispute of 1971 had their case weakened by firms using alternative courier services for mail and by making greater use of alternative technology in the form of the telephone service.

## Cultural influences

We have noted the considerable influences exerted by the state and the level of economic activity upon personnel/HRM activities. It is therefore not surprising that differences in practice can also be traced to cultural variations. Differences may be observed between the operation of personnel management in different countries as the following illustrations will show.

In Britain the function clearly reflects the growth of trade-union activity and a general preference for localized collective bargaining. In the USA the activities of personnel are shaped by prevailing social attitudes which favour the use of law and which tend to be distrustful of trade unions. As a consequence much greater use is made of the law in such matters as the employment contract, equal opportunities and trade union collective bargaining. In addition there is much lower trade union membership than in Britain and therefore much less evidence of traditional industrial relations activity by personnel managers. In fact some companies in the USA have developed personnel strategies which actively discourage trade-union organizations and focus on keeping the unions out by offering attractive welfare provisions and pay packages. In Germany, with its highly centralized system of collective bargaining, industrial relations is not a major concern of the personnel manager. Specialist management functions such as personnel play a much smaller role in Germany than elsewhere, a correspondingly higher status being accorded to line management. There would appear to be little interest in the techniques of personnel management such as the use of job analysis and job descriptions. In major companies in Japan, personnel policies reflect the operation of a dual-labour market, bestowing considerable advantages on a privileged group of employees, including lifetime employment and a whole range of company welfare provisions. (The section on Japanese Management in Chapter 2 has a fuller account.)

Despite these differences there is some evidence of practices converging. We have already noted the influence of Japanese companies in Britain and the interest in single union, 'no-strike' agreements. Many American companies operating in Britain tend to be non-unionized and the type of strategies employed by firms like Hewlett-Packard and IBM (Cases 3.5 and 8.1) have gained currency among personnel practitioners in Britain.

The development of HRM is central to this theme of convergence. The assumption that economic and structural change will push firms towards a common HRM model was investigated as part of a study of HRM practices across Europe (Brewster and Bournois, 1991; Brewster *et al.*, 1991). The study found considerable variation in HRM practice, particularly between Britain and the rest of Europe. The idea of a common model was challenged by different national institutional and legal frameworks. Guest (1990) goes further and puts forward a case that HRM is probably culturally specific to the USA. He likens the core characteristics of HRM to those of the 'American Dream' with its emphasis on individualism, hard work, reward, and fighting the frontier, which in this case is represented both by inefficient practices and Japanese competition. Nonetheless we have seen instances where HRM strategies do work in a non-USA, and indeed a British setting. For an explanation of this we must return to the discussion in Chapter 2 concerning comparative management. In most national settings management practices are derived from a number of influences, some of which will be cultural, while others will relate to more common themes of technology, markets and organizational size.

On a different level altogether, one similarity would appear to exist. Wherever personnel management is practised it has been traditionally dogged by a low status image. In the following section we will explore reasons for this and in our discussion of personnel strategies suggest why this may be changing.

## Organizational aspects of human resource management

In this section we will view the relationship between organization size and personnel activities and focus on the relationship between the personnel function and other management activities in the organization structure. A major theme to emerge in personnel's dealings with management from other functional areas is that of goal conflict. Attempts to resolve such conflict are currently focused upon organizational culture and HRM. We will deal with this aspect at the end of the section.

### Human resource management and organization size

The relationship between the growth of the firm and the development of formalization, differentiation and specialization has already been discussed in Chapter 3. The development of personnel management departments in firms during the early part of this century can be clearly attributed to the increasing size of the organization. A control mechanism was needed, particularly in the areas of recruitment and payment systems, giving rise to specialist positions of 'wages officer' and 'labour officer'. Such positions concerned themselves with recruitment, discipline, timekeeping and general administration of the payment system including the control of bonus payments. This growth of the size of firms was also a major factor in the changes in collective bargaining, placing more emphasis on bargaining within individual firms rather than at industry level. We have already noted how this resulted in the creation of industrial relations specialists.

A comprehensive survey of UK practices noted that whereas only 7% of firms employing fewer than 50 people had personnel specialists, the proportion rose to 93% for firms employing over 2000 people (Daniel and Millward, 1983). Furthermore, we can see that the increasing size of the firm also results in the increasing specialization within the personnel function itself. For example at Ford Motor Company the function is split into two main areas. One group deals with day-to-day industrial relations issues while the other group deals with such issues as training and management development. Within this broad split further specializations occur.

## Human resource management, organization structure and goals

There is growing evidence, not only in Britain, but throughout Europe, that the personnel function has become decentralized. This relates in part to the increasing adoption of HRM approaches with their emphasis on a greater involvement of line managers. However, in Britain, decentralization has also occurred in those firms which retain traditional collective bargaining. A major reason offered for this change is the decreasing role played by employers' associations. They play much less of a role in all aspects of business in Britain than elsewhere. For example, major car companies such as Ford, Vauxhall and Peugeot-Talbot have opted out of membership of their employers' association in Britain, but they have retained membership of associations in other European countries where they operate (Edwards *et al.*, 1992). Despite the trend towards decentralization, several large organizations such as Marks & Spencer retain a large centralized presence.

The spread of HRM practices has been cited for the increase in power and influence among personnel practitioners. Torrington (1989) tends to support that view, but remains somewhat sceptical.

> Most of those in the personnel function who espouse Human Resource Management are doing so in search of enhanced status and power. With the obsession about innovation that currently pervades management thinking, a change of label is a useful indication of innovation, even if you are not too sure there is anything different in the package.
>
> (Torrington, 1989, p. 64)

While there is considerable disagreement as to whether power and influence have increased, there is no disagreement that traditionally the personnel function did not enjoy high status within many organizations. We can identify three problem areas:

- conflict between personnel and other functional managers (these are sometimes referred to generically as line managers);

- the difficulties encountered by personnel managers in proving their worth to the organization either because of the suspicion of line management towards new techniques or because of the way personnel organize their work;
- conflict within personnel management itself between professional and organizational goals.

In general the research has focused on case studies where problems have been identified in the relationship between personnel and other departments. Little is known about how successful personnel departments operate and how they successfully integrate with other functional areas. This may well give a somewhat stereotyped view of the personnel function and ignore a wide range of situations where personnel managers are happy with their role and are seen to be effective. The various cases should be viewed within the limitation.

The line and staff model has often been used to analyse the personnel function, depicting personnel operating in an advisory capacity only.

> The personnel department here is as it should be, as service to the line. For example, if we want more labour they get it, train it, and arrange for it to be paid. They provide information for negotiating too, but I do the real negotiating.
>
> (General Works Manager quoted in Legge, 1978, p. 51)

Legge sees this relationship between personnel and line management as a basis for conflict in that line have a 'confused, hazy and/or stereotyped perception of the potential nature and scope of a personnel department's activities' and 'tend to consider that personnel departments are "out of touch" with the kind of problems and constraints which face them' (Legge, 1978, p. 52). In particular, other managers

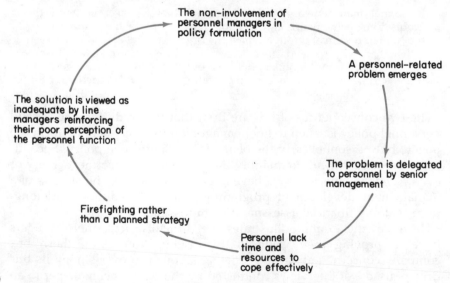

*Figure 8.3* A vicious circle depicting the relationship between personnel and line management. *Source:* adapted from Legge (1978).

feel that personnel do not identify as closely as they do with the profit goals of the organization.

In her case studies Legge saw a vicious circle operating, as illustrated in Figure 8.3. Personnel are not involved in planning and decision-making, resulting in human resource problems that are left to personnel to sort out; pressure of time and lack of resources lead to crisis management resulting in line management having a poor perception of the personnel function and hence its non-involvement in decision-making. The circle is reinforced by the failure on the part of some line managers to recognize the need for a specialist role for personnel, since many personnel activities are carried out by all managers, as in the case of selection and training. Attempts to break free of the circle by personnel specialists adopting specialized techniques based on the behaviourial sciences are often rebuffed by a suspicious line management. In this way carefully constructed appraisal schemes flounder in the face of line management opposition. As a result, Legge sees many personnel managers 'opt for an easy life' and concentrate on a more acceptable welfare role.

In a study of personnel management in manufacturing and the health service, personnel themselves contributed to the kind of problems Karen Legge outlined. Personnel managers enjoyed crisis management and took on a variety of different activities to boost their credibility in the eyes of the rest of management. This resulted in too broad and too heavy a workload with the consequence of ineffectiveness and in-competence. Personnel management were thus unable to contribute effectively to the goals of the organization as identified by line management and re-enforced the vicious circle (Guest and Horwood, 1980).

The question of effectiveness and personnel proving their worth was also raised by Legge.

> Personnel management by definition, is chiefly concerned with the acquisition, maintenance and development of one of the resources (ie, the human resource) through which the organisational ends are achieved rather than with the ends themselves. They are concerned with means rather than ends and inputs rather than outputs, and in situations where there is difficulty in determining the relationship between the two.
>
> (Legge, 1978, p. 60)

The two consequences of this are first, that the credit for a successful personnel policy is taken to line management who actually perform the policy, but personnel carry the blame for an ineffective policy. Second, it is extremely difficult to quantify the outcome of personnel activity or even isolate its effect. As we have already mentioned, the success of a management development programme may be so diffuse and long-term that any financial assessment is impossible.

The following example illustrates the difficulty personnel managers have in proving their value to the organization. A northern bus company concerned about the growing labour turnover among its bus drivers used exit interviews conducted by the personnel manager in an attempt to reduce the number who actually left. The interviews which were conducted whenever a bus driver gave notice of terminating his contract appeared to have very little impact for the first six months, but then the numbers leaving began to fall. Closer examination of this particular situation revealed that during the period when turnover was highest, a bus company in a neighbouring area was recruiting at a higher basic wage, while the time of falling turnover coincided with a downturn in the economy when all job opportunities were much scarcer. In other words, personnel often deal with external forces outside their control.

We can now see that the first two problem areas are linked. The conflict between personnel managers and other managers is a function of personnel's seeming inability to prove their worth.

Our third problem area concerns the potential conflict between organizational and professional goals. Personnel managers are popularly portrayed as a group in the middle, owing allegiance to both the needs of the workforce and the needs of the organization they serve. As we saw from the IPM's definition of personnel management at the beginning of this chapter, there is no conflict in that the good professional is concerned 'to achieve efficiency and justice, neither of which can be achieved without the other'. It is clear that professional high ideals can conflict with the daily pressures of getting the job done. In practice, however, such conflict is rarely felt by personnel practitioners. They generally see themselves as part of the management group and as such subscribe to management goals, even though they do not always operate as line management would like.

The kind of problems identified above can be tackled through the creation of an organization culture which stresses cooperation and consensus. It is to this we now turn.

## The role of organizational culture

We have seen how personnel managers reflect the culture of a particular enterprise. In general terms the activities of personnel, especially those concerned with recruitment, selection and training, ensure that employees fit the prevailing culture of the firm. This takes on a more fundamental aspect in those firms that have identified a mission and build their organization culture around that mission. We deal with such aspects more fully when we deal with organizational cultures in Chapter 3. In such firms the personnel function assumes a role of major importance.

Certain local authorities have made considerable attempts to change the culture of their organizations in accordance with (usually) a guiding political ideology. The focus is usually on the criteria used in the recruitment and selection of new staff, with a special concern for equal opportunities, as the following job advertisement reveals:

As part of Lambeth's Equal Opportunities Policy, applications are welcome from people regardless of race, creed, nationality, age, sex, sexual orientation or responsibility for children or dependents.

(*Guardian*, 20 Nov 1985)

We can see from Case 8.1 that IBM lays great store by selecting the right type of individual, investing heavily in management training and establishing excellent conditions of employment. In cases 2.3 and 3.5 in Nissan and Hewlett-Packard respectively, the importance of selection again emerges. In Hewlett-Packard the culture is sustained by paying attention to management styles as in their technique of 'management by wandering around'. In all these cases the senior management see employment relations as a major route to establishing the kind of company they want.

We have seen already that the development of organizational culture which stresses commitment, quality and flexibility is a central device of HRM. For many organizations this implies a strategic change. It is to the notion of personnel/HRM strategy that we now turn.

## Human resource management strategies

In this section we examine strategic approaches to personnel/HRM. We do so at an interesting time with developments in HRM. We have already noted that HRM not only places great emphasis upon a strategic approach to human resource issues, but also that such strategies aim for total integration within the corporate objectives of the enterprise. Such a strategic approach is a relatively recent phenomenon. Just over a decade ago an examination of a variety of companies revealed that specific personnel and industrial relations policies are notable by their absence. From her case studies Legge concluded:

> In company decision-making, the personnel management considerations involved in production, marketing and finance decisions were not so much overruled (although this also occurred . . .) as went by default.
>
> (Legge, 1978, p. 37)

She noted that where policy did exist it was fragmented, short term and largely reactive. Traditionally, where personnel strategies have existed they have been based around manpower planning. We shall examine this first before attempting to map out some alternative models.

### Manpower planning

This process is concerned with matching future manpower requirements with future manpower availability and involves consideration of both the quantity and the quality of the labour force including the analysis of such factors as the age profile of the staff. A variety of techniques have been used from simple demand-supply models to more sophisticated statistical models of the type used by the Civil Service to plan its own manpower requirements. The output of a manpower planning exercise should set the guidelines for personnel strategies in recruitment, selection, training, retirement and so on. The resulting strategies will vary depending on the relationship of the predicted future demand to predicted future supply.

> Manpower planning represents the basic strategic planning device of personnel management. It enables management to forecast future manpower requirements against current manpower resources and developing strategies to cope with the gap between the two.
>
> **KEY CONCEPT 8.4**
> *Manpower planning*

For example, a firm whose demand for labour exceeds the predicted supply may have to consider changes in its payment strategies with a view to attract more recruits or investigate the possibilities of introducing new technology to replace labour. Where the existing labour supply exceeds the predicted future demands then plans may have to be formulated for early retirement, redundancy or perhaps looking to marketing strategies to increase the demand for the firm's goods and services. Even where demand and supply are evenly matched, then a manpower planning exercise may well give management useful insights into the nature of labour utilization and suggest where improvements can be made.

The reality, of course is much more complex than the kind of model illustrated above. Such complexities are often the result of long lead times and the impact of other variables over which management have little control. The planning of the supply of future medical doctors is an exercise that must incorporate projected birth rates, death rates, take account of the age profile of the nation and examine trends in disease and illness. Given that the training time of future doctors is at least seven years then allowance must be made for drop out rates along the way as well. Even if these complexities are overcome then the exercise can be jeopardized by national cut-backs in health care spending or changes in EC law which extends the pool of available labour.

In the late 1980s management were fed considerable information about 'the demographic time-bomb', a forecast of a declining birth rate and its likely impact on the recruitment of school leavers in the 1990s. Some firms such as Ford Motor Company set up programmes to counteract a shortfall in the future supply of labour by building closer relationships with local schools and by projecting on improved image to the local community. In practice, any likely impact of a declining birth rate was mitigated by a recession and an increasing trend towards smaller workforces. Rather than scratching around for new recruits most companies were more active in making employees redundant.

## Links to corporate strategy

As a result of interest in HRM, there has been renewed discussion of the relationship between personnel/HRM strategy and the corporate objectives of the enterprise. There are obvious examples where a change in business strategy leads to a corresponding change in the personnel strategy. Survival in a recession may depend on either cutting back on operations or developing new areas of operation. In a recession clear policies may need to emerge on redundancy, as we saw with IBM in Case 8.1, or more flexible ways of working are introduced to cut costs. The development of new products and markets calls for new skills which may necessitate recruiting new staff or retraining existing employees. Whenever the 'rules' of the business change there is generally an implication for personnel policy. In higher education, new arrangements for funding have placed emphasis upon the research and publications record of the academic staff. Many of the newer universities, created from the old polytechnic sector, are attempting to build up their research and publications record through the recruitment of staff who can offer them those skills and who can bring with them a healthy publications record. The emphasis is therefore shifting away from teaching to research. This has implications not only for recruitment and selection, but the promotion and development policies for existing staff.

Different product markets call for variations in personnel/HRM strategy. A simple way of illustrating this is to use the Boston Consulting Group matrix that we introduced in Chapter 4. This seems to have found renewed favour among personnel/HRM academics (see, for example, Purcell, 1989).

In a 'cash-cow' product market the emphasis is upon stable, low-cost production to 'milk' the profits. Personnel policies associated with 'cash-cows' are those which ensure stability and continuity and include formalized procedures for job evaluation, a focus on welfare provision to retain staff, and, where unions are involved, highly structured collective bargaining. 'Cash-cows' may be associated with a need to keep costs to a minimum and may be associated with the use of a flexible labour force and high numbers of part-timers. However, as Purcell points out, the very profitability of 'cash-cows' may lead to complacency such as overmanning.

Where 'stars' and 'question marks' are concerned the emphasis shifts to operating a more flexible approach. Personnel priorities become the selection and development of innovative staff and the creation of teams across different functional specialisms. The long-term uncertainty associated with both 'stars' and 'question marks' places emphasis upon the management of change.

For 'dogs' the focus turns to cutting losses. This may mean redundancy programmes and it may involve retraining, transfer and even relocation.

## New approaches to strategy?

> The pressure on human resource managers to be strategic is almost as intense now as the campaign to persuade us to eat healthily. We all believe it is a good thing to be strategic – career progressive for ourselves, prestigious for our profession and it might even do our organizations good as well.
>
> (Herriot and Pinder, 1992, p. 36)

The emergence of HRM was viewed by some as a strategic lifeline to a group of personnel practitioners without a clear strategy. However, we

**Unitarist**
*Traditional unitarist*
*Sophisticated unitarist*

**Pluralist**
*New industrial relations pluralist*
*Opportunistic pluralist*
*Sophisticated pluralist*
*Traditional pluralist*

*Figure 8.4* Approaches to personnel/HRM.

have seen that the classic HRM approach is perhaps more talked about than practised and that there are significant variations. We will attempt to identify some of those variations by constructing a model of personnel/HRM practice in a British context.

We present a model in Figure 8.4, which is based upon the work of Fox (1974a, 1974b), Purcell and Sisson (1983) and Guest (1989, 1990). The model identifies two broad categories, unitarist and pluralist. The unitarist approach emphasizes shared goals while the pluralist approach acknowledges that different groups within the organization may have different goals. We have identified several variations.

The **traditional unitarists** represent management whose predominant view is the opposition to all kinds of trade union groups. Such a strategy can result in direct confrontation as was seen in the much publicized Grunwick dispute of 1976 when the managing director of a film processing plant in Southall denied union recognition to a group to Asian Workers. The ensuing dispute had racial as well as industrial relations implications. The 1980s and 1990s has seen traditional unitarists engage more readily in redundancy programmes and be more willing to use contract labour (Millward *et al.*, 1992). It was predicted that the political and economic changes of the 1980s would encourage the traditional unitarists to emerge from their closets embodied in 'macho-management' stereotypes, with Michael Edwardes (ex of British Leyland) and Ian McGregor (ex of British Steel and the Coal Board) as the hero figures. However such stereotypes perhaps owe more to media distortion than accurate analysis.

The **sophisticated unitarists** are those companies like IBM and Hewlett-Packard, that are the role models for HRM practice. In such companies considerable time and effort is taken to ensure workforce commitment to overall company objectives. Such companies are typified by fairly sophisticated personnel policies in selection, training, reward systems and employee involvement.

**New industrial relations pluralists** are to be found in those firms that espouse the 'single union, no strike philosophy' that we have encountered earlier in the chapter. The model for such companies are the Japanese transplants such as Nissan and Toyota. Many such companies attempt to involve their employees through a works council or similar institution. Probably many managers in this category are aspiring unitarists.

The **opportunistic pluralists** represent those managers in unionized firms who have used the economic and political climate as an opportunity to roll back the influence of the trade unions. They have found no need to adopt the aggressive anti-union stance of the traditional unitarists and are still prepared to work within a pluralist framework. As Kessler and Bayliss write,

> most managers took the line that since they could get what they wanted through negotiations or by acting unilaterally, there was no need to attack the unions.
>
> (Kessler and Bayliss, 1992b, p. 35)

The **sophisticated pluralists** on the other hand see consultation and negotiation with trade unions as the keystone of their personnel policies. Such firms have well-established procedures for determining pay and conditions and often have mechanisms for employee participation. Managers in this category see that change is necessary but prefer it to be agreed with employees rather than imposed upon them. Ferner and Hyman (1992) found such an approach more common in European countries other than Britain, but it can be found here as well. Most of the major oil companies, British Airways and some local governments exhibit such strategies. Perkins Diesels (Case 8.3) also see negotiation as an important part of organization change. The sophisticated pluralist approach suggests that HRM is not incompatible with trade unionism.

**Traditional pluralists** tend not to be strategically oriented preferring instead to adopt the standard reactive response to problems. They manage by 'firefighting', and as such fit in well with our illustrations of personnel management when we discussed the influence of organizational structure and goals upon the personnel/HRM function.

As we have mentioned throughout this chapter, there is much discussion of firms shifting towards an HRM approach. The above classification implies that managers have not one, but several models from which to choose. However, as we saw in our discussion of organizational culture in Chapter 3, culture change is particularly difficult. The adoption of HRM policies is not only costly, but may well meet with resistance from the shopfloor as well as management. It is not by chance that HRM strategies are often associated with greenfield sites. Nonetheless there is enough evidence to suggest that personnel are reacting to changing circumstances. The relative weakness of trade unions has reduced the need for extensive exercises in collective bargaining and conflict management. We have seen how some managers have used this as an opportunity to reduce manning levels and increase labour flexibility. In declining industries there is a reduction in recruitment and training and a focus on redundancy and early retirement. In growth areas there is an increased concern for the selection, development and retention of a core group of employees.

We can see from these models that there is considerable variation in personnel strategy and that the explanation for the variation is a function of a number of key variables. These are the variables that form the basis of the Business in Context model namely, the state, the

The Perkins Engine Group is owned by the Canadian firm, Varity, a company which also controls Massey Ferguson. The company makes diesel engines of all types ranging from seven to 1500 brake horsepower. Its main manufacturing operation, Peterborough Engines, is based in the town of the same name and currently employs nearly three-quarters of the total workforce. Despite the acquisition of Rolls Royce Diesel Engines in 1984 and Lesley Gardner Diesels in 1986, the overall size of the company has been reduced from over 10 000 in the 1970s to 4900 in 1989. Such a change has not been possible without a significant change in personnel strategies and in the work of the personnel function.

In the late 1970s the company appeared to be in a healthy position. The demand for its products was high and the concern was to operate at full capacity. The plant was working seven days a week and the 10 000 employees were working an average of 10% overtime per person. The company was turning out 1000 diesel engine a day with 86% of these for the export market. The company adopted fairly typical personnel and industrial-relations strategies for the engineering industry. Payment-by-results was the norm, training tended to focus on an engineering apprenticeship programme, and industrial-relations negotiation was highly centralized. The main trade union at Perkins (the AUEW) was strong, with a high membership among shop-floor employees. There was a high number of short unofficial disputes that were highly localized. The high demand for the company's product meant that stoppages had to be avoided at all costs. The strategy adopted by the company was for a central personnel department to handle all industrial-relations matters, including the negotiation for local disputes in a bid to formalize procedures and take grievances away from their immediate location. As a consequence, local line management was seldom involved in industrial relations and related personnel issues.

In 1980 the demand for diesel engines fell sharply. In response the management opted for a strict control of all overtime working; the introduction of some short-time working; the setting-up of a series of programmes to introduce changes in working practice that would enhance the competitiveness of the firm; and a mixture of voluntary and compulsory redundancy.

The urgency of change was all the greater because of the company's heavy reliance on export markets and hence competition from diesel engine manufacturers all over the world, who were also competing for a declining market share. The management recognized that such changes could not be made without consultation with the trade unions and the workforce, so that communication became the key to the implementation of the strategic changes. The changes were brought about through a variety of methods.

● All changes were negotiated with the trade union and the AUEW participated fully in the exercise. The union recognized that survival of the firm was the issue, but found the dilemma of protecting jobs for some while sanctioning the redundancy of others difficult to reconcile with traditional trade-union practices. The redundancy issue was particularly difficult in that management could not afford to let all those go who wanted to under a generous voluntary scheme. The financial burden would be too high and such programmes might leave the company understaffed in certain key areas. Compulsory redundancy was therefore inevitable with the subsequent difficult negotiations and disputes.

● The union had also to agree to new work practices. These generally involved the

**CASE 8.3**
*The Perkins Engine Group*

broadening of jobs and the introduction of more flexible work methods through the ending of demarcation agreements. Discussion and negotiation on this issue were specific to individual departments and sections, effectively decentralizing industrial relations. Line management became much more involved in personnel matters as the emphasis on the introduction of new work practices was shifted to man-management at the local level.

- There was a concern that all employees received a clear picture of the threats facing the company and fear that information could easily be distorted. The director took it upon himself to brief personally all senior management and trade-union leaders. Team briefings were held throughout the organization. A company video was produced which examined the current position and explained the need for change. A training-school programme was set up which gave sessions on the firm's position and encouraged feedback.

- A 'Fair Day's Work Charter' was produced which stressed the need for all employees, both staff and hourly paid, to work for the whole day; to achieve output and quality targets set by management; to suggest ways of improving work methods and equipment; and to work cooperatively.

By 1982 employment levels had been reduced to 6000, but it was decided that the strategy had to continue throughout the 1980s, despite the acquisition of new plants such as Rolls Royce. Redundancy became an annual exercise with the usual mix of voluntary and compulsory to preserve key skills. Three new strategies emerged.

First, a major reorganization took place. The company was restructured around autonomous strategic business units operating as independent profit centres. Senior management are given considerable responsibility and scope to enhance the competitiveness of their business unit. Entrepreneurship is encouraged and a fair proportion of senior management salary is tied to performance. There are plans to extend this scheme to all employees at some future date.

Second, considerable emphasis has been placed on the training of employees to widen their range of skills to enhance flexibility and to increase the general level of skill throughout the organization. The company's programme was considered successful enough for them to win a National Training Award in 1987.

Third, new investments have been made in automation to improve quality and reduce staffing costs. Assistance with modernization has been obtained by the company participating in an EC funded project for the furtherance of technology transfer by the dissemination of operating experience and best practice.

As a result of the various changes the company has become much leaner, focusing on the employment of skilled, flexible employees.

(*Source*: Jackson, 1983; Company Information, 1988)

economy, culture, technology, the labour force, organization size, structure, goals and ownership.

## Summary

The role and activities of human resource management (HRM) have emerged largely as a reaction to some problem or crisis and the development of the function is clearly related to economic growth, the increasing size of organizations, government legislation and policy, the growth of the labour movement and developments in collective bargaining. Expectations of the decline of the function in the face of an economy in recession and the decline in numbers and influence of the trade union movement are, as yet, premature. A new role is emerging which gives the former personnel management a new name, HRM, and a new focus, which stresses strategic management. At present, evidence as to the widespread existence and influence of the new role is mixed.

Focus on the activity of HRM in the UK reveals an historic preoccupation with industrial relations, while an analysis of other types of activity reveals a largely intuitive and subjective approach behind a scientific façade.

Traditionally personnel managers have had low status as a result of their historic association with a welfare role and the fact that most of their activities can be carried out by all managers.

Such analyses at the level of the firm may well explain a lack of personnel strategy beyond the basic manpower planning, although initiatives in the direct of HRM may well alter this state of affairs. However, perhaps too much emphasis has been placed upon the problems of the role and more evidence is needed of effective operation and, in particular, the effectiveness of newly styled HRM policies. Indeed, many firms are displaying a greater concern for productivity and cost-effectiveness and are de-emphasizing traditional industrial relations. Traditional approaches can still be found, however in many firms.

## Further reading

An interesting analysis of the role of the personnel specialist that is still relevant today is offered by K. Legge, *Power, Innovation and Problem-solving in Personnel Management* (McGraw-Hill, 1978). A more practical approach to HRM is provided by D. Torrington and L. Hall, *Personnel Management: A New Approach* (Prentice Hall, 1991). Good sources for the change from personnel to HRM are J. Storey (ed.), *New Perspectives on Human Resource Management* (Routledge, 1989), a series of excellent readings, and J. Storey, *Developments in the Management of Human Resources: An Analytical Review* (Basil Blackwell, 1992). A readable approach to industrial relations, including all the more recent developments, is offered by S. Kessler and F. Bayliss, *Contemporary British Industrial Relations* (Macmillan, 1992), while a sweeping review of European developments is provided by A. Ferner and R. Hyman (eds), *Industrial Relations in the New Europe* (Basil Blackwell, 1992).

## Discussion

1   Is there a case for the elimination of all personnel specialists, so that the function can be performed by all managers.

2   Assess the role of the state in the development of the personnel and HRM function. How has that role changed and what has been the impact since 1980?

3   In what way have economic changes affected what personnel/HRM managers do, and the way they go about their activities?

4   How significant is industrial relations today? What changes do you foresee in the main activities?

5   What are the main sources of tension between personnel/HRM and other management groups? What strategies are available to reduce such tensions?

6   To what extent is HRM a separate activity from personnel management?

7   How would you establish a manpower plan for (a) a small expanding computer software firm, (b) a medium-sized firm manufacturing electrical components for the car industry and (c) a new university from the former polytechnic sector? What key issues emerge in each case?

8   Examine the key environmental, organizational and strategic issues in each of the three cases offered in this chapter? What lessons are to be learnt by other firms from the situations faced by these three companies?

9   Do HRM policies need to vary for the public as opposed to the private sector?

# Finance and accounting

In this chapter we examine the role played by the finance and accounting function in the operation of a business. We identify three main functions: the raising of funds or financial management; the contribution of accounting to management control and decision-making, often referred to as management accounting; and the function of financial reporting. We show these three elements in Figure 9.1, and deliberately portray them as overlapping activities. For example, a management which decides on a strategy of business expansion into new markets and new process technologies (a decision based on management accounting calculations) will need to present accounting information to a bank or another potential investor (financial reporting) to persuade them to back the expansion with the necessary capital (financial management).

Accounting procedures and processes are very much a product of the organizational and wider environments in which they operate. We will examine the various economic, legal and social influences on the finance and accounting function, and look at variations resulting from the size of the organization, ownership patterns and organization structure. We shall also look at the accounting practices of large multi-divisional companies by examining the procedures for cost allocation and transfer pricing. We end the chapter by giving a broad overview on the contribution of finance and accounting strategies to overall management strategy.

Throughout this chapter it is the intention to present accounting not as a series of technical calculations but as a management function that is influenced significantly by those who prepare and use accounting information. For example, the determination and disclosure of profit levels will be guided by regulations governing accounting practice. It may also be influenced by forthcoming wage negotiations with trade unions and with a view to minimizing liability for tax. Budgets are determined by management to guide future activities in accordance with plans. The process of budget-setting and resource allocation is also, in many organizations, a product of organizational politics, power and influence.

It is not our intention to give an introduction to bookkeeping and

*Figure 9.1* Finance and accounting activities.

various accounting techniques. There are a range of suitable introductory books that students may consult and we recommend some at the end of this chapter. For those seeking a much broader coverage of the finance and accounting issues in organizations, you should refer to the accompanying accounting text in this series by Berry and Jarvis (1994). Many of the issues are also dealt with in more depth in the series economics text by Neale and Haslam (1994).

## Finance and accounting in business

Accountants form the largest professional group in Britain, and, numerically at least, are much more significant here than elsewhere. A recent survey established the presence of 120 000 qualified accountants in Britain, compared with 20 000 in France, and only 6000 in Japan, and 4000 in the former West Germany (Handy, 1987). Many of those accountants in Britain operate in business either as finance and accounting specialists or as general managers. Professional accountancy is often regarded as a training route for senior management in this country.

As we shall see later, such statistics reflect a difference in the nature of businesses in the various countries and may even be misleading. For example, the management accounting function exists in many German firms, but is performed by business economists. The variations in the number of accountants in different countries are however thought by some to reflect significant cultural differences in the way businesses operate. It has often been claimed that the traditional accountant's attitude to risk aversion can hold back entrepreneurial decision-making and, as we have seen elsewhere in this book, a preoccupation with short-term accounting calculations and financial returns may have damaged the long-term competitiveness of manufacturing industry. This is a theme that has been explored by Hayes and Wheelwright (1984) and in Chapters 5 and 6 of this book.

As stated in our introduction we shall examine the function in terms of the three activities of financial management, management accounting and financial reporting, depicted in Figure 9.1.

## Financial management

Financial management is concerned with the raising of capital to finance the organization's operations and with ensuring that the company can generate sufficient revenue to cover the cost of raising this finance. That cost may be in the form of interest rates payable to banks or dividend paid out to shareholders. There is a clear overlap with management accounting in that the funds must be managed by putting them to the most effective use. For example, investments must be carefully appraised. We may identify four sources of finance: shares, bank lending, internal funding, and the state.

**Shares**   The major source of finance from shares comes in the form of new share issues. Despite the recent publicity given to this through the privatization of such organizations as British Telecom and British Gas, probably less than 10% of all finance comes from share issue (Wilson, 1980). In recent years the creation of the Unlisted Securities Market, whereby firms not large enough to have a full Stock Market listing are able to sell shares, has had significant impact on the financing of small firms. Overall, however shares still play a minor role in the raising of funds and recent evidence suggests that where new share issues do play a part, the money is spent not on investing in current activities, but to fund acquisitions (Mayer, 1988).

The Stock Market was created to encourage potential investors to finance businesses over which they had no direct control, yet for the majority it is simply a secondary market in which shares are bought and sold by investors, with no funding activity involved. A great deal of stock-market activity revolves around the dealings of financial intermediaries. We have discussed their role alongside more general issues relating to the separation of ownership and control in Chapter 3. While funding and share trading are two separate activities, those holding large numbers of shares can influence management decision-making, in that, if sufficient numbers of shares are traded, then the company itself is traded. Managements tend to be aware that new owners may have different agendas from those of their predecessors.

**Banks**   Borrowing from banks is more common than raising finance through share issues, but on the whole British banks are less willing to lend and less willing to take an active role in the management of business activities than their counterparts in other countries. Banks play a much more significant and much more integrated role in France,

Japan, and Germany. In countries such as Germany, lending terms are also more favourable to industrial borrowers both as far as interest rates and the length of the pay-back period is concerned. Not only are British banks somewhat conservative in their lending policies, they are also, when acting as institutional investors, quite likely to sell their shares when things go wrong. Inadvertently, through their activities on the Stock Market, banks may weaken the financial position of a company, which can encourage a takeover bid.

The reluctance of British banks to finance business was argued by the Wilson Report to be a function of the poor performance of British industrial firms, which did not merit investment (Wilson, 1980). There is recent evidence that the banks are conscious of their poor image as far as investment is concerned and all the major high-street banks have engaged in costly advertising and publicity campaigns to attract the business borrower. Managers will always view high interest rates as the major obstacle to bank borrowing. The high interest rates operating in the UK for much of the 1980s and early 1990s as part of the Government's attack on inflation acted as such an obstacle.

**Internal funding**   Many texts play down internal sources of finance, yet all the evidence points to this as the major source of funding for most private companies in Britain, many obtaining as much as 70% of funds this way (Wilson, 1980; Mayer, 1988). The finance will come mainly from the redistribution of profits, although funding can be raised through the sale of assets.

**State funding**   The state in Britain plays a relatively minor role in the funding of business. Apart from the investment in prestige projects such as Concorde and microchips, the activities of the state in Britain have generally been restricted to supporting declining industries and firms and preventing mass unemployment in economically deprived regions. This would seem to be the logic behind the Government's regional policy and its investment in British Steel and British Leyland. Since 1979, the UK Government has espoused a free market economy and such funding activity has been limited. We refer you to Chapters 2 and 5 for a further discussion of such issues.

There are several reasons why management prefer to finance their businesses internally. The major factor is the fear that the involvement of banks and shareholders will weaken their control of the company. This is certainly the case as far as bank borrowing is concerned, but less so for shareholders. However, as we saw in Chapter 3, institutional investors can have considerable influence on management decisions. The shareholding route may be especially resisted by small-business owners fearing a diminution of their control over the business. As we suggested above, there is a major reluctance on the part of British managers to borrow from banks when interest rates are high and when the banks impose short payback periods.

There are a number of other factors which influence the source of finance. The attitude of management to risk may be an important

| The management accounting department plans, coordinates and controls the use of funds in organizations. It involves such activities as budgeting, costing, investment appraisal and the management of cash flows. | **KEY CONCEPT 9.2** *Management accounting* |
|---|---|

factor. A cautious manager may wish to limit the extent of bank borrowing at all costs. The extent to which internal funds can be made available depends on the ability of management to satisfy its shareholders through dividend pay-out. There are also significant differences in the funding of activities between large and small firms, a point we shall return to later in the chapter.

## Management accounting

Management accounting is the application of accounting techniques to provide management with the information to assist in the processes of planning and control. There is a clear overlap with financial management in that management accounting is concerned with the use of funds, and with financial reporting in that management accounting uses the data collected as a basis for its calculations.

In terms of planning, management accounting assists in the formulation of plans for other functional areas. For example, an assessment of future labour costs will assist the process of manpower planning. Predictions of the future cost of raw materials will help in devising appropriate purchasing strategies and, where predicted costs are high, may even stimulate the development of new products using alternative materials. An important contribution to the planning process is the assistance offered by management accounting techniques of investment appraisal in selecting the most appropriate course of action from a range of alternatives. Such techniques are more valuable as environments become increasingly complex.

Management accounting plays a very important role in the wider process of management control. It enables clear parameters to be set in the form of budgets and represents a method by which many problems can be sensed and measured. It is especially useful as a control tool for three reasons. First, the data produced offer management one of the few methods of quantifying the effect of their decisions and of the organization's operations. Second, management accounting integrates the information from all the activities of the business and enables management to view operations as a whole. Third, it deals with the control of funds that are essential to an organization's survival.

We deal with five aspects of management accounting; budgeting, cost accounting, investment appraisal, the management of cash flows, and the contribution of the management accountant to management decisions. There is considerable overlap between these categories. For example, the control of assets would inevitably involve budgetary control, and the contribution to general management decisions would include all the other four categories. Management accounting is central to strategic planning and many of the issues reappear when we discuss strategy at the end of this chapter. For the moment we examine each of the categories in turn.

**Budgeting and budgetary control**   A budget is a quantitative statement of expectations concerning the allocation of resources and performance. The two aspects of budgeting are the establishment of standards and the setting-up of mechanisms to measure and control performance. As a result, budgeting has a central position in the design of most management and accounting information systems.

Budgets are used in many different ways; to allocate funds and supplies, as a means of delegating management authority, as targets to motivate employees, and as a means of control of both spending and performance. For example, the University of East London allocates funds to each department designated as a cost centre. The allocation varies according to the size of the department and the nature of its work, so that science and engineering may get a large capital expenditure budget to purchase essential equipment. Budgets are allocated under a number of headings including equipment, office supplies, library purchases, the funding of conferences for staff and so on. Such a mechanism serves two main purposes. First, it attempts to ensure that expenditure keeps within clearly defined limits. Second, it spreads the complex task of managing this expenditure by delegating to department heads.

Budgets are normally based on historic information, usually last year's budget. In a highly bureaucratic organization, resistant to change, this can cause difficulties when the needs of organization members change. For example, many higher education institutions are slowly coming to terms with the fact that business studies courses have expanded rapidly and now provide them with a large proportion of their total student body. In many cases this is not represented in budget allocation which is based on out-of-date information. The problem is intensified in that the developments in business computing have meant that the capital needs of business studies departments, in the form of computer equipment, have also grown dramatically, while current allocations favour traditional science and engineering courses.

In all organizations there are often significant difficulties in changing the budget allocations. This is because budgeting is a bargaining process dealing with the allocation of scarce resources and those with most to lose have a vested interest in maintaining the status quo. It is for this reason that increasing attention has been given to the behavioural aspects of budgeting (Hopwood, 1974 offers some good examples). The bargaining process can be useful in that it can force management to confront long-held assumptions and face up to underlying tensions which affect decision-making. However there is a danger that conflict will be dysfunctional. This is especially true where budgeting in the form of targets is used as a control device, and more so where it forms the basis of the organization's reward system. In this case and also where scarce resources are at stake there may be a temptation for managers to distort information to place both them and their departments in the most favourable light.

Budgeting is therefore inseparable from the process of organizational politics and the way the organization is structured. In some cases this process have been acknowledged and attempts have been made to introduce some form of participation in the budget planning process.

**Cost accounting** Cost accounting involves the analysis and allocation of costs. In large organizations this can be a complex process involving paper transactions between different units, especially in multi-divisional firms. We return to this aspect when we discuss the influence of organization structure on accounting procedures. The nature of costs varies considerably. Some costs such as rents are relatively fixed, while others such as the amount of raw materials used by a manufacturing firm will vary with the intensity of production. Some costs, such as wages, are highly detailed, while others such as expenditure on hospitality can be relatively vague.

In recent years traditional cost-accounting methods, usually based on historic data, have been challenged, first by high rates of inflation in the 1970s and more recently by other changes. In many manufacturing organizations changes are taking place which are challenging the basis of historical costs and management are having to devise new methods of costing. These changes include the introduction of new manufacturing technology to reduce the cost of production and a renewed emphasis placed upon improving quality, increasing operating efficiency and reducing the uncertainty of materials and components supply. We have referred to these changes elsewhere in this book.

**Investment appraisal** Capital investment involves the commitment of funds now with the expectation of acceptable earnings in the future. Such decisions are made about the purchase or renting of new or additional premises, investment in new equipment, the development of a new product, or even the acquisition of another business. A careful appraisal of such investments is necessary due to the usually large amounts involved and the key impact such investments might have on the future viability of the company. A variety of investment appraisal methods have been devised, including payback, rate of return, net present value (NPV) and yield.

NPV is a popular method since it estimates future returns on investment, but assesses them on current values. Management are therefore able to make more informed judgements. Despite the popularity and frequency of their use, NPV calculations are not without problems. They are difficult to use for long-term investments without management making some rather big assumptions about such things as the future behaviour of markets and the future costs of raw materials. The more assumptions which have to be made then the less accurate the forecasts are likely to be. A problem associated with this is that strong management commitment to a particular investment project may result in a self-fulfilling NPV calculation. The figures are simply made to work to justify the decision. A study of the coal, steel and car industry in Britain in the 1970s concluded that large investments were justified on the basis of highly dubious input data; investment decisions which were subsequently proved unwise (Williams *et al.*, 1986).

**The management of cash flows**   The management of cash flows is concerned with the movement of cash into and out of the organization. This is an important activity since the firm needs to ensure that it has sufficient cash to cover its current expenditure. Many small firms find their severest problems occur with the management of cash flows. A business start-up has a considerable cash outflow to begin with and it may be some time before sufficient revenue is established to cover these initial costs. Several businesses have ceased trading with full order books, simply because they have insufficient incoming cash to pay bank interest charges and so are unable to stay in business and capitalize on their orders.

Cash-flow management can be particularly difficult in times of high inflation, when there is a danger that profits become absorbed by escalating costs. Some firms also experience cash-flow difficulties in expanding economies. In such situations there is a temptation to turn profit, not into cash, but into new investments by budgeting against future profits. Such a situation led Laker Airways to overreach itself by investing in expensive new passenger aircraft at a time when its markets were limited by the restrictive practices of other airlines. The company was forced into liquidation.

A current concern of cash-flow management is the management of stocks. Many manufacturing firms are attempting to reduce their outgoings through a better control of inventory. Strategies employed include the development of close links with a limited number of suppliers and operating such production control methods as 'Just-In-Time'. (Chapter 6 has a fuller discussion of such strategies.)

**General contribution to management decision-making**   Any discussion of the various elements of management activity can give the misleading impression that such activities are discrete. In reality the work of the management accountant does not focus on any one of these activities singly but uses them all in conjunction to assist in the general process of management decision-making on an on-going basis. The accountant would be expected to contribute to most types of management decision,

| KEY CONCEPT 9.3<br>*Financial reporting* | Financial reporting is the presentation of financial information in a form that is useful to interested parties. As well as being a legal requirement of many firms, the publishing of such information is useful in management decision-making, for potential investors, for trade unions and even for a firm's competitors. Since the financial information can be available to such a wide audience, management must decide on the extent of disclosure beyond the minimum required by law. |
|---|---|

and certainly would have an input in major decisions such as plant closure and decisions to make or buy.

## Financial reporting

Financial reporting involves the collection and presentation of data for use in financial management and management accounting. The two major forms of financial statement for companies are the balance sheet and the profit and loss account. The broad content of these two statements is presented in Tables 9.1 and 9.2. The balance sheet represents the summary of a firm's financial position at the end of an accounting period. The profit and loss account provides detail of a firm's income and expenditure throughout the accounting period. The form and content of such statements is determined partly by the demands of the Companies Acts 1948–81 and partly by the recommendations of the Statements of Standard Accounting Practice (SSAPs) issued collectively by the various professional accounting bodies in this country.

As we noted above, such information is particularly useful to management in the planning, organizing and controlling of resources. It is not only management who are interested in the financial information of individual businesses; the following also have need of such information.

- The **State** requires public companies to be accountable and present their accounting information in a standardized form according to the requirements of the various Companies Acts 1948–81. These state that all public companies must present to Companies House,

**Table 9.1**  The content of a typical balance sheet

| Assets | Liabilities |
|---|---|
| *Fixed assets* | *Capital* |
| Buildings | Share capital |
| Plant and equipment | |
| Transport | |
| Assets leased to third parties | |
| | |
| *Current assets* | *Current liabilities* |
| Stock | Creditors |
| Debtors | Loans |
| Bank balance | Overdrafts |
| Cash | |
| Investments | |

**Table 9.2** The content of a typical profit and loss account

| Income | Expenditure |
|---|---|
| Sales revenue | Raw materials |
| Income from investments | Wages |
| | Heating, lighting etc. |
| | Rent and rates |
| | Advertising |
| | Insurance |
| | Depreciation |
| | Tax |
| | Dividend |

a balance sheet, a profit and loss account, a directors' report, and notes on the accounts where necessary. As we shall see later there is some relaxation of these requirements for smaller businesses, but only relating to the extent of information provided. As well as stipulating the various accounts to be presented the law also determines what must be disclosed. The broad content of a balance sheet and a profit and loss account is presented in Tables 9.1 and 9.2 respectively.

The State also requires financial information to levy appropriate taxes on businesses. The nature of the tax laws certainly affects how firms report and most use reporting conventions which minimize their liability for tax.

The accounting information provided by firms under the requirements of the Companies Acts and tax law is used by the State for the purposes of economic planning and forecasting.

- **Investors** need the information to make informed judgements about future investments, as well as needing to protect their existing investments. The accountability of public companies to their investors was the major factor in the development of rules governing disclosure.
- **Employees** may need the information, especially if they are involved in a profit-sharing or share ownership scheme. Published accounts are of course particularly useful to trade unions in planning wage negotiations. In more general terms, a company concerned to involve its employees in the running of the enterprise may see the disclosure of financial information as an important element of the participation process.
- **Creditors** such as banks and suppliers are naturally concerned with the firm's liquidity and need to assess the risk involved in offering credit and of course to safeguard against fraud.

- **Competitors** usually find the financial information particularly useful as a yardstick against which their own performance may be measured, and may derive useful insights into what other firms are doing.
- **Consumers** will use the information to ascertain the risk of placing expensive or long-term contracts and perhaps to assess the fairness of a company's pricing policy.

The major issue in financial reporting is the extent of disclosure. The wide availability of the accounts of public companies certainly influences their content and the way information is presented. Managements have a fair amount of discretion since much of the content of accounts is subject to interpretation, such as allowances for depreciation and the valuation of assets. As a result, firms are often accused of manipulating their financial information to minimize tax liability or to present a strong management case in wage negotiation with trade unions. In addition firms are also conscious that financial information will be available to competitors and may wish to hide certain facts from them. We have already seen in our discussion of management accounting that financial information can be presented in such a way as to legitimize certain courses of action in preference to others. All this reinforces the notion that accounting is a behavioural and political rather than a technical exercise.

## The environmental aspects of finance and accounting

In the last section we saw that financial reporting was greatly influenced by State regulations concerning the disclosure of information for public accountability and for reasons of collecting taxes. In this section we focus on two further environmental influences on the accounting and finance function; the economy and cultural differences.

In keeping with our Business in Context model, influences are two-way. The finance and accounting practices of firms have an impact upon the environment in which they operate. Economic resources in society are often allocated on the basis of accounting information. We have noted elsewhere in this book the growing tendency for firms to engage in the buying and selling of other companies. Financial information is vital to this activity. Company statements are eagerly awaited by trade unions and the information they provide can form the basis of their arguments in the next round of pay talks. The closure of the Cortonwood colliery in South Yorkshire was based on accounting information provided for the management of the National Coal Board. The impact of such closures on the local community is considerable. The impact in this case precipitated a bitter coal-mining strike which lasted over a year. (A discussion of the kind of accounting procedures which resulted in the closure of Cortonwood can be found in Berry *et al.*, 1985. We return to this case at the end of the chapter.)

## The role of the economy

In general, accounting practices will vary according to the nature of the economy in which they operate. For example, in many Third World countries there is little need for sophisticated accounting techniques and systems of basic cash accounting predominate. The raising of finance that we discussed in the previous section is a function of the state of the market and the way this influences profit levels, share prices and bank interest rates. Two specific economic features have held particular interest for accountants: inflation and currency exchange.

The relatively high rates of inflation experienced by the British economy in the 1970s led accountants to rethink the basis for their calculations and made popular the concept of inflation accounting and resulted in a Government report (the Sandilands Committee on Inflation Accounting). A major problem in times of high inflation is that profits can be overstated by basing costs on historic data made largely irrelevant by inflation. In such situations systems of adjusting balance sheets to account for fluctuating prices were developed. While these have less relevance today, inflation accounting techniques are widely used in such countries as Brazil.

Like inflation, fluctuations in currency exchange rates makes historic cost accounting difficult. The affect is particularly significant for those firms reliant on export markets. For example, the Swiss multinationals Nestlés and Ciba Geigy have as much as 98% of their business outside Switzerland (Choi and Mueller, 1978).

## Cultural differences

Many differences can be observed in the accounting practices of different countries. These differences reflect a variety of factors such as the nature of the legal system, the pattern of ownership and control, the system of taxation, the strength of the accountancy profession, and the general social climate.

In France and the former West Germany financial reporting systems are highly prescribed by law, yet there tends to be less emphasis on financial reporting in France largely because the dominance of family ownership, and hence the private nature of many companies. In Britain and the USA reporting requirements are less prescriptive but the information needs of shareholders are much greater, especially in the USA where share ownership is more diffuse. Patterns of ownership are themselves related to the influence of the accounting profession. Public ownership requires accountability and hence accountants play a major role in the auditing of company accounts. Much less auditing is required in France which may account for their relatively low numbers of accountants. In general, a social climate which encourages openness, social responsibility and consumerism, as in the USA, results in significantly different patterns in the disclosure of financial information than those found in a much more closed society such as Switzerland.

There has been considerable pressure for the standardization of accounting practices across countries. Some harmonization has taken place within the EU and this was reflected by certain changes in the financial reporting requirements of British firms. The pressure for standardization comes from a variety of quarters. Financial reports prepared in one country are used by financial analysts and investors in another as part of the growing internationalization of capital. Standardization would greatly assist multinational companies to consolidate their accounts, assess potential acquisitions more effectively and even enable them to transfer accounting staff from one country to another more easily. It should not be forgotten that many of the major accounting firms operate multinationally too and harmonization would greatly assist their operations.

## The organizational aspects of finance and accounting

The nature of any organization impinges significantly upon accounting procedures. This is inevitably shown when changes occur in ownership or in the goals of the enterprise, bringing about changes in the organizational culture. For example, the takeover of one firm by another may well result in the consolidation of accounts and perhaps a change in the accounting practices. The privatization of a number of companies in Britain since the 1980s has changed the nature of the organization from a service centre to a profit centre with a corresponding impact upon accounting practices. In the public sector, significant changes are taking place as well. In Case 4.3 we presented the changes that were occurring in the new universities as a result of incorporation in 1989. One major change has been the withdrawal of local-authority accounting controls and the subsequent elevation of the management accounting function within universities themselves. Another change affecting all public-sector organizations has been the greater emphasis placed on income generation beyond that normally provided. This places an extra burden upon public bodies but may also give them greater flexibility to pursue their own goals.

For the remainder of this section we focus on two organizational issues: the accounting implications of the size of the firm, and the influence of structure on accounting procedures. The two issues are linked as we shall see when we examine the problems of cost allocation and transfer pricing in large multi-divisional firms.

### The accounting requirements of large and small firms

Differences in the size of businesses affects their ability to raise capital, the complexity of their accounting procedures and controls, and the extent of their financial reporting. Differences are therefore to be found in all the three functions of finance and accounting that we identified in Figure 9.1.

Larger firms, not surprisingly, have much more complex accounting procedures and generally employ a number of professional accountants in a specialized functional department. In smaller firms the accounting function is often external to the firm with a subsequent reliance on the advice of an outsider, who may not have the detailed knowledge of an internal management accountant. Larger firms may have the problems of satisfying large numbers of shareholders, but their very size often gives them an advantage in raising funds from external sources. In any event, large and complex organizations can often finance themselves internally through their ability to switch funds from one unit to another. Small firms have much more problems raising finance and tend to be more concerned with the management of cash flows.

As with the proposals to harmonize accounting procedures between nation states there is a lobby to standardize practices across all types of firms irrespective of their size. However, the cost of preparing complex financial statements can be daunting for a small business and the benefits of such information much less than for larger firms. Paradoxically in the light of its general views on harmonization, the EC champions different accounting practices for large and small firms. This was reflected in Britain in the 1981 Companies Act which removed the requirement of smaller firms to produce profit and loss accounts and directors' reports and introduced less onerous requirements for balance sheet information. In reality however, this does not appear to meet the information needs of banks on which small companies are so heavily dependent for finance. To satisfy their lending requirements, banks are insisting on stringent financial control mechanisms in small firms and much more detailed financial reporting than is required by law (Berry *et al.*, 1987). As a result, the pressure for standardization may well come from the banking community.

## Organization structure, cost allocation and transfer pricing

We have already seen how organization structure and accounting procedures tend to reinforce one another, in that a large organization may delegate responsibility and control costs through the creation of individual budget centres. In very large organizations the organization structure generally matches the finance and accounting responsibilities of the firm. A centralized headquarters will act as an investment centre determining new initiatives, as well as allocating profit targets for each division. In turn the divisions will determine targets for each operating unit and designate each one as a cost centre in control of a budget. There are occasions when mismatches can occur, as in the case of a department manager who has no effective budget, and hence limited powers of operation.

The operation of budgetary control can produce a more efficient and effective management control system. It also carries the potential problem of encouraging functional insularity to the detriment of the firm as a whole. Units can become so preoccupied with achieving their own targets and keeping within their own budgets that they may refuse calls for assistance from other units through the fear that this will erode their own performance levels. In some manufacturing firms this has resulted in a total lack of continuity between departments and between production shifts. This has led some firms to examine team-building techniques developed by social psychologists to enhance greater cooperation.

Such problems increase with the size of the firm and with the necessity for funds to flow across many different units of the same organization. The problems come to a head in large multi-divisional firms where each unit operates as a profit centre and is accountable to top management for the achievement of predetermined profit targets. We examine two aspects of this problem: cost allocation and transfer pricing.

The problems of cost allocation occur when central services, such as headquarters administration, research and development, and perhaps maintenance, must be paid for by those units in the organization with the responsibility for generating income and profit. A decision needs to be made on the basis of the apportionment of such costs. Some firms vary cost allocation according to the size of the profit centre, as a proportion of their costs, or the extent to which use is made of the central services. The final criteria is often difficult to measure accurately, but any method is open to challenge by those managers who see their profits eroded by costs which lie outside their control. Some managers are resentful that their efforts are diluted by sections of the firm that do not generate income but merely incur costs. In some cases this has resulted in the marginality of service departments such as personnel and R&D. Once again accounting becomes the focus for political debate at the level of the firm.

Transfer pricing is the process through which goods and services produced in one section of the organization are sold internally for use by another. The need for transfer pricing mechanisms is a function of the development of the multi-divisional firm and associated profit centres. An effectively operated transfer pricing mechanism can contribute to the optimum allocation of a firm's resources and to the motivation of division managers towards efficient operation and hence to the overall prosperity of the organization.

Such mechanisms occur wherever there is a need in one unit of the organization for the services of another. A form of transfer pricing occurs in higher education as the following illustration reveals. Universities and other colleges tend to be organized around specialist subject departments. A department which offers a business studies course may have the need for specialist law inputs which reside outside that department. In many colleges a transfer pricing system has been devised whereby those departments servicing another are allocated points based on the number of hours and students they service. These points with those generated from their own departments form the basis for staffing allocations. A major problem with such a mechanism is that it may encourage departments only to service those areas where they can ensure high rates of return.

This is a similar problem to the one we outlined when we discussed organization structure in Chapter 3. A foundry operating as a profit centre in a manufacturing firm may find that the pressure to meet targets conflicts with the demands placed upon it for goods from other units in the same organization. Management may be faced with the dilemma of having to meet internal demand when higher returns may be obtained through meeting the requirements of customers external to the firm. The issue of transfer pricing is particularly pertinent to the operation of multinational firms and it is to this aspect we now turn.

## Transfer pricing and the multinationals

A great deal of transfer pricing activity occurs between member organizations of large multinational corporations. It has been estimated that as much as 40% of all business trade is accounted for by dealings between members of the same corporation (Choi and Mueller, 1978). While this can cause the kind of organizational political problems outlined above, there are three main reasons for the extensiveness of such activity. These relate to issues of taxation, competition and issues relating to the need of the multinational to protect itself against social, economic and political changes occurring in the host country. These issues should be viewed in conjunction with the discussion on multinationals in Chapter 2.

**Tax reasons**  Through its activities worldwide a multinational company can move profits from high to low tax areas using the transfer pricing mechanism. Firms operating in high tax areas are charged inflated prices for goods and services produced in low tax areas. While this represents only a paper exchange of funds within the same organization it can result in some firms showing a much greater profit than others. In normal circumstances pressure is brought to bear on poorly performing profit centres. Such problems may be avoided by the use of dual reporting systems: one for external consumption and the other for internal use only.

**Competition reasons**  Some multinationals subsidize member firms through the transfer price mechanism. In order that a new company may develop itself in an established market the other firms could supply goods and services at low prices, buying back the finished products at a high price.

**Protection against change**  A multinational will wish to protect itself against those economic and political changes which threaten its prosperity and ultimate existence. Problems caused by high inflation, currency exchange and devaluation in a particular country can be tackled by charging high prices for goods supplied to the subsidiary in that country, and buying goods back at low prices. By operating in this way the multinational keeps finance in the family and prevents it being siphoned off by individual nation states.

The kind of behaviour outlined above has naturally led some multinationals into direct conflict with the governments of those countries in which they operate. A famous case is that of Hoffman-La Roche, the Swiss pharmaceutical company and the patent holder for Librium and

Valium. Through these two products alone, the company has a virtual monopoly of the world tranquillizer market. The British Government in 1971 considered that Hoffman-La Roche was operating against the public interest in this country through its pricing policy on the two tranquillizers in question and called in the Monopolies Commission to investigate. The Commission found that the parent company in Switzerland, Hoffman-La Roche was supplying its British subsidiary, Roche Products, with the active ingredients for Librium and Valium at the transfer price of £370 per kilo and £922 per kilo respectively, out of a total manufacturing cost for Librium of £437 per kilo and for Valium of £979 per kilo. The Commission discovered that the raw materials could be purchased in Italy at a cost of £9 per kilo for Librium and £20 per kilo for Valium. The Commission concluded that Hoffman-La Roche were acting against the interests of the public but were hampered in their investigation by the lack of accounting information from the Swiss parent company; a British government body having no jurisdiction in Switzerland and no access to information produced under totally different rules for financial reporting. The price differences were explained by Hoffman-La Roche in terms of administrative and research costs and a pricing policy based upon what the market would bear. The company probably gained significant tax advantages by operating in this fashion (Stopford *et al.*, 1980).

## Strategic aspects of finance and accounting

The three functions of finance and accounting represent strategies of financing and controlling operations, of distributing resources and power through budget allocation, and of information disclosure. Additionally, financial tools and information are invariably used in the making of strategic decisions in other functional areas, such as the decision to invest in new products or equipment, or to take on extra staff. Financial analyses form the basis of most acquisition attempts.

We can therefore see that the finance and accounting function assists management decision-making on a number of key issues that are central to the viability of the firm. These issues include the sources of funds, investment decisions, acceptable levels of debt, the minimization of tax liability and the extent of the pay out to shareholders.

As with all the functional areas we have discussed in this book there is a growing recognition that the strategies associated with the different activities are linked in some kind of synergistic way. In manufacturing industry evidence is emerging that cost and quality are not necessarily trade-offs but essential ingredients of the same strategy. A greater attention focused on improving product quality can also be successful in lowering costs. This can become a virtuous circle in that extra funds are released for further investment in quality improvement.

Throughout this chapter we have been careful to point out the inexact nature of accounting methods. We can summarize the various limitations on the use of accounting information in strategy formulation.

- Because of the problems of measuring many aspects of business activities, accounting information can be highly subjective.
- Financial statements are summaries. Information is therefore selected and interpreted according to the needs of the compiler and user of financial statements.
- As a result of the above, financial information is often used deliberately to achieve political ends such as the justification of an investment decision or a pay claim.
- There is an added danger in all this in that many assume the data to be scientific and objective, and use them accordingly.
- Because of the bias in accounting to what can effectively be measured, management may place undue emphasis on short-term results and neglect the longer-term implications of strategic decisions, or base too many decisions on historic data which are made redundant by changing circumstances.

A good illustration of the interpretative problems associated with accounting information is offered by the NCB decision to close Cortonwood Colliery as part of its rationalization strategy. A Monopoly and Mergers Commission Report calculated the revenue of the colliery at £44.3 per tonne, while its costs were calculated at £50.5 per tonne. On these figures the mine was clearly unprofitable and losing the Coal Board in excess of £1.7 a year. A study of the accounting methods used by the NCB questioned the basis for many of the costs used, but more significantly suggested that many of the costs such as surface damage and essential services would not be avoided by closing the colliery. If these unavoidable costs are eliminated from the equation as constants, then Cortonwood could be shown to be making a net contribution of £5.45 per tonne of coal mined (Berry *et al.*, 1985).

## Summary

The finance and accounting function in business comprises financial management, management accounting, and financial reporting.

Financial management is concerned with the funding of the business and ensuring such funds can be met by the organization. The major sources of finance are share issues, bank lending, state finance and internally generated funds, usually through the reinvestment of profit. It is this last source that would appear to be most significant for firms in Britain.

Management accounting is concerned with assisting management in planning and control. It involves the preparation and control of budgets, the analysis and allocation of costs, the appraisal of capital investments, the management of cash flows and general contribution to strategic decision-making.

Financial reporting involves the preparation of financial statements such as the balance sheet and profit and loss account and must take account of the needs of the various groups who are to use this information. A major issue is the extent of disclosure.

The finance and accounting function is greatly influenced by the environment in which it operates. Financial reporting is subject to strict state controls and accounting practices have developed to cope with economic changes such as inflation and fluctuations in the value of currency. Despite pressures to harmonize accounting practices there are considerable differences between countries, reflecting a number of cultural influences.

Accounting practices vary also with the size of the organization, with large and small companies having their own special problems. As organizations increase in size and develop appropriate structures, decisions will have to be made on the allocation of costs and transfer pricing. The latter becomes a particularly useful mechanism in the hands of the multinational corporation.

Accounting information forms the basis for most strategic decisions within the organization. Its value should be placed alongside a number of limitations, not least of which are the subjective nature of accounts and the role played by accounting information to justify organizational political decisions.

## Further reading

Two basic accounting texts that are easy to follow are A. Berry and R. Jarvis, *Accounting in a Business Context*, 2nd edn (Chapman & Hall, 1994) and R. Dodge, *Foundations of Business Accounting* (Chapman & Hall, 1993). The first, a companion volume in this series offers an intelligent general approach, while the second focuses more on techniques and activities. A readable text on management accounting that offers a number of useful examples is J. Sizer, *An Insight into Management Accounting* (Penguin, 1989). Organizational issues are well represented by C. Emmanuel *et al.*, *Accounting for Management Control*, 2nd edn (Chapman & Hall, 1990), while a good examination of the behavioural aspects of accounting is presented by A. Hopwood, *Accounting and Human Behaviour* (Accountancy Age Books, 1974). Issues of accounting and finance in small firms are well represented in K. Keasey and R. Watson, *Small Firm Management: Ownership, Finance and Performance* (Blackwell, 1993).

## Discussion

1  What is the value of the professional accountant to business? Why do professional accountants proliferate in Britain?
2  Why is the internal funding of business so popular in this country?
3  What would be the most appropriate methods the following organizations could use to raise revenue to fund new activities: a very small firm just making a mark in the office supplies market; a university; a multinational car manufacturer?
4  What specific contributions can the management accountant make

to strategic decision-making? What limitations can be placed on the value of this contribution?

5  Identify the different needs of the users of accounting information. Can current methods of financial reporting hope to satisfy them all?

6  What are the specific finance and accounting problems and priorities for small as opposed to large companies?

7  What are the advantages and disadvantages to various interested parties associated with cost allocation and transfer pricing activities in multidivisional firms?

8  Identify the behavioural and political nature of management accounting. What problems does this cause and how might they be minimized?

# Conclusions

## 10

It is difficult to draw conclusions from a textbook such as this without recourse to some rather bland and meaningless predictions about such topics as 'the future of business' or 'new developments in business ideas'. Nevertheless, given that the preceding nine chapters have been spent examining business through the workings of a model, it seems appropriate to highlight some of the themes and issues which have emerged. In identifying these issues we run the risk of attracting the kinds of criticisms we have levelled at the attempts of others. We do however temper our thoughts with a few notes of caution.

## Major themes

This book has stressed five major themes.

- Businesses operate through a network of complex interrelationships. To aid our understanding we have simplified the world of business by identifying a number of core business activities and three contexts in which those activities operate; these are the strategic, organizational and environmental contexts. Together, these activities and contexts make up the Business in Context model. The various elements that make up business activities interact with one another as do the various elements which make up the different contexts. In addition, influences go backwards and forwards across the various levels of the model to create the complex patterns of interrelationship.

- The idea that influences operate in several directions is very important to our understanding of business. Businesses are undoubtedly shaped by the various contexts in which they operate. In turn businesses shape the environment in which they operate. The business activities of one firm become part of the competitive environment of another. What we label as the economy is the product of business activity. A firm is said to adopt new technology as if it were a gift from the gods, yet developments in technology are the product of human endeavour and the technology adopted by one firm may well have its origins in the activities of another.

- The various interactions and influences we have described occur in a number of different contexts. We can think too narrowly that the term 'business' only refers to those organizations operating in pursuit of profit. We have stressed throughout this book that business activities occur in all kinds of organization, including schools, hospitals, government offices and charities.
- Business decisions are made by people and as such are subject to a range of behavioural influences and political considerations. While a number of 'rational' techniques have emerged to guide decision-making in each of the business activities, it is often the 'non-rational' factors that are most significant. We use the terms rational and non-rational with caution, in that a decision and decision-making method which may appear less than rational to us, may of course be perfectly rational to the decision-maker.
- Because of the behavioural and political nature of business activities, it is important to acknowledge the existence of a number of different perspectives on business issues. The development of a new method of manufacture is to the manager an attempt to improve the efficiency of the operation. To the worker it may represent a threat to job satisfaction and job security. To the consumer it may mean a more available and cheaper product, but it may also represent unacceptable changes in product design. This rather crude illustration reinforces the necessity of viewing business issues from the perspective of all interested parties. Business ideas often fail simply because managers have not considered the possibility that they may not be acceptable to all concerned.

The notion of different perspectives is a strong theme of the entire Business in Context series. Each of the subsequent books in the series examines the workings of the Business in Context model and a range of related business issues from a different perspective, each with a grounding in a different academic discipline.

## Major issues

A number of major issues common to all business activities seems to have emerged over the last few years.

- There would appear to be a convergence of all types of organization on a business model we have in the past only associated with profit-oriented firms. Educational establishments, local authorities and hospitals are re-examining their methods of management and control and are seeking various methods of income generation.
- A history of business ideas reveals that at various times each of the various activities of business claims the focus of attention. We have been urged to innovate out of the recession, to focus on operating efficiency, to market what the customer requires, and to create a distinctive organization culture around a value system shared by all personnel. There is now a greater realization than ever before of

the need to develop an integrated business strategy and that none of the functional activities can exist in isolation.

- The basis for such integration is a set of core ideas which reappear constantly in the literature and in discussions about business. A major theme is the importance of learning from the good practices of others, which accounts for the interest throughout the late 1970s and the 1980s on cross-cultural research and especially the dissemination of best practice from those economically successful nations like Japan. The core ideas themselves include a concern for improved quality and productivity, a rediscovery of the importance of entrepreneurship, and a focus on achieving business results through people.

## The issues in context

We must temper our enthusiasm for these new business ideas for a number of reasons.

- We have noted throughout this book that the relationships in business between intentions, actions and outcomes are not only difficult to measure but that the complex nature of the business environment makes causal relationships difficult to prove. We saw this in the various attempts to show a link between innovation and economic growth and again in our analysis of the small firms policy of the British Government.
- The history of business ideas is also the history of particular fashions and fads, which have either been short-lived or have persisted only in isolated pockets of resistance. Many firms have embarked upon policies for management-by-objectives, job enrichment, quality circles and the like only to discard them at some later stage. Within the life span of this edition TQM could well have suffered the same fate. The problem is not always the inadequacy of the technique, but is also a function of the conservative nature of management and the insufficient attention paid to its introduction and utilization.
- Many of the new ideas that have emerged are undoubtedly products of the environmental conditions in operation at a particular moment in time. Thus we can attribute Japanization, 'excellent' companies, the rediscovery of entrepreneurship, consensus industrial relations, and the like to a particular economic climate, particular kinds of business operation, the presence (in Britain at any rate) of an ideologically strong government, and the relative weakness of labour. Current pressures on UK businesses are undoubtedly those generated by the early 1990s economic recession, increased international competition and the deregulation of many types of business activity. Such pressures have placed an emphasis on issues relating to innovation, marketing, quality and HRM. The extent to which such notions are viable in the same form in different circumstances is open to question.

- Some of the business developments have their negative side. We have seen the devastating effects on some communities of the growth of regional unemployment and that the current vogue for part-time workers and contract workers has created a secondary labour force which enjoys less security and fewer rights as employees.

There is undoubtedly a tendency for the commentators of any period to regard their time as an age of discontinuity. Our analysis of business reveals much more of a continuity. For many firms, current changes simply pass them by and business goes on much the same as usual apart from the various incremental changes that are bound to occur. An analysis of business over the last 40 years reveals several constants, not least of which is the continuing power of the multinational enterprise. Many of the changes that do occur are products of the environment and are just as likely to change again as the environment itself changes. Undoubtedly there are significant changes that will leave their mark, but these changes are themselves new expressions of the very traditional management goal of enhancing the effectiveness of their operation.

# References

Abernathy, W. J. and Utterback J. M. (1978) Patterns of industrial innovation, ch. 33 of R. R. Rothberg (ed.), *Corporate Strategy and Product Innovation*, 2nd edn, The Free Press, New York.

Adam, G. (1975) Multinational corporations and worldwide sourcing, in H. Radice (ed.), *International Firms and Modern Imperialism*, Penguin, Harmondsworth.

Adcroft, A., Cutler, T., Haslam, C., Williams, J. and Williams, K. (1991) Hanson and ICI: the consequences of financial engineering, *University of East London, Occasional Papers in Business, Economy and Society* No. 2.

Ansoff, H. I. and Stewart, J. M. (1967) Strategies for a technology-based business, *Harvard Business Review*, **45**, Nov.–Dec., pp. 71–83.

Ansoff, H. I. (1968) *Corporate Strategy*, Penguin, Harmondsworth.

Anthony, P. D. (1990) The paradox of management culture or 'He who leads is lost', *Personnel Review*, **19**(4), pp. 3–8.

Armstrong, P., Glyn, A. and Harrison, J. (1984) *Capitalism Since World War Two*, Fontana, London.

Armstrong, P., Glyn, A. and Harrison, J. (1991) *Capitalism Since 1945*, Basil Blackwell, Oxford.

Atkinson, J. (1984) Manpower strategies for flexible organizations, *Personnel Management*, Aug. pp. 28–31.

Baker, M. J. (1991) *Marketing*, 5th edn, Macmillan, London.

Bannock, G. (1981) *The Economics of Small Firms: Return from the Wilderness*, Basil Blackwell, Oxford.

Bassett, P. (1986) *Strike Free*, Macmillan, London.

Beasley, J. E. (1985) Strategies for corporate and business success – a survey, *OMEGA*, **13**, 1, pp. 51–8.

Beer, M., Spector, B., Lawrence, P., Quinn Mills, D. and Walton, R. E. (1984) *Managing Human Assets*, Free Press, New York.

Beer, M., Spector, B., Lawrence, P., Quinn Mills, D. and Walton, R. E. (1985) *Human Resource Management, The General Managers Perspective Text and Cases*, Free Press, New York.

Berle, A. A. (1954) *The Twentieth Century Capitalist Revolution*, Harcourt Brace, New York.

Berle, A. A. and Means, G. C. (1932) *The Modern Corporation and Private Property*, Macmillan, New York.

Berry, A., Citron, D. and Jarvis, R. (1987) *The Information Needs of Bankers Dealing with Large and Small Companies: with Particular Reference to Proposed Changes in Legislation*, Certified Research Report 7, Certified Accountant Publications Ltd, London.

Berry, A. and Jarvis, R. (1994) *Accounting in a Business Context*, 2nd edn, Chapman & Hall, London.

Berry, T., Capps, T., Cooper, D., Hooper, T. and Lowe, T. (1985) NCB accounts – a mine of misinformation, *Accountancy*, Jan., pp. 10–12.

Bhaskar, K. (1980) *The Future of the World Motor Industry*, Kogan Page, London.

Binks, M. and Jennings, A. (1986) New firms as a source of industrial regeneration, in M. Scott (ed.), *Small Firms Growth and Development*, Gower, Aldershot.

Binns, D. (1993) Total Quality Management, organization theory and the New Right: A contribution to the critique or bureaucratic totalitarianism, *University of East London, Occasional Papers on Business, Economy and Society* No. 11.

Bird, D., Beatson, M. and Butcher, S. (1993) Membership of trade unions, *Employment Gazette*, May, pp. 189–96.

Blauner, R. (1964) *Alienation and Freedom*, University of Chicago Press, Chicago.

Bolton, J. (1971) *Small Firms: The Report of the Committee of Inquiry on Small Firms*, HMSO, Cmd 4811, London.

Bowen, A. and Ricketts, M. (1992) *Stimulating Innovation in Industry: The Challenge for the United Kingdom*, Kogan Page/NEDO, London.

Bowen, A., Buxton, T. and Ricketts, M. (1992) The economics of innovation: setting the scene, in A. Bowen and M. Ricketts (eds), *Stimulating Innovation in Industry: The Challenge for the United Kingdom*, Kogan Page/NEDO, London.

Bowen, D. (1992) Bigger is better in Britain's battered industry, *Independent on Sunday*, 26th July.

Bradley, K. and Hill, S. (1983) After Japan: the Quality Circle transplant and productive efficiency, *British Journal of Industrial Relations*, **21**, 3, pp. 291–311.

Braverman, H. (1974) *Labor and Monopoly Capital*, Monthly Review Press, New York.

Brewster, C. and Bournois, F. (1991) Human resource management: a European perspective, *Personnel Review*, **20**, 6, pp. 4–13.

Brewster, C., Hegewisch, A. and Lockhart, J. T. (1991) Researching human resource management: methodology of the Price Waterhouse Cranfield Project on European trends, *Personnel Review*, **20**, 6, pp. 36–40.

Bright, G., Colvin, M., Loveridge, J., Page, R. and Thompson, C. (1983) *Moving Forward: Small Business and the Economy*, Conservative Political Centre, London.

Brittan, S. (1983) The myth of the Kondratieff, *Financial Times*, 7 Apr.

Brossard, M. and Maurice, M. (1976) Is there a universal model of organisational structure? *International Studies of Management and Organization*, **6**, pp. 11–45.

Bruce, M. (1987) Managing people first – bringing the service concept into British Airways, *Independent and Commercial Training*, Mar./Apr.

Buchan, J. (1993) Withdrawal symptoms, *The Independent on Sunday Review*, 23 Apr., pp. 2–5.

Burnham, J. (1941) *The Management Revolution*, Day, New York.

Burns, T. and Stalker, G. M. (1966) *The Management of Innovation*, Tavistock, London.

Burrell, G. and Morgan, G. (1979) *Sociological Paradigms and Organisation Analysis*, Heinemann, London.

Burrows, G. (1986) *No-Strike Agreements and Pendulum Arbitration*, Institute of Personnel Management, London.

Buzzell (1964) *Mathematical Models and Marketing Management*, Harvard University, Boston.

Cannon, T. (1986) *Basic Marketing*, 2nd edn, Holt, Rinehart & Winston, Eastbourne.

Carroll, D. T. (1983) A disappointing search for excellence, *Harvard Business Review*, **63**, Nov.–Dec., pp. 78–88.

Casey, B. (1986) The dual apprenticeship system, *British Journal of Industrial Relations*, **14**, 1, pp. 63–82.

Cecchini, P. (1988) *The European Challenge 1992: The Benefits of a Single Market*, Wildwood House, Aldershot.

Chandler, A. D. (1962) *Strategy and Structure: Chapters in the History of American Capitalism*, MIT Press, Cambridge, Mass.

Chandler, A. D. (1977) *The Visible Hand: The Managerial Revolution in American Business*, Harvard University Press, Cambridge, Mass.

Channon, D. F. (1973) *The Strategy and Structure of British Enterprise*, Macmillan, London.

Child, J. (1969) *The Business Enterprise in Modern Industrial Society*, Collier-Macmillan, London.

Child, J. (1972) Organisational structure, environment and performance: the role of strategic choice, *Sociology*, **6**, pp. 1–21.

Child, J. (1984a) *Organizations: A Guide to Problems and Practice*, 2nd edn, Harper & Row, London.

Child, J. (1984b) New technology and developments in management organization, *OMEGA*, **12**, 3, pp. 211-23.

Child, J. and Kieser, A. (1979) Organization and managerial roles in British and West German companies: an examination of the culture free thesis, in C. J. Lammers and D. J. Hickson (eds), *Organizations Alike and Unlike*, Routledge & Kegan Paul, London.

Child, J., Fores, M., Glover, I. and Lawrence, P. (1983) A price to pay? Professionalism and work organization in Britain and West Germany, *Sociology*, **17**, 1, pp. 63–77.

Childs, D. (1992) *Britain Since 1945: A Political History*, Routledge, London.

Choi, F. D. S. and Mueller, G. G. (1978) *An Introduction to Multinational Accounting*, Prentice Hall Inc. Englewood Cliffs, N.J.

Chong Li Choy (1990) Business in the development of Singapore, ch. 1 in Chong Li Choy *et al.* (eds), *Business, Society and Development in Singapore*, Times Academic Press, Singapore.

Clarke, T. and Pitelis, C. (eds) (1993) *The Political Economy of Privatization*, Routledge, London.

Coleman, T. (1988) Travels with a Rover, *Guardian*, 13 Aug.

Collard, R. and Dale, B. (1985) Quality Circles: Why they break down and why they hold up, *Personnel Management*, Feb., pp. 28–31.

Connon, H. (1992) Glaxo invests in £1bn. hot-house to foster discovery, *Independent*, 9 June, p. 19.

Crouch, C. J. (1978) The changing role of the state in industrial relations in Western Europe, in C. J. Crouch and A. Pizzorno (eds), *The Resurgence of Class Conflict in Western Europe Since 1968*, Vol. 1, Macmillan, London.

Curran, J. (1986) *Bolton Fifteen Years On: A Review and Analysis, of Small Business Research in Britain, 1971–86*, Small Business Trust, London.

Cyert, R. M. and March, J. G. (1963) *A Behavioral Theory of the Firm*, Prentice Hall, Englewood Cliffs, N. J.

DTI, Innovation Advisory Board (1990) *Innovation: City Attitudes and Practices*.

Daft, R. L. (1982) Bureaucratic v non-Bureaucratic structures and the process of innovation and change, in S. B. Bachovach (ed.), *Research in the Sociology of Organizations*, JAI Press, Greenwich.

Damanpour, F., Szabat, K. A. and Evan W. M. (1989) The relationship between types of innovation and organization performance, *Journal of Management Studies*, **26**, 6, Nov., pp. 587–601.

Daniel, W. W. (1987) *Workplace Industrial Relations and Technical Change*, Policy Studies Institute, London.

Daniel, W. W. and Millward, N. (1983) *Workplace Industrial Relations in Britain*, Heinemann, London.

Daniels, C. (1991) *The Management Challenge of Information Technology*, The Economist Intelligence Unit and Business International, London.

Davis, S. M. and Lawrence, P. R. (eds) (1977) *Matrix*, Addison-Wesley, Reading, Mass.

Dawson, S. (1986) *Analysing Organizations*, Macmillan, London.

Dawson, S. (1992) *Analysing Organizations*, 2nd edn, Macmillan, Basingstoke.

Deal, T. E. and Kennedy, A. A. (1982) *Corporate Cultures*, Addison-Wesley, Reading, Mass.

Deming, W. E. (1986) *Out of Crisis: Quality, Productivity and Competitive Position*, Cambridge University Press, Cambridge.

Dhalla, N. K. (1978) Assessing the long-term value of advertising, *Harvard Business Review*, Jan.–Feb., pp. 87–95.

Dilworth, J. B. (1986) *Production and Operations Management: Manufacturing and Non-Manufacturing*, Random House, New York.

Dodge, R. (1993) *Foundations of Business Accounting*, Chapman & Hall, London.

Donovan (1968) *Royal Commission on Trade Unions and Employers Associations 1965–1968*, HMSO, Cmnd 3623, London.

Dore, R. (1973) *British Factory – Japanese Factory*, University of California Press, Berkeley, Calif.

Drucker, P. F. (1964) *Managing for Results*, Harper & Row, New York.

Drucker, P. F. (1968) *The Practice of Management*, Pan Books, London.

Drucker, P. F. (1985) *Innovation and Entrepreneurship*, Heinemann, London.

van Duijn, J. J. (1983) *The Long Wave in Economic Life*, George Allen & Unwin, London.

Earl, M. J. (1989) *Management Strategies for Information Technology*, Prentice Hall International, Hemel Hempstead.

Earl, P. E. (1984) *The Corporate Imagination: How Big Companies Make Mistakes*, Wheatsheaf Books, Brighton.

Ebel, K. H. (1985) Social and Labour Implications of Flexible Manufacturing Systems, *International Labour Review*, **124**, 2, Mar.–Apr., pp. 133–47.

Edwards, P., Hall, M., Hyman, R., Margusen, P., Sisson, K., Waddington, J. and Winchester, D. (1992) Great Britain: still muddling through, in A. Ferner and R. Hyman (eds), *Industrial Relations in the New Europe*, Basil Blackwell, Oxford.

Eilon, S. (1985) Recasting the die, *OMEGA*, **13**, 3, pp. 135–42.

Ekvall, G. (1991) The organizational culture of idea-management: a creative climate for the management of ideas, in J. Henry and D. Walker (eds), *Managing Innovation*, Sage/OU, London.

El-Namaki, M. (1993) *Contemporary Dynamics of Entrepreneurship*, Netherlands International Institute for Management, Netherlands.

Emmanuel, C., Otley, D. and Merchant, K. (1990) *Accounting for Management Control*, 2nd edn, Chapman & Hall, London.

Emery, F. and Thorsrud, E. (1976) *Democracy at Work*, Nijhoff, Leiden.

Employment Department Group (1992) *Small Firms in Britain Report 1992*, HMSO, London.

Evans, H. (1983) *Good Times Bad Times*, Weidenfield & Nicholson, London.

Fagan, M. (1991) Is it right that the scientists should take the decisions?, *Independent*, 10 June, p. 20.

Ferner, A. and Hyman, R. (1992) Industrial relations on the Continent: a model of cooperation?, *Personnel Management*, Aug., **24**, 8, pp. 32–4.

Ferner, A. and Hyman, R. (eds) (1992) *Industrial Relations in the New Europe*, Basil Blackwell, Oxford.

Finniston, M. (1980) *Report of the Committee of Inquiry into the Engineering Profession*, HMSO, London.

Flanders, A. (1964) *The Fawley Productivity Agreements*, Faber & Faber, London.

Fox, A. (1974a) *Beyond Contract: Work, Trust and Power Relations*, Faber & Faber, London.

Fox, A. (1974b) *Man Mismanagement*, Faber & Faber, London.

Foy, N. (1983) The public productivity poser, *Management Today*, July, pp. 67–71.

Freeman, C. (1989) R & D, technical change and investment in the UK, in F. Green (ed.), *The Restructuring of the UK Economy*, Harvester Wheatsheaf, London.

Galbraith, J. K. (1972) *The New Industrial State*, 2nd edn, Penguin, Harmondsworth.

Gailbraith, J. R. (1971) Matrix organization designs, *Business Horizons*, **14**, pp. 29–40.

Galbraith, J. R. and Nathanson, D. A. (1978) *Strategy Implementation: The Role of Structure and Process*, West Publishing Co., St Paul, Minnesota.

Gamble, A. (1985) *Britain in Decline*, Macmillan, London.

Ganguly, P. and Bannock, G. (1985) *UK Small Business Statistics and International Comparisons*, Harper & Row, London.

Glueck, W. F. and Jauch, L. R. (1984) *Business Policy and Strategic Management*, 4th edn, McGraw-Hill, Singapore.

Goldthorpe, J. (1977) Industrial Relations in Great Britain: a critique of Reformism, in T. Clarke and L. Clements (eds), *Trade Unions under Capitalism*, Fontana, Glasgow.

Gould, A. and Keeble, D. (1984) New firms and rural industrialization in East Anglia, *Regional Studies*, **18**, 3, pp. 189–201.

Grant, W. and Marsh, D. (1977) *The CBI*, Hodder & Stoughton, London.

Greater London Council (1983) *Small Firms and the London Industrial Strategy*, Economic Policy Group Strategy Document, No. 4, GLC, London.

Gordan, G. G. and Ditomaso, N. (1992) Predicting corporate performance from organizational culture, *Journal of Management Studies*, **29**, 6, pp. 783–98.

Green, F. (ed.) (1989a) *The Restructuring of the UK Economy*, Harvester Wheatsheaf, London.

Green, F. (1989b) Evaluating structural economic change: Britain in the 1980s, in F. Green (ed.), *The Restructuring of the UK Economy*, Harvester Wheatsheaf, London, Ch. 1.

Griffin, T. (1984) Technological change and craft control in the newspaper industry: an international comparison, *Cambridge Journal of Economics*, **8**, 1, Mar., pp. 41–61.

Guest, D. E. (1982) Has the recession really hit personnel management?, *Personnel Management*, Oct., pp. 36–9.

Guest, D. E. (1989) Human resource management: its implications for industrial relations and trade unions, in J. Storey (ed.), *New Perspectives on Human Resource Management*, Routledge, London.

Guest, D. E. (1990) Human resource management and the American dream, *Journal of Management Studies*, **27**, 4, July, pp. 377-97.

Guest, D. (1991) Personnel management: the end of orthodoxy?, *British Journal of Industrial Relations*, **29**, 2, June, pp. 149–75.

Guest, D. and Horwood, R. (1980) *The Role and Effectiveness of Personnel Management: A Preliminary Report*, The Nancy Seear Fellowship Personnel Management Research Programme: Research Report No. 1, LSE, London.

Hahn, C. (1993) The importance of manufacturing in a robust economy, *RSA Journal*, June, pp. 540–9.

Hampden-Turner, C. (1990) *Corporate Culture Management: From Vicious to Virtuous Circles*, Economist Books, Hutchinson, London.

Hanan, M. (1974) Reorganize your company around its markets, *Harvard Business Review*, Nov.–Dec., pp. 63–74.

Handy, C. (1987) *The Making of Managers: A Report on Management Education, Training and Development in the USA, West Germany, France, Japan and the United Kingdom*, MSC, NEDC and BIM, London.

Handy, C. (1974) *Understanding Organizations*, Harmondsworth, Penguin.

Handy, C. (1993) *Understanding Organizations*, 4th edn, Harmondsworth, Penguin.

Harbison, F. and Myers, C. A. (1959) *Management in the Industrial World: An International Analysis*, McGraw-Hill, New York.

Harris, N. D. (1989) *Service Operations Management*, Cassell, London.

Harrison, P. (1985) *Inside the Third World*, 2nd edn, Harmondsworth, Penguin.

Hayek, F. A. (1984) *1980's Unemployment and the Unions*, Institute for Economic Affairs.

Hayes, R. H. and Schmenner, R. W. (1978) How should you organize manufacturing?, *Harvard Business Review*, Jan.–Feb., pp. 105–18.

Hayes, R. H. and Wheelwright, S. C. (1984) *Restoring our Competitive Edge: Competing Through Manufacturing*, John Wiley, New York.

Heald, D. (1985) Will privatisation of public enterprises solve the problems of control?, *Public Administration*, **63**, Spring, pp. 7–22.

Henry, J. and Walker, D. (eds) (1991) *Managing Innovation*, London, Sage/Open University.

Herriot, P. and Pinder, B. (1992) Human resource strategy in a changing world, *Personnel Management*, **24**, 8, Aug., pp. 36–9.

Herzberg, F. (1968) One more time: how do you motivate employees?, *Harvard Business Review*, **46**, pp. 53–62.

Hetherington, P. (1986) Perfection in the land of rising productivity, *Guardian*, 5 Mar., p. 23.

Hickson, D. J., Pugh, D. S. and Pheysey, D. C. (1969) Operation technology and organization structure: an empirical appraisal, *Administrative Science Quarterly*, **14**, pp. 378–97.

Hill, S. (1991) Why quality circles failed but total quality management succeeded, *British Journal of Industrial Relations*, **29**, 4, pp. 541–68.

Hill, T. (1991) *Production and Operations Management: Text and Cases*, Prentice Hall, London.

Hill, T. (1993) *Manufacturing Strategy: The Strategic Management of the Manufacturing Function*, 2nd edn, Macmillan, London.

Hofer, C. W. and Schendel, D. (1978) *Strategy Formulation: Analytical Concepts*, West Publishing, St Paul, Minnesota.

Hofstede, G. H. (1980a) *Culture's Consequences: International Differences in Work-Related Values*, Sage, London.

Hofstede, G. H. (1980b) Motivation, leadership and organization: do American theories apply abroad?, *Organizational Dynamics*, Summer, pp. 42–63.

Hofstede, G. H. (1986) The usefulness of the organizational culture concept, *Journal of Management Studies*, **23**, 3, May, pp. 253–7.

Höpfl, H., Smith, S. and Spencer, S. (1992) Values and valuations: The conflict between culture change and job cuts, *Personnel Review*, **21**, 1, pp. 24–37.

Hopwood, A. (1974) *Accounting and Human Behaviour*, Accountancy Age Books, London.

Howard, J. A. and Sheth, J. N. (1969) *The Theory of Buyer Behaviour*, John Wiley, New York.

Howells, P. G. A. and Bain, K. (1990) *Financial Markets and Institutions*, Longman, London.

Husband, T. M. (1984) Management and advanced manufacturing technology, *OMEGA*, **12**, 3, pp. 197–201.

Hyman, R. (1972) *Disputes Procedure in Action*, Heinemann, London.

Institute of Personnel Management (1963) Statement on personnel management and personnel policies, *Personnel Management*, March.

Jackson, P. (1983) How Perkins positively tackled the recession, *Personnel Management*, Nov., pp. 24–7.

Jaikumar, R. (1986) Post-industrial manufacturing, *Harvard Business Review*, Nov.–Dec., pp. 69–76.

Jessop, R. (1980) The transformation of the state in Post-war Britain, in R. Scase (ed.) *The State in Western Europe*, Croom-Helm, London.

Jewkes, J. Sawers, D. and Stillerman, R. (1970) *The Sources of Invention*, W. W. Norton, New York.

Johnson, G. and Scholes, K. (1984) *Exploring Corporate Strategy*, Prentice Hall International, London.

Johnson, G. and Scholes, K. (1993) *Exploring Corporate Strategy: Text and Cases*, 3rd edn, Prentice Hall, London.

Kamata, S. (1983) *Japan in the Passing Lane*, Allen & Unwin, London.

Kaplinsky, R. (1983) Firm size and technical change in a dynamic context, *The Journal of Industrial Economics*, **32**, 1, pp. 39–59.

Kay, J. (1992) Innovations in Corporate Strategy, in A. Bowen and M. Ricketts (eds), *Stimulating Innovation in Industry: The Challenge for the United Kingdom*, Kogan Page/NEDO, London.

Kay, J. (1993) *Foundations of Corporate Success: How Business Strategies Add Value*, Oxford University Press, Oxford.

Keasey, K. and Watson, R. (1993) *Small Firm Management: Ownership, Finance and Performance*, Blackwell, Oxford.

Kennedy, C. (1988) Global strategies for 3M, *Long Range Planning*, **21**, 1, pp. 9–17.

Kerr, C., Dunlop, J. T., Harbison, F. and Myers, C. A. (1973) *Industrialism and Industrial Man*, Harmondsworth, Penguin.

Kessler, S. and Bayliss, F. (1992a) The changing face of industrial relations, *Personnel Management*, May, **24**, 5, pp. 34–7.

Kessler, S. and Bayliss, F. (1992b) *Contemporary British Industrial Relations*, Macmillan, London.

Kondratieff, N. D. (1935) The long waves in economic life, *Review of Economic Statistics*, **17**, pp. 105–15.

Kotler, P. (1983) *Principles of Marketing*, 2nd edn, Prentice Hall, Englewood Cliffs N. J.

Kotler, P. (1993) *Principles of Marketing*, 3rd edn, Prentice Hall International, Englewood Cliffs N. J.

Kotler, P. (1993) *Marketing Management: Analysis Planning, Implementation and Control*, 8th edn, Prentice Hall International, Englewood Cliffs N. J.

Kumar, K. (1978) *Prophecy and Progress*, Harmondsworth, Penguin.

Lancaster, G. and Massingham, L. (1992) *Essentials of Marketing*, 2nd edn, McGraw Hill, Maidenhead.

Lane, K. A. (1985) The U.K. machine tool industry, *OMEGA*, **13**, 4, pp. 247–9.

Lawrence, P. (1980) *Managers and Management in West Germany*, Croom Helm, London.

Lawrence, P. R. and Lorsch, J. (1967) *Organization and Environment*, Harvard University Press, Cambridge, Mass.

Legge, K. (1978) *Power, Innovation and Problem-solving in Personnel Management*, McGraw Hill, London.

Legge, K. (1989) Human resource management: a critical analysis, in J. Storey (ed.), *New Perspectives on Human Resource Management*, Routledge, London.

Levitt, T. (1960) Marketing myopia, *Harvard Business Review*, **38**, July–Aug., pp. 24–47.

Levitt, T. (1975) Marketing myopia: retrospective commentary, *Harvard Business Review*, **53**, Sept.–Oct., pp. 177–81.

Levitt, T. (1986) *The Marketing Imagination*, Free Press, New York.

Levy, S. J. (1959) Symbols for sale, *Harvard Business Review*, July–Aug., pp. 117–24.

Lindblom, C. E. (1959) The science of muddling through, *Public Administration Review*, **19**, 2, pp. 79–88.

McCaskey, M. B. (1982) *The Executive Challenge*, Pitman, London.

McClean, M. and Rowland, T. (1985) *The INMOS Saga: A Triumph of National Enterprise*, Frances Pinter, London.

McClelland, D. (1961) *The Achieving Society*, Van Nostrand, Princeton.

McKinlay, A. and Starkey, K. (1992) Strategy and human resource management, *The International Journal of Human Resource Management*, **3**, 3, Dec., pp. 435–50.

Mansfield, E. (1963) Size of firm, market structure and innovation, *Journal of Political Economy*, **71**, 6, Dec., pp. 556–76.

Marris, R. L. (1964) *The Economic Theory of Managerial Capitalism*, Macmillan, London.

Marsden, D., Morris, T., Willman, P. and Wood, S. (1985) *The Car Industry: Labour Relations and Industrial Adjustment*, Tavistock, London.

Martin, R. (1981) *New Technology and Industrial Relations in Fleet Street*, Clarendon Press, Oxford.

Mayer, C. (1988) New issues in corporate finance, *European Economic Review*, June.

Mensch, G. (1979) *Stalemate in Technology*, Ballinger, Cambridge, Mass.

Miliband, R. (1969) *The State in Capitalist Society*, Quartet, London.

Millward, N. and Stevens, M. (1986) *British Workplace Industrial Relations 1980–84*, Gower, Aldershot.

Millward, N., Stevens, S., Smart, D. and Hawes, W. R. (1992) *Workplace Industrial Relations in Transition: The ED/ESRC/PSI/ACAS Surveys*, Dartmouth, Aldershot.

Minkes, A. L. and Nuttall, C. S. (1985) *Business Behaviour and Management Structure*, Croom Helm, Beckenham.

Minkes, A. L. (1987) *The Entrepreneurial Manager*, Harmondsworth, Penguin.

Mintzberg, H. (1973) Strategy making in 3 modes, *California Management Review*, **16**, Winter, pp. 44–53.

Mowery, D. C. and Rosenberg, N. (1989) *Technology and the Pursuit of Economic Growth*, Cambridge University Press, Cambridge.

Narin, F. (1993) Patent citation analysis: the strategic application of technology indicators, *Patent World*, **51**, Apr., pp. 25–30.

National Economic Development Office (1985) *Advanced Manufacturing Technology*, NEDO, May 1985.

Neale, A. and Haslam, C. (1994) *Economics in a Business Context*, 2nd edn., Chapman & Hall, London.

Needle, D. (1984) The selection process in Britain and West Germany: a cross-national study, unpublished MSc thesis, London School of Economics.

Needle, D. and Needle, J. (1991) The value of patents, *Patent World*, **35**, Sept., pp. 20–36.

Nicosia, F. M. (1966) *Consumer Decision Processes: Marketing and Advertising Implications*, Prentice-Hall, Englewood Cliffs, N.J.

Northcott, J. and Rogers, P. (1984) *Microelectronics in British Industry: The Pattern of Change*, Policy Studies Institute, London.

OECD (1993) *Education at a Glance OECD: Indicators*, OECD Publications, Paris.

Ohmae, K. (1982) *The Mind of the Strategist*, Harmondsworth, Penguin.

Oram, S. (1987) Fleet Street moves on: a managerial perspective, *Industrial Relations Journal*, **18**, 2, Summer, pp. 84–9.

Palmer, A. and Worthington, I. (1992) *The Business and Marketing Environment*, McGraw-Hill, Maidenhead.

Parker, R. C. (1982) *The Management of Innovation*, John Wiley & Sons, Chichester.

Pascale, R. T. (1978) Personnel practices and employee attitudes: a study of Japanese and American managed firms in the United States, *Human Relations*, **31**, pp. 597–616.

Pascale, R. and Rohlen, T. P. (1983) The Mazda turnaround, *Journal of Japanese Studies*, **9**, 2, pp. 219–63.

Paul, W. and Robertson, K. (1970) *Job Enrichment and Employee Motivation*, Gower Press, London.

Pavitt, K. (1983) Characteristics of Innovative Activity in British Industry, *OMEGA*, **11**, 2, pp. 113–30.

Peach, L. (1992) Parting by mutual agreement: IBM's transition to manpower cuts, *Personnel Management*, **24**, 3, Mar., pp. 40–3.

Peck, M. J. and Goto, A. (1982) Technology and economic growth: the case of Japan, in M. L. Tushman and W. L. Moore (eds), *Readings in the Management of Innovation*, Pitman Books, London.

Peltu, M. and Land, F. (1987) *Thomson Holidays: TOP Travel Agents Reservation System*, London Business School, London.

Perrow, C. (1961) The analysis of goals in complex organizations, *American Sociological Review*, **26**, pp. 854–66.

Personnel Standards Lead Body (1993) *A Perspective on Personnel*, Personnel Standards Lead Body, London.

Peters, T. J. and Waterman, R. H. (1982) *In Search of Excellence: Lessons from America's Best Run Companies*, Harper & Row, London.

Pettigrew, A. (1973) *The Politics of Organizational Decision-Making*, Tavistock, London.

Pettigrew, A. M. (1979) On studying organizational cultures, *Administrative Science Quarterly*, Dec., **24**, pp. 570–81.

Piore, M. and Sabel, C. (1984) *The Second Industrial Divide: Possibilities for Prosperity*, Basic Books, New York.

Pollert, A. (1987) The flexible firm: a model in search of reality (or a policy in search of a practice)?, *Warwick Papers in Industrial Relations* No 19.

Porter, M. E. (1980) *Competitive Strategy: Techniques for Analyzing Industries and Competitors*, Free Press, New York.

Price, R. and Bain, G. S. (1983) Union growth in Britain: retrospect and prospect, *British Journal of Industrial Relations*, **21**, pp. 339–55.

Pugh, D. S., Hickson, D. J. and Hinings, C. R. (1969) The context of organization structures, *Administrative Science Quarterly*, **14**, pp. 115–26.

Purcell, J. (1989) The impact of corporate strategy on human resource management, in J. Storey (ed.), *New Perspectives on Human Resource Management*, Routledge, London.

Purcell, J. and Sisson, K. (1983) Strategies and practice in the management of industrial relations in G. Bain (ed.), *Industrial Relations in Britain*, Blackwell, Oxford.

Rainnie, A. (1985) Small firms, big problems: the political economy of small business, *Capital and Class*, **25**, Spring, pp. 140–68.

Randlesome, C. (1991) *Business Cultures in Europe*, Butterworth/Heinemann, London.

Ray, C. A. (1986) Corporate culture: the last frontier of control, *Journal of Management Studies*, **23**, 3, May, pp. 287–97.

Rice, A. K. (1958) *Productivity and Social Organization*, Tavistock, London.

Richards, M. D. (1978) *Organizational Goal Structures*, West Publishing, St. Paul, Minnesota.

Rines, M. (1976) Woodville Rubbers 600% bounce, *Marketing*, Sept., pp. 21–3.

Rogers, E. M. (1962) *Diffusion of Innovations*, Free Press, New York.

Rothwell, R. and Zegveld (1981) *Industrial Innovation and Public Policy*, Frances Pinter, London.

Rumelt, R. P. (1974) *Strategy, Structure and Economic Performance*, Harvard University Press, Cambridge, Mass.

Sandberg, W. R. (1984) Norton Villiers Triumph and the Meriden Cooperative, in W. F. Gleuck and L. R. Jauch (eds), *Business Policy and Strategic Management*, 4th edn, McGraw-Hill, Singapore.

Sato, K. and Hoshino, Y. (eds) (1984) *The Anatomy of Japanese Business*, Croom Helm, London.

Scase, R. and Goffee, R. (1980) *The Real World of the Small Business Owner*, Croom Helm, London.

Schmookler, J. (1966) *Invention and Economic Growth*, Harvard University Press, Cambridge, Mass.

Schumpeter, J. A. (1939) *Business Cycles*, McGraw-Hill, London.

Schumpeter, J. A. (1961) *The Theory of Economic Development*, Oxford University Press, Oxford.

Scott, J. P. (1979) *Corporations, Classes and Capitalism*, Hutchinson, London.

Selznick, P. (1949) *TVA and the Grass Roots*, University of California Press, Berkley, Calif.

Sethi, S., Namiki, N. and Swanson, C. (1984) *The False Promise of the Japanese Miracle*, Pitman, London.

Shapiro, B. P. (1977) Can marketing and manufacturing coexist, *Harvard Business Review*, Sept.–Oct., pp. 104–14.

Sheehan R. (1967) Proprietors in the world of big business, *Fortune*, 15 June.

Shonfield, A. (1968) *A Note of Dissent, Royal Commission on Trade Unions and*

*Employers Associations 1965–68*, Report Cmnd 3623, HMSO, London.

Simmonds, K. S. (1986) Marketing as innovation: the eighth paradigm, *Journal of Management Studies*, **23**, 5, Sept., pp. 479–98.

Sizer, J. (1989) *An Insight into Management Accounting*, Harmondsworth, Penguin.

Skinner, W. (1969) Manufacturing – The missing link in corporate strategy, *Harvard Business Review*, May–June, pp. 136–45.

Skinner, W. (1974) The focused factory, *Harvard Business Review*, May–June, pp. 113–21.

Sloan, A. P. (1986) *My Years with General Motors*, Harmondsworth, Penguin.

Smith, R. (1982) Word processing installation, *Employment Gazette*, June, pp. 270–72.

Solow, R. W. (1957) Technical change and the aggregate production function, *Review of Economics and Statistics*, **1**, 3, pp. 312–20.

Sorge, A. and Warner, M. (1980) Manpower training, manufacturing organization and workplace relations in Great Britain and West Germany, *British Journal of Industrial Relations*, Nov., pp. 318–33.

Stanworth, J. and Gray, C. (eds) (1991) *Bolton 20 Years On: The Small Firm in the 1990s*, Paul Chapman Publishing, London.

Starr, M. K. (1972) *Production Management: Systems and Synthesis*, Prentice-Hall Inc. Englewood Cliffs, N. J.

Steedman, H. and Wagner, K. (1987) A second look at productivity, machinery and skills in Britain and Germany, *National Institute Economic Review*, Nov., pp. 84–94.

Stewart, H. and Gallagher, C. C. (1985) Business death and firm size in the U.K., *International Small Business Journal*, **4**, 1.

Stopford, J. M., Channon, D. F. and Constable, J. (1980) *Cases in Strategic Management*, John Wiley and Sons, Chichester.

Storey, J. (ed.) (1989) *New Perspectives on Human Resource Management*, Routledge, London.

Storey, J. (1992) *Developments in the Management of Human Resources: An Analytical Review*, Basil Blackwell, Oxford.

Strang, R. A. (1976) Sales promotion – Fast growth, faulty management, *Harvard Business Review*, July–Aug., pp. 115–24.

Tayles, M. and Woods, M. (1993) Total quality management at Akzo, *Research Update*, **3**, 1, CIMA Research Foundation.

Taylor, D. (1984) Learning from the Japanese, *Employment Gazette*, **92**, 6, June, pp. 279–85.

Taylor, F. W. (1947) *Scientific Management*, Harper & Row, New York.

Thackray, J. (1983) America's robotic rising, *Management Today*, Feb., pp. 54–7.

Thomas, R. E. (1982) *The Government of Business*, Philip Allan, Oxford.

Tighe, C. (1986) Behind the lines at Nissan, *Sunday Times*, 13 Apr., p. 67.

Torrington, D. (1989) Human resource management and personnel function, in J. Storey (ed.), *New Perspectives on Human Resources Management*, Routledge, London.

Torrington, D. and Hall, L. (1991) *Personnel Management: A New Approach*, Prentice Hall, London.

Trist, E. L. and Bamforth, K. W. (1951) Some social and psychological consequences of the Long-Wall method of coal-getting, *Human Relations*, **4**, pp. 3–38.

Trompenaars, F. (1993) *Riding the Waves of Culture: Understanding Cultural Diversity in Business*, The Economist Books, London.

Turner, G. (1971) *The Leyland Papers*, Eyre & Spottiswood, London.

United Nations (1986) *Survey on Flexible Manufacturing Systems*, United Nations, New York.

Walton, R. E. (1987) *Innovating to Compete*, Jossey Bass, San Fransisco.

Wasson, C. R. (1978) *Dynamic Competitive Strategy and Product Life Cycles*, Austin Press, Austin Texas.

Welford, R. and Prescott, K. (1992) *European Business: An Issue-based Approach*, Pitman, London.

Wells, J. (1989) Uneven development and deindustrialization in the UK since 1979, in F. Green (ed.), *The Restructuring of the UK Economy*, Harvester Wheatsheaf, London, ch. 2.

Wheelwright, S. (1981) Japan – where operations really are strategic, *Harvard Business Review*, **59**, July–Aug., pp. 65–72.

White, M. and Trevor, M. (1983) *Under Japanese Management – The Experience of British Workers*, Heinemann, London.

Wiener, M. J. (1981) *English Culture and the Decline of the Industrial Spirit 1850–1980*, Cambridge University Press, Cambridge.

Wild, R. (1985) *Essentials of Production and Operations Management*, Holt Rinehart & Winston, London.

Wilkinson, B. (1986) *The Shopfloor Politics of New Technology*, Gower, Aldershot.

Wilkinson, E. (1983) *Japan Versus Europe*, Harmondsworth, Penguin.

Williams, K., Haslam, C., Wardlow, A. and Williams, J. (1986) Accounting for failure in the nationalised enterprises – coal, steel, and cars since 1970, *Economy and Society*, **15**, 2, May, pp. 167–219.

Williams, K., Haslam, C., Williams, J. and Cutler, T. (1992a) Against lean production, *Economy and Society*, **21**, 3, Aug., pp. 321–54.

Williams, K., Haslam, C., Williams, J., Adcroft, A. and Johal, S. (1992b) Factories or warehouses: Japanese manufacturing foreign direct investment in Britain and the United States, *University of East London, Occasional Papers on Business, Economy and Society*, No 6.

Williams, K., Cutler, T., Williams, J. and Haslam, C. (1987) The end of mass production?, *Economy and Society*, **16**, 3, Aug., pp. 405–39.

Williams, K., Williams, J. and Haslam, C. (1987) *The Breakdown of Austin Rover*, Berg, Leamington Spa.

Williams, V. (1984) Employment implications of new technology, *Employment Gazette*, **92**, 5, May, 210–15.

Williamson, D. T. N. (1972) The anachronistic factory, *Proceedings of the Royal Society*, A331, pp. 139–60.

Wilson (1980) *Report of the Committee to Review the Functioning of Financial Institutions*. HMSO, London.

Winkler, J. T. (1977) The Coming Corporatism in R. Skidelsky (ed.), *The End of the Keynesian Era*, Macmillan, London.

Womack, J., Jones, D. and Roos, D. (1990) *The Machine the Changed the World*, Rawson Associates, New York.

Wong Kwei Cheong (1991) The style of managing in a multicultural society, in J. M. Putti (ed.), *Management: Asian Context*, McGraw-Hill, Singapore, pp. 78–94.

Wood, F. (1993) *Business Accounting, Books 1 and 2*, 6th edn, Pitman, London.

Woodward, J. (1965) *Industrial Organization: Theory and Practice*, Oxford University Press, London.

# Index